THE APOCRYPHA

*The Apocryphal/Deuterocanonical Books
of the Old Testament*

NEW REVISED STANDARD VERSION

THE APOCRYPHA

*The Apocryphal/Deuterocanonical Books
of the Old Testament*

NEW REVISED STANDARD VERSION

CAMBRIDGE
UNIVERSITY PRESS

Minster Text

CAMBRIDGE UNIVERSITY PRESS
Cambridge, New York, Melbourne, Madrid, Cape Town, Singapore, São Paulo, Delhi

Cambridge University Press
The Edinburgh Building, Cambridge CB2 8RU, UK

www.cambridge.org
Information on this title: www.cambridge.org/9780521507769

This edition first published 1992
Reprinted 1998, 2001, 2002, 2004, 2005, 2006, 2009

Printed in the UK by CPI William Clowes Beccles NR34 7TL

Typeset in 8/9pt Monotype Photina 747

ISBN 978-0-521-50776-9

CONTENTS

PREFACE TO THE APOCRYPHAL/DEUTEROCANONICAL BOOKS IN THE NEW REVISED STANDARD VERSION

When the King James or Authorized Version of the Bible was published in 1611, it contained, between the Old and the New Testaments, the books of the Apocrypha. These are books and portions of books that appear in the Latin Vulgate, either as part of the Old Testament or as an appendix, but are not in the Hebrew Bible. With the exception of 2 Esdras, these books appear also in the Greek version of the Old Testament that is known as the Septuagint.

In the course of time printers began to issue editions of the King James Bible without the books of the Apocrypha, and when the American Standard Version of the Bible was published in 1901, it did not include the Apocrypha. After the Revised Standard Version of the Bible was issued in 1952, a request came from the General Convention of the Protestant Episcopal Church that the Standard Bible Committee undertake also the revision of the English translation of the Apocrypha. This work was accomplished in 1957. It was on the basis of this version that the text of a "Common Bible," approved by both Roman Catholics and Protestants, was issued in 1973. Subsequently, in order to include all the texts accepted as Deuterocanonical by Eastern Orthodox Churches, the Standard Bible Committee prepared a version of 3 and 4 Maccabees and Psalm 151; this was issued in 1977. Since the contents of the collection known as Deuterocanonical Books vary among the churches that recognize them as authoritative, in the interest of clear identification they have been arranged in the New Revised Standard Version in four sections (see the Table of Contents).

For the translation of the Apocryphal/Deuterocanonical Books the Committee made use of a number of texts. In the case of most of the books the basic text was the standard edition of the Greek Septuagint prepared by Alfred Rahlfs and published by the Württemberg Bible Society (Stuttgart, 1935). For several of the books the more recently published individual volumes of the Göttingen Septuagint project were utilized. For the book of Tobit it was decided to follow the form of the Greek text found in codex Sinaiticus (supported as it is by evidence from Qumran); where this text is defective, it was supplemented and corrected by other Greek manuscripts. For the three Additions to Daniel (namely, Susanna, the Prayer of Azariah and the Song of the Three Jews, and Bel and the Dragon) the Committee continued to use the Greek version attributed to

Theodotion (the so-called "Theodotion-Daniel"). In translating Ecclesiasticus (Sirach), while constant reference was made to the Hebrew fragments of a large portion of this book (those discovered at Qumran and Masada as well as those recovered from the Cairo Genizah), the Committee generally followed the Greek text (including verse numbers) published by Joseph Ziegler in the Göttingen Septuagint (1965). But in many places the Committee has translated the Hebrew text when this provides a reading that is clearly superior to the Greek; the Syriac and Latin versions were also consulted throughout and occasionally adopted. The basic text adopted in rendering 2 Esdras is the Latin version given in the Biblia Sacra, edited by Robert Weber (Stuttgart, 1971). This was supplemented by consulting the Latin text as edited by R. L. Bensly (1895) and by Bruno Violet (1910), as well as the several Oriental versions of 2 Esdras, namely, the Syriac, Ethiopic, Arabic (two forms, referred to as Arabic 1 and Arabic 2), Armenian, and Georgian versions.

Finally, since the Additions to the Book of Esther are disjointed and unintelligible as they stand in most editions of the Apocrypha, we have provided them with their original context by translating the whole of the Greek version of Esther from Robert Hanhart's Göttingen edition (1983).

For the Committee,
BRUCE M. METZGER

THE NAMES AND ORDER OF
THE APOCRYPHAL/DEUTEROCANONICAL BOOKS

*The Apocryphal/Deuterocanonical Books are listed here
in four groupings, as follows:*

(a) *Books and Additions to Esther and
Daniel that are in the Roman Catholic,
Greek, and Slavonic Bibles.*

Tobit	1
Judith	14
The Additions to the Book of Esther	
(with a translation of the entire Greek text of Esther)	27
Wisdom of Solomon	38
Ecclesiasticus, or the Wisdom of Jesus Son of Sirach	58
Baruch	114
The Letter of Jeremiah (=Baruch ch. 6)	119
The Additions to the Book of Daniel	
The Prayer of Azariah and the Song of the Three Jews	121
Susanna	124
Bel and the Dragon	126
1 Maccabees	127
2 Maccabees	156

(b) *Books in the Greek and Slavonic Bibles;
not in the Roman Catholic Canon*

1 Esdras (= 2 Esdras in Slavonic = 3 Esdras in Appendix to Vulgate)	178
Prayer of Manasseh (in Appendix to Vulgate)	192
Psalm 151, following Psalm 150 in the Greek Bible	193
3 Maccabees	194

(c) *In the Slavonic Bible and in the Latin
Vulgate Appendix*

2 Esdras (= 3 Esdras in Slavonic = 4 Esdras in Vulgate Appendix)	204

(Note: In the Latin Vulgate, Ezra – Nehemiah = 1 and 2 Esdras)

(d) *In an Appendix to the Greek Bible*

4 Maccabees	234

The following abbreviations are used

Tob	Tobit	Song of Thr	Prayer of Azariah and the Song of the Three Jews
Jdt	Judith		
Add Esth	Additions to Esther	Sus	Susanna
Wis	Wisdom	Bel	Bel and the Dragon
Sir	Sirach (Ecclesiasticus)	1 Macc	1 Maccabees
Bar	Baruch	2 Macc	2 Maccabees
1 Esd	1 Esdras	3 Macc	3 Maccabees
2 Esd	2 Esdras	4 Macc	4 Maccabees
Let Jer	Letter of Jeremiah	Pr Man	Prayer of Manasseh

THE
APOCRYPHA

*The Apocryphal/Deuterocanonical Books
of the Old Testament*

TOBIT

1 This book tells the story of Tobit son of Tobiel son of Hananiel son of Aduel son of Gabael son of Raphael son of Raguel of the descendants[a] of Asiel, of the tribe of Naphtali, [2]who in the days of King Shalmaneser[b] of the Assyrians was taken into captivity from Thisbe, which is to the south of Kedesh Naphtali in Upper Galilee, above Asher toward the west, and north of Phogor.

Tobit's Youth and Virtuous Life

[3] I, Tobit, walked in the ways of truth and righteousness all the days of my life. I performed many acts of charity for my kindred and my people who had gone with me in exile to Nineveh in the land of the Assyrians. [4]When I was in my own country, in the land of Israel, while I was still a young man, the whole tribe of my ancestor Naphtali deserted the house of David and Jerusalem. This city had been chosen from among all the tribes of Israel, where all the tribes of Israel should offer sacrifice and where the temple, the dwelling of God, had been consecrated and established for all generations forever.

[5] All my kindred and our ancestral house of Naphtali sacrificed to the calf[c] that King Jeroboam of Israel had erected in Dan and on all the mountains of Galilee. [6]But I alone went often to Jerusalem for the festivals, as it is prescribed for all Israel by an everlasting decree. I would hurry off to Jerusalem with the first fruits of the crops and the firstlings of the flock, the tithes of the cattle, and the first shearings of the sheep. [7]I would give these to the priests, the sons of Aaron, at the altar; likewise the tenth of the grain, wine, olive oil, pomegranates, figs, and the rest of the fruits to the sons of Levi who ministered at Jerusalem. Also for six years I would save up a second tenth in money and go and distribute it in Jerusalem. [8]A third tenth[d] I would give to the orphans and widows and to the converts who had attached themselves to Israel. I would bring it and give it to them in the third year, and we would eat it according to the ordinance decreed concerning it in the law of Moses

and according to the instructions of Deborah, the mother of my father Tobiel,[e] for my father had died and left me an orphan. [9]When I became a man I married a woman,[f] a member of our own family, and by her I became the father of a son whom I named Tobias.

Taken Captive to Nineveh

[10] After I was carried away captive to Assyria and came as a captive to Nineveh, everyone of my kindred and my people ate the food of the Gentiles, [11]but I kept myself from eating the food of the Gentiles. [12]Because I was mindful of God with all my heart, [13]the Most High gave me favor and good standing with Shalmaneser,[b] and I used to buy everything he needed. [14]Until his death I used to go into Media, and buy for him there. While in the country of Media I left bags of silver worth ten talents in trust with Gabael, the brother of Gabri. [15]But when Shalmaneser[b] died, and his son Sennacherib reigned in his place, the highways into Media became unsafe and I could no longer go there.

Courage in Burying the Dead

[16] In the days of Shalmaneser[b] I performed many acts of charity to my kindred, those of my tribe. [17]I would give my food to the hungry and my clothing to the naked; and if I saw the dead body of any of my people thrown out behind the wall of Nineveh, I would bury it. [18]I also buried any whom King Sennacherib put to death when he came fleeing from Judea in those days of judgment that the king of heaven executed upon him because of his blasphemies. For in his anger he put to death many Israelites; but I would secretly remove the bodies and bury them. So when Sennacherib looked for them he could not find them. [19]Then one of the Ninevites went and informed the king about me, that I was burying them; so I hid myself. But when I realized that the king knew about me and that I was being searched for to be put to death, I was afraid

[a] Other ancient authorities lack *of Raphael son of Raguel of the descendants*   [b] Gk *Enemessaros*   [c] Other ancient authorities read *heifer*   [d] *A third tenth* added from other ancient authorities   [e] Lat: Gk *Hananiel*   [f] Other ancient authorities add *Anna*

1

and ran away. [20]Then all my property was confiscated; nothing was left to me that was not taken into the royal treasury except my wife Anna and my son Tobias.

[21] But not forty[g] days passed before two of Sennacherib's[h] sons killed him, and they fled to the mountains of Ararat, and his son Esar-haddon[i] reigned after him. He appointed Ahikar, the son of my brother Hanael[j] over all the accounts of his kingdom, and he had authority over the entire administration. [22]Ahikar interceded for me, and I returned to Nineveh. Now Ahikar was chief cupbearer, keeper of the signet, and in charge of administration of the accounts under King Sennacherib of Assyria; so Esar-haddon[i] reappointed him. He was my nephew and so a close relative.

2 Then during the reign of Esar-haddon[i] I returned home, and my wife Anna and my son Tobias were restored to me. At our festival of Pentecost, which is the sacred festival of weeks, a good dinner was prepared for me and I reclined to eat. [2]When the table was set for me and an abundance of food placed before me, I said to my son Tobias, "Go, my child, and bring whatever poor person you may find of our people among the exiles in Nineveh, who is wholeheartedly mindful of God,[k] and he shall eat together with me. I will wait for you, until you come back." [3]So Tobias went to look for some poor person of our people. When he had returned he said, "Father!" And I replied, "Here I am, my child." Then he went on to say, "Look, father, one of our own people has been murdered and thrown into the market place, and now he lies there strangled." [4]Then I sprang up, left the dinner before even tasting it, and removed the body[l] from the square[m] and laid it[l] in one of the rooms until sunset when I might bury it.[l] [5]When I returned, I washed myself and ate my food in sorrow. [6]Then I remembered the prophecy of Amos, how he said against Bethel,[n]

"Your festivals shall be turned into mourning,
and all your songs into lamentation."

And I wept.

Tobit Becomes Blind

7 When the sun had set, I went and dug a grave and buried him. [8]And my neighbors laughed and said, "Is he still not afraid? He has already been hunted down to be put to death for doing this, and he ran away; yet here he is again burying the dead!" [9]That same night I washed myself and went into my courtyard and slept by the wall of the courtyard; and my face was uncovered because of the heat. [10]I did not know that there were sparrows on the wall; their fresh droppings fell into my eyes and produced white films. I went to physicians to be healed, but the more they treated me with ointments the more my vision was obscured by the white films, until I became completely blind. For four years I remained unable to see. All my kindred were sorry for me, and Ahikar took care of me for two years before he went to Elymais.

Tobit's Wife Earns Their Livelihood

11 At that time, also, my wife Anna earned money at women's work. [12]She used to send what she made to the owners and they would pay wages to her. One day, the seventh of Dystrus, when she cut off a piece she had woven and sent it to the owners, they paid her full wages and also gave her a young goat for a meal. [13]When she returned to me, the goat began to bleat. So I called her and said, "Where did you get this goat? It is surely not stolen, is it? Return it to the owners; for we have no right to eat anything stolen." [14]But she said to me, "It was given to me as a gift in addition to my wages." But I did not believe her, and told her to return it to the owners. I became flushed with anger against her over this. Then she replied to me, "Where are your acts of charity? Where are your righteous deeds? These things are known about you!"[o]

Tobit's Prayer

3 Then with much grief and anguish of heart I wept, and with groaning began to pray:

---

[g] Other ancient authorities read either *forty-five* or *fifty*   [h] Gk *his*   [i] Gk *Sacherdonos*   [j] Other authorities read *Hananael*   [k] Lat: Gk *wholeheartedly mindful*   [l] Gk *him*   [m] Other ancient authorities lack *from the square*   [n] Other ancient authorities read *against Bethlehem*   [o] Or *to you*; Gk *with you*

2 "You are righteous, O Lord,
and all your deeds are just;
all your ways are mercy and truth;
you judge the world.[p]
3 And now, O Lord, remember me
and look favorably upon me.
Do not punish me for my sins
and for my unwitting offenses
and those that my ancestors
committed before you.
They sinned against you,
4 and disobeyed your commandments.
So you gave us over to plunder, exile,
and death,
to become the talk, the byword, and
an object of reproach
among all the nations among whom
you have dispersed us.
5 And now your many judgments are
true
in exacting penalty from me for my
sins.
For we have not kept your
commandments
and have not walked in accordance
with truth before you.
6 So now deal with me as you will;
command my spirit to be taken
from me,
so that I may be released from the
face of the earth and become
dust.
For it is better for me to die than to
live,
because I have had to listen to
undeserved insults,
and great is the sorrow within me.
Command, O Lord, that I be released
from this distress;
release me to go to the eternal
home,
and do not, O Lord, turn your face
away from me.
For it is better for me to die
than to see so much distress in my
life
and to listen to insults."

Sarah Falsely Accused

7 On the same day, at Ecbatana in Media,
it also happened that Sarah, the daughter
of Raguel, was reproached by one of her
father's maids. 8For she had been married
to seven husbands, and the wicked demon
Asmodeus had killed each of them before
they had been with her as is customary for
wives. So the maid said to her, "You are
the one who kills[q] your husbands! See, you
have already been married to seven husbands and have not borne the name of[r] a
single one of them. 9Why do you beat us?
Because your husbands are dead? Go with
them! May we never see a son or daughter
of yours!"

Sarah's Prayer for Death

10 On that day she was grieved in spirit
and wept. When she had gone up to her
father's upper room, she intended to hang
herself. But she thought it over and said,
"Never shall they reproach my father, saying to him, 'You had only one beloved
daughter but she hanged herself because of
her distress.' And I shall bring my father in
his old age down in sorrow to Hades. It is
better for me not to hang myself, but to
pray the Lord that I may die and not listen
to these reproaches anymore." 11At that
same time, with hands outstretched toward
the window, she prayed and said,
"Blessed are you, merciful God!
Blessed is your name forever;
let all your works praise you
forever.
12 And now, Lord,[s] I turn my face to
you,
and raise my eyes toward you.
13 Command that I be released from the
earth
and not listen to such reproaches
any more.
14 You know, O Master, that I am
innocent
of any defilement with a man,
15 and that I have not disgraced my
name
or the name of my father in the
land of my exile.
I am my father's only child;
he has no other child to be his
heir;
and he has no close relative or other
kindred
for whom I should keep myself as
wife.
Already seven husbands of mine have
died.
Why should I still live?

[p] Other ancient authorities read *you render true and righteous judgment forever* [q] Other ancient authorities read *strangles* [r] Other ancient authorities read *have had no benefit from* [s] Other ancient authorities lack *Lord*

But if it is not pleasing to you,
    O Lord, to take my life,
    hear me in my disgrace."

An Answer to Prayer

16 At that very moment, the prayers of both of them were heard in the glorious presence of God. [17]So Raphael was sent to heal both of them: Tobit, by removing the white films from his eyes, so that he might see God's light with his eyes; and Sarah, daughter of Raguel, by giving her in marriage to Tobias son of Tobit, and by setting her free from the wicked demon Asmodeus. For Tobias was entitled to have her before all others who had desired to marry her. At the same time that Tobit returned from the courtyard into his house, Sarah daughter of Raguel came down from her upper room.

Tobit Gives Instructions to His Son

4 That same day Tobit remembered the money that he had left in trust with Gabael at Rages in Media, [2]and he said to himself, "Now I have asked for death. Why do I not call my son Tobias and explain to him about the money before I die?" [3]Then he called his son Tobias, and when he came to him he said, "My son, when I die,[t] give me a proper burial. Honor your mother and do not abandon her all the days of her life. Do whatever pleases her, and do not grieve her in anything. [4]Remember her, my son, because she faced many dangers for you while you were in her womb. And when she dies, bury her beside me in the same grave.

5 "Revere the Lord all your days, my son, and refuse to sin or to transgress his commandments. Live uprightly all the days of your life, and do not walk in the ways of wrongdoing; [6]for those who act in accordance with truth will prosper in all their activities. To all those who practice righteousness[u] [7]give alms from your possessions, and do not let your eye begrudge the gift when you make it. Do not turn your face away from anyone who is poor, and the face of God will not be turned away from you. [8]If you have many possessions, make your gift from them in proportion; if few, do not be afraid to give according to the little you have. [9]So you will be laying up a good treasure for yourself against the day of necessity. [10]For almsgiving delivers from death and keeps you from going into the Darkness. [11]Indeed, almsgiving, for all who practice it, is an excellent offering in the presence of the Most High.

12 "Beware, my son, of every kind of fornication. First of all, marry a woman from among the descendants of your ancestors; do not marry a foreign woman, who is not of your father's tribe; for we are the descendants of the prophets. Remember, my son, that Noah, Abraham, Isaac, and Jacob, our ancestors of old, all took wives from among their kindred. They were blessed in their children, and their posterity will inherit the land. [13]So now, my son, love your kindred, and in your heart do not disdain your kindred, the sons and daughters of your people, by refusing to take a wife for yourself from among them. For in pride there is ruin and great confusion. And in idleness there is loss and dire poverty, because idleness is the mother of famine.

14 "Do not keep over until the next day the wages of those who work for you, but pay them at once. If you serve God you will receive payment. Watch yourself, my son, in everything you do, and discipline yourself in all your conduct. [15]And what you hate, do not do to anyone. Do not drink wine to excess or let drunkenness go with you on your way. [16]Give some of your food to the hungry, and some of your clothing to the naked. Give all your surplus as alms, and do not let your eye begrudge your giving of alms. [17]Place your bread on the grave of the righteous, but give none to sinners. [18]Seek advice from every wise person and do not despise any useful counsel. [19]At all times bless the Lord God, and ask him that your ways may be made straight and that all your paths and plans may prosper. For none of the nations has understanding, but the Lord himself will give them good counsel; but if he chooses otherwise, he casts down to deepest Hades. So now, my child, remember these commandments, and do not let them be erased from your heart.

Money Left in Trust with Gabael

20 "And now, my son, let me explain to you that I left ten talents of silver in trust

---

[t] Lat   [u] The text of codex Sinaiticus goes directly from verse 6 to verse 19, reading *To those who practice righteousness [19]the Lord will give good counsel.* In order to fill the lacuna verses 7 to 18 are derived from other ancient authorities

with Gabael son of Gabrias, at Rages in Media. ²¹Do not be afraid, my son, because we have become poor. You have great wealth if you fear God and flee from every sin and do what is good in the sight of the Lord your God."

The Angel Raphael

5 Then Tobias answered his father Tobit, "I will do everything that you have commanded me, father; ²but how can I obtain the money^v from him, since he does not know me and I do not know him? What evidence^w am I to give him so that he will recognize and trust me, and give me the money? Also, I do not know the roads to Media, or how to get there." ³Then Tobit answered his son Tobias, "He gave me his bond and I gave him my bond. I^x divided his in two; we each took one part, and I put one with the money. And now twenty years have passed since I left this money in trust. So now, my son, find yourself a trustworthy man to go with you, and we will pay him wages until you return. But get back the money from Gabael."^{y}

4 So Tobias went out to look for a man to go with him to Media, someone who was acquainted with the way. He went out and found the angel Raphael standing in front of him; but he did not perceive that he was an angel of God. ⁵Tobias^z said to him, "Where do you come from, young man?" "From your kindred, the Israelites," he replied, "and I have come here to work." Then Tobias^a said to him, "Do you know the way to go to Media?" ⁶"Yes," he replied, "I have been there many times; I am acquainted with it and know all the roads. I have often traveled to Media, and would stay with our kinsman Gabael who lives in Rages of Media. It is a journey of two days from Ecbatana to Rages; for it lies in a mountainous area, while Ecbatana is in the middle of the plain." ⁷Then Tobias said to him, "Wait for me, young man, until I go in and tell my father; for I do need you to travel with me, and I will pay you your wages." ⁸He replied, "All right, I will wait; but do not take too long."

9 So Tobias^a went in to tell his father Tobit and said to him, "I have just found a man who is one of our own Israelite kindred!" He replied, "Call the man in, my son,

so that I may learn about his family and to what tribe he belongs, and whether he is trustworthy enough to go with you."

10 Then Tobias went out and called him, and said, "Young man, my father is calling for you." So he went in to him, and Tobit greeted him first. He replied, "Joyous greetings to you!" But Tobit retorted, "What joy is left for me any more? I am a man without eyesight; I cannot see the light of heaven, but I lie in darkness like the dead who no longer see the light. Although still alive, I am among the dead. I hear people but I cannot see them." But the young man^a said, "Take courage; the time is near for God to heal you; take courage." Then Tobit said to him, "My son Tobias wishes to go to Media. Can you accompany him and guide him? I will pay your wages, brother." He answered, "I can go with him and I know all the roads, for I have often gone to Media and have crossed all its plains, and I am familiar with its mountains and all of its roads."

11 Then Tobit^a said to him, "Brother, of what family are you and from what tribe? Tell me, brother." ¹²He replied, "Why do you need to know my tribe?" But Tobit^a said, "I want to be sure, brother, whose son you are and what your name is." ¹³He replied, "I am Azariah, the son of the great Hananiah, one of your relatives." ¹⁴Then Tobit said to him, "Welcome! God save you, brother. Do not feel bitter toward me, brother, because I wanted to be sure about your ancestry. It turns out that you are a kinsman, and of good and noble lineage. For I knew Hananiah and Nathan,^{b} the two sons of Shemeliah,^{c} and they used to go with me to Jerusalem and worshiped with me there, and were not led astray. Your kindred are good people; you come of good stock. Hearty welcome!"

15 Then he added, "I will pay you a drachma a day as wages, as well as expenses for yourself and my son. So go with my son, ¹⁶and^d I will add something to your wages." Raphael^z answered, "I will go with him; so do not fear. We shall leave in good health and return to you in good health, because the way is safe." ¹⁷So Tobit^a said to him, "Blessings be upon you, brother."

Then he called his son and said to him, "Son, prepare supplies for the journey and

^{v} Gk *it* ^{w} Gk *sign* ^{x} Other authorities read *He* ^{y} Gk *from him* ^{z} Gk *He* ^{a} Gk *he* ^{b} Other ancient authorities read *Jathan* or *Nathaniah* ^{c} Other ancient authorities read *Shemaiah* ^{d} Other ancient authorities add *when you return safely*

5

set out with your brother. May God in heaven bring you safely there and return you in good health to me; and may his angel, my son, accompany you both for your safety."

Before he went out to start his journey, he kissed his father and mother. Tobit then said to him, "Have a safe journey."

18 But his mother*ᵉ* began to weep, and said to Tobit, "Why is it that you have sent my child away? Is he not the staff of our hand as he goes in and out before us? ¹⁹Do not heap money upon money, but let it be a ransom for our child. ²⁰For the life that is given to us by the Lord is enough for us." ²¹Tobit*ᶠ* said to her, "Do not worry; our child will leave in good health and return to us in good health. Your eyes will see him on the day when he returns to you in good health. Say no more! Do not fear for them, my sister. ²²For a good angel will accompany him; his journey will be successful, and he will come back in good health."

6 ¹So she stopped weeping.

Journey to Rages

The young man went out and the angel went with him; ²and the dog came out with him and went along with them. So they both journeyed along, and when the first night overtook them they camped by the Tigris river. ³Then the young man went down to wash his feet in the Tigris river. Suddenly a large fish leaped up from the water and tried to swallow the young man's foot, and he cried out. ⁴But the angel said to the young man, "Catch hold of the fish and hang on to it!" So the young man grasped the fish and drew it up on the land. ⁵Then the angel said to him, "Cut open the fish and take out its gall, heart, and liver. Keep them with you, but throw away the intestines. For its gall, heart, and liver are useful as medicine." ⁶So after cutting open the fish the young man gathered together the gall, heart, and liver; then he roasted and ate some of the fish, and kept some to be salted.

The two continued on their way together until they were near Media.*ᵍ* ⁷Then the young man questioned the angel and said to him, "Brother Azariah, what medicinal value is there in the fish's heart and liver, and in the gall?" ⁸He replied, "As for the fish's heart and liver, you must burn them to make a smoke in the presence of a man or woman afflicted by a demon or evil spirit, and every affliction will flee away and never remain with that person any longer. ⁹And as for the gall, anoint a person's eyes where white films have appeared on them; blow upon them, upon the white films, and the eyes*ʰ* will be healed."

Raphael's Instructions

10 When he entered Media and already was approaching Ecbatana,*ⁱ* ¹¹Raphael said to the young man, "Brother Tobias." "Here I am," he answered. Then Raphael*ʲ* said to him, "We must stay this night in the home of Raguel. He is your relative, and he has a daughter named Sarah. ¹²He has no male heir and no daughter except Sarah only, and you, as next of kin to her, have before all other men a hereditary claim on her. Also it is right for you to inherit her father's possessions. Moreover, the girl is sensible, brave, and very beautiful, and her father is a good man." ¹³He continued, "You have every right to take her in marriage. So listen to me, brother; tonight I will speak to her father about the girl, so that we may take her to be your bride. When we return from Rages we will celebrate her marriage. For I know that Raguel can by no means keep her from you or promise her to another man without incurring the penalty of death according to the decree of the book of Moses. Indeed he knows that you, rather than any other man, are entitled to marry his daughter. So now listen to me, brother, and tonight we shall speak concerning the girl and arrange her engagement to you. And when we return from Rages we will take her and bring her back with us to your house."

14 Then Tobias said in answer to Raphael, "Brother Azariah, I have heard that she already has been married to seven husbands and that they died in the bridal chamber. On the night when they went in to her, they would die. I have heard people saying that it was a demon that killed them. ¹⁵It does not harm her, but it kills anyone who desires to approach her. So now, since I am the only son my father has, I am afraid that I may die and bring my father's and mother's life down to their grave, grieving

ᵉOther ancient authorities add *Anna*   ᶠGk *He*   ᵍOther ancient authorities read *Ecbatana*   ʰGk *they*
ⁱOther ancient authorities read *Rages*   ʲGk *he*

6

for me—and they have no other son to bury them."

16 But Raphael[k] said to him, "Do you not remember your father's orders when he commanded you to take a wife from your father's house? Now listen to me, brother, and say no more about this demon. Take her. I know that this very night she will be given to you in marriage. [17]When you enter the bridal chamber, take some of the fish's liver and heart, and put them on the embers of the incense. An odor will be given off; [18]the demon will smell it and flee, and will never be seen near her any more. Now when you are about to go to bed with her, both of you must first stand up and pray, imploring the Lord of heaven that mercy and safety may be granted to you. Do not be afraid, for she was set apart for you before the world was made. You will save her, and she will go with you. I presume that you will have children by her, and they will be as brothers to you. Now say no more!" When Tobias heard the words of Raphael and learned that she was his kinswoman,[l] related through his father's lineage, he loved her very much, and his heart was drawn to her.

Arrival at the Home of Raguel

7 Now when they[m] entered Ecbatana, Tobias[k] said to him, "Brother Azariah, take me straight to our brother Raguel." So he took him to Raguel's house, where they found him sitting beside the courtyard door. They greeted him first, and he replied, "Joyous greetings, brothers; welcome and good health!" Then he brought them into his house. [2]He said to his wife Edna, "How much the young man resembles my kinsman Tobit!" [3]Then Edna questioned them, saying, "Where are you from, brothers?" They answered, "We belong to the descendants of Naphtali who are exiles in Nineveh." [4]She said to them, "Do you know our kinsman Tobit?" And they replied, "Yes, we know him." Then she asked them, "Is he[n] in good health?" [5]They replied, "He is alive and in good health." And Tobias added, "He is my father!" [6]At that Raguel jumped up and kissed him and wept. [7]He also spoke to him as follows, "Blessings on you, my child, son of a good and noble father![o] O most miserable of calamities that such an upright and beneficent man has become blind!" He then embraced his kinsman Tobias and wept. [8]His wife Edna also wept for him, and their daughter Sarah likewise wept. [9]Then Raguel[k] slaughtered a ram from the flock and received them very warmly.

Marriage of Tobias and Sarah

When they had bathed and washed themselves and had reclined to dine, Tobias said to Raphael, "Brother Azariah, ask Raguel to give me my kinswoman[l] Sarah." [10]But Raguel overheard it and said to the lad, "Eat and drink, and be merry tonight. For no one except you, brother, has the right to marry my daughter Sarah. Likewise I am not at liberty to give her to any other man than yourself, because you are my nearest relative. But let me explain to you the true situation more fully, my child. [11]I have given her to seven men of our kinsmen, and all died on the night when they went in to her. But now, my child, eat and drink, and the Lord will act on behalf of you both." But Tobias said, "I will neither eat nor drink anything until you settle the things that pertain to me." So Raguel said, "I will do so. She is given to you in accordance with the decree in the book of Moses, and it has been decreed from heaven that she be given to you. Take your kinswoman;[l] from now on you are her brother and she is your sister. She is given to you from today and forever. May the Lord of heaven, my child, guide and prosper you both this night and grant you mercy and peace." [12]Then Raguel summoned his daughter Sarah. When she came to him he took her by the hand and gave her to Tobias,[p] saying, "Take her to be your wife in accordance with the law and decree written in the book of Moses. Take her and bring her safely to your father. And may the God of heaven prosper your journey with his peace." [13]Then he called her mother and told her to bring writing material; and he wrote out a copy of a marriage contract, to the effect that he gave her to him as wife according to the decree of the law of Moses. [14]Then they began to eat and drink.

15 Raguel called his wife Edna and said to her, "Sister, get the other room ready,

---

[k] Gk *he*   [l] Gk *sister*   [m] Other ancient authorities read *he*   [n] Other ancient authorities add *alive and*   [o] Other ancient authorities add *When he heard that Tobit had lost his sight, he was stricken with grief and wept. Then he said,*   [p] Gk *him*

and take her there." [16]So she went and made the bed in the room as he had told her, and brought Sarah[q] there. She wept for her daughter.[q] Then, wiping away the tears,[r] she said to her, "Take courage, my daughter; the Lord of heaven grant you joy[s] in place of your sorrow. Take courage, my daughter." Then she went out.

Tobias Routs the Demon

8 When they had finished eating and drinking they wanted to retire; so they took the young man and brought him into the bedroom. [2]Then Tobias remembered the words of Raphael, and he took the fish's liver and heart out of the bag where he had them and put them on the embers of the incense. [3]The odor of the fish so repelled the demon that he fled to the remotest parts[t] of Egypt. But Raphael followed him, and at once bound him there hand and foot.

4 When the parents[u] had gone out and shut the door of the room, Tobias got out of bed and said to Sarah,[q] "Sister, get up, and let us pray and implore our Lord that he grant us mercy and safety." [5]So she got up, and they began to pray and implore that they might be kept safe. Tobias[v] began by saying,

"Blessed are you, O God of our
    ancestors,
and blessed is your name in all
    generations forever.
Let the heavens and the whole
    creation bless you forever.
[6] You made Adam, and for him you
    made his wife Eve
as a helper and support.
From the two of them the human
    race has sprung.
You said, 'It is not good that the man
    should be alone;
let us make a helper for him like
    himself.'
[7] I now am taking this kinswoman of
    mine,
not because of lust,
    but with sincerity.
Grant that she and I may find mercy
and that we may grow old
    together."
[8]And they both said, "Amen, Amen." [9]Then they went to sleep for the night.

But Raguel arose and called his servants to him, and they went and dug a grave, [10]for he said, "It is possible that he will die and we will become an object of ridicule and derision." [11]When they had finished digging the grave, Raguel went into his house and called his wife, [12]saying, "Send one of the maids and have her go in to see if he is alive. But if he is dead, let us bury him without anyone knowing it." [13]So they sent the maid, lit a lamp, and opened the door; and she went in and found them sound asleep together. [14]Then the maid came out and informed them that he was alive and that nothing was wrong. [15]So they blessed the God of heaven, and Raguel[u] said,

"Blessed are you, O God, with every
    pure blessing;
let all your chosen ones bless you.[w]
Let them bless you forever.
[16] Blessed are you because you have
    made me glad.
It has not turned out as I expected,
but you have dealt with us
    according to your great mercy.
[17] Blessed are you because you had
    compassion
on two only children.
Be merciful to them, O Master, and
    keep them safe;
bring their lives to fulfillment
    in happiness and mercy."
[18]Then he ordered his servants to fill in the grave before daybreak.

Wedding Feast

19 After this he asked his wife to bake many loaves of bread; and he went out to the herd and brought two steers and four rams and ordered them to be slaughtered. So they began to make preparations. [20]Then he called for Tobias and swore on oath to him in these words:[x] "You shall not leave here for fourteen days, but shall stay here eating and drinking with me; and you shall cheer up my daughter, who has been depressed. [21]Take at once half of what I own and return in safety to your father; the other half will be yours when my wife and I die. Take courage, my child. I am your father and Edna is your mother, and we belong to you as well as to your wife[y] now and forever. Take courage, my child."

[q] Gk *her*   [r] Other ancient authorities read *the tears of her daughter*   [s] Other ancient authorities read *favor* [t] Or *fled through the air to the parts*   [u] Gk *they*   [v] Gk *He*   [w] Other ancient authorities lack this line   [x] Other ancient authorities read *Tobias and said to him*   [y] Gk *sister*

The Money Recovered

9 Then Tobias called Raphael and said to him, 2"Brother Azariah, take four servants and two camels with you and travel to Rages. Go to the home of Gabael, give him the bond, get the money, and then bring him with you to the wedding celebration. 4For you know that my father must be counting the days, and if I delay even one day I will upset him very much. 3You are witness to the oath Raguel has sworn, and I cannot violate his oath."[z] 5So Raphael with the four servants and two camels went to Rages in Media and stayed with Gabael. Raphael[a] gave him the bond and informed him that Tobit's son Tobias had married and was inviting him to the wedding celebration. So Gabael[b] got up and counted out to him the money bags, with their seals intact; then they loaded them on the camels.[c] 6In the morning they both got up early and went to the wedding celebration. When they came into Raguel's house they found Tobias reclining at table. He sprang up and greeted Gabael,[d] who wept and blessed him with the words, "Good and noble son of a father good and noble, upright and generous! May the Lord grant the blessing of heaven to you and your wife, and to your wife's father and mother. Blessed be God, for I see in Tobias the very image of my cousin Tobit."

Anxiety of the Parents

10 Now, day by day, Tobit kept counting how many days Tobias[b] would need for going and for returning. And when the days had passed and his son did not appear, 2he said, "Is it possible that he has been detained? Or that Gabael has died, and there is no one to give him the money?" 3And he began to worry. 4His wife Anna said, "My child has perished and is no longer among the living." And she began to weep and mourn for her son, saying, 5"Woe to me, my child, the light of my eyes, that I let you make the journey." 6But Tobit kept saying to her, "Be quiet and stop worrying, my dear;[e] he is all right. Probably something unexpected has happened there. The man who went with him is trustworthy and is one of our own kin. Do not grieve for him, my dear;[e] he will soon be here."

7She answered him, "Be quiet yourself! Stop trying to deceive me! My child has perished." She would rush out every day and watch the road her son had taken, and would heed no one.[f] When the sun had set she would go in and mourn and weep all night long, getting no sleep at all.

Tobias and Sarah Start for Home

Now when the fourteen days of the wedding celebration had ended that Raguel had sworn to observe for his daughter, Tobias came to him and said, "Send me back, for I know that my father and mother do not believe that they will see me again. So I beg of you, father, to let me go so that I may return to my own father. I have already explained to you how I left him." 8But Raguel said to Tobias, "Stay, my child, stay with me; I will send messengers to your father Tobit and they will inform him about you." 9But he said, "No! I beg you to send me back to my father." 10So Raguel promptly gave Tobias his wife Sarah, as well as half of all his property: male and female slaves, oxen and sheep, donkeys and camels, clothing, money, and household goods. 11Then he saw them safely off; he embraced Tobias[d] and said, "Farewell, my child; have a safe journey. The Lord of heaven prosper you and your wife Sarah, and may I see children of yours before I die." 12Then he kissed his daughter Sarah and said to her, "My daughter, honor your father-in-law and your mother-in-law,[g] since from now on they are as much your parents as those who gave you birth. Go in peace, daughter, and may I hear a good report about you as long as I live." Then he bade them farewell and let them go. Then Edna said to Tobias, "My child and dear brother, the Lord of heaven bring you back safely, and may I live long enough to see children of you and of my daughter Sarah before I die. In the sight of the Lord I entrust my daughter to you; do nothing to grieve her all the days of your life. Go in peace, my child. From now on I am your mother and Sarah is your beloved wife.[e] May we all prosper together all the days of our lives." Then she kissed them both and saw them safely off. 13Tobias parted from Raguel with happiness and joy, praising the Lord of heaven and earth, King over

---

[z] In other ancient authorities verse 3 precedes verse 4   [a] Gk He   [b] Gk he   [c] Other ancient authorities lack *on the camels*   [d] Gk *him*   [e] Gk *sister*   [f] Other ancient authorities read *and she would eat nothing*   [g] Other ancient authorities lack parts of *Then . . . mother-in-law*

all, because he had made his journey a success. Finally, he blessed Raguel and his wife Edna, and said, "I have been commanded by the Lord to honor you all the days of my life."[h]

Homeward Journey

11 When they came near to Kaserin, which is opposite Nineveh, Raphael said, [2]"You are aware of how we left your father. [3]Let us run ahead of your wife and prepare the house while they are still on the way." [4]As they went on together Raphael[i] said to him, "Have the gall ready." And the dog[j] went along behind them.

5 Meanwhile Anna sat looking intently down the road by which her son would come. [6]When she caught sight of him coming, she said to his father, "Look, your son is coming, and the man who went with him!"

Tobit's Sight Restored

7 Raphael said to Tobias, before he had approached his father, "I know that his eyes will be opened. [8]Smear the gall of the fish on his eyes; the medicine will make the white films shrink and peel off from his eyes, and your father will regain his sight and see the light."

9 Then Anna ran up to her son and threw her arms around him, saying, "Now that I have seen you, my child, I am ready to die." And she wept. [10]Then Tobit got up and came stumbling out through the courtyard door. Tobias went up to him, [11]with the gall of the fish in his hand, and holding him firmly, he blew into his eyes, saying, "Take courage, father." With this he applied the medicine on his eyes, [12]and it made them smart.[h] [13]Next, with both his hands he peeled off the white films from the corners of his eyes. Then Tobit[i] saw his son and[k] threw his arms around him, [14]and he wept and said to him, "I see you, my son, the light of my eyes!" Then he said,

"Blessed be God,
    and blessed be his great name,
    and blessed be all his holy angels.
May his holy name be blessed[l]

throughout all the ages.
[15] Though he afflicted me,
    he has had mercy upon me.[m]
    Now I see my son Tobias!"

So Tobit went in rejoicing and praising God at the top of his voice. Tobias reported to his father that his journey had been successful, that he had brought the money, that he had married Raguel's daughter Sarah, and that she was, indeed, on her way there, very near to the gate of Nineveh.

16 Then Tobit, rejoicing and praising God, went out to meet his daughter-in-law at the gate of Nineveh. When the people of Nineveh saw him coming, walking along in full vigor and with no one leading him, they were amazed. [17]Before them all, Tobit acknowledged that God had been merciful to him and had restored his sight. When Tobit met Sarah the wife of his son Tobias, he blessed her saying, "Come in, my daughter, and welcome. Blessed be your God who has brought you to us, my daughter. Blessed be your father and your mother, blessed be my son Tobias, and blessed be you, my daughter. Come in now to your home, and welcome, with blessing and joy. Come in, my daughter." So on that day there was rejoicing among all the Jews who were in Nineveh. [18]Ahikar and his nephew Nadab were also present to share Tobit's joy. With merriment they celebrated Tobias's wedding feast for seven days, and many gifts were given to him.[n]

Raphael's Wages

12 When the wedding celebration was ended, Tobit called his son Tobias and said to him, "My child, see to paying the wages of the man who went with you, and give him a bonus as well." [2]He replied, "Father, how much shall I pay him? It would do no harm to give him half of the possessions brought back with me. [3]For he has led me back to you safely, he cured my wife, he brought the money back with me, and he healed you. How much extra shall I give him as a bonus?" [4]Tobit said, "He deserves, my child, to receive half of all that he brought back." [5]So Tobias[i] called him and said, "Take for your wages half of all that you brought back, and farewell."

---

[h] Lat: Meaning of Gk uncertain   [i] Gk he   [j] Codex Sinaiticus reads And the Lord   [k] Other ancient authorities lack saw his son and   [l] Codex Sinaiticus reads May his great name be upon us and blessed be all the angels   [m] Lat: Gk lacks this line   [n] Other ancient authorities lack parts of this sentence

Raphael's Exhortation

6 Then Raphael[o] called the two of them privately and said to them, "Bless God and acknowledge him in the presence of all the living for the good things he has done for you. Bless and sing praise to his name. With fitting honor declare to all people the deeds[p] of God. Do not be slow to acknowledge him. [7]It is good to conceal the secret of a king, but to acknowledge and reveal the works of God, and with fitting honor to acknowledge him. Do good and evil will not overtake you. [8]Prayer with fasting[q] is good, but better than both is almsgiving with righteousness. A little with righteousness is better than wealth with wrongdoing.[r] It is better to give alms than to lay up gold. [9]For almsgiving saves from death and purges away every sin. Those who give alms will enjoy a full life, [10]but those who commit sin and do wrong are their own worst enemies.

Raphael Discloses His Identity

11 "I will now declare the whole truth to you and will conceal nothing from you. Already I have declared it to you when I said, 'It is good to conceal the secret of a king, but to reveal with due honor the works of God.' [12]So now when you and Sarah prayed, it was I who brought and read[s] the record of your prayer before the glory of the Lord, and likewise whenever you would bury the dead. [13]And that time when you did not hesitate to get up and leave your dinner to go and bury the dead, [14]I was sent to you to test you. And at the same time God sent me to heal you and Sarah your daughter-in-law. [15]I am Raphael, one of the seven angels who stand ready and enter before the glory of the Lord."

16 The two of them were shaken; they fell face down, for they were afraid. [17]But he said to them, "Do not be afraid; peace be with you. Bless God forevermore. [18]As for me, when I was with you, I was not acting on my own will, but by the will of God. Bless him each and every day; sing his praises. [19]Although you were watching me, I really did not eat or drink anything—but what you saw was a vision. [20]So now get up from the ground,[t] and acknowledge God. See, I am ascending to him who sent me.

Write down all these things that have happened to you." And he ascended. [21]Then they stood up, and could see him no more. [22]They kept blessing God and singing his praises, and they acknowledged God for these marvelous deeds of his, when an angel of God had appeared to them.

Tobit's Thanksgiving to God

13 Then Tobit[o] said:
"Blessed be God who lives
forever,
because his kingdom[u] lasts
throughout all ages.
2 For he afflicts, and he shows mercy;
he leads down to Hades in the
lowest regions of the earth,
and he brings up from the great
abyss,[v]
and there is nothing that can
escape his hand.
3 Acknowledge him before the nations,
O children of Israel;
for he has scattered you among
them.
4 He has shown you his greatness
even there.
Exalt him in the presence of every
living being,
because he is our Lord and he is
our God;
he is our Father and he is God
forever.
5 He will afflict[w] you for your iniquities,
but he will again show mercy on
all of you.
He will gather you from all the
nations
among whom you have been
scattered.
6 If you turn to him with all your heart
and with all your soul,
to do what is true before him,
then he will turn to you
and will no longer hide his face
from you.
So now see what he has done for
you;
acknowledge him at the top of your
voice.
Bless the Lord of righteousness,
and exalt the King of the ages.[x]

[o] Gk *he* [p] Gk *words;* other ancient authorities read *words of the deeds* [q] Codex Sinaiticus *with sincerity* [r] Lat [s] Lat: Gk lacks *and read* [t] Other ancient authorities read *now bless the Lord on earth* [u] Other ancient authorities read *forever, and his kingdom* [v] Gk *from destruction* [w] Other ancient authorities read *He afflicted* [x] The lacuna in codex Sinaiticus, verses 6b to 10a, is filled in from other ancient authorities

In the land of my exile I acknowledge
    him,
and show his power and majesty to
    a nation of sinners:
'Turn back, you sinners, and do what
    is right before him;
perhaps he may look with favor
    upon you and show you
    mercy.'
7 As for me, I exalt my God,
    and my soul rejoices in the King of
    heaven.
8 Let all people speak of his majesty,
    and acknowledge him in Jerusalem.
9 O Jerusalem, the holy city,
    he afflicted[y] you for the deeds of
    your hands,[z]
    but will again have mercy on the
    children of the righteous.
10 Acknowledge the Lord, for he is good,[a]
    and bless the King of the ages,
    so that his tent[b] may be rebuilt in
    you in joy.
May he cheer all those within you who
    are captives,
    and love all those within you who
    are distressed,
    to all generations forever.
11 A bright light will shine to all the
    ends of the earth;
    many nations will come to you
    from far away,
    the inhabitants of the remotest parts of
    the earth to your holy name,
    bearing gifts in their hands for the
    King of heaven.
Generation after generation will give
    joyful praise in you;
    the name of the chosen city will
    endure forever.
12 Cursed are all who speak a harsh
    word against you;
    cursed are all who conquer you
    and pull down your walls,
all who overthrow your towers
    and set your homes on fire.
    But blessed forever will be all who
    revere you.[c]
13 Go, then, and rejoice over the children
    of the righteous,
    for they will be gathered together
    and will praise the Lord of the ages.
14 Happy are those who love you,

and happy are those who rejoice in
    your prosperity.
Happy also are all people who grieve
    with you
    because of your afflictions;
for they will rejoice with you
    and witness all your glory forever.
15 My soul blesses[d] the Lord, the great
    King!
16   For Jerusalem will be built[e] as his
    house for all ages.
How happy I will be if a remnant of
    my descendants should survive
    to see your glory and acknowledge
    the King of heaven.
The gates of Jerusalem will be built
    with sapphire and emerald,
    and all your walls with precious
    stones.
The towers of Jerusalem will be built
    with gold,
    and their battlements with pure
    gold.
The streets of Jerusalem will be paved
    with ruby and with stones of Ophir.
17 The gates of Jerusalem will sing
    hymns of joy,
    and all her houses will cry,
    'Hallelujah!
Blessed be the God of Israel!'
    and the blessed will bless the holy
    name forever and ever."

Tobit's Final Counsel

14 So ended Tobit's words of praise.
2 Tobit[f] died in peace when he
was one hundred twelve years old, and was
buried with great honor in Nineveh. He was
sixty-two[g] years old when he lost his eyesight, and after regaining it he lived in prosperity, giving alms and continually blessing
God and acknowledging God's majesty.

3 When he was about to die, he called
his son Tobias and the seven sons of Tobias[h]
and gave this command: "My son, take
your children 4and hurry off to Media, for I
believe the word of God that Nahum spoke
about Nineveh, that all these things will
take place and overtake Assyria and Nineveh.
Indeed, everything that was spoken by the
prophets of Israel, whom God sent, will
occur. None of all their words will fail, but

---

[y] Other ancient authorities read *will afflict*   [z] Other ancient authorities read *your children*   [a] Other ancient
authorities read *Lord worthily*   [b] Or *tabernacle*   [c] Other ancient authorities read *who build you up*   [d] Or *O my
soul, bless*   [e] Other ancient authorities add *for a city*   [f] Gk *He*   [g] Other ancient authorities read *fifty-eight*
[h] Lat: Gk lacks *and the seven sons of Tobias*

all will come true at their appointed times.
So it will be safer in Media than in Assyria
and Babylon. For I know and believe that
whatever God has said will be fulfilled and
will come true; not a single word of the
prophecies will fail. All of our kindred,
inhabitants of the land of Israel, will be scattered and taken as captives from the good
land; and the whole land of Israel will be
desolate, even Samaria and Jerusalem will
be desolate. And the temple of God in it will
be burned to the ground, and it will be desolate for a while.[i]
5 "But God will again have mercy on
them, and God will bring them back into
the land of Israel; and they will rebuild the
temple of God, but not like the first one until
the period when the times of fulfillment
shall come. After this they all will return
from their exile and will rebuild Jerusalem
in splendor; and in it the temple of God will
be rebuilt, just as the prophets of Israel have
said concerning it. [6]Then the nations in the
whole world will all be converted and worship God in truth. They will all abandon
their idols, which deceitfully have led them
into their error; [7]and in righteousness they
will praise the eternal God. All the Israelites
who are saved in those days and are truly
mindful of God will be gathered together;
they will go to Jerusalem and live in safety
forever in the land of Abraham, and it will
be given over to them. Those who sincerely
love God will rejoice, but those who commit
sin and injustice will vanish from all the
earth. [8,9]So now, my children, I command
you, serve God faithfully and do what is
pleasing in his sight. Your children are also
to be commanded to do what is right and to
give alms, and to be mindful of God and to
bless his name at all times with sincerity
and with all their strength. So now, my son,
leave Nineveh; do not remain here. [10]On
whatever day you bury your mother beside
me, do not stay overnight within the
confines of the city. For I see that there is
much wickedness within it, and that much
deceit is practiced within it, while the people are without shame. See, my son, what
Nadab did to Ahikar who had reared him.
Was he not, while still alive, brought down
into the earth? For God repaid him to his
face for this shameful treatment. Ahikar
came out into the light, but Nadab went
into the eternal darkness, because he tried
to kill Ahikar. Because he gave alms,
Ahikar[j] escaped the fatal trap that Nadab
had set for him, but Nadab fell into it himself, and was destroyed. [11]So now, my children, see what almsgiving accomplishes,
and what injustice does—it brings death!
But now my breath fails me."

Death of Tobit and Anna

Then they laid him on his bed, and he
died; and he received an honorable funeral.
[12]When Tobias's mother died, he buried
her beside his father. Then he and his wife
and children[k] returned to Media and settled
in Ecbatana with Raguel his father-in-law.
[13]He treated his parents-in-law[l] with great
respect in their old age, and buried them in
Ecbatana of Media. He inherited both the
property of Raguel and that of his father
Tobit. [14]He died highly respected at the age
of one hundred seventeen[m] years. [15]Before
he died he heard[n] of the destruction of
Nineveh, and he saw its prisoners being led
into Media, those whom King Cyaxares[o] of
Media had taken captive. Tobias[p] praised
God for all he had done to the people of
Nineveh and Assyria; before he died he
rejoiced over Nineveh, and he blessed the
Lord God forever and ever. Amen.[q]

[i] Lat: Other ancient authorities read *of God will be in distress and will be burned for a while* [j] Gk *he*; other ancient authorities read *Manasses* [k] Codex Sinaiticus lacks *and children* [l] Gk *them* [m] Other authorities read other numbers [n] Codex Sinaiticus reads *saw and heard* [o] Cn: Codex Sinaiticus *Ahikar*; other ancient authorities read *Nebuchadnezzar and Ahasuerus* [p] Gk *He* [q] Other ancient authorities lack *Amen*

JUDITH

Arphaxad Fortifies Ecbatana

1 It was the twelfth year of the reign of Nebuchadnezzar, who ruled over the Assyrians in the great city of Nineveh. In those days Arphaxad ruled over the Medes in Ecbatana. ²He built walls around Ecbatana with hewn stones three cubits thick and six cubits long; he made the walls seventy cubits high and fifty cubits wide. ³At its gates he raised towers one hundred cubits high and sixty cubits wide at the foundations. ⁴He made its gates seventy cubits high and forty cubits wide to allow his armies to march out in force and his infantry to form their ranks. ⁵Then King Nebuchadnezzar made war against King Arphaxad in the great plain that is on the borders of Ragau. ⁶There rallied to him all the people of the hill country and all those who lived along the Euphrates, the Tigris, and the Hydaspes, and, on the plain, Arioch, king of the Elymeans. Thus, many nations joined the forces of the Chaldeans.ᵃ

Nebuchadnezzar Issues an Ultimatum

7 Then Nebuchadnezzar, king of the Assyrians, sent messengers to all who lived in Persia and to all who lived in the west, those who lived in Cilicia and Damascus, Lebanon and Antilebanon, and all who lived along the seacoast, ⁸and those among the nations of Carmel and Gilead, and Upper Galilee and the great plain of Esdraelon, ⁹and all who were in Samaria and its towns, and beyond the Jordan as far as Jerusalem and Bethany and Chelous and Kadesh and the river of Egypt, and Tahpanhes and Raamses and the whole land of Goshen, ¹⁰even beyond Tanis and Memphis, and all who lived in Egypt as far as the borders of Ethiopia. ¹¹But all who lived in the whole region disregarded the summons of Nebuchadnezzar, king of the Assyrians, and refused to join him in the war; for they were not afraid of him, but regarded him as only one man.ᵇ So they sent back his messengers empty-handed and in disgrace. 12 Then Nebuchadnezzar became very angry with this whole region, and swore by his throne and kingdom that he would take revenge on the whole territory of Cilicia and Damascus and Syria, that he would kill with his sword also all the inhabitants of the land of Moab, and the people of Ammon, and all Judea, and every one in Egypt, as far as the coasts of the two seas.

Arphaxad Is Defeated

13 In the seventeenth year he led his forces against King Arphaxad and defeated him in battle, overthrowing the whole army of Arphaxad and all his cavalry and all his chariots. ¹⁴Thus he took possession of his towns and came to Ecbatana, captured its towers, plundered its markets, and turned its glory into disgrace. ¹⁵He captured Arphaxad in the mountains of Ragau and struck him down with his spears, thus destroying him once and for all. ¹⁶Then he returned to Nineveh, he and all his combined forces, a vast body of troops; and there he and his forces rested and feasted for one hundred twenty days.

The Expedition against the West

2 In the eighteenth year, on the twenty-second day of the first month, there was talk in the palace of Nebuchadnezzar, king of the Assyrians, about carrying out his revenge on the whole region, just as he had said. ²He summoned all his ministers and all his nobles and set before them his secret plan and recounted fully, with his own lips, all the wickedness of the region.ᶜ ³They decided that every one who had not obeyed his command should be destroyed.

4 When he had completed his plan, Nebuchadnezzar, king of the Assyrians, called Holofernes, the chief general of his army, second only to himself, and said to him, ⁵"Thus says the Great King, the lord of the whole earth: Leave my presence and take with you men confident in their strength, one hundred twenty thousand foot soldiers and twelve thousand cavalry. ⁶March out against all the land to the west, because they disobeyed my orders. ⁷Tell them to prepare earth and water, for I am coming against them in my anger, and will cover the whole face of the earth with the feet of my troops, to whom I will hand them over to be plundered. ⁸Their wounded shall fill their ravines and gullies, and the swelling

---

ᵃ Syr: Gk *Cheleoudites*   ᵇ Or *a man*   ᶜ Meaning of Gk uncertain

14

river shall be filled with their dead. ⁹I will lead them away captive to the ends of the whole earth. ¹⁰You shall go and seize all their territory for me in advance. They must yield themselves to you, and you shall hold them for me until the day of their punishment. ¹¹But to those who resist show no mercy, but hand them over to slaughter and plunder throughout your whole region. ¹²For as I live, and by the power of my kingdom, what I have spoken I will accomplish by my own hand. ¹³And you—take care not to transgress any of your lord's commands, but carry them out exactly as I have ordered you; do it without delay."

Campaign of Holofernes

14 So Holofernes left the presence of his lord, and summoned all the commanders, generals, and officers of the Assyrian army. ¹⁵He mustered the picked troops by divisions as his lord had ordered him to do, one hundred twenty thousand of them, together with twelve thousand archers on horseback, ¹⁶and he organized them as a great army is marshaled for a campaign. ¹⁷He took along a vast number of camels and donkeys and mules for transport, and innumerable sheep and oxen and goats for food; ¹⁸also ample rations for everyone, and a huge amount of gold and silver from the royal palace.

19 Then he set out with his whole army, to go ahead of King Nebuchadnezzar and to cover the whole face of the earth to the west with their chariots and cavalry and picked foot soldiers. ²⁰Along with them went a mixed crowd like a swarm of locusts, like the dust*d* of the earth—a multitude that could not be counted.

21 They marched for three days from Nineveh to the plain of Bectileth, and camped opposite Bectileth near the mountain that is to the north of Upper Cilicia. ²²From there Holofernes*e* took his whole army, the infantry, cavalry, and chariots, and went up into the hill country. ²³He ravaged Put and Lud, and plundered all the Rassisites and the Ishmaelites on the border of the desert, south of the country of the Chelleans. ²⁴Then he followed*f* the Euphrates and passed through Mesopotamia and destroyed all the

fortified towns along the brook Abron, as far as the sea. ²⁵He also seized the territory of Cilicia, and killed everyone who resisted him. Then he came to the southern borders of Japheth, facing Arabia. ²⁶He surrounded all the Midianites, and burned their tents and plundered their sheepfolds. ²⁷Then he went down into the plain of Damascus during the wheat harvest, and burned all their fields and destroyed their flocks and herds and sacked their towns and ravaged their lands and put all their young men to the sword.

28 So fear and dread of him fell upon all the people who lived along the seacoast, at Sidon and Tyre, and those who lived in Sur and Ocina and all who lived in Jamnia. Those who lived in Azotus and Ascalon feared him greatly.

Entreaties for Peace

3 They therefore sent messengers to him to sue for peace in these words: ²"We, the servants of Nebuchadnezzar, the Great King, lie prostrate before you. Do with us whatever you will. ³See, our buildings and all our land and all our wheat fields and our flocks and herds and all our encampments*g* lie before you; do with them as you please. ⁴Our towns and their inhabitants are also your slaves; come and deal with them as you see fit."

5 The men came to Holofernes and told him all this. ⁶Then he went down to the seacoast with his army and stationed garrisons in the fortified towns and took picked men from them as auxiliaries. ⁷These people and all in the countryside welcomed him with garlands and dances and tambourines. ⁸Yet he demolished all their shrines*h* and cut down their sacred groves; for he had been commissioned to destroy all the gods of the land, so that all nations should worship Nebuchadnezzar alone, and that all their dialects and tribes should call upon him as a god.

9 Then he came toward Esdraelon, near Dothan, facing the great ridge of Judea; ¹⁰he camped between Geba and Scythopolis, and remained for a whole month in order to collect all the supplies for his army.

---

d Gk *sand*   *e* Gk *he*   *f* Or *crossed*   *g* Gk *all the sheepfolds of our tents*   *h* Syr: Gk *borders*

Judea on the Alert

4 When the Israelites living in Judea heard of everything that Holofernes, the general of Nebuchadnezzar, the king of the Assyrians, had done to the nations, and how he had plundered and destroyed all their temples, ²they were therefore greatly terrified at his approach; they were alarmed both for Jerusalem and for the temple of the Lord their God. ³For they had only recently returned from exile, and all the people of Judea had just now gathered together, and the sacred vessels and the altar and the temple had been consecrated after their profanation. ⁴So they sent word to every district of Samaria, and to Kona, Beth-horon, Belmain, and Jericho, and to Choba and Aesora, and the valley of Salem. ⁵They immediately seized all the high hilltops and fortified the villages on them and stored up food in preparation for war—since their fields had recently been harvested.

6 The high priest, Joakim, who was in Jerusalem at the time, wrote to the people of Bethulia and Betomesthaim, which faces Esdraelon opposite the plain near Dothan, ⁷ordering them to seize the mountain passes, since by them Judea could be invaded; and it would be easy to stop any who tried to enter, for the approach was narrow, wide enough for only two at a time to pass.

Prayer and Penance

8 So the Israelites did as they had been ordered by the high priest Joakim and the senate of the whole people of Israel, in session at Jerusalem. ⁹And every man of Israel cried out to God with great fervor, and they humbled themselves with much fasting. ¹⁰They and their wives and their children and their cattle and every resident alien and hired laborer and purchased slave—they all put sackcloth around their waists. ¹¹And all the Israelite men, women, and children living at Jerusalem prostrated themselves before the temple and put ashes on their heads and spread out their sackcloth before the Lord. ¹²They even draped the altar with sackcloth and cried out in unison, praying fervently to the God of Israel not to allow their infants to be carried off and their wives to be taken as booty, and the towns they had inherited to be destroyed, and the sanctuary to be profaned and desecrated to the malicious joy of the Gentiles.

13 The Lord heard their prayers and had regard for their distress; for the people fasted many days throughout Judea and in Jerusalem before the sanctuary of the Lord Almighty. ¹⁴The high priest Joakim and all the priests who stood before the Lord and ministered to the Lord, with sackcloth around their loins, offered the daily burnt offerings, the votive offerings, and freewill offerings of the people. ¹⁵With ashes on their turbans, they cried out to the Lord with all their might to look with favor on the whole house of Israel.

Council against the Israelites

5 It was reported to Holofernes, the general of the Assyrian army, that the people of Israel had prepared for war and had closed the mountain passes and fortified all the high hilltops and set up barricades in the plains. ²In great anger he called together all the princes of Moab and the commanders of Ammon and all the governors of the coastland, ³and said to them, "Tell me, you Canaanites, what people is this that lives in the hill country? What towns do they inhabit? How large is their army, and in what does their power and strength consist? Who rules over them as king and leads their army? ⁴And why have they alone, of all who live in the west, refused to come out and meet me?"

Achior's Report

5 Then Achior, the leader of all the Ammonites, said to him, "May my lord please listen to a report from the mouth of your servant, and I will tell you the truth about this people that lives in the mountain district near you. No falsehood shall come from your servant's mouth. ⁶These people are descended from the Chaldeans. ⁷At one time they lived in Mesopotamia, because they did not wish to follow the gods of their ancestors who were in Chaldea. ⁸Since they had abandoned the ways of their ancestors, and worshiped the God of heaven, the God they had come to know, their ancestors*ʲ* drove them out from the presence of their gods. So they fled to Mesopotamia, and lived there for a long time. ⁹Then their God commanded them to leave the place where they were living and go to the land of Canaan. There they settled, and grew very prosperous in gold and silver and very much livestock. ¹⁰When a famine spread over the

---

ʲ Gk *they*

land of Canaan they went down to Egypt and lived there as long as they had food. There they became so great a multitude that their race could not be counted. [11]So the king of Egypt became hostile to them; he exploited them and forced them to make bricks. [12]They cried out to their God, and he afflicted the whole land of Egypt with incurable plagues. So the Egyptians drove them out of their sight. [13]Then God dried up the Red Sea before them, [14]and he led them by the way of Sinai and Kadesh-barnea. They drove out all the people of the desert, [15]and took up residence in the land of the Amorites, and by their might destroyed all the inhabitants of Heshbon; and crossing over the Jordan they took possession of all the hill country. [16]They drove out before them the Canaanites, the Perizzites, the Jebusites, the Shechemites, and all the Gergesites, and lived there a long time.

17 "As long as they did not sin against their God they prospered, for the God who hates iniquity is with them. [18]But when they departed from the way he had prescribed for them, they were utterly defeated in many battles and were led away captive to a foreign land. The temple of their God was razed to the ground, and their towns were occupied by their enemies. [19]But now they have returned to their God, and have come back from the places where they were scattered, and have occupied Jerusalem, where their sanctuary is, and have settled in the hill country, because it was uninhabited.

20 "So now, my master and lord, if there is any oversight in this people and they sin against their God and we find out their offense, then we can go up and defeat them. [21]But if they are not a guilty nation, then let my lord pass them by; for their Lord and God will defend them, and we shall become the laughingstock of the whole world."

22 When Achior had finished saying these things, all the people standing around the tent began to complain; Holofernes' officers and all the inhabitants of the seacoast and Moab insisted that he should be cut to pieces. [23]They said, "We are not afraid of the Israelites; they are a people with no strength or power for making war. [24]Therefore let us go ahead, Lord Holofernes, and your vast army will swallow them up."

Achior Handed over to the Israelites

6 When the disturbance made by the people outside the council had died down, Holofernes, the commander of the Assyrian army, said to Achior[j] in the presence of all the foreign contingents:

2 "Who are you, Achior and you mercenaries of Ephraim, to prophesy among us as you have done today and tell us not to make war against the people of Israel because their God will defend them? What god is there except Nebuchadnezzar? He will send his forces and destroy them from the face of the earth. Their God will not save them; [3]we the king's[k] servants will destroy them as one man. They cannot resist the might of our cavalry. [4]We will overwhelm them;[l] their mountains will be drunk with their blood, and their fields will be full of their dead. Not even their footprints will survive our attack; they will utterly perish. So says King Nebuchadnezzar, lord of the whole earth. For he has spoken; none of his words shall be in vain.

5 "As for you, Achior, you Ammonite mercenary, you have said these words in a moment of perversity; you shall not see my face again from this day until I take revenge on this race that came out of Egypt. [6]Then at my return the sword of my army and the spear[m] of my servants shall pierce your sides, and you shall fall among their wounded. [7]Now my slaves are going to take you back into the hill country and put you in one of the towns beside the passes. [8]You will not die until you perish along with them. [9]If you really hope in your heart that they will not be taken, then do not look downcast! I have spoken, and none of my words shall fail to come true."

10 Then Holofernes ordered his slaves, who waited on him in his tent, to seize Achior and take him away to Bethulia and hand him over to the Israelites. [11]So the slaves took him and led him out of the camp into the plain, and from the plain they went up into the hill country and came to the springs below Bethulia. [12]When the men of the town saw them,[n] they seized their weapons and ran out of the town to the top of the hill, and all the slingers kept them from coming up by throwing stones at them. [13]So having taken shelter below the hill, they bound Achior and left him

---

[j]Other ancient authorities add *and to all the Moabites*　　[k]Gk *his*　　[l]Other ancient authorities add *with it*
[m]Lat Syr: Gk *people*　　[n]Other ancient authorities add *on the top of the hill*

lying at the foot of the hill, and returned to their master.

14 Then the Israelites came down from their town and found him; they untied him and brought him into Bethulia and placed him before the magistrates of their town, [15]who in those days were Uzziah son of Micah, of the tribe of Simeon, and Chabris son of Gothoniel, and Charmis son of Melchiel. [16]They called together all the elders of the town, and all their young men and women ran to the assembly. They set Achior in the midst of all their people, and Uzziah questioned him about what had happened. [17]He answered and told them what had taken place at the council of Holofernes, and all that he had said in the presence of the Assyrian leaders, and all that Holofernes had boasted he would do against the house of Israel. [18]Then the people fell down and worshiped God, and cried out:

19 "O Lord God of heaven, see their arrogance, and have pity on our people in their humiliation, and look kindly today on the faces of those who are consecrated to you."

20 Then they reassured Achior, and praised him highly. [21]Uzziah took him from the assembly to his own house and gave a banquet for the elders; and all that night they called on the God of Israel for help.

The Campaign against Bethulia

7 The next day Holofernes ordered his whole army, and all the allies who had joined him, to break camp and move against Bethulia, and to seize the passes up into the hill country and make war on the Israelites. [2]So all their warriors marched off that day; their fighting forces numbered one hundred seventy thousand infantry and twelve thousand cavalry, not counting the baggage and the foot soldiers handling it, a very great multitude. [3]They encamped in the valley near Bethulia, beside the spring, and they spread out in breadth over Dothan as far as Balbaim and in length from Bethulia to Cyamon, which faces Esdraelon.

4 When the Israelites saw their vast numbers, they were greatly terrified and said to one another, "They will now strip clean the whole land; neither the high mountains nor the valleys nor the hills will bear their weight." [5]Yet they all seized their weapons, and when they had kindled fires on their towers, they remained on guard all that night.

6 On the second day Holofernes led out all his cavalry in full view of the Israelites in Bethulia. [7]He reconnoitered the approaches to their town, and visited the springs that supplied their water; he seized them and set guards of soldiers over them, and then returned to his army.

8 Then all the chieftains of the Edomites and all the leaders of the Moabites and the commanders of the coastland came to him and said, [9]"Listen to what we have to say, my lord, and your army will suffer no losses. [10]This people, the Israelites, do not rely on their spears but on the height of the mountains where they live, for it is not easy to reach the tops of their mountains. [11]Therefore, my lord, do not fight against them in regular formation, and not a man of your army will fall. [12]Remain in your camp, and keep all the men in your forces with you; let your servants take possession of the spring of water that flows from the foot of the mountain, [13]for this is where all the people of Bethulia get their water. So thirst will destroy them, and they will surrender their town. Meanwhile, we and our people will go up to the tops of the nearby mountains and camp there to keep watch to see that no one gets out of the town. [14]They and their wives and children will waste away with famine, and before the sword reaches them they will be strewn about in the streets where they live. [15]Thus you will pay them back with evil, because they rebelled and did not receive you peaceably."

16 These words pleased Holofernes and all his attendants, and he gave orders to do as they had said. [17]So the army of the Ammonites moved forward, together with five thousand Assyrians, and they encamped in the valley and seized the water supply and the springs of the Israelites. [18]And the Edomites and Ammonites went up and encamped in the hill country opposite Dothan; and they sent some of their men toward the south and the east, toward Egrebeh, which is near Chusi beside the Wadi Mochmur. The rest of the Assyrian army encamped in the plain, and covered the whole face of the land. Their tents and supply trains spread out in great number, and they formed a vast multitude.

The Distress of the Israelites

19 The Israelites then cried out to the
Lord their God, for their courage failed,
because all their enemies had surrounded
them, and there was no way of escape from
them. [20]The whole Assyrian army, their
infantry, chariots, and cavalry, surrounded
them for thirty-four days, until all the
water containers of every inhabitant of
Bethulia were empty; [21]their cisterns were
going dry, and on no day did they have
enough water to drink, for their drinking
water was rationed. [22]Their children were
listless, and the women and young men
fainted from thirst and were collapsing in
the streets of the town and in the gate-
ways; they no longer had any strength.

23 Then all the people, the young men,
the women, and the children, gathered
around Uzziah and the rulers of the town
and cried out with a loud voice, and said
before all the elders, [24]"Let God judge
between you and us! You have done us a
great injury in not making peace with the
Assyrians. [25]For now we have no one to
help us; God has sold us into their hands, to
be strewn before them in thirst and exhaustion. [26]Now summon them and surrender
the whole town as booty to the army of
Holofernes and to all his forces. [27]For it
would be better for us to be captured by
them.[o] We shall indeed become slaves, but
our lives will be spared, and we shall not
witness our little ones dying before our eyes,
and our wives and children drawing their
last breath. [28]We call to witness against you
heaven and earth and our God, the Lord of
our ancestors, who punishes us for our sins
and the sins of our ancestors; do today the
things that we have described!"

29 Then great and general lamentation
arose throughout the assembly, and they
cried out to the Lord God with a loud voice.
[30]But Uzziah said to them, "Courage, my
brothers and sisters![p] Let us hold out for five
days more; by that time the Lord our God
will turn his mercy to us again, for he will
not forsake us utterly. [31]But if these days
pass by, and no help comes for us, I will do
as you say."

32 Then he dismissed the people to their
various posts, and they went up on the
walls and towers of their town. The women
and children he sent home. In the town
they were in great misery.

The Character of Judith

8 Now in those days Judith heard about
these things: she was the daughter of
Merari son of Ox son of Joseph son of Oziel
son of Elkiah son of Ananias son of Gideon
son of Raphain son of Ahitub son of Elijah son
of Hilkiah son of Eliab son of Nathanael son
of Salamiel son of Sarasadai son of Israel.
[2]Her husband Manasseh, who belonged to
her tribe and family, had died during the
barley harvest. [3]For as he stood overseeing
those who were binding sheaves in the
field, he was overcome by the burning
heat, and took to his bed and died in his
town Bethulia. So they buried him with his
ancestors in the field between Dothan and
Balamon. [4]Judith remained as a widow for
three years and four months [5]at home
where she set up a tent for herself on the
roof of her house. She put sackcloth
around her waist and dressed in widow's
clothing. [6]She fasted all the days of her
widowhood, except the day before the sabbath and the sabbath itself, the day before
the new moon and the day of the new
moon, and the festivals and days of rejoicing of the house of Israel. [7]She was beautiful in appearance, and was very lovely to
behold. Her husband Manasseh had left her
gold and silver, men and women slaves,
livestock, and fields; and she maintained
this estate. [8]No one spoke ill of her, for she
feared God with great devotion.

Judith and the Elders

9 When Judith heard the harsh words
spoken by the people against the ruler,
because they were faint for lack of water,
and when she heard all that Uzziah said to
them, and how he promised them under
oath to surrender the town to the
Assyrians after five days, [10]she sent her
maid, who was in charge of all she possessed, to summon Uzziah and[q] Chabris and
Charmis, the elders of her town. [11]They
came to her, and she said to them:

"Listen to me, rulers of the people of
Bethulia! What you have said to the people
today is not right; you have even sworn and
pronounced this oath between God and
you, promising to surrender the town to
our enemies unless the Lord turns and helps
us within so many days. [12]Who are you
to put God to the test today, and to set

[o] Other ancient authorities add *than to die of thirst* [p] Gk *Courage, brothers* [q] Other ancient authorities lack *Uzziah and* (see verses 28 and 35)

yourselves up in the place of[r] God in human affairs? [13]You are putting the Lord Almighty to the test, but you will never learn anything! [14]You cannot plumb the depths of the human heart or understand the workings of the human mind; how do you expect to search out God, who made all these things, and find out his mind or comprehend his thought? No, my brothers, do not anger the Lord our God. [15]For if he does not choose to help us within these five days, he has power to protect us within any time he pleases, or even to destroy us in the presence of our enemies. [16]Do not try to bind the purposes of the Lord our God; for God is not like a human being, to be threatened, or like a mere mortal, to be won over by pleading. [17]Therefore, while we wait for his deliverance, let us call upon him to help us, and he will hear our voice, if it pleases him.

18 "For never in our generation, nor in these present days, has there been any tribe or family or people or town of ours that worships gods made with hands, as was done in days gone by. [19]That was why our ancestors were handed over to the sword and to pillage, and so they suffered a great catastrophe before our enemies. [20]But we know no other god but him, and so we hope that he will not disdain us or any of our nation. [21]For if we are captured, all Judea will be captured and our sanctuary will be plundered; and he will make us pay for its desecration with our blood. [22]The slaughter of our kindred and the captivity of the land and the desolation of our inheritance—all this he will bring on our heads among the Gentiles, wherever we serve as slaves; and we shall be an offense and a disgrace in the eyes of those who acquire us. [23]For our slavery will not bring us into favor, but the Lord our God will turn it to dishonor.

24 "Therefore, my brothers, let us set an example for our kindred, for their lives depend upon us, and the sanctuary—both the temple and the altar—rests upon us. [25]In spite of everything let us give thanks to the Lord our God, who is putting us to the test as he did our ancestors. [26]Remember what he did with Abraham, and how he tested Isaac, and what happened to Jacob in Syrian Mesopotamia, while he was tending the sheep of Laban, his mother's brother. [27]For he has not tried us with fire, as he did them, to search their hearts, nor

has he taken vengeance on us; but the Lord scourges those who are close to him in order to admonish them."

28 Then Uzziah said to her, "All that you have said was spoken out of a true heart, and there is no one who can deny your words. [29]Today is not the first time your wisdom has been shown, but from the beginning of your life all the people have recognized your understanding, for your heart's disposition is right. [30]But the people were so thirsty that they compelled us to do for them what we have promised, and made us take an oath that we cannot break. [31]Now since you are a God-fearing woman, pray for us, so that the Lord may send us rain to fill our cisterns. Then we will no longer feel faint from thirst."

32 Then Judith said to them, "Listen to me. I am about to do something that will go down through all generations of our descendants. [33]Stand at the town gate tonight so that I may go out with my maid; and within the days after which you have promised to surrender the town to our enemies, the Lord will deliver Israel by my hand. [34]Only, do not try to find out what I am doing; for I will not tell you until I have finished what I am about to do."

35 Uzziah and the rulers said to her, "Go in peace, and may the Lord God go before you, to take vengeance on our enemies." [36]So they returned from the tent and went to their posts.

The Prayer of Judith

9 Then Judith prostrated herself, put ashes on her head, and uncovered the sackcloth she was wearing. At the very time when the evening incense was being offered in the house of God in Jerusalem, Judith cried out to the Lord with a loud voice, and said,

2 "O Lord God of my ancestor Simeon, to whom you gave a sword to take revenge on those strangers who had torn off a virgin's clothing[s] to defile her, and exposed her thighs to put her to shame, and polluted her womb to disgrace her; for you said, 'It shall not be done'—yet they did it; [3]so you gave up their rulers to be killed, and their bed, which was ashamed of the deceit they had practiced, was stained with blood, and you struck down slaves along with princes, and princes on their thrones. [4]You gave up their

---

[r] Or *above*   [s] Cn: Gk *loosed her womb*

wives for booty and their daughters to captivity, and all their booty to be divided among your beloved children who burned with zeal for you and abhorred the pollution of their blood and called on you for help. O God, my God, hear me also, a widow.

5 "For you have done these things and those that went before and those that followed. You have designed the things that are now, and those that are to come. What you had in mind has happened; ⁶the things you decided on presented themselves and said, 'Here we are!' For all your ways are prepared in advance, and your judgment is with foreknowledge.

7 "Here now are the Assyrians, a greatly increased force, priding themselves in their horses and riders, boasting in the strength of their foot soldiers, and trusting in shield and spear, in bow and sling. They do not know that you are the Lord who crushes wars; the Lord is your name. ⁸Break their strength by your might, and bring down their power in your anger; for they intend to defile your sanctuary, and to pollute the tabernacle where your glorious name resides, and to break off the horns*ᵗ* of your altar with the sword. ⁹Look at their pride, and send your wrath upon their heads. Give to me, a widow, the strong hand to do what I plan. ¹⁰By the deceit of my lips strike down the slave with the prince and the prince with his servant; crush their arrogance by the hand of a woman.

11 "For your strength does not depend on numbers, nor your might on the powerful. But you are the God of the lowly, helper of the oppressed, upholder of the weak, protector of the forsaken, savior of those without hope. ¹²Please, please, God of my father, God of the heritage of Israel, Lord of heaven and earth, Creator of the waters, King of all your creation, hear my prayer! ¹³Make my deceitful words bring wound and bruise on those who have planned cruel things against your covenant, and against your sacred house, and against Mount Zion, and against the house your children possess. ¹⁴Let your whole nation and every tribe know and understand that you are God, the God of all power and might, and that there is no other who protects the people of Israel but you alone!"

Judith Prepares to Go to Holofernes

10 When Judith*ᵘ* had stopped crying out to the God of Israel, and had ended all these words, ²she rose from where she lay prostrate. She called her maid and went down into the house where she lived on sabbaths and on her festal days. ³She removed the sackcloth she had been wearing, took off her widow's garments, bathed her body with water, and anointed herself with precious ointment. She combed her hair, put on a tiara, and dressed herself in the festive attire that she used to wear while her husband Manasseh was living. ⁴She put sandals on her feet, and put on her anklets, bracelets, rings, earrings, and all her other jewelry. Thus she made herself very beautiful, to entice the eyes of all the men who might see her. ⁵She gave her maid a skin of wine and a flask of oil, and filled a bag with roasted grain, dried fig cakes, and fine bread;*ᵛ* then she wrapped up all her dishes and gave them to her to carry.

6 Then they went out to the town gate of Bethulia and found Uzziah standing there with the elders of the town, Chabris and Charmis. ⁷When they saw her transformed in appearance and dressed differently, they were very greatly astounded at her beauty and said to her, ⁸"May the God of our ancestors grant you favor and fulfill your plans, so that the people of Israel may glory and Jerusalem may be exalted." She bowed down to God.

9 Then she said to them, "Order the gate of the town to be opened for me so that I may go out and accomplish the things you have just said to me." So they ordered the young men to open the gate for her, as she requested. ¹⁰When they had done this, Judith went out, accompanied by her maid. The men of the town watched her until she had gone down the mountain and passed through the valley, where they lost sight of her.

Judith Is Captured

11 As the women*ʷ* were going straight on through the valley, an Assyrian patrol met her ¹²and took her into custody. They asked her, "To what people do you belong, and where are you coming from, and where are you going?" She replied, "I am a daughter of the Hebrews, but I am fleeing from

---

ᵗ Syr: Gk *horn*   *ᵘ* Gk *she*   *ᵛ* Other ancient authorities add *and cheese*   *ʷ* Gk *they*

them, for they are about to be handed over to you to be devoured. ¹³I am on my way to see Holofernes the commander of your army, to give him a true report; I will show him a way by which he can go and capture all the hill country without losing one of his men, captured or slain."

14 When the men heard her words, and observed her face—she was in their eyes marvelously beautiful—they said to her, ¹⁵"You have saved your life by hurrying down to see our lord. Go at once to his tent; some of us will escort you and hand you over to him. ¹⁶When you stand before him, have no fear in your heart, but tell him what you have just said, and he will treat you well."

17 They chose from their number a hundred men to accompany her and her maid, and they brought them to the tent of Holofernes. ¹⁸There was great excitement in the whole camp, for her arrival was reported from tent to tent. They came and gathered around her as she stood outside the tent of Holofernes, waiting until they told him about her. ¹⁹They marveled at her beauty and admired the Israelites, judging them by her. They said to one another, "Who can despise these people, who have women like this among them? It is not wise to leave one of their men alive, for if we let them go they will be able to beguile the whole world!"

Judith Is Brought before Holofernes

20 Then the guards of Holofernes and all his servants came out and led her into the tent. ²¹Holofernes was resting on his bed under a canopy that was woven with purple and gold, emeralds and other precious stones. ²²When they told him of her, he came to the front of the tent, with silver lamps carried before him. ²³When Judith came into the presence of Holofernes^x and his servants, they all marveled at the beauty of her face. She prostrated herself and did obeisance to him, but his slaves raised her up.

11   Then Holofernes said to her, "Take courage, woman, and do not be afraid in your heart, for I have never hurt anyone who chose to serve Nebuchadnezzar, king of all the earth. ²Even now, if your people who live in the hill country had not slighted me, I would never have lifted my

spear against them. They have brought this on themselves. ³But now tell me why you have fled from them and have come over to us. In any event, you have come to safety. Take courage! You will live tonight and ever after. ⁴No one will hurt you. Rather, all will treat you well, as they do the servants of my lord King Nebuchadnezzar."

Judith Explains Her Presence

5 Judith answered him, "Accept the words of your slave, and let your servant speak in your presence. I will say nothing false to my lord this night. ⁶If you follow out the words of your servant, God will accomplish something through you, and my lord will not fail to achieve his purposes. ⁷By the life of Nebuchadnezzar, king of the whole earth, and by the power of him who has sent you to direct every living being! Not only do human beings serve him because of you, but also the animals of the field and the cattle and the birds of the air will live, because of your power, under Nebuchadnezzar and all his house. ⁸For we have heard of your wisdom and skill, and it is reported throughout the whole world that you alone are the best in the whole kingdom, the most informed and the most astounding in military strategy.

9 "Now as for Achior's speech in your council, we have heard his words, for the people of Bethulia spared him and he told them all he had said to you. ¹⁰Therefore, lord and master, do not disregard what he said, but keep it in your mind, for it is true. Indeed our nation cannot be punished, nor can the sword prevail against them, unless they sin against their God.

11 "But now, in order that my lord may not be defeated and his purpose frustrated, death will fall upon them, for a sin has overtaken them by which they are about to provoke their God to anger when they do what is wrong. ¹²Since their food supply is exhausted and their water has almost given out, they have planned to kill their livestock and have determined to use all that God by his laws has forbidden them to eat. ¹³They have decided to consume the first fruits of the grain and the tithes of the wine and oil, which they had consecrated and set aside for the priests who minister in the presence of our God in Jerusalem—things it is not lawful for any of the people even to touch

---

^x Gk *him*

with their hands. [14]Since even the people in Jerusalem have been doing this, they have sent messengers there in order to bring back permission from the council of the elders. [15]When the response reaches them and they act upon it, on that very day they will be handed over to you to be destroyed.

16 "So when I, your slave, learned all this, I fled from them. God has sent me to accomplish with you things that will astonish the whole world wherever people shall hear about them. [17]Your servant is indeed God-fearing and serves the God of heaven night and day. So, my lord, I will remain with you; but every night your servant will go out into the valley and pray to God. He will tell me when they have committed their sins. [18]Then I will come and tell you, so that you may go out with your whole army, and not one of them will be able to withstand you. [19]Then I will lead you through Judea, until you come to Jerusalem; there I will set your throne.[y] You will drive them like sheep that have no shepherd, and no dog will so much as growl at you. For this was told me to give me foreknowledge; it was announced to me, and I was sent to tell you."

20 Her words pleased Holofernes and all his servants. They marveled at her wisdom and said, [21]"No other woman from one end of the earth to the other looks so beautiful or speaks so wisely!" [22]Then Holofernes said to her, "God has done well to send you ahead of the people, to strengthen our hands and bring destruction on those who have despised my lord. [23]You are not only beautiful in appearance, but wise in speech. If you do as you have said, your God shall be my God, and you shall live in the palace of King Nebuchadnezzar and be renowned throughout the whole world."

Judith as a Guest of Holofernes

12 Then he commanded them to bring her in where his silver dinnerware was kept, and ordered them to set a table for her with some of his own delicacies, and with some of his own wine to drink. [2]But Judith said, "I cannot partake of them, or it will be an offense; but I will have enough with the things I brought with me." [3]Holofernes said to her, "If your supply runs out, where can we get you more of the same? For none of your people

are here with us." [4]Judith replied, "As surely as you live, my lord, your servant will not use up the supplies I have with me before the Lord carries out by my hand what he has determined."

5 Then the servants of Holofernes brought her into the tent, and she slept until midnight. Toward the morning watch she got up [6]and sent this message to Holofernes: "Let my lord now give orders to allow your servant to go out and pray." [7]So Holofernes commanded his guards not to hinder her. She remained in the camp three days. She went out each night to the valley of Bethulia, and bathed at the spring in the camp.[z] [8]After bathing, she prayed the Lord God of Israel to direct her way for the triumph of his[a] people. [9]Then she returned purified and stayed in the tent until she ate her food toward evening.

Judith Attends Holofernes' Banquet

10 On the fourth day Holofernes held a banquet for his personal attendants only, and did not invite any of his officers. [11]He said to Bagoas, the eunuch who had charge of his personal affairs, "Go and persuade the Hebrew woman who is in your care to join us and to eat and drink with us. [12]For it would be a disgrace if we let such a woman go without having intercourse with her. If we do not seduce her, she will laugh at us."

13 So Bagoas left the presence of Holofernes, and approached her and said, "Let this pretty girl not hesitate to come to my lord to be honored in his presence, and to enjoy drinking wine with us, and to become today like one of the Assyrian women who serve in the palace of Nebuchadnezzar." [14]Judith replied, "Who am I to refuse my lord? Whatever pleases him I will do at once, and it will be a joy to me until the day of my death." [15]So she proceeded to dress herself in all her woman's finery. Her maid went ahead and spread for her on the ground before Holofernes the lambskins she had received from Bagoas for her daily use in reclining. 16 Then Judith came in and lay down. Holofernes' heart was ravished with her and his passion was aroused, for he had been waiting for an opportunity to seduce her from the day he first saw her. [17]So Holofernes said to her, "Have a drink and be merry with us!" [18]Judith said, "I will

[y] Or *chariot*   [z] Other ancient authorities lack *in the camp*   [a] Other ancient authorities read *her*

gladly drink, my lord, because today is the greatest day in my whole life." [19]Then she took what her maid had prepared and ate and drank before him. [20]Holofernes was greatly pleased with her, and drank a great quantity of wine, much more than he had ever drunk in any one day since he was born.

Judith Beheads Holofernes

13 When evening came, his slaves quickly withdrew. Bagoas closed the tent from outside and shut out the attendants from his master's presence. They went to bed, for they all were weary because the banquet had lasted so long. [2]But Judith was left alone in the tent, with Holofernes stretched out on his bed, for he was dead drunk.

3 Now Judith had told her maid to stand outside the bedchamber and to wait for her to come out, as she did on the other days; for she said she would be going out for her prayers. She had said the same thing to Bagoas. [4]So everyone went out, and no one, either small or great, was left in the bedchamber. Then Judith, standing beside his bed, said in her heart, "O Lord God of all might, look in this hour on the work of my hands for the exaltation of Jerusalem. [5]Now indeed is the time to help your heritage and to carry out my design to destroy the enemies who have risen up against us."

6 She went up to the bedpost near Holofernes' head, and took down his sword that hung there. [7]She came close to his bed, took hold of the hair of his head, and said, "Give me strength today, O Lord God of Israel!" [8]Then she struck his neck twice with all her might, and cut off his head. [9]Next she rolled his body off the bed and pulled down the canopy from the posts. Soon afterward she went out and gave Holofernes' head to her maid, [10]who placed it in her food bag.

Judith Returns to Bethulia

Then the two of them went together, as they were accustomed to do for prayer. They passed through the camp, circled around the valley, and went up the mountain to Bethulia, and came to its gates. [11]From a distance Judith called out to the sentries at the gates, "Open, open the gate!

God, our God, is with us, still showing his power in Israel and his strength against our enemies, as he has done today!"

12 When the people of her town heard her voice, they hurried down to the town gate and summoned the elders of the town. [13]They all ran together, both small and great, for it seemed unbelievable that she had returned. They opened the gate and welcomed them. Then they lit a fire to give light, and gathered around them. [14]Then she said to them with a loud voice, "Praise God, O praise him! Praise God, who has not withdrawn his mercy from the house of Israel, but has destroyed our enemies by my hand this very night!"

15 Then she pulled the head out of the bag and showed it to them, and said, "See here, the head of Holofernes, the commander of the Assyrian army, and here is the canopy beneath which he lay in his drunken stupor. The Lord has struck him down by the hand of a woman. [16]As the Lord lives, who has protected me in the way I went, I swear that it was my face that seduced him to his destruction, and that he committed no sin with me, to defile and shame me."

17 All the people were greatly astonished. They bowed down and worshiped God, and said with one accord, "Blessed are you our God, who have this day humiliated the enemies of your people."

18 Then Uzziah said to her, "O daughter, you are blessed by the Most High God above all other women on earth; and blessed be the Lord God, who has created the heavens and the earth, who has guided you to cut off the head of the leader of our enemies. [19]Your praise[b] will never depart from the hearts of those who remember the power of God. [20]May God grant this to be a perpetual honor to you, and may he reward you with blessings, because you risked your own life when our nation was brought low, and you averted our ruin, walking in the straight path before our God." And all the people said, "Amen. Amen."

Judith's Counsel

14 Then Judith said to them, "Listen to me, my friends. Take this head and hang it upon the parapet of your wall. [2]As soon as day breaks and the sun rises on the earth, each of you take up your weapons, and let every able-bodied man go out

[b] Other ancient authorities read *hope*

of the town; set a captain over them, as if you were going down to the plain against the Assyrian outpost; only do not go down. ³Then they will seize their arms and go into the camp and rouse the officers of the Assyrian army. They will rush into the tent of Holofernes and will not find him. Then panic will come over them, and they will flee before you. ⁴Then you and all who live within the borders of Israel will pursue them and cut them down in their tracks. ⁵But before you do all this, bring Achior the Ammonite to me so that he may see and recognize the man who despised the house of Israel and sent him to us as if to his death."

6 So they summoned Achior from the house of Uzziah. When he came and saw the head of Holofernes in the hand of one of the men in the assembly of the people, he fell down on his face in a faint. ⁷When they raised him up he threw himself at Judith's feet, and did obeisance to her, and said, "Blessed are you in every tent of Judah! In every nation those who hear your name will be alarmed. ⁸Now tell me what you have done during these days."

So Judith told him in the presence of the people all that she had done, from the day she left until the moment she began speaking to them. ⁹When she had finished, the people raised a great shout and made a joyful noise in their town. ¹⁰When Achior saw all that the God of Israel had done, he believed firmly in God. So he was circumcised, and joined the house of Israel, remaining so to this day.

Holofernes' Death Is Discovered
11 As soon as it was dawn they hung the head of Holofernes on the wall. Then they all took their weapons, and they went out in companies to the mountain passes. ¹²When the Assyrians saw them they sent word to their commanders, who then went to the generals and the captains and to all their other officers. ¹³They came to Holofernes' tent and said to the steward in charge of all his personal affairs, "Wake up our lord, for the slaves have been so bold as to come down against us to give battle, to their utter destruction."

14 So Bagoas went in and knocked at the entry of the tent, for he supposed that he was sleeping with Judith. ¹⁵But when no

one answered, he opened it and went into the bedchamber and found him sprawled on the floor dead, with his head missing. ¹⁶He cried out with a loud voice and wept and groaned and shouted, and tore his clothes. ¹⁷Then he went to the tent where Judith had stayed, and when he did not find her, he rushed out to the people and shouted, ¹⁸"The slaves have tricked us! One Hebrew woman has brought disgrace on the house of King Nebuchadnezzar. Look, Holofernes is lying on the ground, and his head is missing!"

19 When the leaders of the Assyrian army heard this, they tore their tunics and were greatly dismayed, and their loud cries and shouts rose up throughout the camp.

The Assyrians Flee in Panic
15 When the men in the tents heard it, they were amazed at what had happened. ²Overcome with fear and trembling, they did not wait for one another, but with one impulse all rushed out and fled by every path across the plain and through the hill country. ³Those who had camped in the hills around Bethulia also took to flight. Then the Israelites, everyone that was a soldier, rushed out upon them. ⁴Uzziah sent men to Betomasthaim*ᶜ* and Choba and Kola, and to all the frontiers of Israel, to tell what had taken place and to urge all to rush out upon the enemy to destroy them. ⁵When the Israelites heard it, with one accord they fell upon the enemy,*ᵈ* and cut them down as far as Choba. Those in Jerusalem and all the hill country also came, for they were told what had happened in the camp of the enemy. The men in Gilead and in Galilee outflanked them with great slaughter, even beyond Damascus and its borders. ⁶The rest of the people of Bethulia fell upon the Assyrian camp and plundered it, acquiring great riches. ⁷And the Israelites, when they returned from the slaughter, took possession of what remained. Even the villages and towns in the hill country and in the plain got a great amount of booty, since there was a vast quantity of it.

The Israelites Celebrate Their Victory
8 Then the high priest Joakim and the elders of the Israelites who lived in Jerusalem came to witness the good things that

ᶜ Other ancient authorities add *and Bebai*   ᵈ Gk *them*

the Lord had done for Israel, and to see Judith and to wish her well. ⁹When they met her, they all blessed her with one accord and said to her, "You are the glory of Jerusalem, you are the great boast of Israel, you are the great pride of our nation! ¹⁰You have done all this with your own hand; you have done great good to Israel, and God is well pleased with it. May the Almighty Lord bless you forever!" And all the people said, "Amen."

11 All the people plundered the camp for thirty days. They gave Judith the tent of Holofernes and all his silver dinnerware, his beds, his bowls, and all his furniture. She took them and loaded her mules and hitched up her carts and piled the things on them.

12 All the women of Israel gathered to see her, and blessed her, and some of them performed a dance in her honor. She took ivy-wreathed wands in her hands and distributed them to the women who were with her; ¹³and she and those who were with her crowned themselves with olive wreaths. She went before all the people in the dance, leading all the women, while all the men of Israel followed, bearing their arms and wearing garlands and singing hymns.

Judith Offers Her Hymn of Praise

14 Judith began this thanksgiving before all Israel, and all the people loudly sang this song of praise. ¹And Judith said,

16

Begin a song to my God with
    tambourines,
sing to my Lord with cymbals.
Raise to him a new psalm;ᵉ
exalt him, and call upon his name.
² For the Lord is a God who crushes
    wars;
he sets up his camp among his
    people;
he delivered me from the hands of
    my pursuers.
³ The Assyrian came down from the
    mountains of the north;
he came with myriads of his
    warriors;
their numbers blocked up the wadis,
    and their cavalry covered the hills.
⁴ He boasted that he would burn up my
    territory,

and kill my young men with the
    sword,
and dash my infants to the ground,
and seize my children as booty,
and take my virgins as spoil.
⁵ But the Lord Almighty has foiled them
    by the hand of a woman.ᶠ
⁶ For their mighty one did not fall by
    the hands of the young men,
nor did the sons of the Titans strike
    him down,
nor did tall giants set upon him;
but Judith daughter of Merari
with the beauty of her countenance
    undid him.
⁷ For she put away her widow's
    clothing
to exalt the oppressed in Israel.
She anointed her face with perfume;
⁸ she fastened her hair with a tiara
and put on a linen gown to beguile
    him.
⁹ Her sandal ravished his eyes,
her beauty captivated his mind,
and the sword severed his neck!
¹⁰ The Persians trembled at her boldness,
the Medes were daunted at her
    daring.
¹¹ Then my oppressed people shouted;
my weak people cried out,ᵍ and the
    enemyʰ trembled;
they lifted up their voices, and the
    enemyʰ were turned back.
¹² Sons of slave-girls pierced them
    through
and wounded them like the children
    of fugitives;
they perished before the army of my
    Lord.
¹³ I will sing to my God a new song:
O Lord, you are great and glorious,
wonderful in strength, invincible.
¹⁴ Let all your creatures serve you,
for you spoke, and they were made.
You sent forth your spirit,ⁱ and it
    formed them;ʲ
there is none that can resist your
    voice.
¹⁵ For the mountains shall be shaken to
    their foundations with the waters;

ᵉ Other ancient authorities read *a psalm and praise*   ᶠ Other ancient authorities add *he has confounded them*
ᵍ Other ancient authorities read *feared*   ʰ Gk *they*   ⁱ Or *breath*   ʲ Other ancient authorities read *they were created*

before your glance the rocks shall
  melt like wax.
But to those who fear you
  you show mercy.
16 For every sacrifice as a fragrant
  offering is a small thing,
and the fat of all whole burnt
  offerings to you is a very little
  thing;
but whoever fears the Lord is great
  forever.

17 Woe to the nations that rise up
  against my people!
The Lord Almighty will take
  vengeance on them in the day
  of judgment;
he will send fire and worms into their
  flesh;
they shall weep in pain forever.

18 When they arrived at Jerusalem, they
worshiped God. As soon as the people were
purified, they offered their burnt offerings,
their freewill offerings, and their gifts.
19Judith also dedicated to God all the possessions of Holofernes, which the people
had given her; and the canopy that she had
taken for herself from his bedchamber she

gave as a votive offering. 20For three
months the people continued feasting in
Jerusalem before the sanctuary, and Judith
remained with them.

The Renown and Death of Judith

21 After this they all returned home to
their own inheritances. Judith went to
Bethulia, and remained on her estate. For
the rest of her life she was honored
throughout the whole country. 22Many
desired to marry her, but she gave herself
to no man all the days of her life after her
husband Manasseh died and was gathered
to his people. 23She became more and more
famous, and grew old in her husband's
house, reaching the age of one hundred
five. She set her maid free. She died in
Bethulia, and they buried her in the cave of
her husband Manasseh; 24and the house of
Israel mourned her for seven days. Before
she died she distributed her property to all
those who were next of kin to her husband
Manasseh, and to her own nearest kindred.
25No one ever again spread terror among
the Israelites during the lifetime of Judith,
or for a long time after her death.

ESTHER

(The Greek Version Containing the Additional Chapters)

Note. The deuterocanonical portions of the Book of Esther are several additional passages found in the Greek translation of the
Hebrew Book of Esther, a translation that differs also in other respects from the Hebrew text (the latter is translated in the
NRSV Old Testament). The disordered chapter numbers come from the displacement of the additions to the end of the canoni-
cal Book of Esther by Jerome in his Latin translation and from the subsequent division of the Bible into chapters by Stephen
Langton, who numbered the additions consecutively as though they formed a direct continuation of the Hebrew text. So that
the additions may be read in their proper context, the whole of the Greek version is here translated, though certain familiar
names are given according to their Hebrew rather than their Greek form; for example, Mordecai and Vashti instead of
Mardocheus and Astin. The order followed is that of the Greek text, but the chapter and verse numbers conform to those of the
King James or Authorized Version. The additions, conveniently indicated by the letters A—F, are located as follows: A, before
1.1; B, after 3.13; C and D, after 4.17; E, after 8.12; F, after 10.3.

ADDITION A

Mordecai's Dream

11 *a* 2In the second year of the reign of
Artaxerxes the Great, on the first
day of Nisan, Mordecai son of Jair son of
Shimei*b* son of Kish, of the tribe of Benjamin,
had a dream. 3He was a Jew living in the
city of Susa, a great man, serving in the
court of the king. 4He was one of the cap-

tives whom King Nebuchadnezzar of
Babylon had brought from Jerusalem with
King Jeconiah of Judea. And this was his
dream: 5Noises*c* and confusion, thunders
and earthquake, tumult on the earth! 6Then
two great dragons came forward, both
ready to fight, and they roared terribly. 7At
their roaring every nation prepared for war,
to fight against the righteous nation. 8It was
a day of darkness and gloom, of tribulation

---

a Chapters 11.2—12.6 correspond to chapter A 1–17 in some translations.   *b* Gk *Semeios*   *c* Or *Voices*

and distress, affliction and great tumult on the earth! [9]And the whole righteous nation was troubled; they feared the evils that threatened them,[d] and were ready to perish. [10]Then they cried out to God; and at their outcry, as though from a tiny spring, there came a great river, with abundant water; [11]light came, and the sun rose, and the lowly were exalted and devoured those held in honor.

12 Mordecai saw in this dream what God had determined to do, and after he awoke he had it on his mind, seeking all day to understand it in every detail.

A Plot against the King

12 Now Mordecai took his rest in the courtyard with Gabatha and Tharra, the two eunuchs of the king who kept watch in the courtyard. [2]He overheard their conversation and inquired into their purposes, and learned that they were preparing to lay hands on King Artaxerxes; and he informed the king concerning them. [3]Then the king examined the two eunuchs, and after they had confessed it, they were led away to execution. [4]The king made a permanent record of these things, and Mordecai wrote an account of them. [5]And the king ordered Mordecai to serve in the court, and rewarded him for these things. [6]But Haman son of Hammedatha, a Bougean, who was in great honor with the king, determined to injure Mordecai and his people because of the two eunuchs of the king.

END OF ADDITION A

Artaxerxes' Banquet

1 It was after this that the following things happened in the days of Artaxerxes, the same Artaxerxes who ruled over one hundred twenty-seven provinces from India to Ethiopia.[e] [2]In those days, when King Artaxerxes was enthroned in the city of Susa, [3]in the third year of his reign, he gave a banquet for his Friends and other persons of various nations, the Persians and Median nobles, and the governors of the provinces. [4]After this, when he had displayed to them the riches of his kingdom and the splendor of his bountiful celebration during the course of one hundred eighty

days, [5]at the end of the festivity[f] the king gave a drinking party for the people of various nations who lived in the city. This was held for six days in the courtyard of the royal palace, [6]which was adorned with curtains of fine linen and cotton, held by cords of purple linen attached to gold and silver blocks on pillars of marble and other stones. Gold and silver couches were placed on a mosaic floor of emerald, mother-of-pearl, and marble. There were coverings of gauze, embroidered in various colors, with roses arranged around them. [7]The cups were of gold and silver, and a miniature cup was displayed, made of ruby, worth thirty thousand talents. There was abundant sweet wine, such as the king himself drank. [8]The drinking was not according to a fixed rule; but the king wished to have it so, and he commanded his stewards to comply with his pleasure and with that of the guests.

9 Meanwhile, Queen Vashti[g] gave a drinking party for the women in the palace where King Artaxerxes was.

Dismissal of Queen Vashti

10 On the seventh day, when the king was in good humor, he told Haman, Bazan, Tharra, Boraze, Zatholtha, Abataza, and Tharaba, the seven eunuchs who served King Artaxerxes, [11]to escort the queen to him in order to proclaim her as queen and to place the diadem on her head, and to have her display her beauty to all the governors and the people of various nations, for she was indeed a beautiful woman. [12]But Queen Vashti[g] refused to obey him and would not come with the eunuchs. This offended the king and he became furious. [13]He said to his Friends, "This is how Vashti[g] has answered me.[h] Give therefore your ruling and judgment on this matter." [14]Arkesaeus, Sarsathaeus, and Malesear, then the governors of the Persians and Medes who were closest to the king—Arkesaeus, Sarsathaeus, and Malesear, who sat beside him in the chief seats—came to him [15]and told him what must be done to Queen Vashti[g] for not obeying the order that the king had sent her by the eunuchs. [16]Then Muchaeus said to the king and the governors, "Queen Vashti[g] has insulted not only the king but also all the king's governors and officials" [17](for he had reported to them

---

[d] Gk *their own evils*   [e] Other ancient authorities lack *to Ethiopia*   [f] Gk *marriage feast*   [g] Gk *Astin*   [h] Gk *Astin has said thus and so*

what the queen had said and how she had defied the king). "And just as she defied King Artaxerxes, [18]so now the other ladies who are wives of the Persian and Median governors, on hearing what she has said to the king, will likewise dare to insult their husbands. [19]If therefore it pleases the king, let him issue a royal decree, inscribed in accordance with the laws of the Medes and Persians so that it may not be altered, that the queen may no longer come into his presence; but let the king give her royal rank to a woman better than she. [20]Let whatever law the king enacts be proclaimed in his kingdom, and thus all women will give honor to their husbands, rich and poor alike." [21]This speech pleased the king and the governors, and the king did as Muchaeus had recommended. [22]The king sent the decree into all his kingdom, to every province in its own language, so that in every house respect would be shown to every husband.

Esther Becomes Queen

2 After these things, the king's anger abated, and he no longer was concerned about Vashti[i] or remembered what he had said and how he had condemned her. [2]Then the king's servants said, "Let beautiful and virtuous girls be sought out for the king. [3]The king shall appoint officers in all the provinces of his kingdom, and they shall select beautiful young virgins to be brought to the harem in Susa, the capital. Let them be entrusted to the king's eunuch who is in charge of the women, and let ointments and whatever else they need be given them. [4]And the woman who pleases the king shall be queen instead of Vashti."[i] This pleased the king, and he did so.

5 Now there was a Jew in Susa the capital whose name was Mordecai son of Jair son of Shimei[j] son of Kish, of the tribe of Benjamin; [6]he had been taken captive from Jerusalem among those whom King Nebuchadnezzar of Babylon had captured. [7]And he had a foster child, the daughter of his father's brother, Aminadab, and her name was Esther. When her parents died, he brought her up to womanhood as his own. The girl was beautiful in appearance. [8]So, when the decree of the king was proclaimed, and many girls were gathered in Susa the capital in custody of Gai, Esther also was brought to Gai, who had custody of the women. [9]The girl pleased him and won his favor, and he quickly provided her with ointments and her portion of food,[k] as well as seven maids chosen from the palace; he treated her and her maids with special favor in the harem. [10]Now Esther had not disclosed her people or country, for Mordecai had commanded her not to make it known. [11]And every day Mordecai walked in the courtyard of the harem, to see what would happen to Esther.

12 Now the period after which a girl was to go to the king was twelve months. During this time the days of beautification are completed—six months while they are anointing themselves with oil of myrrh, and six months with spices and ointments for women. [13]Then she goes in to the king; she is handed to the person appointed, and goes with him from the harem to the king's palace. [14]In the evening she enters and in the morning she departs to the second harem, where Gai the king's eunuch is in charge of the women; and she does not go in to the king again unless she is summoned by name.

15 When the time was fulfilled for Esther daughter of Aminadab, the brother of Mordecai's father, to go in to the king, she neglected none of the things that Gai, the eunuch in charge of the women, had commanded. Now Esther found favor in the eyes of all who saw her. [16]So Esther went in to King Artaxerxes in the twelfth month, which is Adar, in the seventh year of his reign. [17]And the king loved Esther and she found favor beyond all the other virgins, so he put on her the queen's diadem. [18]Then the king gave a banquet lasting seven days for all his Friends and the officers to celebrate his marriage to Esther; and he granted a remission of taxes to those who were under his rule.

The Plot Discovered

19 Meanwhile Mordecai was serving in the courtyard. [20]Esther had not disclosed her country—such were the instructions of Mordecai; but she was to fear God and keep his laws, just as she had done when she was with him. So Esther did not change her mode of life.

21 Now the king's eunuchs, who were chief bodyguards, were angry because of Mordecai's advancement, and they plotted

[i] Gk *Astin* [j] Gk *Semeios* [k] Gk lacks *of food*

29

to kill King Artaxerxes. 22The matter
became known to Mordecai, and he
warned Esther, who in turn revealed the
plot to the king. 23He investigated the two
eunuchs and hanged them. Then the king
ordered a memorandum to be deposited in
the royal library in praise of the goodwill
shown by Mordecai.

Mordecai Refuses to Do Obeisance

3 After these events King Artaxerxes
promoted Haman son of Hammedatha,
a Bougean, advancing him and granting
him precedence over all the king's[l] Friends.
2So all who were at court used to do obeisance to Haman,[m] for so the king had commanded to be done. Mordecai, however, did
not do obeisance. 3Then the king's courtiers
said to Mordecai, "Mordecai, why do you
disobey the king's command?" 4Day after
day they spoke to him, but he would not listen to them. Then they informed Haman
that Mordecai was resisting the king's command. Mordecai had told them that he was
a Jew. 5So when Haman learned that
Mordecai was not doing obeisance to him,
he became furiously angry, 6and plotted to
destroy all the Jews under Artaxerxes' rule.
7 In the twelfth year of King Artaxerxes
Haman[n] came to a decision by casting lots,
taking the days and the months one by
one, to fix on one day to destroy the whole
race of Mordecai. The lot fell on the fourteenth[o] day of the month of Adar.

Decree against the Jews

8 Then Haman[n] said to King Artaxerxes,
"There is a certain nation scattered among
the other nations in all your kingdom; their
laws are different from those of every other
nation, and they do not keep the laws of
the king. It is not expedient for the king to
tolerate them. 9If it pleases the king, let it
be decreed that they are to be destroyed,
and I will pay ten thousand talents of silver
into the king's treasury." 10So the king took
off his signet ring and gave it to Haman to
seal the decree[p] that was to be written
against the Jews. 11The king told Haman,
"Keep the money, and do whatever you
want with that nation."
12 So on the thirteenth day of the first
month the king's secretaries were summoned, and in accordance with Haman's
instructions they wrote in the name of
King Artaxerxes to the magistrates and the
governors in every province from India to
Ethiopia. There were one hundred twenty-
seven provinces in all, and the governors
were addressed each in his own language.
13Instructions were sent by couriers
throughout all the empire of Artaxerxes to
destroy the Jewish people on a given day of
the twelfth month, which is Adar, and to
plunder their goods.

ADDITION B

The King's Letter

13[q] This is a copy of the letter: "The
Great King, Artaxerxes, writes the
following to the governors of the hundred
twenty-seven provinces from India to
Ethiopia and to the officials under them:
2 "Having become ruler of many
nations and master of the whole world (not
elated with presumption of authority but
always acting reasonably and with kindness), I have determined to settle the lives
of my subjects in lasting tranquility and, in
order to make my kingdom peaceable and
open to travel throughout all its extent, to
restore the peace desired by all people.
3 "When I asked my counselors how
this might be accomplished, Haman—who
excels among us in sound judgment, and is
distinguished for his unchanging goodwill
and steadfast fidelity, and has attained the
second place in the kingdom— 4pointed out
to us that among all the nations in the
world there is scattered a certain hostile
people, who have laws contrary to those of
every nation and continually disregard the
ordinances of kings, so that the unifying of
the kingdom that we honorably intend
cannot be brought about. 5We understand
that this people, and it alone, stands constantly in opposition to every nation, per-
versely following a strange manner of life
and laws, and is ill-disposed to our government, doing all the harm they can so that
our kingdom may not attain stability.
6 "Therefore we have decreed that those
indicated to you in the letters written by
Haman, who is in charge of affairs and is
our second father, shall all—wives and
children included—be utterly destroyed by
the swords of their enemies, without pity or

[l] Gk *all his* [m] Gk *him* [n] Gk *he* [o] Other ancient witnesses read *thirteenth*; see 8.12 [p] Gk lacks *the decree*
[q] Chapter 13.1–7 corresponds to chapter B 1–7 in some translations.

restraint, on the fourteenth day of the twelfth month, Adar, of this present year, [7]so that those who have long been hostile and remain so may in a single day go down in violence to Hades, and leave our government completely secure and untroubled hereafter."

END OF ADDITION B

3 [14]Copies of the document were posted in every province, and all the nations were ordered to be prepared for that day. [15]The matter was expedited also in Susa. And while the king and Haman caroused together, the city of Susa[r] was thrown into confusion.

Mordecai Seeks Esther's Aid

4 When Mordecai learned of all that had been done, he tore his clothes, put on sackcloth, and sprinkled himself with ashes; then he rushed through the street of the city, shouting loudly: "An innocent nation is being destroyed!" [2]He got as far as the king's gate, and there he stopped, because no one was allowed to enter the courtyard clothed in sackcloth and ashes. [3]And in every province where the king's proclamation had been posted there was a loud cry of mourning and lamentation among the Jews, and they put on sackcloth and ashes. [4]When the queen's[s] maids and eunuchs came and told her, she was deeply troubled by what she heard had happened, and sent some clothes to Mordecai to put on instead of sackcloth; but he would not consent. [5]Then Esther summoned Hachratheus, the eunuch who attended her, and ordered him to get accurate information for her from Mordecai.[t]

7 So Mordecai told him what had happened and how Haman had promised to pay ten thousand talents into the royal treasury to bring about the destruction of the Jews. [8]He also gave him a copy of what had been posted in Susa for their destruction, to show to Esther; and he told him to charge her to go in to the king and plead for his favor in behalf of the people. "Remember," he said, "the days when you were an ordinary person, being brought up

under my care—for Haman, who stands next to the king, has spoken against us and demands our death. Call upon the Lord; then speak to the king in our behalf, and save us from death."

9 Hachratheus went in and told Esther all these things. [10]And she said to him, "Go to Mordecai and say, [11]'All nations of the empire know that if any man or woman goes to the king inside the inner court without being called, there is no escape for that person. Only the one to whom the king stretches out the golden scepter is safe—and it is now thirty days since I was called to go to the king.'"

12 When Hachratheus delivered her entire message to Mordecai, [13]Mordecai told him to go back and say to her, "Esther, do not say to yourself that you alone among all the Jews will escape alive. [14]For if you keep quiet at such a time as this, help and protection will come to the Jews from another quarter, but you and your father's family will perish. Yet, who knows whether it was not for such a time as this that you were made queen?" [15]Then Esther gave the messenger this answer to take back to Mordecai: [16]"Go and gather all the Jews who are in Susa and fast on my behalf; for three days and nights do not eat or drink, and my maids and I will also go without food. After that I will go to the king, contrary to the law, even if I must die." [17]So Mordecai went away and did what Esther had told him to do.

ADDITION C

Mordecai's Prayer

13 [8u]Then Mordecai[v] prayed to the Lord, calling to remembrance all the works of the Lord.

9 He said, "O Lord, Lord, you rule as King over all things, for the universe is in your power and there is no one who can oppose you when it is your will to save Israel, [10]for you have made heaven and earth and every wonderful thing under heaven. [11]You are Lord of all, and there is no one who can resist you, the Lord. [12]You know all things; you know, O Lord, that it

---

[r] Gk *the city*   [s] Gk *When her*   [t] Other ancient witnesses add [6]*So Hachratheus went out to Mordecai in the street of the city opposite the city gate.*   [u] Chapters 13.8—15.16 correspond to chapters C 1–30 and D 1–16 in some translations.   [v] Gk *he*

was not in insolence or pride or for any love of glory that I did this, and refused to bow down to this proud Haman; ¹³for I would have been willing to kiss the soles of his feet to save Israel! ¹⁴But I did this so that I might not set human glory above the glory of God, and I will not bow down to anyone but you, who are my Lord; and I will not do these things in pride. ¹⁵And now, O Lord God and King, God of Abraham, spare your people; for the eyes of our foes are upon us^w to annihilate us, and they desire to destroy the inheritance that has been yours from the beginning. ¹⁶Do not neglect your portion, which you redeemed for yourself out of the land of Egypt. ¹⁷Hear my prayer, and have mercy upon your inheritance; turn our mourning into feasting that we may live and sing praise to your name, O Lord; do not destroy the lips^x of those who praise you."

18 And all Israel cried out mightily, for their death was before their eyes.

Esther's Prayer

14 Then Queen Esther, seized with deadly anxiety, fled to the Lord. ²She took off her splendid apparel and put on the garments of distress and mourning, and instead of costly perfumes she covered her head with ashes and dung, and she utterly humbled her body; every part that she loved to adorn she covered with her tangled hair. ³She prayed to the Lord God of Israel, and said: "O my Lord, you only are our king; help me, who am alone and have no helper but you, ⁴for my danger is in my hand. ⁵Ever since I was born I have heard in the tribe of my family that you, O Lord, took Israel out of all the nations, and our ancestors from among all their forebears, for an everlasting inheritance, and that you did for them all that you promised. ⁶And now we have sinned before you, and you have handed us over to our enemies ⁷because we glorified their gods. You are righteous, O Lord! ⁸And now they are not satisfied that we are in bitter slavery, but they have covenanted with their idols ⁹to abolish what your mouth has ordained, and to destroy your inheritance, to stop the mouths of those who praise you and to quench your altar and the glory of your house, ¹⁰to open the mouths of the nations for the praise of vain idols, and to magnify forever a mortal king.

11 "O Lord, do not surrender your scepter to what has no being; and do not let them laugh at our downfall; but turn their plan against them, and make an example of him who began this against us. ¹²Remember, O Lord; make yourself known in this time of our affliction, and give me courage, O King of the gods and Master of all dominion! ¹³Put eloquent speech in my mouth before the lion, and turn his heart to hate the man who is fighting against us, so that there may be an end of him and those who agree with him. ¹⁴But save us by your hand, and help me, who am alone and have no helper but you, O Lord. ¹⁵You have knowledge of all things, and you know that I hate the splendor of the wicked and abhor the bed of the uncircumcised and of any alien. ¹⁶You know my necessity—that I abhor the sign of my proud position, which is upon my head on days when I appear in public. I abhor it like a filthy rag, and I do not wear it on the days when I am at leisure. ¹⁷And your servant has not eaten at Haman's table, and I have not honored the king's feast or drunk the wine of libations. ¹⁸Your servant has had no joy since the day that I was brought here until now, except in you, O Lord God of Abraham. ¹⁹O God, whose might is over all, hear the voice of the despairing, and save us from the hands of evildoers. And save me from my fear!"

END OF ADDITION C

_____

ADDITION D

Esther Is Received by the King

15 On the third day, when she ended her prayer, she took off the garments in which she had worshiped, and arrayed herself in splendid attire. ²Then, majestically adorned, after invoking the aid of the all-seeing God and Savior, she took two maids with her; ³on one she leaned gently for support, ⁴while the other followed, carrying her train. ⁵She was radiant with perfect beauty, and she looked happy, as if beloved, but her heart was frozen with fear. ⁶When she had gone through all the doors, she stood before the king. He was seated on his royal throne, clothed in the

^w Gk for they are eying us   *^x Gk mouth*

full array of his majesty, all covered with gold and precious stones. He was most terrifying.

7 Lifting his face, flushed with splendor, he looked at her in fierce anger. The queen faltered, and turned pale and faint, and collapsed on the head of the maid who went in front of her. [8]Then God changed the spirit of the king to gentleness, and in alarm he sprang from his throne and took her in his arms until she came to herself. He comforted her with soothing words, and said to her, [9]"What is it, Esther? I am your husband.[y] Take courage; [10]You shall not die, for our law applies only to our subjects.[z] Come near."

11 Then he raised the golden scepter and touched her neck with it; [12]he embraced her, and said, "Speak to me." [13]She said to him, "I saw you, my lord, like an angel of God, and my heart was shaken with fear at your glory. [14]For you are wonderful, my lord, and your countenance is full of grace." [15]And while she was speaking, she fainted and fell. [16]Then the king was agitated, and all his servants tried to comfort her.

END OF ADDITION D

---

5 [a] [3]The king said to her, "What do you wish, Esther? What is your request? It shall be given you, even to half of my kingdom." [4]And Esther said, "Today is a special day for me. If it pleases the king, let him and Haman come to the dinner that I shall prepare today." [5]Then the king said, "Bring Haman quickly, so that we may do as Esther desires." So they both came to the dinner that Esther had spoken about. [6]While they were drinking wine, the king said to Esther, "What is it, Queen Esther? It shall be granted you." [7]She said, "My petition and request is: [8]if I have found favor in the sight of the king, let the king and Haman come to the dinner that I shall prepare them, and tomorrow I will do as I have done today."

Haman's Plot against Mordecai

9 So Haman went out from the king joyful and glad of heart. But when he saw Mordecai the Jew in the courtyard, he was filled with anger. [10]Nevertheless, he went home and summoned his friends and his

wife Zosara. [11]And he told them about his riches and the honor that the king had bestowed on him, and how he had advanced him to be the first in the kingdom. [12]And Haman said, "The queen did not invite anyone to the dinner with the king except me; and I am invited again tomorrow. [13]But these things give me no pleasure as long as I see Mordecai the Jew in the courtyard." [14]His wife Zosara and his friends said to him, "Let a gallows be made, fifty cubits high, and in the morning tell the king to have Mordecai hanged on it. Then, go merrily with the king to the dinner." This advice pleased Haman, and so the gallows was prepared.

Mordecai's Reward from the King

6 That night the Lord took sleep from the king, so he gave orders to his secretary to bring the book of daily records, and to read to him. [2]He found the words written about Mordecai, how he had told the king about the two royal eunuchs who were on guard and sought to lay hands on King Artaxerxes. [3]The king said, "What honor or dignity did we bestow on Mordecai?" The king's servants said, "You have not done anything for him." [4]While the king was inquiring about the goodwill shown by Mordecai, Haman was in the courtyard. The king asked, "Who is in the courtyard?" Now Haman had come to speak to the king about hanging Mordecai on the gallows that he had prepared. [5]The servants of the king answered, "Haman is standing in the courtyard." And the king said, "Summon him." [6]Then the king said to Haman, "What shall I do for the person whom I wish to honor?" And Haman said to himself, "Whom would the king wish to honor more than me?" [7]So he said to the king, "For a person whom the king wishes to honor, [8]let the king's servants bring out the fine linen robe that the king has worn, and the horse on which the king rides, [9]and let both be given to one of the king's honored Friends, and let him robe the person whom the king loves and mount him on the horse, and let it be proclaimed through the open square of the city, saying, 'Thus shall it be done to everyone whom the king honors.'" [10]Then the king said to Haman, "You have made an excellent suggestion! Do just as you have said for Mordecai the Jew, who is

---

[y] Gk *brother*   [z] Meaning of Gk uncertain   [a] In Greek, Chapter D replaces verses 1 and 2 in Hebrew.

33

on duty in the courtyard. And let nothing be omitted from what you have proposed." [11]So Haman got the robe and the horse; he put the robe on Mordecai and made him ride through the open square of the city, proclaiming, "Thus shall it be done to everyone whom the king wishes to honor." [12]Then Mordecai returned to the courtyard, and Haman hurried back to his house, mourning and with his head covered. [13]Haman told his wife Zosara and his friends what had befallen him. His friends and his wife said to him, "If Mordecai is of the Jewish people, and you have begun to be humiliated before him, you will surely fall. You will not be able to defend yourself, because the living God is with him."

Haman at Esther's Banquet

14 While they were still talking, the eunuchs arrived and hurriedly brought Haman to the banquet that Esther had prepared. 7 [1]So the king and Haman went in to drink with the queen. [2]And the second day, as they were drinking wine, the king said, "What is it, Queen Esther? What is your petition and what is your request? It shall be granted to you, even to half of my kingdom." [3]She answered and said, "If I have found favor with the king, let my life be granted me at my petition, and my people at my request. [4]For we have been sold, I and my people, to be destroyed, plundered, and made slaves—we and our children—male and female slaves. This has come to my knowledge. Our antagonist brings shame on[b] the king's court." [5]Then the king said, "Who is the person that would dare to do this thing?" [6]Esther said, "Our enemy is this evil man Haman!" At this, Haman was terrified in the presence of the king and queen.

Punishment of Haman

7 The king rose from the banquet and went into the garden, and Haman began to beg for his life from the queen, for he saw that he was in serious trouble. [8]When the king returned from the garden, Haman had thrown himself on the couch, pleading with the queen. The king said, "Will he dare even assault my wife in my own house?" Haman, when he heard, turned away his face. [9]Then Bugathan, one of the eunuchs, said to the king, "Look, Haman has even prepared a gallows for Mordecai, who gave information of concern to the king; it is standing at Haman's house, a gallows fifty cubits high." So the king said, "Let Haman be hanged on that." [10]So Haman was hanged on the gallows he had prepared for Mordecai. With that the anger of the king abated.

Royal Favor Shown the Jews

8 On that very day King Artaxerxes granted to Esther all the property of the persecutor[c] Haman. Mordecai was summoned by the king, for Esther had told the king[d] that he was related to her. [2]The king took the ring that had been taken from Haman, and gave it to Mordecai; and Esther set Mordecai over everything that had been Haman's.

3 Then she spoke once again to the king and, falling at his feet, she asked him to avert all the evil that Haman had planned against the Jews. [4]The king extended his golden scepter to Esther, and she rose and stood before the king. [5]Esther said, "If it pleases you, and if I have found favor, let an order be sent rescinding the letters that Haman wrote and sent to destroy the Jews in your kingdom. [6]How can I look on the ruin of my people? How can I be safe if my ancestral nation[e] is destroyed?" [7]The king said to Esther, "Now that I[f] have granted all of Haman's property to you and have hanged him on a tree because he acted against the Jews, what else do you request? [8]Write in my name what you think best and seal it with my ring; for whatever is written at the king's command and sealed with my ring cannot be contravened."

9 The secretaries were summoned on the twenty-third day of the first month, that is, Nisan, in the same year; and all that he commanded with respect to the Jews was given in writing to the administrators and governors of the provinces from India to Ethiopia, one hundred twenty-seven provinces, to each province in its own language. [10]The edict was written[g] with the king's authority and sealed with his ring, and sent out by couriers. [11]He ordered the Jews in every city to observe their own laws, to defend themselves, and to act as they wished against their opponents and enemies [12]on a certain day, the thirteenth of the twelfth month, which is Adar, throughout all the kingdom of Artaxerxes.

[b] Gk is not worthy of   [c] Gk slanderer   [d] Gk him   [e] Gk country   [f] Gk If I   [g] Gk It was written

---

ADDITION E

The Decree of Artaxerxes

16[h] The following is a copy of this letter:

"The Great King, Artaxerxes, to the governors of the provinces from India to Ethiopia, one hundred twenty-seven provinces, and to those who are loyal to our government, greetings.

2 "Many people, the more they are honored with the most generous kindness of their benefactors, the more proud do they become, [3]and not only seek to injure our subjects, but in their inability to stand prosperity, they even undertake to scheme against their own benefactors. [4]They not only take away thankfulness from others, but, carried away by the boasts of those who know nothing of goodness, they even assume that they will escape the evil-hating justice of God, who always sees everything. [5]And often many of those who are set in places of authority have been made in part responsible for the shedding of innocent blood, and have been involved in irremediable calamities, by the persuasion of friends who have been entrusted with the administration of public affairs, [6]when these persons by the false trickery of their evil natures beguile the sincere goodwill of their sovereigns.

7 "What has been wickedly accomplished through the pestilent behavior of those who exercise authority unworthily can be seen, not so much from the more ancient records that we hand on, as from investigation of matters close at hand.[i] [8]In the future we will take care to render our kingdom quiet and peaceable for all, [9]by changing our methods and always judging what comes before our eyes with more equitable consideration. [10]For Haman son of Hammedatha, a Macedonian (really an alien to the Persian blood, and quite devoid of our kindliness), having become our guest, [11]enjoyed so fully the goodwill that we have for every nation that he was called our father and was continually bowed down to by all as the person second to the royal throne. [12]But, unable to restrain his arrogance, he undertook to deprive us of our kingdom and our life,[j] [13]and with intricate craft and deceit asked for the destruc-

tion of Mordecai, our savior and perpetual benefactor, and of Esther, the blameless partner of our kingdom, together with their whole nation. [14]He thought that by these methods he would catch us undefended and would transfer the kingdom of the Persians to the Macedonians.

15 "But we find that the Jews, who were consigned to annihilation by this thrice-accursed man, are not evildoers, but are governed by most righteous laws [16]and are children of the living God, most high, most mighty,[k] who has directed the kingdom both for us and for our ancestors in the most excellent order.

17 "You will therefore do well not to put in execution the letters sent by Haman son of Hammedatha, [18]since he, the one who did these things, has been hanged at the gate of Susa with all his household—for God, who rules over all things, has speedily inflicted on him the punishment that he deserved.

19 "Therefore post a copy of this letter publicly in every place, and permit the Jews to live under their own laws. [20]And give them reinforcements, so that on the thirteenth day of the twelfth month, Adar, on that very day, they may defend themselves against those who attack them at the time of oppression. [21]For God, who rules over all things, has made this day to be a joy for his chosen people instead of a day of destruction for them.

22 "Therefore you shall observe this with all good cheer as a notable day among your commemorative festivals, [23]so that both now and hereafter it may represent deliverance for you[l] and the loyal Persians, but that it may be a reminder of destruction for those who plot against us.

24 "Every city and country, without exception, that does not act accordingly shall be destroyed in wrath with spear and fire. It shall be made not only impassable for human beings, but also most hateful to wild animals and birds for all time.

END OF ADDITION E

---

8 [13]"Let copies of the decree be posted conspicuously in all the kingdom, and let all the Jews be ready on that day to fight against their enemies."

---

[h] Chapter 16.1–24 corresponds to chapter E 1–24 in some translations.   [i] Gk *matters beside* (your) *feet*   [j] Gk *our spirit*   [k] Gk *greatest*   [l] Other ancient authorities read *for us*

14 So the messengers on horseback set out with all speed to perform what the king had commanded; and the decree was published also in Susa. [15]Mordecai went out dressed in the royal robe and wearing a gold crown and a turban of purple linen. The people in Susa rejoiced on seeing him. [16]And the Jews had light and gladness [17]in every city and province wherever the decree was published; wherever the proclamation was made, the Jews had joy and gladness, a banquet and a holiday. And many of the Gentiles were circumcised and became Jews out of fear of the Jews.

Victory of the Jews

9 Now on the thirteenth day of the twelfth month, which is Adar, the decree written by the king arrived. [2]On that same day the enemies of the Jews perished; no one resisted, because they feared them. [3]The chief provincial governors, the princes, and the royal secretaries were paying honor to the Jews, because fear of Mordecai weighed upon them. [4]The king's decree required that Mordecai's name be held in honor throughout the kingdom.[m] [6]Now in the city of Susa the Jews killed five hundred people, [7]including Pharsannestain, Delphon, Phasga, [8]Pharadatha, Barea, Sarbacha, [9]Marmasima, Aruphaeus, Arsaeus, Zabutheus, [10]the ten sons of Haman son of Hammedatha, the Bougean, the enemy of the Jews—and they indulged[n] themselves in plunder.

11 That very day the number of those killed in Susa was reported to the king. [12]The king said to Esther, "In Susa, the capital, the Jews have destroyed five hundred people. What do you suppose they have done in the surrounding countryside? Whatever more you ask will be done for you." [13]And Esther said to the king, "Let the Jews be allowed to do the same tomorrow. Also, hang up the bodies of Haman's ten sons." [14]So he permitted this to be done, and handed over to the Jews of the city the bodies of Haman's sons to hang up. [15]The Jews who were in Susa gathered on the fourteenth and killed three hundred people, but took no plunder.

16 Now the other Jews in the kingdom gathered to defend themselves, and got relief from their enemies. They destroyed fifteen thousand of them, but did not engage in plunder. [17]On the fourteenth day they rested and made that same day a day of rest, celebrating it with joy and gladness. [18]The Jews who were in Susa, the capital, came together also on the fourteenth, but did not rest. They celebrated the fifteenth with joy and gladness. [19]On this account then the Jews who are scattered around the country outside Susa keep the fourteenth of Adar as a joyful holiday, and send presents of food to one another, while those who live in the large cities keep the fifteenth day of Adar as their joyful holiday, also sending presents to one another.

The Festival of Purim

20 Mordecai recorded these things in a book, and sent it to the Jews in the kingdom of Artaxerxes both near and far, [21]telling them that they should keep the fourteenth and fifteenth days of Adar, [22]for on these days the Jews got relief from their enemies. The whole month (namely, Adar), in which their condition had been changed from sorrow into gladness and from a time of distress to a holiday, was to be celebrated as a time for feasting[o] and gladness and for sending presents of food to their friends and to the poor.

23 So the Jews accepted what Mordecai had written to them [24]—how Haman son of Hammedatha, the Macedonian,[p] fought against them, how he made a decree and cast lots[q] to destroy them, [25]and how he went in to the king, telling him to hang Mordecai; but the wicked plot he had devised against the Jews came back upon himself, and he and his sons were hanged. [26]Therefore these days were called "Purim," because of the lots (for in their language this is the word that means "lots"). And so, because of what was written in this letter, and because of what they had experienced in this affair and what had befallen them, Mordecai established this festival,[r] [27]and the Jews took upon themselves, upon their descendants, and upon all who would join them, to observe it without fail.[s] These days of Purim should be a memorial and kept from generation to generation, in every city,

---

[m] Meaning of Gk uncertain. Some ancient authorities add verse 5, *So the Jews struck down all their enemies with the sword, killing and destroying them, and they did as they pleased to those who hated them.*   [n] Other ancient authorities read *did not indulge*   [o] Gk *of weddings*   [p] Other ancient witnesses read *the Bougean*   [q] Gk *a lot*   [r] Gk *he established* (it)   [s] Meaning of Gk uncertain

family, and country. [28]These days of Purim were to be observed for all time, and the commemoration of them was never to cease among their descendants.

29 Then Queen Esther daughter of Aminadab along with Mordecai the Jew wrote down what they had done, and gave full authority to the letter about Purim.[t] [31]And Mordecai and Queen Esther established this decision on their own responsibility, pledging their own well-being to the plan.[u] [32]Esther established it by a decree forever, and it was written for a memorial.

10 The king levied a tax upon his kingdom both by land and sea. [2]And as for his power and bravery, and the wealth and glory of his kingdom, they were recorded in the annals of the kings of the Persians and the Medes. [3]Mordecai acted with authority on behalf of King Artaxerxes and was great in the kingdom, as well as honored by the Jews. His way of life was such as to make him beloved to his whole nation.

ADDITION F

Mordecai's Dream Fulfilled

4 [v]And Mordecai said, "These things have come from God; [5]for I remember the dream that I had concerning these matters, and none of them has failed to be fulfilled. [6]There was the little spring that became a river, and there was light and sun and abundant water—the river is Esther, whom the king married and made queen. [7]The two dragons are Haman and myself. [8]The nations are those that gathered to destroy the name of the Jews. [9]And my nation, this is Israel, who cried out to God and was saved. The Lord has saved his people; the Lord has rescued us from all these evils; God has done great signs and wonders, wonders that have never happened among the nations. [10]For this purpose he made two lots, one for the people of God and one for all the nations, [11]and these two lots came to the hour and moment and day of decision before God and among all the nations. [12]And God remembered his people and vindicated his inheritance. [13]So they will observe these days in the month of Adar, on the fourteenth and fifteenth[w] of that month, with an assembly and joy and gladness before God, from generation to generation forever among his people Israel."

Postscript

11 [1]In the fourth year of the reign of Ptolemy and Cleopatra, Dositheus, who said that he was a priest and a Levite,[x] and his son Ptolemy brought to Egypt[y] the preceding Letter about Purim, which they said was authentic and had been translated by Lysimachus son of Ptolemy, one of the residents of Jerusalem.

END OF ADDITION F

---

[t]Verse 30 in Heb is lacking in Gk: *Letters were sent to all the Jews, to the one hundred twenty-seven provinces of the kingdom of Ahasuerus, in words of peace and truth.* [u]Meaning of Gk uncertain   [v]Chapter 10.4–13 and 11.1 correspond to chapter F 1–11 in some translations.   [w]Other ancient authorities lack *and fifteenth* [x]Or *priest, and Levitas* [y]Cn: Gk *brought in*

THE WISDOM OF SOLOMON

Exhortation to Uprightness

1 Love righteousness, you rulers of the earth,
think of the Lord in goodness
and seek him with sincerity of heart;

2 because he is found by those who do
not put him to the test,
and manifests himself to those who do
not distrust him.

3 For perverse thoughts separate people
from God,
and when his power is tested, it
exposes the foolish;

4 because wisdom will not enter a
deceitful soul,
or dwell in a body enslaved to sin.

5 For a holy and disciplined spirit will
flee from deceit,
and will leave foolish thoughts behind,
and will be ashamed at the approach
of unrighteousness.

6 For wisdom is a kindly spirit,
but will not free blasphemers from the
guilt of their words;
because God is witness of their inmost
feelings,
and a true observer of their hearts,
and a hearer of their tongues.

7 Because the spirit of the Lord has filled
the world,
and that which holds all things
together knows what is said,

8 therefore those who utter unrighteous
things will not escape notice,
and justice, when it punishes, will not
pass them by.

9 For inquiry will be made into the
counsels of the ungodly,
and a report of their words will come
to the Lord,
to convict them of their lawless deeds;

10 because a jealous ear hears all things,
and the sound of grumbling does not
go unheard.

11 Beware then of useless grumbling,
and keep your tongue from slander;
because no secret word is without
result,[a]
and a lying mouth destroys the soul.

12 Do not invite death by the error of
your life,
or bring on destruction by the works
of your hands;

13 because God did not make death,
and he does not delight in the death
of the living.

14 For he created all things so that they
might exist;
the generative forces[b] of the world are
wholesome,
and there is no destructive poison in
them,
and the dominion[c] of Hades is not on
earth.

15 For righteousness is immortal.

Life as the Ungodly See It

16 But the ungodly by their words and
deeds summoned death;[d]
considering him a friend, they pined
away
and made a covenant with him,
because they are fit to belong to his
company.

2 For they reasoned unsoundly, saying
to themselves,
"Short and sorrowful is our life,
and there is no remedy when a life
comes to its end,
and no one has been known to return
from Hades.

2 For we were born by mere chance,
and hereafter we shall be as though
we had never been,
for the breath in our nostrils is smoke,
and reason is a spark kindled by the
beating of our hearts;

3 when it is extinguished, the body will
turn to ashes,
and the spirit will dissolve like empty
air.

4 Our name will be forgotten in time,
and no one will remember our works;
our life will pass away like the traces
of a cloud,
and be scattered like mist
that is chased by the rays of the sun
and overcome by its heat.

5 For our allotted time is the passing of
a shadow,
and there is no return from our death,
because it is sealed up and no one
turns back.

[a] Or *will go unpunished*   [b] Or *the creatures*   [c] Or *palace*   [d] Gk *him*

38

6 "Come, therefore, let us enjoy the good
 things that exist,
and make use of the creation to the
 full as in youth.
7 Let us take our fill of costly wine and
 perfumes,
and let no flower of spring pass us by.
8 Let us crown ourselves with rosebuds
 before they wither.
9 Let none of us fail to share in our
 revelry;
everywhere let us leave signs of
 enjoyment,
because this is our portion, and this
 our lot.
10 Let us oppress the righteous poor man;
let us not spare the widow
or regard the gray hairs of the aged.
11 But let our might be our law of right,
for what is weak proves itself to be
 useless.

12 "Let us lie in wait for the righteous
 man,
because he is inconvenient to us and
 opposes our actions;
he reproaches us for sins against the
 law,
and accuses us of sins against our
 training.
13 He professes to have knowledge of God,
and calls himself a child*e* of the Lord.
14 He became to us a reproof of our
 thoughts;
15 the very sight of him is a burden to us,
because his manner of life is unlike
 that of others,
and his ways are strange.
16 We are considered by him as
 something base,
and he avoids our ways as unclean;
he calls the last end of the righteous
 happy,
and boasts that God is his father.
17 Let us see if his words are true,
and let us test what will happen at
 the end of his life;
18 for if the righteous man is God's child,
 he will help him,
and will deliver him from the hand of
 his adversaries.
19 Let us test him with insult and
 torture,
so that we may find out how gentle
 he is,
and make trial of his forbearance.

20 Let us condemn him to a shameful
 death,
for, according to what he says, he will
 be protected."

Error of the Wicked

21 Thus they reasoned, but they were led
 astray,
for their wickedness blinded them,
22 and they did not know the secret
 purposes of God,
nor hoped for the wages of holiness,
nor discerned the prize for blameless
 souls;
23 for God created us for incorruption,
and made us in the image of his own
 eternity,*f*
24 but through the devil's envy death
 entered the world,
and those who belong to his company
 experience it.

The Destiny of the Righteous

3 But the souls of the righteous are in
 the hand of God,
and no torment will ever touch them.
2 In the eyes of the foolish they seemed
 to have died,
and their departure was thought to be
 a disaster,
3 and their going from us to be their
 destruction;
but they are at peace.
4 For though in the sight of others they
 were punished,
their hope is full of immortality.
5 Having been disciplined a little, they
 will receive great good,
because God tested them and found
 them worthy of himself;
6 like gold in the furnace he tried them,
and like a sacrificial burnt offering he
 accepted them.
7 In the time of their visitation they will
 shine forth,
and will run like sparks through the
 stubble.
8 They will govern nations and rule over
 peoples,
and the Lord will reign over them
 forever.
9 Those who trust in him will
 understand truth,
and the faithful will abide with him in
 love,

e Or *servant*　　*f* Other ancient authorities read *nature*

because grace and mercy are upon his
holy ones,
and he watches over his elect.[g]

The Destiny of the Ungodly

10 But the ungodly will be punished as
their reasoning deserves,
those who disregarded the righteous[h]
and rebelled against the Lord;
11 for those who despise wisdom and
instruction are miserable.
Their hope is vain, their labors are
unprofitable,
and their works are useless.
12 Their wives are foolish, and their
children evil;
13 their offspring are accursed.

On Childlessness

For blessed is the barren woman who
is undefiled,
who has not entered into a sinful
union;
she will have fruit when God
examines souls.
14 Blessed also is the eunuch whose
hands have done no lawless
deed,
and who has not devised wicked
things against the Lord;
for special favor will be shown him for
his faithfulness,
and a place of great delight in the
temple of the Lord.
15 For the fruit of good labors is
renowned,
and the root of understanding does
not fail.
16 But children of adulterers will not
come to maturity,
and the offspring of an unlawful union
will perish.
17 Even if they live long they will be
held of no account,
and finally their old age will be
without honor.
18 If they die young, they will have no
hope
and no consolation on the day of
judgment.
19 For the end of an unrighteous
generation is grievous.

4 Better than this is childlessness with
virtue,
for in the memory of virtue[i] is
immortality,
because it is known both by God and
by mortals.
2 When it is present, people imitate[j] it,
and they long for it when it has gone;
throughout all time it marches,
crowned in triumph,
victor in the contest for prizes that are
undefiled.
3 But the prolific brood of the ungodly
will be of no use,
and none of their illegitimate seedlings
will strike a deep root
or take a firm hold.
4 For even if they put forth boughs for
a while,
standing insecurely they will be
shaken by the wind,
and by the violence of the winds they
will be uprooted.
5 The branches will be broken off before
they come to maturity,
and their fruit will be useless,
not ripe enough to eat, and good for
nothing.
6 For children born of unlawful unions
are witnesses of evil against
their parents when God
examines them.[k]
7 But the righteous, though they die
early, will be at rest.
8 For old age is not honored for length
of time,
or measured by number of years;
9 but understanding is gray hair for
anyone,
and a blameless life is ripe old age.
10 There were some who pleased God
and were loved by him,
and while living among sinners were
taken up.
11 They were caught up so that evil
might not change their
understanding
or guile deceive their souls.
12 For the fascination of wickedness
obscures what is good,
and roving desire perverts the innocent
mind.
13 Being perfected in a short time, they
fulfilled long years;

---

[g] Text of this line uncertain; omitted by some ancient authorities. Compare 4.15   [h] Or *what is right*   [i] Gk *it*
[j] Other ancient authorities read *honor*   [k] Gk *at their examination*

14 for their souls were pleasing to the
　　Lord,
　therefore he took them quickly from
　　the midst of wickedness.
15 Yet the peoples saw and did not
　　understand,
　or take such a thing to heart,
　that God's grace and mercy are with
　　his elect,
　and that he watches over his holy
　　ones.

The Triumph of the Righteous

16 The righteous who have died will
　　condemn the ungodly who are
　　living,
　and youth that is quickly perfected[l]
　　will condemn the prolonged old
　　age of the unrighteous.
17 For they will see the end of the wise,
　and will not understand what the
　　Lord purposed for them,
　and for what he kept them safe.
18 The unrighteous[m] will see, and will
　　have contempt for them,
　but the Lord will laugh them to scorn.
　After this they will become dishonored
　　corpses,
　and an outrage among the dead
　　forever;
19 because he will dash them speechless
　　to the ground,
　and shake them from the foundations;
　they will be left utterly dry and
　　barren,
　and they will suffer anguish,
　and the memory of them will perish.

The Final Judgment

20 They will come with dread when their
　　sins are reckoned up,
　and their lawless deeds will convict
　　them to their face.

5 Then the righteous will stand with
　　great confidence
in the presence of those who have
　　oppressed them
and those who make light of their
　　labors.
2 When the unrighteous[n] see them, they
　　will be shaken with dreadful
　　fear,
　and they will be amazed at the
　　unexpected salvation of the
　　righteous.

3 They will speak to one another in
　　repentance,
　and in anguish of spirit they will
　　groan, and say,
4 "These are persons whom we once
　　held in derision
　and made a byword of reproach—fools
　　that we were!
　We thought that their lives were
　　madness
　and that their end was without honor.
5 Why have they been numbered among
　　the children of God?
　And why is their lot among the
　　saints?
6 So it was we who strayed from the
　　way of truth,
　and the light of righteousness did not
　　shine on us,
　and the sun did not rise upon us.
7 We took our fill of the paths of
　　lawlessness and destruction,
　and we journeyed through trackless
　　deserts,
　but the way of the Lord we have not
　　known.
8 What has our arrogance profited us?
　And what good has our boasted
　　wealth brought us?

9 "All those things have vanished like a
　　shadow,
　and like a rumor that passes by;
10 like a ship that sails through the
　　billowy water,
　and when it has passed no trace can
　　be found,
　no track of its keel in the waves;
11 or as, when a bird flies through the
　　air,
　no evidence of its passage is found;
　the light air, lashed by the beat of its
　　pinions
　and pierced by the force of its rushing
　　flight,
　is traversed by the movement of its
　　wings,
　and afterward no sign of its coming is
　　found there;
12 or as, when an arrow is shot at a
　　target,
　the air, thus divided, comes together
　　at once,
　so that no one knows its pathway.
13 So we also, as soon as we were born,
　　ceased to be,

---

l Or *ended*　　*m* Gk *They*　　*n* Gk *they*

41

and we had no sign of virtue to show,
but were consumed in our
wickedness."
¹⁴ Because the hope of the ungodly is
like thistledown*°* carried by the
wind,
and like a light frost*°* driven away by
a storm;
it is dispersed like smoke before the
wind,
and it passes like the remembrance of
a guest who stays but a day.

The Reward of the Righteous
¹⁵ But the righteous live forever,
and their reward is with the Lord;
the Most High takes care of them.
¹⁶ Therefore they will receive a glorious
crown
and a beautiful diadem from the hand
of the Lord,
because with his right hand he will
cover them,
and with his arm he will shield them.
¹⁷ The Lord*°* will take his zeal as his
whole armor,
and will arm all creation to repel*°* his
enemies;
¹⁸ he will put on righteousness as a
breastplate,
and wear impartial justice as a helmet;
¹⁹ he will take holiness as an invincible
shield,
²⁰ and sharpen stern wrath for a sword,
and creation will join with him to
fight against his frenzied foes.
²¹ Shafts of lightning will fly with true
aim,
and will leap from the clouds to the
target, as from a well-drawn
bow,
²² and hailstones full of wrath will be
hurled as from a catapult;
the water of the sea will rage against
them,
and rivers will relentlessly overwhelm
them;
²³ a mighty wind will rise against them,
and like a tempest it will winnow
them away.
Lawlessness will lay waste the whole
earth,
and evildoing will overturn the thrones
of rulers.

Kings Should Seek Wisdom
6 Listen therefore, O kings, and
understand;
learn, O judges of the ends of the
earth.
² Give ear, you that rule over
multitudes,
and boast of many nations.
³ For your dominion was given you
from the Lord,
and your sovereignty from the Most
High;
he will search out your works and
inquire into your plans.
⁴ Because as servants of his kingdom
you did not rule rightly,
or keep the law,
or walk according to the purpose of
God,
⁵ he will come upon you terribly and
swiftly,
because severe judgment falls on those
in high places.
⁶ For the lowliest may be pardoned in
mercy,
but the mighty will be mightily tested.
⁷ For the Lord of all will not stand in
awe of anyone,
or show deference to greatness;
because he himself made both small and
great,
and he takes thought for all alike.
⁸ But a strict inquiry is in store for the
mighty.
⁹ To you then, O monarchs, my words
are directed,
so that you may learn wisdom and
not transgress.
¹⁰ For they will be made holy who
observe holy things in holiness,
and those who have been taught them
will find a defense.
¹¹ Therefore set your desire on my
words;
long for them, and you will be
instructed.

Description of Wisdom
¹² Wisdom is radiant and unfading,
and she is easily discerned by those
who love her,
and is found by those who seek her.
¹³ She hastens to make herself known to
those who desire her.

° Other ancient authorities read *dust*   *°* Other ancient authorities read *spider's web*   *°* Gk *He*   *°* Or *punish*

¹⁴ One who rises early to seek her will
   have no difficulty,
   for she will be found sitting at the
   gate.
¹⁵ To fix one's thought on her is perfect
   understanding,
   and one who is vigilant on her
   account will soon be free from
   care,
¹⁶ because she goes about seeking those
   worthy of her,
   and she graciously appears to them in
   their paths,
   and meets them in every thought.

¹⁷ The beginning of wisdom[s] is the most
   sincere desire for instruction,
   and concern for instruction is love of
   her,
¹⁸ and love of her is the keeping of her
   laws,
   and giving heed to her laws is
   assurance of immortality,
¹⁹ and immortality brings one near to God;
²⁰ so the desire for wisdom leads to a
   kingdom.

²¹ Therefore if you delight in thrones and
   scepters, O monarchs over the
   peoples,
   honor wisdom, so that you may reign
   forever.
²² I will tell you what wisdom is and
   how she came to be,
   and I will hide no secrets from you,
   but I will trace her course from the
   beginning of creation,
   and make knowledge of her clear,
   and I will not pass by the truth;
²³ nor will I travel in the company of
   sickly envy,
   for envy[t] does not associate with
   wisdom.
²⁴ The multitude of the wise is the
   salvation of the world,
   and a sensible king is the stability of
   any people.
²⁵ Therefore be instructed by my words,
   and you will profit.

Solomon Like Other Mortals

7 I also am mortal, like everyone else,
   a descendant of the first-formed
   child of earth;

and in the womb of a mother I was
   molded into flesh,
² within the period of ten months,
   compacted with blood,
   from the seed of a man and the
   pleasure of marriage.
³ And when I was born, I began to
   breathe the common air,
   and fell upon the kindred earth;
   my first sound was a cry, as is true of
   all.
⁴ I was nursed with care in swaddling
   cloths.
⁵ For no king has had a different
   beginning of existence;
⁶ there is for all one entrance into life,
   and one way out.

Solomon's Respect for Wisdom
⁷ Therefore I prayed, and understanding
   was given me;
   I called on God, and the spirit of
   wisdom came to me.
⁸ I preferred her to scepters and thrones,
   and I accounted wealth as nothing in
   comparison with her.
⁹ Neither did I liken to her any priceless
   gem,
   because all gold is but a little sand in
   her sight,
   and silver will be accounted as clay
   before her.
¹⁰ I loved her more than health and
   beauty,
   and I chose to have her rather than
   light,
   because her radiance never ceases.
¹¹ All good things came to me along
   with her,
   and in her hands uncounted wealth.
¹² I rejoiced in them all, because wisdom
   leads them;
   but I did not know that she was their
   mother.
¹³ I learned without guile and I impart
   without grudging;
   I do not hide her wealth,
¹⁴ for it is an unfailing treasure for
   mortals;
   those who get it obtain friendship with
   God,
   commended for the gifts that come
   from instruction.

[s] Gk *Her beginning*   [t] Gk *this*

Solomon Prays for Wisdom

¹⁵ May God grant me to speak with
  judgment,
  and to have thoughts worthy of what
    I have received;
  for he is the guide even of wisdom
    and the corrector of the wise.
¹⁶ For both we and our words are in his
    hand,
  as are all understanding and skill in
    crafts.
¹⁷ For it is he who gave me unerring
    knowledge of what exists,
  to know the structure of the world
    and the activity of the
    elements;
¹⁸ the beginning and end and middle of
    times,
  the alternations of the solstices and
    the changes of the seasons,
¹⁹ the cycles of the year and the
    constellations of the stars,
²⁰ the natures of animals and the
    tempers of wild animals,
  the powers of spirits*ᵘ* and the thoughts
    of human beings,
  the varieties of plants and the virtues
    of roots;
²¹ I learned both what is secret and
    what is manifest,
²² for wisdom, the fashioner of all things,
    taught me.

The Nature of Wisdom

There is in her a spirit that is
    intelligent, holy,
  unique, manifold, subtle,
  mobile, clear, unpolluted,
  distinct, invulnerable, loving the good,
    keen,
  irresistible, ²³beneficent, humane,
  steadfast, sure, free from anxiety,
  all-powerful, overseeing all,
  and penetrating through all spirits
    that are intelligent, pure, and
    altogether subtle.
²⁴ For wisdom is more mobile than any
    motion;
  because of her pureness she pervades
    and penetrates all things.
²⁵ For she is a breath of the power of God,
  and a pure emanation of the glory of
    the Almighty;
  therefore nothing defiled gains
    entrance into her.

²⁶ For she is a reflection of eternal light,
  a spotless mirror of the working of
    God,
  and an image of his goodness.
²⁷ Although she is but one, she can do
    all things,
  and while remaining in herself, she
    renews all things;
  in every generation she passes into
    holy souls
  and makes them friends of God, and
    prophets;
²⁸ for God loves nothing so much as the
    person who lives with wisdom.
²⁹ She is more beautiful than the sun,
  and excels every constellation of the
    stars.
  Compared with the light she is found
    to be superior,
³⁰ for it is succeeded by the night,
  but against wisdom evil does not
    prevail.

8 She reaches mightily from one end of
  the earth to the other,
  and she orders all things well.

Solomon's Love for Wisdom

² I loved her and sought her from my
    youth;
  I desired to take her for my bride,
  and became enamored of her beauty.
³ She glorifies her noble birth by living
    with God,
  and the Lord of all loves her.
⁴ For she is an initiate in the knowledge
    of God,
  and an associate in his works.
⁵ If riches are a desirable possession in
    life,
  what is richer than wisdom, the active
    cause of all things?
⁶ And if understanding is effective,
  who more than she is fashioner of
    what exists?
⁷ And if anyone loves righteousness,
  her labors are virtues;
  for she teaches self-control and
    prudence,
  justice and courage;
  nothing in life is more profitable for
    mortals than these.
⁸ And if anyone longs for wide
    experience,
  she knows the things of old, and
    infers the things to come;

ᵘ Or *winds*

she understands turns of speech and
   the solutions of riddles;
she has foreknowledge of signs and
   wonders
and of the outcome of seasons and
   times.

Wisdom Indispensable to Rulers
9 Therefore I determined to take her to
   live with me,
knowing that she would give me good
   counsel
and encouragement in cares and grief.
¹⁰ Because of her I shall have glory
   among the multitudes
and honor in the presence of the
   elders, though I am young.
¹¹ I shall be found keen in judgment,
and in the sight of rulers I shall be
   admired.
¹² When I am silent they will wait for
   me,
and when I speak they will give heed;
if I speak at greater length,
they will put their hands on their
   mouths.
¹³ Because of her I shall have
   immortality,
and leave an everlasting remembrance
   to those who come after me.
¹⁴ I shall govern peoples,
and nations will be subject to me;
¹⁵ dread monarchs will be afraid of me
   when they hear of me;
among the people I shall show myself
   capable, and courageous in
   war.
¹⁶ When I enter my house, I shall find
   rest with her;
for companionship with her has no
   bitterness,
and life with her has no pain, but
   gladness and joy.
¹⁷ When I considered these things
   inwardly,
and pondered in my heart
that in kinship with wisdom there is
   immortality,
¹⁸ and in friendship with her, pure
   delight,
and in the labors of her hands,
   unfailing wealth,
and in the experience of her company,
   understanding,
and renown in sharing her words,

I went about seeking how to get her
   for myself.
¹⁹ As a child I was naturally gifted,
and a good soul fell to my lot;
²⁰ or rather, being good, I entered an
   undefiled body.
²¹ But I perceived that I would not
   possess wisdom unless God
   gave her to me—
and it was a mark of insight to know
   whose gift she was—
so I appealed to the Lord and implored
   him,
and with my whole heart I said:

Solomon's Prayer for Wisdom

9 "O God of my ancestors and Lord of
   mercy,
who have made all things by your
   word,
² and by your wisdom have formed
   humankind
to have dominion over the creatures
   you have made,
³ and rule the world in holiness and
   righteousness,
and pronounce judgment in
   uprightness of soul,
⁴ give me the wisdom that sits by your
   throne,
and do not reject me from among
   your servants.
⁵ For I am your servantᵛ the son of
   your serving girl,
a man who is weak and short-lived,
with little understanding of judgment
   and laws;
⁶ for even one who is perfect among
   human beings
will be regarded as nothing without the
   wisdom that comes from you.
⁷ You have chosen me to be king of
   your people
and to be judge over your sons and
   daughters.
⁸ You have given command to build a
   temple on your holy mountain,
and an altar in the city of your
   habitation,
a copy of the holy tent that you
   prepared from the beginning.
⁹ With you is wisdom, she who knows
   your works
and was present when you made the
   world;

ᵛ Gk *slave*

she understands what is pleasing in
  your sight
and what is right according to your
  commandments.
¹⁰ Send her forth from the holy heavens,
and from the throne of your glory
  send her,
that she may labor at my side,
and that I may learn what is pleasing
  to you.
¹¹ For she knows and understands all
  things,
and she will guide me wisely in my
  actions
and guard me with her glory.
¹² Then my works will be acceptable,
and I shall judge your people justly,
and shall be worthy of the throne[w] of
  my father.
¹³ For who can learn the counsel of
  God?
Or who can discern what the Lord
  wills?
¹⁴ For the reasoning of mortals is
  worthless,
and our designs are likely to fail;
¹⁵ for a perishable body weighs down the
  soul,
and this earthy tent burdens the
  thoughtful[x] mind.
¹⁶ We can hardly guess at what is on
  earth,
and what is at hand we find with
  labor;
but who has traced out what is in the
  heavens?
¹⁷ Who has learned your counsel,
unless you have given wisdom
and sent your holy spirit from on
  high?
¹⁸ And thus the paths of those on earth
  were set right,
and people were taught what pleases
  you,
and were saved by wisdom."

The Work of Wisdom from Adam to Moses

10 Wisdom[y] protected the first-formed
  father of the world, when he
  alone had been created;
she delivered him from his
  transgression,
² and gave him strength to rule all things.
³ But when an unrighteous man
departed from her in his anger,

he perished because in rage he killed
  his brother.
⁴ When the earth was flooded because
  of him, wisdom again saved it,
steering the righteous man by a paltry
  piece of wood.

⁵ Wisdom[y] also, when the nations in
  wicked agreement had been put
  to confusion,
recognized the righteous man and
  preserved him blameless before
  God,
and kept him strong in the face of his
  compassion for his child.

⁶ Wisdom[y] rescued a righteous man
  when the ungodly were
  perishing;
he escaped the fire that descended on
  the Five Cities.[z]
⁷ Evidence of their wickedness still remains:
a continually smoking wasteland,
plants bearing fruit that does not
  ripen,
and a pillar of salt standing as a
  monument to an unbelieving
  soul.
⁸ For because they passed wisdom by,
they not only were hindered from
  recognizing the good,
but also left for humankind a
  reminder of their folly,
so that their failures could never go
  unnoticed.

⁹ Wisdom rescued from troubles those
  who served her.
¹⁰ When a righteous man fled from his
  brother's wrath,
she guided him on straight paths;
she showed him the kingdom of God,
and gave him knowledge of holy
  things;
she prospered him in his labors,
and increased the fruit of his toil.
¹¹ When his oppressors were covetous,
she stood by him and made him rich.
¹² She protected him from his enemies,
and kept him safe from those who lay
  in wait for him;
in his arduous contest she gave him
  the victory,
so that he might learn that godliness
  is more powerful than anything
  else.

---

[w] Gk *thrones*   [x] Or *anxious*   [y] Gk *She*   [z] Or *on Pentapolis*

¹³ When a righteous man was sold,
  wisdom^a did not desert him,
 but delivered him from sin.
 She descended with him into the
  dungeon,
¹⁴ and when he was in prison she did
  not leave him,
 until she brought him the scepter of a
  kingdom
 and authority over his masters.
 Those who accused him she showed
  to be false,
 and she gave him everlasting honor.

Wisdom Led the Israelites out of Egypt
¹⁵ A holy people and blameless race
 wisdom delivered from a nation of
  oppressors.
¹⁶ She entered the soul of a servant of
  the Lord,
 and withstood dread kings with
  wonders and signs.
¹⁷ She gave to holy people the reward of
  their labors;
 she guided them along a marvelous
  way,
 and became a shelter to them by day,
 and a starry flame through the night.
¹⁸ She brought them over the Red Sea,
 and led them through deep waters;
¹⁹ but she drowned their enemies,
 and cast them up from the depth of
  the sea.
²⁰ Therefore the righteous plundered the
  ungodly;
 they sang hymns, O Lord, to your
  holy name,
 and praised with one accord your
  defending hand;
²¹ for wisdom opened the mouths of
  those who were mute,
 and made the tongues of infants speak
  clearly.

Wisdom Led the Israelites through the Desert
11 Wisdom^b prospered their works by
  the hand of a holy prophet.
² They journeyed through an
  uninhabited wilderness,
 and pitched their tents in untrodden
  places.
³ They withstood their enemies and
  fought off their foes.
⁴ When they were thirsty, they called
  upon you,

and water was given them out of
  flinty rock,
and from hard stone a remedy for
  their thirst.
⁵ For through the very things by which
  their enemies were punished,
they themselves received benefit in
  their need.
⁶ Instead of the fountain of an ever-
  flowing river,
stirred up and defiled with blood
⁷ in rebuke for the decree to kill the infants,
you gave them abundant water
  unexpectedly,
⁸ showing by their thirst at that time
how you punished their enemies.
⁹ For when they were tried, though
  they were being disciplined in
  mercy,
they learned how the ungodly were
  tormented when judged in
  wrath.
¹⁰ For you tested them as a parent^c does
  in warning,
but you examined the ungodly^d as a
  stern king does in
  condemnation.
¹¹ Whether absent or present, they were
  equally distressed,
¹² for a twofold grief possessed them,
and a groaning at the memory of
  what had occurred.
¹³ For when they heard that through
  their own punishments
the righteous^e had received benefit,
  they perceived it was the Lord's
  doing.
¹⁴ For though they had mockingly
  rejected him who long before
  had been cast out and exposed,
at the end of the events they marveled
  at him,
when they felt thirst in a different
  way from the righteous.

Punishment of the Wicked
¹⁵ In return for their foolish and wicked
  thoughts,
which led them astray to worship
  irrational serpents and
  worthless animals,
you sent upon them a multitude of
  irrational creatures to punish
  them,

---

^a Gk *she* ^b Gk *She* ^c Gk *a father* ^d Gk *those* ^e Gk *they*

16 so that they might learn that one is
     punished by the very things by
     which one sins.
17 For your all-powerful hand,
     which created the world out of
       formless matter,
     did not lack the means to send upon
       them a multitude of bears, or
       bold lions,
18 or newly-created unknown beasts full
       of rage,
     or such as breathe out fiery breath,
     or belch forth a thick pall of smoke,
     or flash terrible sparks from their eyes;
19 not only could the harm they did
       destroy people,[f]
     but the mere sight of them could kill
       by fright.
20 Even apart from these, people[g] could
       fall at a single breath
     when pursued by justice
     and scattered by the breath of your
       power.
     But you have arranged all things by
       measure and number and
       weight.

God Is Powerful and Merciful
21 For it is always in your power to
       show great strength,
     and who can withstand the might of
       your arm?
22 Because the whole world before you is
       like a speck that tips the scales,
     and like a drop of morning dew that
       falls on the ground.
23 But you are merciful to all, for you
       can do all things,
     and you overlook people's sins, so that
       they may repent.
24 For you love all things that exist,
     and detest none of the things that you
       have made,
     for you would not have made
       anything if you had hated it.
25 How would anything have endured if
       you had not willed it?
     Or how would anything not called
       forth by you have been
       preserved?
26 You spare all things, for they are
       yours, O Lord, you who love the
       living.

12 For your immortal spirit is in all
       things.
2 Therefore you correct little by little
       those who trespass,
     and you remind and warn them of
       the things through which they
       sin,
     so that they may be freed from
       wickedness and put their trust
       in you, O Lord.

The Sins of the Canaanites
3 Those who lived long ago in your
       holy land
4 you hated for their detestable practices,
     their works of sorcery and unholy
       rites,
5 their merciless slaughter[h] of children,
     and their sacrificial feasting on human
       flesh and blood.
     These initiates from the midst of a
       heathen cult,[i]
6 these parents who murder helpless
       lives,
     you willed to destroy by the hands of
       our ancestors,
7 so that the land most precious of all
       to you
     might receive a worthy colony of the
       servants[j] of God.
8 But even these you spared, since they
       were but mortals,
     and sent wasps[k] as forerunners of
       your army
     to destroy them little by little,
9 though you were not unable to give
       the ungodly into the hands of
       the righteous in battle,
     or to destroy them at one blow by
       dread wild animals or your
       stern word.
10 But judging them little by little you
       gave them an opportunity to
       repent,
     though you were not unaware that
       their origin[l] was evil
     and their wickedness inborn,
     and that their way of thinking would
       never change.
11 For they were an accursed race from
       the beginning,
     and it was not through fear of anyone
       that you left them unpunished
       for their sins.

---

[f] Gk them   [g] Gk they   [h] Gk slaughterers   [i] Meaning of Gk uncertain   [j] Or children   [k] Or hornets   [l] Or nature

God Is Sovereign

12 For who will say, "What have you done?"
or will resist your judgment?
Who will accuse you for the destruction of nations that you made?
Or who will come before you to plead as an advocate for the unrighteous?
13 For neither is there any god besides you, whose care is for all people,[m]
to whom you should prove that you have not judged unjustly;
14 nor can any king or monarch confront you about those whom you have punished.
15 You are righteous and you rule all things righteously,
deeming it alien to your power
to condemn anyone who does not deserve to be punished.
16 For your strength is the source of righteousness,
and your sovereignty over all causes you to spare all.
17 For you show your strength when people doubt the completeness of your power,
and you rebuke any insolence among those who know it.[n]
18 Although you are sovereign in strength, you judge with mildness,
and with great forbearance you govern us;
for you have power to act whenever you choose.

God's Lessons for Israel

19 Through such works you have taught your people
that the righteous must be kind,
and you have filled your children with good hope,
because you give repentance for sins.
20 For if you punished with such great care and indulgence[o]
the enemies of your servants[p] and those deserving of death,
granting them time and opportunity to give up their wickedness,
21 with what strictness you have judged your children,
to whose ancestors you gave oaths and covenants full of good promises!
22 So while chastening us you scourge our enemies ten thousand times more,
so that, when we judge, we may meditate upon your goodness,
and when we are judged, we may expect mercy.

The Punishment of the Egyptians

23 Therefore those who lived unrighteously, in a life of folly,
you tormented through their own abominations.
24 For they went far astray on the paths of error,
accepting as gods those animals that even their enemies[q] despised;
they were deceived like foolish infants.
25 Therefore, as though to children who cannot reason,
you sent your judgment to mock them.
26 But those who have not heeded the warning of mild rebukes
will experience the deserved judgment of God.
27 For when in their suffering they became incensed
at those creatures that they had thought to be gods, being punished by means of them,
they saw and recognized as the true God the one whom they had before refused to know.
Therefore the utmost condemnation came upon them.

The Foolishness of Nature Worship

13 For all people who were ignorant of God were foolish by nature;
and they were unable from the good things that are seen to know the one who exists,
nor did they recognize the artisan while paying heed to his works;
2 but they supposed that either fire or wind or swift air,
or the circle of the stars, or turbulent water,

[m] Or *all things* [n] Meaning of Gk uncertain [o] Other ancient authorities lack *and indulgence*; others read *and entreaty* [p] Or *children* [q] Gk *they*

or the luminaries of heaven were the
      gods that rule the world.
3 If through delight in the beauty of
      these things people assumed
      them to be gods,
let them know how much better than
      these is their Lord,
for the author of beauty created them.
4 And if people^r were amazed at their
      power and working,
let them perceive from them
      how much more powerful is the one
      who formed them.
5 For from the greatness and beauty of
      created things
comes a corresponding perception of
      their Creator.
6 Yet these people are little to be
      blamed,
for perhaps they go astray
while seeking God and desiring to find
      him.
7 For while they live among his works,
      they keep searching,
and they trust in what they see,
      because the things that are
      seen are beautiful.
8 Yet again, not even they are to be
      excused;
9 for if they had the power to know so
      much
that they could investigate the world,
how did they fail to find sooner the
      Lord of these things?

The Foolishness of Idolatry
10 But miserable, with their hopes set on
      dead things, are those
who give the name "gods" to the
      works of human hands,
gold and silver fashioned with skill,
and likenesses of animals,
or a useless stone, the work of an
      ancient hand.
11 A skilled woodcutter may saw down a
      tree easy to handle
and skillfully strip off all its bark,
and then with pleasing workmanship
make a useful vessel that serves life's
      needs,
12 and burn the cast-off pieces of his
      work
to prepare his food, and eat his fill.
13 But a cast-off piece from among them,
      useful for nothing,

a stick crooked and full of knots,
he takes and carves with care in his
      leisure,
and shapes it with skill gained in
      idleness;^s
he forms it in the likeness of a human
      being,
14 or makes it like some worthless
      animal,
giving it a coat of red paint and
      coloring its surface red
and covering every blemish in it with
      paint;
15 then he makes a suitable niche for it,
and sets it in the wall, and fastens it
      there with iron.
16 He takes thought for it, so that it may
      not fall,
because he knows that it cannot help
      itself,
for it is only an image and has need
      of help.
17 When he prays about possessions and
      his marriage and children,
he is not ashamed to address a lifeless
      thing.
18 For health he appeals to a thing that
      is weak;
for life he prays to a thing that is dead;
for aid he entreats a thing that is
      utterly inexperienced;
for a prosperous journey, a thing that
      cannot take a step;
19 for money-making and work and
      success with his hands
he asks strength of a thing whose
      hands have no strength.

Folly of a Navigator Praying to an Idol
14 Again, one preparing to sail and
      about to voyage over raging
      waves
calls upon a piece of wood more
      fragile than the ship that
      carries him.
2 For it was desire for gain that planned
      that vessel,
and wisdom was the artisan who built it;
3 but it is your providence, O Father,
      that steers its course,
because you have given it a path in
      the sea,
and a safe way through the waves,
4 showing that you can save from every
      danger,

---

^r Gk *they*   ^s Other ancient authorities read *with intelligent skill*

so that even a person who lacks skill
　　may put to sea.
5 It is your will that works of your
　　wisdom should not be without
　　effect;
therefore people trust their lives even
　　to the smallest piece of wood,
and passing through the billows on a
　　raft they come safely to land.
6 For even in the beginning, when
　　arrogant giants were perishing,
the hope of the world took refuge on
　　a raft,
and guided by your hand left to the
　　world the seed of a new
　　generation.
7 For blessed is the wood by which
　　righteousness comes.

8 But the idol made with hands is
　　accursed, and so is the one
　　who made it—
he for having made it, and the
　　perishable thing because it was
　　named a god.
9 For equally hateful to God are the
　　ungodly and their ungodliness;
10 for what was done will be punished
　　together with the one who
　　did it.
11 Therefore there will be a visitation also
　　upon the heathen idols,
because, though part of what God
　　created, they became an
　　abomination,
snares for human souls
and a trap for the feet of the foolish.

The Origin and Evils of Idolatry
12 For the idea of making idols was the
　　beginning of fornication,
and the invention of them was the
　　corruption of life;
13 for they did not exist from the
　　beginning,
nor will they last forever.
14 For through human vanity they
　　entered the world,
and therefore their speedy end has
　　been planned.

15 For a father, consumed with grief at
　　an untimely bereavement,
made an image of his child, who had
　　been suddenly taken from him;

he now honored as a god what was
　　once a dead human being,
and handed on to his dependants
　　secret rites and initiations.
16 Then the ungodly custom, grown
　　strong with time, was kept as
　　a law,
and at the command of monarchs
　　carved images were worshiped.
17 When people could not honor
　　monarchs[t] in their presence,
　　since they lived at a distance,
they imagined their appearance far
　　away,
and made a visible image of the king
　　whom they honored,
so that by their zeal they might flatter
　　the absent one as though
　　present.

18 Then the ambition of the artisan
　　impelled
even those who did not know the
　　king to intensify their worship.
19 For he, perhaps wishing to please his
　　ruler,
skillfully forced the likeness to take
　　more beautiful form,
20 and the multitude, attracted by the
　　charm of his work,
now regarded as an object of worship
　　the one whom shortly before
　　they had honored as a human
　　being.
21 And this became a hidden trap for
　　humankind,
because people, in bondage to
　　misfortune or to royal
　　authority,
bestowed on objects of stone or wood
　　the name that ought not to be
　　shared.

22 Then it was not enough for them to
　　err about the knowledge of
　　God,
but though living in great strife due to
　　ignorance,
they call such great evils peace.
23 For whether they kill children in their
　　initiations, or celebrate secret
　　mysteries,
or hold frenzied revels with strange
　　customs,
24 they no longer keep either their lives
　　or their marriages pure,

---

[t] Gk *them*

but they either treacherously kill one
another, or grieve one another
by adultery,
25 and all is a raging riot of blood and
murder, theft and deceit,
corruption, faithlessness,
tumult, perjury,
26 confusion over what is good,
forgetfulness of favors,
defiling of souls, sexual perversion,
disorder in marriages, adultery, and
debauchery.
27 For the worship of idols not to be
named
is the beginning and cause and end of
every evil.
28 For their worshipers" either rave in
exultation,
or prophesy lies, or live unrighteously,
or readily commit perjury;
29 for because they trust in lifeless idols
they swear wicked oaths and expect to
suffer no harm.
30 But just penalties will overtake them
on two counts:
because they thought wrongly about
God in devoting themselves to
idols,
and because in deceit they swore
unrighteously through contempt
for holiness.
31 For it is not the power of the things
by which people swear,ᵛ
but the just penalty for those who sin,
that always pursues the transgression
of the unrighteous.

Benefits of Worshiping the True God

15 But you, our God, are kind and
true,
patient, and ruling all thingsʷ in
mercy.
2 For even if we sin we are yours,
knowing your power;
but we will not sin, because we know
that you acknowledge us as
yours.
3 For to know you is complete
righteousness,
and to know your power is the root
of immortality.
4 For neither has the evil intent of
human art misled us,
nor the fruitless toil of painters,
a figure stained with varied colors,

5 whose appearance arouses yearning in
fools,
so that they desireˣ the lifeless form of
a dead image.
6 Lovers of evil things and fit for such
objects of hopeʸ
are those who either make or desire
or worship them.

The Foolishness of Worshiping Clay Idols
7 A potter kneads the soft earth
and laboriously molds each vessel for
our service,
fashioning out of the same clay
both the vessels that serve clean uses
and those for contrary uses, making
all alike;
but which shall be the use of each
of them
the worker in clay decides.
8 With misspent toil, these workers form a
futile god from the same clay—
these mortals who were made of earth
a short time before
and after a little while go to the earth
from which all mortals are
taken,
when the time comes to return the
souls that were borrowed.
9 But the workers are not concerned
that mortals are destined to die
or that their life is brief,
but they compete with workers in gold
and silver,
and imitate workers in copper;
and they count it a glorious thing to
mold counterfeit gods.
10 Their heart is ashes, their hope is
cheaper than dirt,
and their lives are of less worth than
clay,
11 because they failed to know the one
who formed them
and inspired them with active souls
and breathed a living spirit into them.
12 But they considered our existence an
idle game,
and life a festival held for profit,
for they say one must get money
however one can, even by base
means.
13 For these persons, more than all
others, know that they sin
when they make from earthy matter
fragile vessels and carved images.

" Gk *they*   ᵛ Or *of the oaths people swear*   ʷ Or *ruling the universe*   ˣ Gk *and he desires*   ʸ Gk *such hopes*

14 But most foolish, and more miserable
     than an infant,
are all the enemies who oppressed
     your people.
15 For they thought that all their
     heathen idols were gods,
though these have neither the use of
     their eyes to see with,
nor nostrils with which to draw
     breath,
nor ears with which to hear,
nor fingers to feel with,
and their feet are of no use for
     walking.
16 For a human being made them,
and one whose spirit is borrowed
     formed them;
for none can form gods that are like
     themselves.
17 People are mortal, and what they
     make with lawless hands is
     dead;
for they are better than the objects
     they worship,
since*z* they have life, but the idols*a*
     never had.

Serpents in the Desert
18 Moreover, they worship even the most
     hateful animals,
which are worse than all others when
     judged by their lack of
     intelligence;
19 and even as animals they are not so
     beautiful in appearance that
     one would desire them,
but they have escaped both the praise
     of God and his blessing.

16 Therefore those people*b* were
     deservedly punished through
     such creatures,
and were tormented by a multitude of
     animals.
2 Instead of this punishment you
     showed kindness to your
     people,
and you prepared quails to eat,
a delicacy to satisfy the desire of appetite;
3 in order that those people, when they
     desired food,
might lose the least remnant of
     appetite*c*
because of the odious creatures sent to
     them,

while your people,*b* after suffering want
     a short time,
might partake of delicacies.
4 For it was necessary that upon those
     oppressors inescapable want
     should come,
while to these others it was merely
     shown how their enemies were
     being tormented.

5 For when the terrible rage of wild
     animals came upon your
     people*d*
and they were being destroyed by the
     bites of writhing serpents,
your wrath did not continue to the
     end;
6 they were troubled for a little while as
     a warning,
and received a symbol of deliverance
     to remind them of your law's
     command.

7 For the one who turned toward it was
     saved, not by the thing that
     was beheld,
but by you, the Savior of all.
8 And by this also you convinced our
     enemies
that it is you who deliver from every
     evil.
9 For they were killed by the bites of
     locusts and flies,
and no healing was found for them,
because they deserved to be punished
     by such things.
10 But your children were not conquered
     even by the fangs of venomous
     serpents,
for your mercy came to their help and
     healed them.
11 To remind them of your oracles they
     were bitten,
and then were quickly delivered,
so that they would not fall into deep
     forgetfulness
and become unresponsive*e* to your
     kindness.
12 For neither herb nor poultice cured
     them,
but it was your word, O Lord, that
     heals all people.
13 For you have power over life and death;
you lead mortals down to the gates of
     Hades and back again.

z Other ancient authorities read *of which*   *a* Gk *but they*   *b* Gk *they*   *c* Gk *loathed the necessary appetite*   *d* Gk
them   *e* Meaning of Gk uncertain

¹⁴ A person in wickedness kills another,
but cannot bring back the departed
spirit,
or set free the imprisoned soul.

Disastrous Storms Strike Egypt
¹⁵ To escape from your hand is
impossible;
¹⁶ for the ungodly, refusing to know you,
were flogged by the strength of your
arm,
pursued by unusual rains and hail
and relentless storms,
and utterly consumed by fire.
¹⁷ For—most incredible of all—in water,
which quenches all things,
the fire had still greater effect,
for the universe defends the righteous.
¹⁸ At one time the flame was restrained,
so that it might not consume the creatures
sent against the ungodly,
but that seeing this they might know
that they were being pursued by the
judgment of God;
¹⁹ and at another time even in the midst
of water it burned more
intensely than fire,
to destroy the crops of the unrighteous
land.

The Israelites Receive Manna
²⁰ Instead of these things you gave your
people food of angels,
and without their toil you supplied
them from heaven with bread
ready to eat,
providing every pleasure and suited to
every taste.
²¹ For your sustenance manifested your
sweetness toward your children;
and the bread, ministering^f to the
desire of the one who took it,
was changed to suit everyone's liking.
²² Snow and ice withstood fire without
melting,
so that they might know that the
crops of their enemies
were being destroyed by the fire that
blazed in the hail
and flashed in the showers of rain;
²³ whereas the fire,^g in order that the
righteous might be fed,
even forgot its native power.

²⁴ For creation, serving you who made it,
exerts itself to punish the unrighteous,
and in kindness relaxes on behalf of
those who trust in you.
²⁵ Therefore at that time also, changed
into all forms,
it served your all-nourishing bounty,
according to the desire of those who
had need,^h
²⁶ so that your children, whom you
loved, O Lord, might learn
that it is not the production of crops
that feeds humankind
but that your word sustains those
who trust in you.
²⁷ For what was not destroyed by fire
was melted when simply warmed by a
fleeting ray of the sun,
²⁸ to make it known that one must rise
before the sun to give you
thanks,
and must pray to you at the dawning
of the light;
²⁹ for the hope of an ungrateful person
will melt like wintry frost,
and flow away like waste water.

Terror Strikes the Egyptians at Night

17 Great are your judgments and hard
to describe;
therefore uninstructed souls have gone
astray.
² For when lawless people supposed that
they held the holy nation in
their power,
they themselves lay as captives of
darkness and prisoners of long
night,
shut in under their roofs, exiles from
eternal providence.
³ For thinking that in their secret sins
they were unobserved
behind a dark curtain of forgetfulness,
they were scattered, terribly^i alarmed,
and appalled by specters.
⁴ For not even the inner chamber that
held them protected them from
fear,
but terrifying sounds rang out around
them,
and dismal phantoms with gloomy
faces appeared.
⁵ And no power of fire was able to give
light,

---

^f Gk *and it, ministering*   ^g Gk *this*   ^h Or *who made supplication*   ^i Other ancient authorities read *unobserved,
they were darkened behind a dark curtain of forgetfulness, terribly*

nor did the brilliant flames of the stars
　　avail to illumine that hateful night.
6 Nothing was shining through to them
　　except a dreadful, self-kindled fire,
　　and in terror they deemed the things
　　　　that they saw
　　to be worse than that unseen
　　　　appearance.
7 The delusions of their magic art lay
　　　　humbled,
　　and their boasted wisdom was
　　　　scornfully rebuked.
8 For those who promised to drive off
　　　　the fears and disorders of a sick
　　　　soul
　　were sick themselves with ridiculous
　　　　fear.
9 For even if nothing disturbing
　　　　frightened them,
　　yet, scared by the passing of wild animals
　　　　and the hissing of snakes
10 they perished in trembling fear,
　　refusing to look even at the air,
　　　　though it nowhere could be
　　　　avoided.
11 For wickedness is a cowardly thing,
　　　　condemned by its own
　　　　testimony;[j]
　　distressed by conscience, it has always
　　　　exaggerated[k] the difficulties.
12 For fear is nothing but a giving up of the
　　　　helps that come from reason;
13 and hope, defeated by this inward
　　　　weakness,
　　prefers ignorance of what causes the
　　　　torment.
14 But throughout the night, which was
　　　　really powerless
　　and which came upon them from the
　　　　recesses of powerless Hades,
　　they all slept the same sleep,
15 and now were driven by monstrous
　　　　specters,
　　and now were paralyzed by their
　　　　souls' surrender;
　　for sudden and unexpected fear
　　　　overwhelmed them.
16 And whoever was there fell down,
　　and thus was kept shut up in a prison
　　　　not made of iron;
17 for whether they were farmers or
　　　　shepherds
　　or workers who toiled in the wilderness,
　　they were seized, and endured the
　　　　inescapable fate;

for with one chain of darkness they
　　　　all were bound.
18 Whether there came a whistling wind,
　　or a melodious sound of birds in wide-
　　　　spreading branches,
　　or the rhythm of violently rushing
　　　　water,
19 or the harsh crash of rocks hurled
　　　　down,
　　or the unseen running of leaping
　　　　animals,
　　or the sound of the most savage
　　　　roaring beasts,
　　or an echo thrown back from a
　　　　hollow of the mountains,
　　it paralyzed them with terror.
20 For the whole world was illumined
　　　　with brilliant light,
　　and went about its work unhindered,
21 while over those people alone heavy
　　　　night was spread,
　　an image of the darkness that was
　　　　destined to receive them;
　　but still heavier than darkness were
　　　　they to themselves.

Light Shines on the Israelites

18 But for your holy ones there was
　　very great light.
　　Their enemies[l] heard their voices but
　　　　did not see their forms,
　　and counted them happy for not
　　　　having suffered,
2 and were thankful that your holy
　　　　ones,[l] though previously
　　　　wronged, were doing them no
　　　　injury;
　　and they begged their pardon for
　　　　having been at variance with
　　　　them.[j]
3 Therefore you provided a flaming pillar
　　　　of fire
　　as a guide for your people's[m]
　　　　unknown journey,
　　and a harmless sun for their glorious
　　　　wandering.
4 For their enemies[n] deserved to be
　　　　deprived of light and
　　　　imprisoned in darkness,
　　those who had kept your children
　　　　imprisoned,
　　through whom the imperishable light
　　　　of the law was to be given to
　　　　the world.

[j] Meaning of Gk uncertain　[k] Other ancient authorities read *anticipated*　[l] Gk *They*　[m] Gk *their*　[n] Gk *those persons*

55

Threat of Annihilation in the Desert

The Death of the Egyptian Firstborn

5 When they had resolved to kill the
    infants of your holy ones,
and one child had been abandoned
    and rescued,
you in punishment took away a
    multitude of their children;
and you destroyed them all together
    by a mighty flood.
6 That night was made known
    beforehand to our ancestors,
so that they might rejoice in sure
    knowledge of the oaths in
    which they trusted.
7 The deliverance of the righteous and
    the destruction of their enemies
were expected by your people.
8 For by the same means by which you
    punished our enemies
you called us to yourself and glorified
    us.
9 For in secret the holy children of good
    people offered sacrifices,
and with one accord agreed to the
    divine law,
so that the saints would share alike
    the same things,
both blessings and dangers;
and already they were singing the
    praises of the ancestors.*o*
10 But the discordant cry of their enemies
    echoed back,
and their piteous lament for their
    children was spread abroad.
11 The slave was punished with the same
    penalty as the master,
and the commoner suffered the same
    loss as the king;
12 and they all together, by the one
    form*p* of death,
had corpses too many to count.
For the living were not sufficient even
    to bury them,
since in one instant their most valued
    children had been destroyed.
13 For though they had disbelieved
    everything because of their
    magic arts,
yet, when their firstborn were
    destroyed, they acknowledged
    your people to be God's child.
14 For while gentle silence enveloped all
    things,
and night in its swift course was now
    half gone,

15 your all-powerful word leaped from
    heaven, from the royal throne,
into the midst of the land that was
    doomed,
a stern warrior
16 carrying the sharp sword of your
    authentic command,
and stood and filled all things with
    death,
and touched heaven while standing on
    the earth.
17 Then at once apparitions in dreadful
    dreams greatly troubled them,
and unexpected fears assailed them;
18 and one here and another there,
    hurled down half dead,
made known why they were dying;
19 for the dreams that disturbed them
    forewarned them of this,
so that they might not perish without
    knowing why they suffered.

Threat of Annihilation in the Desert

20 The experience of death touched also
    the righteous,
and a plague came upon the
    multitude in the desert,
but the wrath did not long continue.
21 For a blameless man was quick to act
    as their champion;
he brought forward the shield of his
    ministry,
prayer and propitiation by incense;
he withstood the anger and put an
    end to the disaster,
showing that he was your servant.
22 He conquered the wrath*q* not by
    strength of body,
not by force of arms,
but by his word he subdued the
    avenger,
appealing to the oaths and covenants
    given to our ancestors.
23 For when the dead had already fallen
    on one another in heaps,
he intervened and held back the wrath,
and cut off its way to the living.
24 For on his long robe the whole world
    was depicted,
and the glories of the ancestors were
    engraved on the four rows of
    stones,
and your majesty was on the diadem
    upon his head.

---

o Other ancient authorities read *dangers, the ancestors already leading the songs of praise*   *p* Gk *name*   *q* Cn: Gk *multitude*

²⁵ To these the destroyer yielded, these
        he^r feared;
  for merely to test the wrath was
        enough.

The Red Sea

19
But the ungodly were assailed to
      the end by pitiless anger,
for God^s knew in advance even their
      future actions:
² how, though they themselves had
      permitted^t your people to depart
  and hastily sent them out,
  they would change their minds and
      pursue them.
³ For while they were still engaged in
      mourning,
  and were lamenting at the graves of
      their dead,
  they reached another foolish decision,
  and pursued as fugitives those whom
      they had begged and compelled
      to leave.
⁴ For the fate they deserved drew them
      on to this end,
  and made them forget what had
      happened,
  in order that they might fill up the
      punishment that their torments
      still lacked,
⁵ and that your people might experience^u
      an incredible journey,
  but they themselves might meet a
      strange death.

God Guides and Protects His People

⁶ For the whole creation in its nature
      was fashioned anew,
  complying with your commands,
  so that your children^v might be kept
      unharmed.
⁷ The cloud was seen overshadowing the
      camp,
  and dry land emerging where water
      had stood before,
  an unhindered way out of the Red
      Sea,
  and a grassy plain out of the raging
      waves,
⁸ where those protected by your hand
      passed through as one nation,
  after gazing on marvelous wonders.
⁹ For they ranged like horses,

and leaped like lambs,
  praising you, O Lord, who delivered them.
¹⁰ For they still recalled the events of
      their sojourn,
  how instead of producing animals the
      earth brought forth gnats,
  and instead of fish the river spewed
      out vast numbers of frogs.
¹¹ Afterward they saw also a new kind^w
      of birds,
  when desire led them to ask for
      luxurious food;
¹² for, to give them relief, quails came up
      from the sea.

The Punishment of the Egyptians

¹³ The punishments did not come upon
      the sinners
  without prior signs in the violence of
      thunder,
  for they justly suffered because of their
      wicked acts;
  for they practiced a more bitter hatred
      of strangers.
¹⁴ Others had refused to receive strangers
      when they came to them,
  but these made slaves of guests who
      were their benefactors.
¹⁵ And not only so—but, while
      punishment of some sort will
      come upon the former
  for having received strangers with
      hostility,
¹⁶ the latter, having first received them
      with festal celebrations,
  afterward afflicted with terrible
      sufferings
  those who had already shared the
      same rights.
¹⁷ They were stricken also with loss of
      sight—
  just as were those at the door of the
      righteous man—
  when, surrounded by yawning
      darkness,
  all of them tried to find the way
      through their own doors.

A New Harmony in Nature

¹⁸ For the elements changed^x places with
      one another,
  as on a harp the notes vary the
      nature of the rhythm,

---

^r Other ancient authorities read *they*   ^s Gk *he*   ^t Other ancient authorities read *had changed their minds to
permit*   ^u Other ancient authorities read *accomplish*   ^v Or *servants*   ^w Or *production*   ^x Gk *changing*

while each note remains the same.[y]
This may be clearly inferred from the
sight of what took place.
[19] For land animals were transformed
into water creatures,
and creatures that swim moved over
to the land.
[20] Fire even in water retained its normal
power,
and water forgot its fire-quenching
nature.
[21] Flames, on the contrary, failed to
consume

the flesh of perishable creatures that
walked among them,
nor did they melt[z] the crystalline,
quick-melting kind of heavenly
food.

Conclusion
[22] For in everything, O Lord, you have
exalted and glorified your
people,
and you have not neglected to help
them at all times and in all
places.

[y] Meaning of Gk uncertain   [z] Cn: Gk *nor could be melted*

ECCLESIASTICUS, OR THE WISDOM OF JESUS SON OF

SIRACH

THE PROLOGUE

Many great teachings have been given to us through the Law and the Prophets and the others[a] that followed them, and for these we should praise Israel for instruction and wisdom. Now, those who read the scriptures must not only themselves understand them, but must also as lovers of learning be able through the spoken and written word to help the outsiders. So my grandfather Jesus, who had devoted himself especially to the reading of the Law and the Prophets and the other books of our ancestors, and had acquired considerable proficiency in them, was himself also led to write something pertaining to instruction and wisdom, so that by becoming familiar also with his book[b] those who love learning might make even greater progress in living according to the law.

You are invited therefore to read it with goodwill and attention, and to be indulgent in cases where, despite our diligent labor in translating, we may seem to have rendered some phrases imperfectly. For what was originally expressed in Hebrew does not have exactly the same sense when translated into another language. Not only this book, but even the Law itself, the Prophecies, and the rest of the books differ not a little when read in the original.

When I came to Egypt in the thirty-eighth year of the reign of Euergetes and stayed for some time, I found opportunity for no little instruction.[c] It seemed highly necessary that I should myself devote some diligence and labor to the translation of this book. During that time I have applied my skill day and night to complete and publish the book for those living abroad who wished to gain learning and are disposed to live according to the law.

[a] Or *other books*   [b] Gk *with these things*   [c] Other ancient authorities read *I found a copy affording no little instruction*

58

In Praise of Wisdom

1 All wisdom is from the Lord,
  and with him it remains
  forever.
2 The sand of the sea, the drops of rain,
  and the days of eternity—who can
  count them?
3 The height of heaven, the breadth of
  the earth,
  the abyss, and wisdom[d]—who can
  search them out?
4 Wisdom was created before all other
  things,
  and prudent understanding from
  eternity.[e]
6 The root of wisdom—to whom has it
  been revealed?
  Her subtleties—who knows them?[f]
8 There is but one who is wise, greatly
  to be feared,
  seated upon his throne—the Lord.
9 It is he who created her;
  he saw her and took her measure;
  he poured her out upon all his
  works,
10 upon all the living according to his gift;
  he lavished her upon those who
  love him.[g]

Fear of the Lord Is True Wisdom

11 The fear of the Lord is glory and
  exultation,
  and gladness and a crown of
  rejoicing.
12 The fear of the Lord delights the
  heart,
  and gives gladness and joy and long
  life.[h]
13 Those who fear the Lord will have a
  happy end;
  on the day of their death they will
  be blessed.

14 To fear the Lord is the beginning of
  wisdom;
  she is created with the faithful in
  the womb.

15 She made[i] among human beings an
  eternal foundation,
  and among their descendants she
  will abide faithfully.
16 To fear the Lord is fullness of wisdom;
  she inebriates mortals with her fruits;
17 she fills their[j] whole house with
  desirable goods,
  and their[j] storehouses with her
  produce.
18 The fear of the Lord is the crown of
  wisdom,
  making peace and perfect health to
  flourish.[k]
19 She rained down knowledge and
  discerning comprehension,
  and she heightened the glory of
  those who held her fast.
20 To fear the Lord is the root of wisdom,
  and her branches are long life.[l]

22 Unjust anger cannot be justified,
  for anger tips the scale to one's
  ruin.
23 Those who are patient stay calm until
  the right moment,
  and then cheerfulness comes back to
  them.
24 They hold back their words until the
  right moment;
  then the lips of many tell of their
  good sense.

25 In the treasuries of wisdom are wise
  sayings,
  but godliness is an abomination to a
  sinner.
26 If you desire wisdom, keep the
  commandments,
  and the Lord will lavish her upon
  you.
27 For the fear of the Lord is wisdom
  and discipline,
  fidelity and humility are his delight.

28 Do not disobey the fear of the Lord;
  do not approach him with a divided
  mind.

---

[d] Other ancient authorities read *the depth of the abyss*   [e] Other ancient authorities add as verse 5, *The source of wisdom is God's word in the highest heaven, and her ways are the eternal commandments.*   [f] Other ancient authorities add as verse 7, *The knowledge of wisdom—to whom was it manifested? And her abundant experience—who has understood it?*   [g] Other ancient authorities add *Love of the Lord is glorious wisdom; to those to whom he appears he apportions her, that they may see him.*   [h] Other ancient authorities add *The fear of the Lord is a gift from the Lord; also for love he makes firm paths.*   [i] Gk *made as a nest*   [j] Other ancient authorities read *her*   [k] Other ancient authorities add *Both are gifts of God for peace; glory opens out for those who love him. He saw her and took her measure.*   [l] Other ancient authorities add as verse 21, *The fear of the Lord drives away sins; and where it abides, it will turn away all anger.*

29 Do not be a hypocrite before others,
   and keep watch over your lips.
30 Do not exalt yourself, or you may fall
   and bring dishonor upon yourself.
The Lord will reveal your secrets
   and overthrow you before the whole
      congregation,
because you did not come in the fear
      of the Lord,
   and your heart was full of deceit.

Duties toward God

2 My child, when you come to serve the
   Lord,
   prepare yourself for testing.*m*
2 Set your heart right and be steadfast,
   and do not be impetuous in time of
      calamity.
3 Cling to him and do not depart,
   so that your last days may be
      prosperous.
4 Accept whatever befalls you,
   and in times of humiliation be patient.
5 For gold is tested in the fire,
   and those found acceptable, in the
      furnace of humiliation.*n*
6 Trust in him, and he will help you;
   make your ways straight, and hope
      in him.

7 You who fear the Lord, wait for his
      mercy;
   do not stray, or else you may fall.
8 You who fear the Lord, trust in him,
   and your reward will not be lost.
9 You who fear the Lord, hope for good
      things,
   for lasting joy and mercy.*o*
10 Consider the generations of old and see:
   has anyone trusted in the Lord and
      been disappointed?
Or has anyone persevered in the fear
   of the Lord*p* and been forsaken?
Or has anyone called upon him and
      been neglected?
11 For the Lord is compassionate and
      merciful;
   he forgives sins and saves in time of
      distress.

12 Woe to timid hearts and to slack
      hands,

and to the sinner who walks a
   double path!
13 Woe to the fainthearted who have no
      trust!
   Therefore they will have no shelter.
14 Woe to you who have lost your
      nerve!
   What will you do when the Lord's
      reckoning comes?

15 Those who fear the Lord do not
      disobey his words,
   and those who love him keep his
      ways.
16 Those who fear the Lord seek to
      please him,
   and those who love him are filled
      with his law.
17 Those who fear the Lord prepare their
      hearts,
   and humble themselves before him.
18 Let us fall into the hands of the Lord,
   but not into the hands of mortals;
for equal to his majesty is his mercy,
   and equal to his name are his
      works.*q*

Duties toward Parents

3 Listen to me your father, O children;
   act accordingly, that you may
      be kept in safety.
2 For the Lord honors a father above his
      children,
   and he confirms a mother's right
      over her children.
3 Those who honor their father atone
      for sins,
4 and those who respect their mother
      are like those who lay up
         treasure.
5 Those who honor their father will
      have joy in their own children,
   and when they pray they will be heard.
6 Those who respect their father will
      have long life,
   and those who honor*r* their mother
      obey the Lord;
7 they will serve their parents as their
      masters.*s*
8 Honor your father by word and deed,
   that his blessing may come upon
      you.

m Or *trials*   *n* Other ancient authorities add *in sickness and poverty put your trust in him*   *o* Other ancient
authorities add *For his reward is an everlasting gift with joy.*   *p* Gk *of him*   *q* Syr: Gk lacks this line   *r* Heb:
Other ancient authorities read *comfort*   *s* In other ancient authorities this line is preceded by *Those who fear
the Lord honor their father,*

⁹ For a father's blessing strengthens the
  houses of the children,
  but a mother's curse uproots their
  foundations.
¹⁰ Do not glorify yourself by dishonoring
   your father,
   for your father's dishonor is no
   glory to you.
¹¹ The glory of one's father is one's own
   glory,
   and it is a disgrace for children not
   to respect their mother.

¹² My child, help your father in his old age,
   and do not grieve him as long as
   he lives;
¹³ even if his mind fails, be patient with
   him;
   because you have all your faculties
   do not despise him.
¹⁴ For kindness to a father will not be
   forgotten,
   and will be credited to you against
   your sins;
¹⁵ in the day of your distress it will be
   remembered in your favor;
   like frost in fair weather, your sins
   will melt away.
¹⁶ Whoever forsakes a father is like a
   blasphemer,
   and whoever angers a mother is
   cursed by the Lord.

Humility
¹⁷ My child, perform your tasks with
   humility;ᵗ
   then you will be loved by those
   whom God accepts.
¹⁸ The greater you are, the more you
   must humble yourself;
   so you will find favor in the sight
   of the Lord.ᵘ
²⁰ For great is the might of the Lord;
   but by the humble he is glorified.
²¹ Neither seek what is too difficult for you,
   nor investigate what is beyond your
   power.
²² Reflect upon what you have been
   commanded,
   for what is hidden is not your concern.
²³ Do not meddle in matters that are
   beyond you,
   for more than you can understand
   has been shown you.

²⁴ For their conceit has led many astray,
   and wrong opinion has impaired
   their judgment.
²⁵ Without eyes there is no light;
   without knowledge there is no
   wisdom.ᵛ
²⁶ A stubborn mind will fare badly at the
   end,
   and whoever loves danger will
   perish in it.
²⁷ A stubborn mind will be burdened by
   troubles,
   and the sinner adds sin to sins.
²⁸ When calamity befalls the proud, there
   is no healing,
   for an evil plant has taken root in
   him.
²⁹ The mind of the intelligent appreciates
   proverbs,
   and an attentive ear is the desire of
   the wise.

Alms for the Poor
³⁰ As water extinguishes a blazing fire,
   so almsgiving atones for sin.
³¹ Those who repay favors give thought
   to the future;
   when they fall they will find
   support.

Duties toward the Poor and the Oppressed
4 My child, do not cheat the poor of
   their living,
   and do not keep needy eyes waiting.
² Do not grieve the hungry,
   or anger one in need.
³ Do not add to the troubles of the
   desperate,
   or delay giving to the needy.
⁴ Do not reject a suppliant in distress,
   or turn your face away from the
   poor.
⁵ Do not avert your eye from the needy,
   and give no one reason to curse you;
⁶ for if in bitterness of soul some should
   curse you,
   their Creator will hear their prayer.
⁷ Endear yourself to the congregation;
   bow your head low to the great.
⁸ Give a hearing to the poor,
   and return their greeting politely.

ᵗ Heb: Gk *meekness*   ᵘ Other ancient authorities add as verse 19, *Many are lofty and renowned, but to the humble he reveals his secrets.*   ᵛ Heb: Other ancient authorities lack verse 25

9 Rescue the oppressed from the
   oppressor;
   and do not be hesitant in giving a
   verdict.
10 Be a father to orphans,
   and be like a husband to their
   mother;
   you will then be like a son of the
   Most High,
   and he will love you more than
   does your mother.

The Rewards of Wisdom
11 Wisdom teaches[w] her children
   and gives help to those who seek
   her.
12 Whoever loves her loves life,
   and those who seek her from early
   morning are filled with joy.
13 Whoever holds her fast inherits glory,
   and the Lord blesses the place she[x]
   enters.
14 Those who serve her minister to the
   Holy One;
   the Lord loves those who love her.
15 Those who obey her will judge the
   nations,
   and all who listen to her will live
   secure.
16 If they remain faithful, they will
   inherit her;
   their descendants will also obtain
   her.
17 For at first she will walk with them
   on tortuous paths;
   she will bring fear and dread upon
   them,
   and will torment them by her
   discipline
   until she trusts them,[y]
   and she will test them with her
   ordinances.
18 Then she will come straight back to
   them again and gladden them,
   and will reveal her secrets to them.
19 If they go astray she will forsake
   them,
   and hand them over to their ruin.

20 Watch for the opportune time, and
   beware of evil,
   and do not be ashamed to be
   yourself.

21 For there is a shame that leads to sin,
   and there is a shame that is glory
   and favor.
22 Do not show partiality, to your own
   harm,
   or deference, to your downfall.
23 Do not refrain from speaking at the
   proper moment,[z]
   and do not hide your wisdom.[a]
24 For wisdom becomes known
   through speech,
   and education through the words of
   the tongue.
25 Never speak against the truth,
   but be ashamed of your ignorance.
26 Do not be ashamed to confess your
   sins,
   and do not try to stop the current
   of a river.
27 Do not subject yourself to a fool,
   or show partiality to a ruler.
28 Fight to the death for truth,
   and the Lord God will fight for you.

29 Do not be reckless in your speech,
   or sluggish and remiss in your
   deeds.
30 Do not be like a lion in your home,
   or suspicious of your servants.
31 Do not let your hand be stretched out
   to receive
   and closed when it is time to give.

Precepts for Everyday Living
5 Do not rely on your wealth,
   or say, "I have enough."
2 Do not follow your inclination and
   strength
   in pursuing the desires of your
   heart.
3 Do not say, "Who can have power over
   me?"
   for the Lord will surely punish you.
4 Do not say, "I sinned, yet what has
   happened to me?"
   for the Lord is slow to anger.
5 Do not be so confident of forgiveness[b]
   that you add sin to sin.
6 Do not say, "His mercy is great,
   he will forgive[c] the multitude of my
   sins,"
   for both mercy and wrath are with him,

---

[w] Heb Syr: Gk *exalts*   [x] Or *he*   [y] Or *until they remain faithful in their heart*   [z] Heb: Gk *at a time of salvation*
[a] So some Gk Mss and Heb Syr Lat: Other Gk Mss lack *and do not hide your wisdom*   [b] Heb: Gk *atonement*
[c] Heb: Gk *he* (or *it*) *will atone for*

and his anger will rest on sinners.
7 Do not delay to turn back to the Lord,
and do not postpone it from day to
day;
for suddenly the wrath of the Lord
will come upon you,
and at the time of punishment you
will perish.
8 Do not depend on dishonest wealth,
for it will not benefit you on the
day of calamity.

9 Do not winnow in every wind,
or follow every path.*d*
10 Stand firm for what you know,
and let your speech be consistent.
11 Be quick to hear,
but deliberate in answering.
12 If you know what to say, answer your
neighbor;
but if not, put your hand over your
mouth.

13 Honor and dishonor come from
speaking,
and the tongue of mortals may be
their downfall.
14 Do not be called double-tongued*e*
and do not lay traps with your
tongue;
for shame comes to the thief,
and severe condemnation to the
double-tongued.
15 In great and small matters cause no
harm,*f*

6 1 and do not become an enemy
instead of a friend;
for a bad name incurs shame and
reproach;
so it is with the double-tongued
sinner.

2 Do not fall into the grip of passion,*g*
or you may be torn apart as by a
bull.*h*
3 Your leaves will be devoured and your
fruit destroyed,
and you will be left like a withered
tree.
4 Evil passion destroys those who have
it,
and makes them the laughingstock
of their enemies.

Friendship, False and True
5 Pleasant speech multiplies friends,
and a gracious tongue multiplies
courtesies.
6 Let those who are friendly with you
be many,
but let your advisers be one in a
thousand.
7 When you gain friends, gain them
through testing,
and do not trust them hastily.
8 For there are friends who are such
when it suits them,
but they will not stand by you in
time of trouble.
9 And there are friends who change into
enemies,
and tell of the quarrel to your
disgrace.
10 And there are friends who sit at your
table,
but they will not stand by you in
time of trouble.
11 When you are prosperous, they
become your second self,
and lord it over your servants;
12 but if you are brought low, they turn
against you,
and hide themselves from you.
13 Keep away from your enemies,
and be on guard with your friends.

14 Faithful friends are a sturdy shelter:
whoever finds one has found a
treasure.
15 Faithful friends are beyond price;
no amount can balance their worth.
16 Faithful friends are life-saving medicine;
and those who fear the Lord will
find them.
17 Those who fear the Lord direct their
friendship aright,
for as they are, so are their
neighbors also.

Blessings of Wisdom
18 My child, from your youth choose
discipline,
and when you have gray hair you
will still find wisdom.
19 Come to her like one who plows and
sows,

---

d Gk adds *so it is with the double-tongued sinner* (see 6.1)   *e* Heb: Gk *a slanderer*   *f* Heb Syr: Gk *be ignorant*
g Heb: Meaning of Gk uncertain   *h* Meaning of Gk uncertain

and wait for her good harvest.
For when you cultivate her you will
toil but little,
and soon you will eat of her
produce.
20 She seems very harsh to the
undisciplined;
fools cannot remain with her.
21 She will be like a heavy stone to test
them,
and they will not delay in casting
her aside.
22 For wisdom is like her name;
she is not readily perceived by
many.

23 Listen, my child, and accept my
judgment;
do not reject my counsel.
24 Put your feet into her fetters,
and your neck into her collar.
25 Bend your shoulders and carry her,
and do not fret under her bonds.
26 Come to her with all your soul,
and keep her ways with all your
might.
27 Search out and seek, and she will
become known to you;
and when you get hold of her, do
not let her go.
28 For at last you will find the rest she
gives,
and she will be changed into joy for
you.
29 Then her fetters will become for you a
strong defense,
and her collar a glorious robe.
30 Her yoke*i* is a golden ornament,
and her bonds a purple cord.
31 You will wear her like a glorious robe,
and put her on like a splendid
crown.*j*

32 If you are willing, my child, you can
be disciplined,
and if you apply yourself you will
become clever.
33 If you love to listen you will gain
knowledge,
and if you pay attention you will
become wise.
34 Stand in the company of the elders.
Who is wise? Attach yourself to
such a one.
35 Be ready to listen to every godly
discourse,

and let no wise proverbs escape
you.
36 If you see an intelligent person, rise
early to visit him;
let your foot wear out his doorstep.
37 Reflect on the statutes of the Lord,
and meditate at all times on his
commandments.
It is he who will give insight to*k* your
mind,
and your desire for wisdom will be
granted.

Miscellaneous Advice

7 Do no evil, and evil will never
overtake you.
2 Stay away from wrong, and it will
turn away from you.
3 Do*l* not sow in the furrows of
injustice,
and you will not reap a sevenfold
crop.

4 Do not seek from the Lord high office,
or the seat of honor from the king.
5 Do not assert your righteousness
before the Lord,
or display your wisdom before the
king.
6 Do not seek to become a judge,
or you may be unable to root out
injustice;
you may be partial to the powerful,
and so mar your integrity.
7 Commit no offense against the public,
and do not disgrace yourself among
the people.

8 Do not commit a sin twice;
not even for one will you go
unpunished.
9 Do not say, "He will consider the
great number of my gifts,
and when I make an offering to the
Most High God, he will accept
it."
10 Do not grow weary when you pray;
do not neglect to give alms.
11 Do not ridicule a person who is
embittered in spirit,
for there is One who humbles and
exalts.
12 Do not devise*m* a lie against your
brother,
or do the same to a friend.

---

i Heb: Gk *Upon her*   *j* Heb: Gk *crown of gladness*   *k* Heb: Gk *will confirm*   *l* Gk *My child, do*   *m* Heb: Gk *plow*

13 Refuse to utter any lie,
for it is a habit that results in no good.
14 Do not babble in the assembly of the elders,
and do not repeat yourself when you pray.

15 Do not hate hard labor
or farm work, which was created by the Most High.
16 Do not enroll in the ranks of sinners;
remember that retribution does not delay.
17 Humble yourself to the utmost,
for the punishment of the ungodly is fire and worms.[n]

Relations with Others

18 Do not exchange a friend for money,
or a real brother for the gold of Ophir.
19 Do not dismiss[o] a wise and good wife,
for her charm is worth more than gold.
20 Do not abuse slaves who work faithfully,
or hired laborers who devote themselves to their task.
21 Let your soul love intelligent slaves;[p]
do not withhold from them their freedom.

22 Do you have cattle? Look after them;
if they are profitable to you, keep them.
23 Do you have children? Discipline them,
and make them obedient[q] from their youth.
24 Do you have daughters? Be concerned for their chastity,[r]
and do not show yourself too indulgent with them.
25 Give a daughter in marriage, and you complete a great task;
but give her to a sensible man.
26 Do you have a wife who pleases you?[s] Do not divorce her;
but do not trust yourself to one whom you detest.

27 With all your heart honor your father,
and do not forget the birth pangs of your mother.
28 Remember that it was of your parents[t] you were born;
how can you repay what they have given to you?

29 With all your soul fear the Lord,
and revere his priests.
30 With all your might love your Maker,
and do not neglect his ministers.
31 Fear the Lord and honor the priest,
and give him his portion, as you have been commanded:
the first fruits, the guilt offering, the gift of the shoulders,
the sacrifice of sanctification, and the first fruits of the holy things.

32 Stretch out your hand to the poor,
so that your blessing may be complete.
33 Give graciously to all the living;
do not withhold kindness even from the dead.
34 Do not avoid those who weep,
but mourn with those who mourn.
35 Do not hesitate to visit the sick,
because for such deeds you will be loved.
36 In all you do, remember the end of your life,
and then you will never sin.

Prudence and Common Sense

8 Do not contend with the powerful,
or you may fall into their hands.
2 Do not quarrel with the rich,
in case their resources outweigh yours;
for gold has ruined many,
and has perverted the minds of kings.
3 Do not argue with the loud of mouth,
and do not heap wood on their fire.

4 Do not make fun of one who is ill-bred,
or your ancestors may be insulted.
5 Do not reproach one who is turning away from sin;
remember that we all deserve punishment.
6 Do not disdain one who is old,
for some of us are also growing old.
7 Do not rejoice over anyone's death;
remember that we must all die.

[n] Heb *for the expectation of mortals is worms* [o] Heb: Gk *deprive yourself of* [p] Heb *Love a wise slave as yourself* [q] Gk *bend their necks* [r] Gk *body* [s] Heb Syr lack *who pleases you* [t] Gk *them*

8 Do not slight the discourse of the sages,
     but busy yourself with their maxims;
   because from them you will learn
     discipline
   and how to serve princes.
9 Do not ignore the discourse of the
     aged,
     for they themselves learned from
       their parents;*u*
   from them you learn how to understand
     and to give an answer when the
       need arises.

10 Do not kindle the coals of sinners,
     or you may be burned in their
       flaming fire.
11 Do not let the insolent bring you to
     your feet,
     or they may lie in ambush against
       your words.
12 Do not lend to one who is stronger
     than you;
     but if you do lend anything, count
       it as a loss.
13 Do not give surety beyond your means;
     but if you give surety, be prepared
       to pay.

14 Do not go to law against a judge,
     for the decision will favor him
       because of his standing.
15 Do not go traveling with the reckless,
     or they will be burdensome to you;
   for they will act as they please,
     and through their folly you will
       perish with them.
16 Do not pick a fight with the quick-
       tempered,
     and do not journey with them
       through lonely country,
   because bloodshed means nothing to
     them,
     and where no help is at hand, they
       will strike you down.
17 Do not consult with fools,
     for they cannot keep a secret.
18 In the presence of strangers do
       nothing that is to be kept
       secret,
     for you do not know what they will
       divulge.*v*
19 Do not reveal your thoughts to anyone,
     or you may drive away your
       happiness.*w*

Advice Concerning Women

9 Do not be jealous of the wife of your
     bosom,
     or you will teach her an evil lesson
       to your own hurt.
2 Do not give yourself to a woman
     and let her trample down your
       strength.
3 Do not go near a loose woman,
     or you will fall into her snares.
4 Do not dally with a singing girl,
     or you will be caught by her tricks.
5 Do not look intently at a virgin,
     or you may stumble and incur
       penalties for her.
6 Do not give yourself to prostitutes,
     or you may lose your inheritance.
7 Do not look around in the streets of a
       city,
     or wander about in its deserted
       sections.
8 Turn away your eyes from a shapely
       woman,
     and do not gaze at beauty
       belonging to another;
   many have been seduced by a
     woman's beauty,
     and by it passion is kindled like a fire.
9 Never dine with another man's wife,
     or revel with her at wine;
   or your heart may turn aside to her,
     and in blood*x* you may be plunged
       into destruction.

Choice of Friends
10 Do not abandon old friends,
     for new ones cannot equal them.
   A new friend is like new wine;
     when it has aged, you can drink it
       with pleasure.

11 Do not envy the success of sinners,
     for you do not know what their end
       will be like.
12 Do not delight in what pleases the
       ungodly;
     remember that they will not be held
       guiltless all their lives.

13 Keep far from those who have power
       to kill,
     and you will not be haunted by the
       fear of death.

---

u Or *ancestors*   *v* Or *it will bring forth*   *w* Heb: Gk *and let him not return a favor to you*   *x* Heb: Gk *by your spirit*

But if you approach them, make no
   misstep,
   or they may rob you of your life.
Know that you are stepping among
   snares,
   and that you are walking on the
   city battlements.

¹⁴ As much as you can, aim to know
   your neighbors,
   and consult with the wise.
¹⁵ Let your conversation be with
   intelligent people,
   and let all your discussion be about
   the law of the Most High.
¹⁶ Let the righteous be your dinner
   companions,
   and let your glory be in the fear of
   the Lord.

Concerning Rulers

¹⁷ A work is praised for the skill of the
   artisan;
   so a people's leader is proved wise
   by his words.
¹⁸ The loud of mouth are feared in their
   city,
   and the one who is reckless in
   speech is hated.

10 A wise magistrate educates his
   people,
   and the rule of an intelligent person
   is well ordered.
² As the people's judge is, so are his
   officials;
   as the ruler of the city is, so are all
   its inhabitants.
³ An undisciplined king ruins his people,
   but a city becomes fit to live in
   through the understanding of
   its rulers.
⁴ The government of the earth is in the
   hand of the Lord,
   and over it he will raise up the
   right leader for the time.
⁵ Human success is in the hand of the
   Lord,
   and it is he who confers honor
   upon the lawgiver.*ᵍ*

The Sin of Pride

⁶ Do not get angry with your neighbor
   for every injury,
   and do not resort to acts of
   insolence.
⁷ Arrogance is hateful to the Lord and
   to mortals,
   and injustice is outrageous to both.
⁸ Sovereignty passes from nation to
   nation
   on account of injustice and
   insolence and wealth.*ᶻ*
⁹ How can dust and ashes be proud?
   Even in life the human body
   decays.*ᵃ*
¹⁰ A long illness baffles the physician;*ᵇ*
   the king of today will die tomorrow.
¹¹ For when one is dead
   he inherits maggots and vermin*ᶜ*
   and worms.
¹² The beginning of human pride is to
   forsake the Lord;
   the heart has withdrawn from its
   Maker.
¹³ For the beginning of pride is sin,
   and the one who clings to it pours
   out abominations.
   Therefore the Lord brings upon them
   unheard-of calamities,
   and destroys them completely.
¹⁴ The Lord overthrows the thrones of
   rulers,
   and enthrones the lowly in their
   place.
¹⁵ The Lord plucks up the roots of the
   nations,*ᵈ*
   and plants the humble in their
   place.
¹⁶ The Lord lays waste the lands of the
   nations,
   and destroys them to the
   foundations of the earth.
¹⁷ He removes some of them and
   destroys them,
   and erases the memory of them
   from the earth.
¹⁸ Pride was not created for human
   beings,
   or violent anger for those born of
   women.

ᵍ Heb: Gk *scribe*   *ᶻ* Other ancient authorities add here or after verse 9a, *Nothing is more wicked than one who loves money, for such a person puts his own soul up for sale.*   *ᵃ* Heb: Meaning of Gk uncertain   *ᵇ* Heb Lat: Meaning of Gk uncertain   *ᶜ* Heb: Gk *wild animals*   *ᵈ* Other ancient authorities read *proud nations*

Persons Deserving Honor

19 Whose offspring are worthy of honor?
   Human offspring.
   Whose offspring are worthy of honor?
   Those who fear the Lord.
   Whose offspring are unworthy of
   honor?
   Human offspring.
   Whose offspring are unworthy of honor?
   Those who break the
   commandments.
20 Among family members their leader is
   worthy of honor,
   but those who fear the Lord are
   worthy of honor in his eyes.*

22 The rich, and the eminent, and the poor—
   their glory is the fear of the Lord.
23 It is not right to despise one who is
   intelligent but poor,
   and it is not proper to honor one
   who is sinful.
24 The prince and the judge and the
   ruler are honored,
   but none of them is greater than
   the one who fears the Lord.
25 Free citizens will serve a wise servant,
   and an intelligent person will not
   complain.

Concerning Humility

26 Do not make a display of your wisdom
   when you do your work,
   and do not boast when you are in
   need.
27 Better is the worker who has goods in
   plenty
   than the boaster who lacks bread.

28 My child, honor yourself with
   humility,
   and give yourself the esteem you
   deserve.
29 Who will acquit those who condemn*f*
   themselves?
   And who will honor those who
   dishonor themselves?*g*
30 The poor are honored for their
   knowledge,
   while the rich are honored for their
   wealth.
31 One who is honored in poverty, how
   much more in wealth!
   And one dishonored in wealth, how
   much more in poverty!

The Deceptiveness of Appearances

11 The wisdom of the humble lifts
   their heads high,
   and seats them among the great.
2 Do not praise individuals for their
   good looks,
   or loathe anyone because of
   appearance alone.
3 The bee is small among flying
   creatures,
   but what it produces is the best of
   sweet things.
4 Do not boast about wearing fine
   clothes,
   and do not exalt yourself when you
   are honored;
   for the works of the Lord are
   wonderful,
   and his works are concealed from
   humankind.
5 Many kings have had to sit on the
   ground,
   but one who was never thought of
   has worn a crown.
6 Many rulers have been utterly
   disgraced,
   and the honored have been handed
   over to others.

Deliberation and Caution

7 Do not find fault before you
   investigate;
   examine first, and then criticize.
8 Do not answer before you listen,
   and do not interrupt when another
   is speaking.
9 Do not argue about a matter that
   does not concern you,
   and do not sit with sinners when
   they judge a case.

10 My child, do not busy yourself with
   many matters;
   if you multiply activities, you will
   not be held blameless.
   If you pursue, you will not overtake,
   and by fleeing you will not escape.
11 There are those who work and
   struggle and hurry,
   but are so much the more in want.
12 There are others who are slow and
   need help,
   who lack strength and abound in
   poverty;

---

e Other ancient authorities add as verse 21, *The fear of the Lord is the beginning of acceptance; obduracy and pride are the beginning of rejection.*   *f* Heb: Gk *sin against*   *g* Heb Lat: Gk *their own life*

but the eyes of the Lord look kindly
   upon them;
he lifts them out of their lowly
   condition
¹³ and raises up their heads
   to the amazement of the many.

¹⁴ Good things and bad, life and death,
   poverty and wealth, come from the
   Lord.*ʰ*
¹⁷ The Lord's gift remains with the
   devout,
   and his favor brings lasting success.
¹⁸ One becomes rich through diligence
   and self-denial,
   and the reward allotted to him is
   this:
¹⁹ when he says, "I have found rest,
   and now I shall feast on my goods!"
he does not know how long it will be
   until he leaves them to others and
   dies.

²⁰ Stand by your agreement and attend
   to it,
   and grow old in your work.
²¹ Do not wonder at the works of a
   sinner,
   but trust in the Lord and keep at
   your job;
for it is easy in the sight of the Lord
   to make the poor rich suddenly, in
   an instant.
²² The blessing of the Lord is*ⁱ* the reward
   of the pious,
   and quickly God causes his blessing
   to flourish.
²³ Do not say, "What do I need,
   and what further benefit can be
   mine?"
²⁴ Do not say, "I have enough,
   and what harm can come to me
   now?"
²⁵ In the day of prosperity, adversity is
   forgotten,
   and in the day of adversity,
   prosperity is not remembered.
²⁶ For it is easy for the Lord on the day
   of death
   to reward individuals according to
   their conduct.
²⁷ An hour's misery makes one forget
   past delights,

and at the close of one's life one's
   deeds are revealed.
²⁸ Call no one happy before his death;
   by how he ends, a person becomes
   known.*ʲ*

Care in Choosing Friends
²⁹ Do not invite everyone into your
   home,
   for many are the tricks of the
   crafty.
³⁰ Like a decoy partridge in a cage, so is
   the mind of the proud,
   and like spies they observe your
   weakness;*ᵏ*
³¹ for they lie in wait, turning good into
   evil,
   and to worthy actions they attach
   blame.
³² From a spark many coals are kindled,
   and a sinner lies in wait to shed
   blood.
³³ Beware of scoundrels, for they devise
   evil,
   and they may ruin your reputation
   forever.
³⁴ Receive strangers into your home and
   they will stir up trouble for
   you,
   and will make you a stranger to
   your own family.

12

If you do good, know to whom
   you do it,
   and you will be thanked for your
   good deeds.
² Do good to the devout, and you will
   be repaid—
   if not by them, certainly by the
   Most High.
³ No good comes to one who persists in
   evil
   or to one who does not give alms.
⁴ Give to the devout, but do not help
   the sinner.
⁵ Do good to the humble, but do not
   give to the ungodly;
hold back their bread, and do not give
   it to them,
   for by means of it they might
   subdue you;

ʰ Other ancient authorities add as verses 15 and 16, *¹⁵Wisdom, understanding, and knowledge of the law come from the Lord; affection and the ways of good works come from him. ¹⁶Error and darkness were created with sinners; evil grows old with those who take pride in malice.* *ⁱ* Heb: Gk *is in* *ʲ* Heb: Gk *and through his children a person becomes known* *ᵏ* Heb: Gk *downfall*

then you will receive twice as much
  evil
for all the good you have done to
  them.
6 For the Most High also hates sinners
  and will inflict punishment on the
  ungodly.[*l*]
7 Give to the one who is good, but do
  not help the sinner.
8 A friend is not known[*m*] in prosperity,
  nor is an enemy hidden in
  adversity.
9 One's enemies are friendly[*n*] when one
  prospers,
  but in adversity even one's friend
  disappears.
10 Never trust your enemy,
  for like corrosion in copper, so is his
  wickedness.
11 Even if he humbles himself and walks
  bowed down,
  take care to be on your guard
  against him.
Be to him like one who polishes a
  mirror,
  to be sure it does not become
  completely tarnished.
12 Do not put him next to you,
  or he may overthrow you and take
  your place.
Do not let him sit at your right hand,
  or else he may try to take your
  own seat,
and at last you will realize the truth
  of my words,
  and be stung by what I have said.

13 Who pities a snake charmer when he
  is bitten,
  or all those who go near wild
  animals?
14 So no one pities a person who
  associates with a sinner
  and becomes involved in the other's
  sins.
15 He stands by you for a while,
  but if you falter, he will not be
  there.
16 An enemy speaks sweetly with his lips,
  but in his heart he plans to throw
  you into a pit;
an enemy may have tears in his eyes,
  but if he finds an opportunity he
  will never have enough of your
  blood.

17 If evil comes upon you, you will find
  him there ahead of you;
  pretending to help, he will trip you
  up.
18 Then he will shake his head, and clap
  his hands,
  and whisper much, and show his
  true face.

Caution Regarding Associates

13 Whoever touches pitch gets dirty,
  and whoever associates with
  a proud person becomes like
  him.
2 Do not lift a weight too heavy for
  you,
  or associate with one mightier and
  richer than you.
How can the clay pot associate with
  the iron kettle?
The pot will strike against it and be
  smashed.
3 A rich person does wrong, and even
  adds insults;
  a poor person suffers wrong, and
  must add apologies.
4 A rich person[*o*] will exploit you if you
  can be of use to him,
  but if you are in need he will
  abandon you.
5 If you own something, he will live
  with you;
  he will drain your resources without
  a qualm.
6 When he needs you he will deceive
  you,
  and will smile at you and
  encourage you;
  he will speak to you kindly and say,
  "What do you need?"
7 He will embarrass you with his
  delicacies,
  until he has drained you two or
  three times,
  and finally he will laugh at you.
Should he see you afterwards, he will
  pass you by
  and shake his head at you.

8 Take care not to be led astray
  and humiliated when you are
  enjoying yourself.[*p*]
9 When an influential person invites
  you, be reserved,

[*l*] Other ancient authorities add *and he is keeping them for the day of their punishment*   [*m*] Other ancient authorities read *punished*   [*n*] Heb: Gk *grieved*   [*o*] Gk *He*   [*p*] Other ancient authorities read *in your folly*

and he will invite you more
insistently.

¹⁰ Do not be forward, or you may be
rebuffed;
do not stand aloof, or you will be
forgotten.

¹¹ Do not try to treat him as an equal,
or trust his lengthy conversations;
for he will test you by prolonged talk,
and while he smiles he will be
examining you.

¹² Cruel are those who do not keep your
secrets;
they will not spare you harm or
imprisonment.

¹³ Be on your guard and very careful,
for you are walking about with
your own downfall.*q*

¹⁵ Every creature loves its like,
and every person the neighbor.

¹⁶ All living beings associate with their
own kind,
and people stick close to those like
themselves.

¹⁷ What does a wolf have in common
with a lamb?
No more has a sinner with the
devout.

¹⁸ What peace is there between a hyena
and a dog?
And what peace between the rich
and the poor?

¹⁹ Wild asses in the wilderness are the
prey of lions;
likewise the poor are feeding
grounds for the rich.

²⁰ Humility is an abomination to the
proud;
likewise the poor are an
abomination to the rich.

²¹ When the rich person totters, he is
supported by friends,
but when the humble*r* falls, he is
pushed away even by friends.

²² If the rich person slips, many come to
the rescue;
he speaks unseemly words, but they
justify him.
If the humble person slips, they even
criticize him;
he talks sense, but is not given a
hearing.

²³ The rich person speaks and all are
silent;
they extol to the clouds what he
says.
The poor person speaks and they say,
"Who is this fellow?"
And should he stumble, they even
push him down.

²⁴ Riches are good if they are free from
sin;
poverty is evil only in the opinion
of the ungodly.

²⁵ The heart changes the countenance,
either for good or for evil.*s*

²⁶ The sign of a happy heart is a
cheerful face,
but to devise proverbs requires
painful thinking.

14 Happy are those who do not
blunder with their lips,
and need not suffer remorse for sin.

² Happy are those whose hearts do not
condemn them,
and who have not given up their hope.

Responsible Use of Wealth

³ Riches are inappropriate for a small-
minded person;
and of what use is wealth to a
miser?

⁴ What he denies himself he collects for
others;
and others will live in luxury on his
goods.

⁵ If one is mean to himself, to whom
will he be generous?
He will not enjoy his own riches.

⁶ No one is worse than one who is
grudging to himself;
this is the punishment for his
meanness.

⁷ If ever he does good, it is by mistake;
and in the end he reveals his
meanness.

⁸ The miser is an evil person;
he turns away and disregards
people.

⁹ The eye of the greedy person is not
satisfied with his share;
greedy injustice withers the soul.

¹⁰ A miser begrudges bread,
and it is lacking at his table.

q Other ancient authorities add as verse 14, *When you hear these things in your sleep, wake up! During all your life love the Lord, and call on him for your salvation.* *r* Other ancient authorities read *poor* *s* Other ancient authorities add *and a glad heart makes a cheerful countenance*

¹¹ My child, treat yourself well, according
　　to your means,
　　and present worthy offerings to the
　　　Lord.
¹² Remember that death does not tarry,
　　and the decree^t of Hades has not
　　　been shown to you.
¹³ Do good to friends before you die,
　　and reach out and give to them as
　　　much as you can.
¹⁴ Do not deprive yourself of a day's
　　enjoyment;
　　do not let your share of desired
　　　good pass by you.
¹⁵ Will you not leave the fruit of your
　　labors to another,
　　and what you acquired by toil to be
　　　divided by lot?
¹⁶ Give, and take, and indulge yourself,
　　because in Hades one cannot look
　　　for luxury.
¹⁷ All living beings become old like a
　　garment,
　　for the decree^u from of old is, "You
　　　must die!"
¹⁸ Like abundant leaves on a spreading
　　tree
　　that sheds some and puts forth
　　　others,
　　so are the generations of flesh and
　　　blood:
　　one dies and another is born.
¹⁹ Every work decays and ceases to exist,
　　and the one who made it will pass
　　　away with it.

The Happiness of Seeking Wisdom
²⁰ Happy is the person who meditates
　　on^v wisdom
　　and reasons intelligently,
²¹ who^w reflects in his heart on her ways
　　and ponders her secrets,
²² pursuing her like a hunter,
　　and lying in wait on her paths;
²³ who peers through her windows
　　and listens at her doors;
²⁴ who camps near her house
　　and fastens his tent peg to her
　　　walls;
²⁵ who pitches his tent near her,
　　and so occupies an excellent lodging
　　　place;
²⁶ who places his children under her
　　shelter,

and lodges under her boughs;
²⁷ who is sheltered by her from the heat,
　　and dwells in the midst of her
　　　glory.

15 Whoever fears the Lord will do
　　this,
　　and whoever holds to the law will
　　　obtain wisdom.^x
² She will come to meet him like a
　　mother,
　　and like a young bride she will
　　　welcome him.
³ She will feed him with the bread of
　　learning,
　　and give him the water of wisdom
　　　to drink.
⁴ He will lean on her and not fall,
　　and he will rely on her and not be
　　　put to shame.
⁵ She will exalt him above his
　　neighbors,
　　and will open his mouth in the
　　　midst of the assembly.
⁶ He will find gladness and a crown of
　　rejoicing,
　　and will inherit an everlasting
　　　name.
⁷ The foolish will not obtain her,
　　and sinners will not see her.
⁸ She is far from arrogance,
　　and liars will never think of her.
⁹ Praise is unseemly on the lips of a
　　sinner,
　　for it has not been sent from the Lord.
¹⁰ For in wisdom must praise be uttered,
　　and the Lord will make it prosper.

Freedom of Choice
¹¹ Do not say, "It was the Lord's doing
　　that I fell away";
　　for he does not do^y what he hates.
¹² Do not say, "It was he who led me
　　astray";
　　for he has no need of the sinful.
¹³ The Lord hates all abominations;
　　such things are not loved by those
　　　who fear him.
¹⁴ It was he who created humankind in
　　the beginning,
　　and he left them in the power of
　　　their own free choice.
¹⁵ If you choose, you can keep the
　　commandments,

---

^t Heb Syr: Gk *covenant*　　^u Heb: Gk *covenant*　　^v Other ancient authorities read *dies in*　　^w The structure
adopted in verses 21–27 follows the Heb　　^x Gk *her*　　^y Heb: Gk *you ought not to do*

and to act faithfully is a matter of
  your own choice.
16 He has placed before you fire and
  water;
  stretch out your hand for whichever
  you choose.
17 Before each person are life and death,
  and whichever one chooses will be
  given.
18 For great is the wisdom of the Lord;
  he is mighty in power and sees
  everything;
19 his eyes are on those who fear him,
  and he knows every human action.
20 He has not commanded anyone to be
  wicked,
  and he has not given anyone
  permission to sin.

God's Punishment of Sinners

16 Do not desire a multitude of
  worthless² children,
  and do not rejoice in ungodly
  offspring.
2 If they multiply, do not rejoice in
  them,
  unless the fear of the Lord is in
  them.
3 Do not trust in their survival,
  or rely on their numbers;ᵃ
  for one can be better than a
  thousand,
  and to die childless is better than to
  have ungodly children.
4 For through one intelligent person a
  city can be filled with people,
  but through a clan of outlaws it
  becomes desolate.

5 Many such things my eye has seen,
  and my ear has heard things more
  striking than these.
6 In an assembly of sinners a fire is
  kindled,
  and in a disobedient nation wrath
  blazes up.
7 He did not forgive the ancient giants
  who revolted in their might.

8 He did not spare the neighbors of Lot,
  whom he loathed on account of
  their arrogance.
9 He showed no pity on the doomed
  nation,
  on those dispossessed because of
  their sins;ᵇ
10 or on the six hundred thousand foot
  soldiers
  who assembled in their
  stubbornness.ᶜ
11 Even if there were only one stiff-necked
  person,
  it would be a wonder if he remained
  unpunished.
  For mercy and wrath are with the
  Lord;ᵈ
  he is mighty to forgive—but he also
  pours out wrath.
12 Great as is his mercy, so also is his
  chastisement;
  he judges a person according to
  his or her deeds.
13 The sinner will not escape with
  plunder,
  and the patience of the godly will
  not be frustrated.
14 He makes room for every act of
  mercy;
  everyone receives in accordance
  with his or her deeds.ᵉ

17 Do not say, "I am hidden from the
  Lord,
  and who from on high has me in
  mind?
  Among so many people I am
  unknown,
  for what am I in a boundless
  creation?
18 Lo, heaven and the highest heaven,
  the abyss and the earth, tremble at
  his visitation!ᶠ
19 The very mountains and the foundations
  of the earth
  quiver and quake when he looks
  upon them.
20 But no human mind can grasp this,
  and who can comprehend his ways?

ᶻHeb: Gk *unprofitable*   ᵃOther ancient authorities add *For you will groan in untimely mourning, and will know
of their sudden end.*   ᵇOther ancient authorities add *All these things he did to the hard-hearted nations, and by
the multitude of his holy ones he was not appeased.*   ᶜOther ancient authorities add *Chastising, showing mercy,
striking, healing, the Lord persisted in mercy and discipline.*   ᵈGk *him*   ᵉOther ancient authorities add* ¹⁵The
Lord hardened Pharaoh so that he did not recognize him, in order that his works might be known under heaven.* ¹⁶*His
mercy is manifest to the whole of creation, and he divided his light and darkness with a plumb line.*   ᶠOther ancient
authorities add *The whole world past and present is in his will.*

21 Like a tempest that no one can see,
so most of his works are concealed.[g]
22 Who is to announce his acts of justice?
Or who can await them? For his decree[h] is far off."[i]
23 Such are the thoughts of one devoid of understanding;
a senseless and misguided person thinks foolishly.

God's Wisdom Seen in Creation

24 Listen to me, my child, and acquire knowledge,
and pay close attention to my words.
25 I will impart discipline precisely[j]
and declare knowledge accurately.

26 When the Lord created[k] his works from the beginning,
and, in making them, determined their boundaries,
27 he arranged his works in an eternal order,
and their dominion[l] for all generations.
They neither hunger nor grow weary,
and they do not abandon their tasks.
28 They do not crowd one another,
and they never disobey his word.
29 Then the Lord looked upon the earth,
and filled it with his good things.
30 With all kinds of living beings he covered its surface,
and into it they must return.

17 The Lord created human beings out of earth,
and makes them return to it again.
2 He gave them a fixed number of days,
but granted them authority over everything on the earth.[m]
3 He endowed them with strength like his own,[n]
and made them in his own image.
4 He put the fear of them[o] in all living beings,
and gave them dominion over beasts and birds.[p]
6 Discretion and tongue and eyes,
ears and a mind for thinking he gave them.
7 He filled them with knowledge and understanding,
and showed them good and evil.
8 He put the fear of him into[q] their hearts
to show them the majesty of his works.[r]
10 And they will praise his holy name,
9 to proclaim the grandeur of his works.
11 He bestowed knowledge upon them,
and allotted to them the law of life.[s]
12 He established with them an eternal covenant,
and revealed to them his decrees.
13 Their eyes saw his glorious majesty,
and their ears heard the glory of his voice.
14 He said to them, "Beware of all evil."
And he gave commandment to each of them concerning the neighbor.
15 Their ways are always known to him;
they will not be hid from his eyes.[t]
17 He appointed a ruler for every nation,
but Israel is the Lord's own portion.[u]
19 All their works are as clear as the sun before him,
and his eyes are ever upon their ways.
20 Their iniquities are not hidden from him,
and all their sins are before the Lord.[v]

[g] Meaning of Gk uncertain: Heb Syr *If I sin, no eye can see me, and if I am disloyal all in secret, who is to know?* [h] Heb *the decree*: Gk *the covenant* [i] Other ancient authorities add *and a scrutiny for all comes at the end* [j] Gk *by weight* [k] Heb: Gk *judged* [l] Or *elements* [m] Lat: Gk *it* [n] Lat: Gk *proper to them* [o] Syr: Gk *him* [p] Other ancient authorities add as verse 5, *They obtained the use of the five faculties of the Lord; as sixth he distributed to them the gift of mind, and as seventh, reason, the interpreter of one's faculties.* [q] Other ancient authorities read *He set his eye upon* [r] Other ancient authorities add *and he gave them to boast of his marvels forever* [s] Other ancient authorities add *so that they may know that they who are alive now are mortal* [t] Other ancient authorities add [16]*Their ways from youth tend toward evil, and they are unable to make for themselves hearts of flesh in place of their stony hearts.* [17]*For in the division of the nations of the whole earth, he appointed* [u] Other ancient authorities add as verse 18, *whom, being his firstborn, he brings up with discipline, and allotting to him the light of his love, he does not neglect him.* [v] Other ancient authorities add as verse 21, *But the Lord, who is gracious and knows how they are formed, has neither left them nor abandoned them, but has spared them.*

22 One's almsgiving is like a signet ring
with the Lord,[w]
and he will keep a person's kindness
like the apple of his eye.[x]
23 Afterward he will rise up and repay them,
and he will bring their recompense
on their heads.
24 Yet to those who repent he grants a
return,
and he encourages those who are
losing hope.

A Call to Repentance
25 Turn back to the Lord and forsake
your sins;
pray in his presence and lessen your
offense.
26 Return to the Most High and turn
away from iniquity,[y]
and hate intensely what he abhors.
27 Who will sing praises to the Most
High in Hades
in place of the living who give thanks?
28 From the dead, as from one who does
not exist, thanksgiving has
ceased;
those who are alive and well sing
the Lord's praises.
29 How great is the mercy of the Lord,
and his forgiveness for those who
return to him!
30 For not everything is within human
capability,
since human beings are not immortal.
31 What is brighter than the sun? Yet it
can be eclipsed.
So flesh and blood devise evil.
32 He marshals the host of the height of
heaven;
but all human beings are dust and
ashes.

The Majesty of God
18 He who lives forever created the
whole universe;
2 the Lord alone is just.[z]
4 To none has he given power to
proclaim his works;
and who can search out his mighty
deeds?

5 Who can measure his majestic power?
And who can fully recount his
mercies?
6 It is not possible to diminish or
increase them,
nor is it possible to fathom the
wonders of the Lord.
7 When human beings have finished,
they are just beginning,
and when they stop, they are still
perplexed.
8 What are human beings, and of what
use are they?
What is good in them, and what is
evil?
9 The number of days in their life is
great if they reach one
hundred years.[a]
10 Like a drop of water from the sea and
a grain of sand,
so are a few years among the days
of eternity.
11 That is why the Lord is patient with
them
and pours out his mercy upon
them.
12 He sees and recognizes that their end
is miserable;
therefore he grants them forgiveness
all the more.
13 The compassion of human beings is
for their neighbors,
but the compassion of the Lord is
for every living thing.
He rebukes and trains and teaches
them,
and turns them back, as a shepherd
his flock.
14 He has compassion on those who
accept his discipline
and who are eager for his precepts.

The Right Spirit in Giving Alms
15 My child, do not mix reproach with
your good deeds,
or spoil your gift by harsh words.
16 Does not the dew give relief from the
scorching heat?
So a word is better than a gift.
17 Indeed, does not a word surpass a
good gift?

[w] Gk *him*   [x] Other ancient authorities add *apportioning repentance to his sons and daughters*   [y] Other ancient authorities add *for he will lead you out of darkness to the light of health.*   [z] Other ancient authorities add *and there is no other beside him;* [3] *he steers the world with the span of his hand, and all things obey his will; for he is king of all things by his power, separating among them the holy things from the profane.*   [a] Other ancient authorities add *but the death of each one is beyond the calculation of all*

Both are to be found in a gracious
person.
18 A fool is ungracious and abusive,
and the gift of a grudging giver
makes the eyes dim.

The Need of Reflection and Self-control
19 Before you speak, learn;
and before you fall ill, take care of
your health.
20 Before judgment comes, examine
yourself;
and at the time of scrutiny you will
find forgiveness.
21 Before falling ill, humble yourself;
and when you have sinned, repent.
22 Let nothing hinder you from paying a
vow promptly,
and do not wait until death to be
released from it.
23 Before making a vow, prepare yourself;
do not be like one who puts the
Lord to the test.
24 Think of his wrath on the day of death,
and of the moment of vengeance
when he turns away his face.
25 In the time of plenty think of the time
of hunger;
in days of wealth think of poverty
and need.
26 From morning to evening conditions
change;
all things move swiftly before the Lord.

27 One who is wise is cautious in
everything;
when sin is all around, one guards
against wrongdoing.
28 Every intelligent person knows wisdom,
and praises the one who finds her.
29 Those who are skilled in words
become wise themselves,
and pour forth apt proverbs.[b]

Self-Control[c]
30 Do not follow your base desires,
but restrain your appetites.
31 If you allow your soul to take pleasure
in base desire,
it will make you the laughingstock
of your enemies.

32 Do not revel in great luxury,
or you may become impoverished
by its expense.
33 Do not become a beggar by feasting
with borrowed money,
when you have nothing in your
purse.[d]

19 The one who does this[e] will not
become rich;
one who despises small things will
fail little by little.
2 Wine and women lead intelligent men
astray,
and the man who consorts with
prostitutes is reckless.
3 Decay and worms will take possession
of him,
and the reckless person will be
snatched away.

Against Loose Talk
4 One who trusts others too quickly has
a shallow mind,
and one who sins does wrong to
himself.
5 One who rejoices in wickedness[f] will
be condemned,[g]
6 but one who hates gossip has less
evil.
7 Never repeat a conversation,
and you will lose nothing at all.
8 With friend or foe do not report it,
and unless it would be a sin for
you, do not reveal it;
9 for someone may have heard you and
watched you,
and in time will hate you.
10 Have you heard something? Let it die
with you.
Be brave, it will not make you burst!
11 Having heard something, the fool
suffers birth pangs
like a woman in labor with a child.
12 Like an arrow stuck in a person's
thigh,
so is gossip inside a fool.

13 Question a friend; perhaps he did not
do it;
or if he did, so that he may not do
it again.

---

b Other ancient authorities add *Better is confidence in the one Lord than clinging with a dead heart to a dead one.*
c This heading is included in the Gk text. d Other ancient authorities add *for you will be plotting against your own life* e Heb: Gk *A worker who is a drunkard* f Other ancient authorities read *heart* g Other ancient authorities add *but one who withstands pleasures crowns his life.* h *One who controls the tongue will live without strife.*

¹⁴ Question a neighbor; perhaps he did
not say it;
or if he said it, so that he may not
repeat it.
¹⁵ Question a friend, for often it is
slander;
so do not believe everything you
hear.
¹⁶ A person may make a slip without
intending it.
Who has not sinned with his
tongue?
¹⁷ Question your neighbor before you
threaten him;
and let the law of the Most High
take its course.ʰ

True and False Wisdom

²⁰ The whole of wisdom is fear of the
Lord,
and in all wisdom there is the
fulfillment of the law.ⁱ
²² The knowledge of wickedness is not
wisdom,
nor is there prudence in the counsel
of sinners.
²³ There is a cleverness that is detestable,
and there is a fool who merely
lacks wisdom.
²⁴ Better are the God-fearing who lack
understanding
than the highly intelligent who
transgress the law.
²⁵ There is a cleverness that is exact but
unjust,
and there are people who abuse
favors to gain a verdict.
²⁶ There is the villain bowed down in
mourning,
but inwardly he is full of deceit.
²⁷ He hides his face and pretends not to
hear,
but when no one notices, he will
take advantage of you.
²⁸ Even if lack of strength keeps him
from sinning,
he will nevertheless do evil when he
finds the opportunity.
²⁹ A person is known by his appearance,

and a sensible person is known
when first met, face to face.
³⁰ A person's attire and hearty laughter,
and the way he walks, show what
he is.

Silence and Speech

20 There is a rebuke that is untimely,
and there is the person who is
wise enough to keep silent.
² How much better it is to rebuke than
to fume!
³ And the one who admits his fault will
be kept from failure.
⁴ Like a eunuch lusting to violate a girl
is the person who does right under
compulsion.
⁵ Some people keep silent and are
thought to be wise,
while others are detested for being
talkative.
⁶ Some people keep silent because they
have nothing to say,
while others keep silent because
they know when to speak.
⁷ The wise remain silent until the right
moment,
but a boasting fool misses the right
moment.
⁸ Whoever talks too much is detested,
and whoever pretends to authority
is hated.ʲ

Paradoxes

⁹ There may be good fortune for a
person in adversity,
and a windfall may result in a loss.
¹⁰ There is the gift that profits you
nothing,
and the gift to be paid back double.
¹¹ There are losses for the sake of glory,
and there are some who have raised
their heads from humble
circumstances.
¹² Some buy much for little,
but pay for it seven times over.

ʰ Other ancient authorities add *and do not be angry.* ¹⁸*The fear of the Lord is the beginning of acceptance, and wisdom obtains his love.* ¹⁹*The knowledge of the Lord's commandments is life-giving discipline; and those who do what is pleasing to him enjoy the fruit of the tree of immortality.* ⁱ Other ancient authorities add *and the knowledge of his omnipotence.* ²¹*When a slave says to his master, "I will not act as you wish," even if later he does it, he angers the one who supports him.* ʲ Other ancient authorities add *How good it is to show repentance when you are reproved, for so you will escape deliberate sin!*

13 The wise make themselves beloved by
only few words,[k]
but the courtesies of fools are wasted.
14 A fool's gift will profit you nothing,[l]
for he looks for recompense
sevenfold.[m]
15 He gives little and upbraids much;
he opens his mouth like a town crier.
Today he lends and tomorrow he asks
it back;
such a one is hateful to God and
humans.[n]
16 The fool says, "I have no friends,
and I get no thanks for my good deeds.
Those who eat my bread are evil-
tongued."
17 How many will ridicule him, and how
often![o]

Inappropriate Speech

18 A slip on the pavement is better than
a slip of the tongue;
the downfall of the wicked will
occur just as speedily.
19 A coarse person is like an
inappropriate story,
continually on the lips of the ignorant.
20 A proverb from a fool's lips will be
rejected,
for he does not tell it at the proper
time.

21 One may be prevented from sinning
by poverty;
so when he rests he feels no remorse.
22 One may lose his life through shame,
or lose it because of human respect.[p]
23 Another out of shame makes promises
to a friend,
and so makes an enemy for nothing.

Lying

24 A lie is an ugly blot on a person;
it is continually on the lips of the
ignorant.
25 A thief is preferable to a habitual liar,
but the lot of both is ruin.
26 A liar's way leads to disgrace,
and his shame is ever with him.

PROVERBIAL SAYINGS[q]

27 The wise person advances himself by
his words,
and one who is sensible pleases the
great.
28 Those who cultivate the soil heap up
their harvest,
and those who please the great
atone for injustice.
29 Favors and gifts blind the eyes of the
wise;
like a muzzle on the mouth they
stop reproofs.
30 Hidden wisdom and unseen treasure,
of what value is either?
31 Better are those who hide their folly
than those who hide their wisdom.[r]

Various Sins

21 Have you sinned, my child? Do so
no more,
but ask forgiveness for your past
sins.
2 Flee from sin as from a snake;
for if you approach sin, it will bite
you.
Its teeth are lion's teeth,
and can destroy human lives.
3 All lawlessness is like a two-edged
sword;
there is no healing for the wound it
inflicts.

4 Panic and insolence will waste away
riches;
thus the house of the proud will be
laid waste.[s]
5 The prayer of the poor goes from their
lips to the ears of God,[t]
and his judgment comes speedily.
6 Those who hate reproof walk in the
sinner's steps,
but those who fear the Lord repent
in their heart.
7 The mighty in speech are widely
known;
when they slip, the sensible person
knows it.

---

[k] Heb: Gk *by words*   [l] Other ancient authorities add *so it is with the envious who give under compulsion*   [m] Syr:
Gk *he has many eyes* instead of *one*   [n] Other ancient authorities lack *to God and humans*   [o] Other ancient
authorities add *for he has not honestly received what he has, and what he does not have is unimportant to him*
[p] Other ancient authorities read *his foolish look*   [q] This heading is included in the Gk text.   [r] Other ancient
authorities add *32 Unwearied endurance in seeking the Lord is better than a masterless charioteer of one's own life.*
[s] Other ancient authorities read *uprooted*   [t] Gk *his ears*

8 Whoever builds his house with other
people's money
is like one who gathers stones for
his burial mound.ᵘ
9 An assembly of the wicked is like a
bundle of tow,
and their end is a blazing fire.
10 The way of sinners is paved with
smooth stones,
but at its end is the pit of Hades.

Wisdom and Foolishness
11 Whoever keeps the law controls his
thoughts,
and the fulfillment of the fear of the
Lord is wisdom.
12 The one who is not clever cannot be
taught,
but there is a cleverness that
increases bitterness.
13 The knowledge of the wise will
increase like a flood,
and their counsel like a life-giving
spring.
14 The mindᵛ of a fool is like a broken
jar;
it can hold no knowledge.

15 When an intelligent person hears a
wise saying,
he praises it and adds to it;
when a foolʷ hears it, he laughs atˣ it
and throws it behind his back.
16 A fool's chatter is like a burden on a
journey,
but delight is found in the speech of
the intelligent.
17 The utterance of a sensible person is
sought in the assembly,
and they ponder his words in their
minds.

18 Like a house in ruins is wisdom to a
fool,
and to the ignorant, knowledge is
talk that has no meaning.
19 To a senseless person education is
fetters on his feet,
and like manacles on his right
hand.
20 A fool raises his voice when he
laughs,
but the wiseʸ smile quietly.

21 To the sensible person education is like
a golden ornament,
and like a bracelet on the right
arm.

22 The foot of a fool rushes into a house,
but an experienced person waits
respectfully outside.
23 A boor peers into the house from the
door,
but a cultivated person remains
outside.
24 It is ill-mannered for a person to listen
at a door;
the discreet would be grieved by the
disgrace.

25 The lips of babblers speak of what is
not their concern,ᶻ
but the words of the prudent are
weighed in the balance.
26 The mind of fools is in their mouth,
but the mouth of the wise is inᵃ
their mind.
27 When an ungodly person curses an
adversary,ᵇ
he curses himself.
28 A whisperer degrades himself
and is hated in his neighborhood.

The Idler

22 The idler is like a filthy stone,
and every one hisses at his
disgrace.
2 The idler is like the filth of dunghills;
anyone that picks it up will shake it
off his hand.

Degenerate Children
3 It is a disgrace to be the father of an
undisciplined son,
and the birth of a daughter is a
loss.
4 A sensible daughter obtains a husband
of her own,
but one who acts shamefully is a
grief to her father.
5 An impudent daughter disgraces father
and husband,
and is despised by both.
6 Like music in time of mourning is ill-
timed conversation,

ᵘ Other ancient authorities read *for the winter* ᵛ Syr Lat: Gk *entrails* ʷ Syr: Gk *reveler* ˣ Syr: Gk *dislikes*
ʸ Syr Lat: Gk *clever* ᶻ Other ancient authorities read *of strangers speak of these things* ᵃ Other ancient
authorities omit *in* ᵇ Or *curses Satan*

but a thrashing and discipline are at
     all times wisdom.*c*

Wisdom and Folly

9 Whoever teaches a fool is like one
     who glues potsherds together,
     or who rouses a sleeper from deep
     slumber.
10 Whoever tells a story to a fool tells it
     to a drowsy man;
     and at the end he will say, "What
     is it?"
11 Weep for the dead, for he has left the
     light behind;
     and weep for the fool, for he has
     left intelligence behind.
Weep less bitterly for the dead, for he
     is at rest;
     but the life of the fool is worse than
     death.
12 Mourning for the dead lasts seven days,
     but for the foolish or the ungodly it
     lasts all the days of their lives.

13 Do not talk much with a senseless
     person
     or visit an unintelligent person.*d*
Stay clear of him, or you may have
     trouble,
     and be spattered when he shakes
     himself off.
Avoid him and you will find rest,
     and you will never be wearied by
     his lack of sense.
14 What is heavier than lead?
     And what is its name except "Fool"?
15 Sand, salt, and a piece of iron
     are easier to bear than a stupid
     person.

16 A wooden beam firmly bonded into a
     building
     is not loosened by an earthquake;
so the mind firmly resolved after due
     reflection
     will not be afraid in a crisis.
17 A mind settled on an intelligent
     thought
     is like stucco decoration that makes
     a wall smooth.
18 Fences*e* set on a high place

will not stand firm against the wind;
so a timid mind with a fool's resolve
     will not stand firm against any fear.

The Preservation of Friendship

19 One who pricks the eye brings tears,
     and one who pricks the heart
     makes clear its feelings.
20 One who throws a stone at birds
     scares them away,
     and one who reviles a friend
     destroys a friendship.
21 Even if you draw your sword against
     a friend,
     do not despair, for there is a way
     back.
22 If you open your mouth against your
     friend,
     do not worry, for reconciliation is
     possible.
But as for reviling, arrogance,
     disclosure of secrets, or a
     treacherous blow—
     in these cases any friend will take
     to flight.

23 Gain the trust of your neighbor in his
     poverty,
     so that you may rejoice with him
     in his prosperity.
Stand by him in time of distress,
     so that you may share with him in
     his inheritance.*f*
24 The vapor and smoke of the furnace
     precede the fire;
     so insults precede bloodshed.
25 I am not ashamed to shelter a friend,
     and I will not hide from him.
26 But if harm should come to me
     because of him,
     whoever hears of it will beware of
     him.

A Prayer for Help against Sinning

27 Who will set a guard over my mouth,
     and an effective seal upon my lips,
     so that I may not fall because of
     them,
     and my tongue may not destroy
     me?

---

c Other ancient authorities add *7Children who are brought up in a good life conceal the lowly birth of their parents.* *8 Children who are disdainfully and boorishly haughty stain the nobility of their kindred.* *d* Other ancient authorities add *For being without sense he will despise everything about you* *e* Other ancient authorities read *Pebbles* *f* Other ancient authorities add *For one should not always despise restricted circumstances, or admire a rich person who is stupid.*

23

O Lord, Father and Master of my life,
do not abandon me to their designs,
and do not let me fall because of
them!

2 Who will set whips over my thoughts,
and the discipline of wisdom over
my mind,
so as not to spare me in my errors,
and not overlook my*ᵍ* sins?

3 Otherwise my mistakes may be
multiplied,
and my sins may abound,
and I may fall before my adversaries,
and my enemy may rejoice over
me.*ʰ*

4 O Lord, Father and God of my life,
do not give me haughty eyes,

5 and remove evil desire from me.

6 Let neither gluttony nor lust overcome
me,
and do not give me over to
shameless passion.

DISCIPLINE OF THE TONGUE*ⁱ*

7 Listen, my children, to instruction
concerning the mouth;
the one who observes it will never
be caught.

8 Sinners are overtaken through their
lips;
by them the reviler and the
arrogant are tripped up.

9 Do not accustom your mouth to
oaths,
nor habitually utter the name of the
Holy One;

10 for as a servant who is constantly
under scrutiny
will not lack bruises,
so also the person who always swears
and utters the Name
will never be cleansed*ʲ* from sin.

11 The one who swears many oaths is
full of iniquity,
and the scourge will not leave his
house.
If he swears in error, his sin remains
on him,
and if he disregards it, he sins
doubly;
if he swears a false oath, he will not
be justified,
for his house will be filled with
calamities.

Foul Language

12 There is a manner of speaking
comparable to death;*ᵏ*
may it never be found in the
inheritance of Jacob!
Such conduct will be far from the
godly,
and they will not wallow in sins.

13 Do not accustom your mouth to
coarse, foul language,
for it involves sinful speech.

14 Remember your father and mother
when you sit among the great,
or you may forget yourself in their
presence,
and behave like a fool through bad
habit;
then you will wish that you had
never been born,
and you will curse the day of your
birth.

15 Those who are accustomed to using
abusive language
will never become disciplined as
long as they live.

Concerning Sexual Sins

16 Two kinds of individuals multiply sins,
and a third incurs wrath.
Hot passion that blazes like a fire
will not be quenched until it burns
itself out;
one who commits fornication with his
near of kin
will never cease until the fire burns
him up.

17 To a fornicator all bread is sweet;
he will never weary until he dies.

18 The one who sins against his marriage
bed
says to himself, "Who can see me?
Darkness surrounds me, the walls hide
me,
and no one sees me. Why should I
worry?
The Most High will not remember
sins."

19 His fear is confined to human eyes
and he does not realize that the
eyes of the Lord
are ten thousand times brighter
than the sun;
they look upon every aspect of human
behavior

ᵍ Gk *their*   *ʰ* Other ancient authorities add *From them the hope of your mercy is remote*   *ⁱ* This heading is included in the Gk text.   *ʲ* Syr *be free*   *ᵏ* Other ancient authorities read *clothed about with death*

and see into hidden corners.
20 Before the universe was created, it was
known to him,
and so it is since its completion.
21 This man will be punished in the
streets of the city,
and where he least suspects it, he
will be seized.

22 So it is with a woman who leaves her
husband
and presents him with an heir by
another man.
23 For first of all, she has disobeyed the
law of the Most High;
second, she has committed an
offense against her husband;
and third, through her fornication she
has committed adultery
and brought forth children by
another man.
24 She herself will be brought before the
assembly,
and her punishment will extend to
her children.
25 Her children will not take root,
and her branches will not bear fruit.
26 She will leave behind an accursed
memory
and her disgrace will never be
blotted out.
27 Those who survive her will recognize
that nothing is better than the fear
of the Lord,
and nothing sweeter than to heed the
commandments of the Lord.*l*

THE PRAISE OF WISDOM*m*

24 Wisdom praises herself,
and tells of her glory in
the midst of her people.
2 In the assembly of the Most High she
opens her mouth,
and in the presence of his hosts she
tells of her glory:
3 "I came forth from the mouth of the
Most High,
and covered the earth like a mist.
4 I dwelt in the highest heavens,
and my throne was in a pillar of
cloud.
5 Alone I compassed the vault of heaven

and traversed the depths of the abyss.
6 Over waves of the sea, over all the
earth,
and over every people and nation I
have held sway.*n*
7 Among all these I sought a resting
place;
in whose territory should I abide?

8 "Then the Creator of all things gave
me a command,
and my Creator chose the place for
my tent.
He said, 'Make your dwelling in Jacob,
and in Israel receive your
inheritance.'
9 Before the ages, in the beginning, he
created me,
and for all the ages I shall not
cease to be.
10 In the holy tent I ministered before him,
and so I was established in Zion.
11 Thus in the beloved city he gave me a
resting place,
and in Jerusalem was my domain.
12 I took root in an honored people,
in the portion of the Lord, his
heritage.

13 "I grew tall like a cedar in Lebanon,
and like a cypress on the heights of
Hermon.
14 I grew tall like a palm tree in En-
gedi,*o*
and like rosebushes in Jericho;
like a fair olive tree in the field,
and like a plane tree beside water*p* I
grew tall.
15 Like cassia and camel's thorn I gave
forth perfume,
and like choice myrrh I spread my
fragrance,
like galbanum, onycha, and stacte,
and like the odor of incense in the
tent.
16 Like a terebinth I spread out my
branches,
and my branches are glorious and
graceful.
17 Like the vine I bud forth delights,
and my blossoms become glorious
and abundant fruit.*q*

---

l Other ancient authorities add as verse 28, *It is a great honor to follow God, and to be received by him is long life.*
m This heading is included in the Gk text.   *n* Other ancient authorities read *I have acquired a possession*
o Other ancient authorities read *on the beaches*   *p* Other ancient authorities omit *beside water*   *q* Other
ancient authorities add as verse 18, *I am the mother of beautiful love, of fear, of knowledge, and of holy hope;
being eternal, I am given to all my children, to those who are named by him.*

19 "Come to me, you who desire me,
  and eat your fill of my fruits.
20 For the memory of me is sweeter than
    honey,
  and the possession of me sweeter
    than the honeycomb.
21 Those who eat of me will hunger for
    more,
  and those who drink of me will
    thirst for more.
22 Whoever obeys me will not be put to
    shame,
  and those who work with me will
    not sin."

Wisdom and the Law
23 All this is the book of the covenant of
    the Most High God,
  the law that Moses commanded us
  as an inheritance for the
    congregations of Jacob.*r*
25 It overflows, like the Pishon, with
    wisdom,
  and like the Tigris at the time of
    the first fruits.
26 It runs over, like the Euphrates, with
    understanding,
  and like the Jordan at harvest time.
27 It pours forth instruction like the Nile,*s*
  like the Gihon at the time of
    vintage.
28 The first man did not know wisdom*t*
    fully,
  nor will the last one fathom her.
29 For her thoughts are more abundant
    than the sea,
  and her counsel deeper than the
    great abyss.

30 As for me, I was like a canal from a
    river,
  like a water channel into a garden.
31 I said, "I will water my garden
  and drench my flower-beds."
  And lo, my canal became a river,
  and my river a sea.
32 I will again make instruction shine
    forth like the dawn,
  and I will make it clear from far
    away.
33 I will again pour out teaching like
    prophecy,

  and leave it to all future
    generations.
34 Observe that I have not labored for
    myself alone,
  but for all who seek wisdom.*t*

Those Who Are Worthy of Praise

25 I take pleasure in three things,
    and they are beautiful in
  the sight of God and of
    mortals:*u*
agreement among brothers and sisters,
  friendship among neighbors,
  and a wife and a husband who live
    in harmony.
2 I hate three kinds of people,
  and I loathe their manner of life:
  a pauper who boasts, a rich person
    who lies,
  and an old fool who commits
    adultery.

3 If you gathered nothing in your
    youth,
  how can you find anything in your
    old age?
4 How attractive is sound judgment in
    the gray-haired,
  and for the aged to possess good
    counsel!
5 How attractive is wisdom in the aged,
  and understanding and counsel in
    the venerable!
6 Rich experience is the crown of the
    aged,
  and their boast is the fear of the
    Lord.

7 I can think of nine whom I would
    call blessed,
  and a tenth my tongue proclaims:
  a man who can rejoice in his children;
  a man who lives to see the
    downfall of his foes.
8 Happy the man who lives with a
    sensible wife,
  and the one who does not plow
    with ox and ass together.*v*
  Happy is the one who does not sin
    with the tongue,
  and the one who has not served an
    inferior.

---

r Other ancient authorities add as verse 24, "*Do not cease to be strong in the Lord, cling to him so that he may strengthen you; the Lord Almighty alone is God, and besides him there is no savior.*"   *s* Syr: Gk *It makes instruction shine forth like light*   *t* Gk *her*   *u* Syr Lat: Gk *In three things I was beautiful and I stood in beauty before the Lord and mortals.*   *v* Heb Syr: Gk lacks *and the one who does not plow with ox and ass together*

9 Happy is the one who finds a friend,[w]
  and the one who speaks to attentive
    listeners.
10 How great is the one who finds wisdom!
  But none is superior to the one
    who fears the Lord.
11 Fear of the Lord surpasses everything;
  to whom can we compare the one
    who has it?[x]

Some Extreme Forms of Evil
13 Any wound, but not a wound of the
    heart!
  Any wickedness, but not the
    wickedness of a woman!
14 Any suffering, but not suffering from
    those who hate!
  And any vengeance, but not the
    vengeance of enemies!
15 There is no venom[y] worse than a
    snake's venom,[y]
  and no anger worse than a
    woman's[z] wrath.

The Evil of a Wicked Woman
16 I would rather live with a lion and a
    dragon
  than live with an evil woman.
17 A woman's wickedness changes her
    appearance,
  and darkens her face like that of a
    bear.
18 Her husband sits[a] among the
    neighbors,
  and he cannot help sighing[b] bitterly.
19 Any iniquity is small compared to a
    woman's iniquity;
  may a sinner's lot befall her!
20 A sandy ascent for the feet of the aged—
  such is a garrulous wife to a quiet
    husband.
21 Do not be ensnared by a woman's
    beauty,
  and do not desire a woman for her
    possessions.[c]
22 There is wrath and impudence and
    great disgrace
  when a wife supports her husband.
23 Dejected mind, gloomy face,
  and wounded heart come from an
    evil wife.

Drooping hands and weak knees
  come from the wife who does not
    make her husband happy.
24 From a woman sin had its beginning,
  and because of her we all die.
25 Allow no outlet to water,
  and no boldness of speech to an evil
    wife.
26 If she does not go as you direct,
  separate her from yourself.

The Joy of a Good Wife
26 Happy is the husband of a good
    wife;
  the number of his days will be
    doubled.
2 A loyal wife brings joy to her
    husband,
  and he will complete his years in peace.
3 A good wife is a great blessing;
  she will be granted among the
    blessings of the man who fears
    the Lord.
4 Whether rich or poor, his heart is
    content,
  and at all times his face is cheerful.

The Worst of Evils: A Wicked Wife
5 Of three things my heart is frightened,
  and of a fourth I am in great fear:[d]
  Slander in the city, the gathering of a
    mob,
  and false accusation—all these are
    worse than death.
6 But it is heartache and sorrow when
  a wife is jealous of a rival,
  and a tongue-lashing makes it
    known to all.
7 A bad wife is a chafing yoke;
  taking hold of her is like grasping a
    scorpion.
8 A drunken wife arouses great anger;
  she cannot hide her shame.
9 The haughty stare betrays an unchaste
    wife;
  her eyelids give her away.

10 Keep strict watch over a headstrong
    daughter,
  or else, when she finds liberty, she
    will make use of it.

---

[w] Lat Syr: Gk *good sense*   [x] Other ancient authorities add as verse 12, *The fear of the Lord is the beginning of love for him, and faith is the beginning of clinging to him.*   [y] Syr: Gk *head*   [z] Other ancient authorities read *an enemy's*   [a] Heb Syr: Gk *loses heart*   [b] Other ancient authorities read *and listening he sighs*   [c] Heb Syr: Other Gk authorities read *for her beauty*   [d] Syr: Meaning of Gk uncertain

11 Be on guard against her impudent eye,
  and do not be surprised if she sins
    against you.
12 As a thirsty traveler opens his mouth
  and drinks from any water near him,
  so she will sit in front of every tent peg
  and open her quiver to the arrow.

The Blessing of a Good Wife
13 A wife's charm delights her husband,
  and her skill puts flesh on his bones.
14 A silent wife is a gift from the Lord,
  and nothing is so precious as her
    self-discipline.
15 A modest wife adds charm to charm,
  and no scales can weigh the value
    of her chastity.
16 Like the sun rising in the heights of
    the Lord,
  so is the beauty of a good wife in
    her well-ordered home.
17 Like the shining lamp on the holy
    lampstand,
  so is a beautiful face on a stately figure.
18 Like golden pillars on silver bases,
  so are shapely legs and steadfast feet.

—————

Other ancient authorities add verses 19–27:

19 *My child, keep sound the bloom of your
    youth,*
  *and do not give your strength to
    strangers.*
20 *Seek a fertile field within the whole plain,*
  and sow it with your own seed,
    trusting in your fine stock.
21 *So your offspring will prosper,*
  *and, having confidence in their good
    descent, will grow great.*
22 *A prostitute is regarded as spittle,*
  *and a married woman as a tower of
    death to her lovers.*
23 *A godless wife is given as a portion to a
    lawless man,*
  *but a pious wife is given to the man
    who fears the Lord.*
24 *A shameless woman constantly acts
    disgracefully,*
  *but a modest daughter will even be
    embarrassed before her husband.*
25 *A headstrong wife is regarded as a dog,*
  *but one who has a sense of shame will
    fear the Lord.*

26 *A wife honoring her husband will seem
    wise to all,*
  *but if she dishonors him in her pride she
    will be known to all as ungodly.*
  Happy is the husband of a good wife;
  *for the number of his years will be
    doubled.*
27 *A loud-voiced and garrulous wife is like a
    trumpet sounding the charge,*
  *and every person like this lives in the
    anarchy of war.*

—————

Three Depressing Things
28 At two things my heart is grieved,
  and because of a third anger comes
    over me:
  a warrior in want through poverty,
  intelligent men who are treated
    contemptuously,
  and a man who turns back from
    righteousness to sin—
  the Lord will prepare him for the sword!

The Temptations of Commerce
29 A merchant can hardly keep from
    wrongdoing,
  nor is a tradesman innocent of sin.

27 Many have committed sin for gain,[e]
  and those who seek to get
    rich will avert their eyes.
2 As a stake is driven firmly into a
    fissure between stones,
  so sin is wedged in between selling
    and buying.
3 If a person is not steadfast in the fear
    of the Lord,
  his house will be quickly overthrown.

Tests in Life
4 When a sieve is shaken, the refuse appears;
  so do a person's faults when he speaks.
5 The kiln tests the potter's vessels;
  so the test of a person is in his
    conversation.
6 Its fruit discloses the cultivation of a tree;
  so a person's speech discloses the
    cultivation of his mind.
7 Do not praise anyone before he speaks,
  for this is the way people are tested.

———

[e] Other ancient authorities read *a trifle*

Reward and Retribution

8 If you pursue justice, you will attain it
    and wear it like a glorious robe.
9 Birds roost with their own kind,
    so honesty comes home to those
    who practice it.
10 A lion lies in wait for prey;
    so does sin for evildoers.

Varieties of Speech

11 The conversation of the godly is
    always wise,
    but the fool changes like the moon.
12 Among stupid people limit your time,
    but among thoughtful people linger
    on.
13 The talk of fools is offensive,
    and their laughter is wantonly sinful.
14 Their cursing and swearing make
    one's hair stand on end,
    and their quarrels make others stop
    their ears.
15 The strife of the proud leads to
    bloodshed,
    and their abuse is grievous to hear.

Betraying Secrets

16 Whoever betrays secrets destroys
    confidence,
    and will never find a congenial friend.
17 Love your friend and keep faith with
    him;
    but if you betray his secrets, do not
    follow after him.
18 For as a person destroys his enemy,
    so you have destroyed the friendship
    of your neighbor.
19 And as you allow a bird to escape
    from your hand,
    so you have let your neighbor go,
    and will not catch him again.
20 Do not go after him, for he is too far off,
    and has escaped like a gazelle from
    a snare.
21 For a wound may be bandaged,
    and there is reconciliation after abuse,
    but whoever has betrayed secrets is
    without hope.

Hypocrisy and Retribution

22 Whoever winks the eye plots mischief,
    and those who know him will keep
    their distance.

23 In your presence his mouth is all
    sweetness,
    and he admires your words;
    but later he will twist his speech
    and with your own words he will
    trip you up.
24 I have hated many things, but him
    above all;
    even the Lord hates him.
25 Whoever throws a stone straight up
    throws it on his own head,
    and a treacherous blow opens up
    many wounds.
26 Whoever digs a pit will fall into it,
    and whoever sets a snare will be
    caught in it.
27 If a person does evil, it will roll back
    upon him,
    and he will not know where it
    came from.
28 Mockery and abuse issue from the proud,
    but vengeance lies in wait for them
    like a lion.
29 Those who rejoice in the fall of the godly
    will be caught in a snare,
    and pain will consume them before
    their death.

Anger and Vengeance

30 Anger and wrath, these also are
    abominations,
    yet a sinner holds on to them.

28 The vengeful will face the Lord's
    vengeance,
    for he keeps a strict account of[f]
    their sins.
2 Forgive your neighbor the wrong he
    has done,
    and then your sins will be pardoned
    when you pray.
3 Does anyone harbor anger against
    another,
    and expect healing from the Lord?
4 If one has no mercy toward another
    like himself,
    can he then seek pardon for his
    own sins?
5 If a mere mortal harbors wrath,
    who will make an atoning sacrifice
    for his sins?
6 Remember the end of your life, and
    set enmity aside;
    remember corruption and death, and
    be true to the commandments.
7 Remember the commandments, and do

[f] Other ancient authorities read *for he firmly establishes*

not be angry with your
neighbor;
remember the covenant of the Most
High, and overlook faults.

8 Refrain from strife, and your sins will
be fewer;
for the hot-tempered kindle strife,
9 and the sinner disrupts friendships
and sows discord among those who
are at peace.
10 In proportion to the fuel, so will the
fire burn,
and in proportion to the obstinacy,
so will strife increase;[g]
in proportion to a person's strength
will be his anger,
and in proportion to his wealth he
will increase his wrath.
11 A hasty quarrel kindles a fire,
and a hasty dispute sheds blood.

The Evil Tongue
12 If you blow on a spark, it will glow;
if you spit on it, it will be put out;
yet both come out of your mouth.

13 Curse the gossips and the double-
tongued,
for they destroy the peace of many.
14 Slander[h] has shaken many,
and scattered them from nation to
nation;
it has destroyed strong cities,
and overturned the houses of the
great.
15 Slander[h] has driven virtuous women
from their homes,
and deprived them of the fruit of
their toil.
16 Those who pay heed to slander[i] will
not find rest,
nor will they settle down in peace.
17 The blow of a whip raises a welt,
but a blow of the tongue crushes
the bones.
18 Many have fallen by the edge of the
sword,
but not as many as have fallen
because of the tongue.
19 Happy is the one who is protected
from it,
who has not been exposed to its anger,
who has not borne its yoke,
and has not been bound with its fetters.

20 For its yoke is a yoke of iron,
and its fetters are fetters of bronze;
21 its death is an evil death,
and Hades is preferable to it.
22 It has no power over the godly;
they will not be burned in its flame.
23 Those who forsake the Lord will fall
into its power;
it will burn among them and will
not be put out.
It will be sent out against them like a
lion;
like a leopard it will mangle them.
24a As you fence in your property with
thorns,
25b so make a door and a bolt for your
mouth.
24b As you lock up your silver and gold,
25a so make balances and scales for
your words.
26 Take care not to err with your tongue,[j]
and fall victim to one lying in wait.

On Lending and Borrowing
29 The merciful lend to their
neighbors;
by holding out a helping hand they
keep the commandments.
2 Lend to your neighbor in his time of
need;
repay your neighbor when a loan
falls due.
3 Keep your promise and be honest with
him,
and on every occasion you will find
what you need.
4 Many regard a loan as a windfall,
and cause trouble to those who help
them.
5 One kisses another's hands until he
gets a loan,
and is deferential in speaking of his
neighbor's money;
but at the time for repayment he delays,
and pays back with empty promises,
and finds fault with the time.
6 If he can pay, his creditor[k] will hardly
get back half,
and will regard that as a windfall.
If he cannot pay, the borrower[k] has
robbed the other of his money,
and he has needlessly made him an
enemy;
he will repay him with curses and
reproaches,

---

[g] Other ancient authorities read *burn*   [h] Gk *A third tongue*   [i] Gk *it*   [j] Gk *with it*   [k] Gk *he*

and instead of glory will repay him
  with dishonor.
7 Many refuse to lend, not because of
    meanness,
  but from fear[j] of being defrauded
    needlessly.

8 Nevertheless, be patient with someone
    in humble circumstances,
  and do not keep him waiting for
    your alms.
9 Help the poor for the commandment's
    sake,
  and in their need do not send them
    away empty-handed.
10 Lose your silver for the sake of a
    brother or a friend,
  and do not let it rust under a stone
    and be lost.
11 Lay up your treasure according to the
    commandments of the Most
    High,
  and it will profit you more than
    gold.
12 Store up almsgiving in your treasury,
  and it will rescue you from every
    disaster;
13 better than a stout shield and a sturdy
    spear,
  it will fight for you against the enemy.

On Guaranteeing Debts
14 A good person will be surety for his
    neighbor,
  but the one who has lost all sense
    of shame will fail him.
15 Do not forget the kindness of your
    guarantor,
  for he has given his life for you.
16 A sinner wastes the property of his
    guarantor,
17   and the ungrateful person abandons
    his rescuer.
18 Being surety has ruined many who
    were prosperous,
  and has tossed them about like
    waves of the sea;
  it has driven the influential into exile,
  and they have wandered among
    foreign nations.
19 The sinner comes to grief through surety;
  his pursuit of gain involves him in
    lawsuits.

20 Assist your neighbor to the best of
    your ability,
  but be careful not to fall yourself.

Home and Hospitality
21 The necessities of life are water, bread,
    and clothing,
  and also a house to assure privacy.
22 Better is the life of the poor under
    their own crude roof
  than sumptuous food in the house
    of others.
23 Be content with little or much,
  and you will hear no reproach for
    being a guest.[m]
24 It is a miserable life to go from house
    to house;
  as a guest you should not open
    your mouth;
25 you will play the host and provide
    drink without being thanked,
  and besides this you will hear rude
    words like these:
26 "Come here, stranger, prepare the table;
  let me eat what you have there."
27 "Be off, stranger, for an honored guest
    is here;
  my brother has come for a visit,
  and I need the guest-room."
28 It is hard for a sensible person to bear
    scolding about lodging[n] and the
    insults of the moneylender.

CONCERNING CHILDREN[o]

30 He who loves his son will whip
    him often,
  so that he may rejoice at the way
    he turns out.
2 He who disciplines his son will profit
    by him,
  and will boast of him among
    acquaintances.
3 He who teaches his son will make his
    enemies envious,
  and will glory in him among his
    friends.
4 When the father dies he will not seem
    to be dead,
  for he has left behind him one like
    himself,
5 whom in his life he looked upon with
    joy
  and at death, without grief.

[j] Other ancient authorities read *many refuse to lend, therefore, because of such meanness; they are afraid*   [m] Lat:
Gk *reproach from your family*; other ancient authorities lack this line   [n] Or *scolding from the household*   [o] This
heading is included in the Gk text.

6 He has left behind him an avenger
against his enemies,
and one to repay the kindness of
his friends.

7 Whoever spoils his son will bind up
his wounds,
and will suffer heartache at every cry.
8 An unbroken horse turns out stubborn,
and an unchecked son turns out
headstrong.
9 Pamper a child, and he will terrorize you;
play with him, and he will grieve you.
10 Do not laugh with him, or you will
have sorrow with him,
and in the end you will gnash your
teeth.
11 Give him no freedom in his youth,
and do not ignore his errors.
12 Bow down his neck in his youth,[p]
and beat his sides while he is young,
or else he will become stubborn and
disobey you,
and you will have sorrow of soul
from him.[q]
13 Discipline your son and make his yoke
heavy,[r]
so that you may not be offended by
his shamelessness.

14 Better off poor, healthy, and fit
than rich and afflicted in body.
15 Health and fitness are better than any
gold,
and a robust body than countless riches.
16 There is no wealth better than health
of body,
and no gladness above joy of heart.
17 Death is better than a life of misery,
and eternal sleep[s] than chronic sickness.

Concerning Foods[t]

18 Good things poured out upon a mouth
that is closed
are like offerings of food placed
upon a grave.
19 Of what use to an idol is a sacrifice?
For it can neither eat nor smell.
So is the one punished by the Lord;
20 he sees with his eyes and groans
as a eunuch groans when
embracing a girl.[u]
21 Do not give yourself over to sorrow,
and do not distress yourself
deliberately.
22 A joyful heart is life itself,
and rejoicing lengthens one's life
span.
23 Indulge yourself[v] and take comfort,
and remove sorrow far from you,
for sorrow has destroyed many,
and no advantage ever comes from it.
24 Jealousy and anger shorten life,
and anxiety brings on premature old
age.
25 Those who are cheerful and merry at
table
will benefit from their food.

Right Attitude toward Riches

31 Wakefulness over wealth wastes
away one's flesh,
and anxiety about it drives away sleep.
2 Wakeful anxiety prevents slumber,
and a severe illness carries off sleep.[w]
3 The rich person toils to amass a fortune,
and when he rests he fills himself
with his dainties.
4 The poor person toils to make a
meager living,
and if ever he rests he becomes needy.

5 One who loves gold will not be justified;
one who pursues money will be led
astray[x] by it.
6 Many have come to ruin because of gold,
and their destruction has met them
face to face.
7 It is a stumbling block to those who
are avid for it,
and every fool will be taken captive
by it.
8 Blessed is the rich person who is
found blameless,
and who does not go after gold.
9 Who is he, that we may praise him?
For he has done wonders among his
people.
10 Who has been tested by it and been
found perfect?
Let it be for him a ground for boasting.
Who has had the power to transgress
and did not transgress,

[p] Other ancient authorities lack this line and the preceding line [q] Other ancient authorities lack this line [r] Heb: Gk *take pains with him* [s] Other ancient authorities lack *eternal sleep* [t] This heading is included in the Gk text; other ancient authorities place the heading before verse 16 [u] Other ancient authorities add *So is the person who does right under compulsion* [v] Other ancient authorities read *Beguile yourself* [w] Other ancient authorities read *sleep carries off a severe illness* [x] Heb Syr: Gk *pursues destruction will be filled*

and to do evil and did not do it?
[11] His prosperity will be established,[y]
    and the assembly will proclaim his
        acts of charity.

Table Etiquette

[12] Are you seated at the table of the
        great?[z]
    Do not be greedy at it,
    and do not say, "How much food
        there is here!"
[13] Remember that a greedy eye is a bad
        thing.
    What has been created more greedy
        than the eye?
    Therefore it sheds tears for any reason.
[14] Do not reach out your hand for
        everything you see,
    and do not crowd your neighbor[a] at
        the dish.
[15] Judge your neighbor's feelings by your
        own,
    and in every matter be thoughtful.
[16] Eat what is set before you like a well
        brought-up person,[b]
    and do not chew greedily, or you
        will give offense.
[17] Be the first to stop, as befits good
        manners,
    and do not be insatiable, or you
        will give offense.
[18] If you are seated among many persons,
    do not help yourself[c] before they do.

[19] How ample a little is for a well-
        disciplined person!
    He does not breathe heavily when
        in bed.
[20] Healthy sleep depends on moderate eating;
    he rises early, and feels fit.
    The distress of sleeplessness and of nausea
        and colic are with the glutton.
[21] If you are overstuffed with food,
    get up to vomit, and you will have
        relief.
[22] Listen to me, my child, and do not
        disregard me,
    and in the end you will appreciate
        my words.
    In everything you do be moderate,[d]
    and no sickness will overtake you.
[23] People bless the one who is liberal
        with food,

and their testimony to his generosity
    is trustworthy.
[24] The city complains of the one who is
        stingy with food,
    and their testimony to his stinginess
        is accurate.

Temperance in Drinking Wine

[25] Do not try to prove your strength by
        wine-drinking,
    for wine has destroyed many.
[26] As the furnace tests the work of the
        smith,[e]
    so wine tests hearts when the
        insolent quarrel.
[27] Wine is very life to human beings
    if taken in moderation.
    What is life to one who is without wine?
    It has been created to make people
        happy.
[28] Wine drunk at the proper time and in
        moderation
    is rejoicing of heart and gladness of
        soul.
[29] Wine drunk to excess leads to
        bitterness of spirit,
    to quarrels and stumbling.
[30] Drunkenness increases the anger of a
        fool to his own hurt,
    reducing his strength and adding
        wounds.
[31] Do not reprove your neighbor at a
        banquet of wine,
    and do not despise him in his
        merrymaking;
    speak no word of reproach to him,
    and do not distress him by making
        demands of him.

Etiquette at a Banquet

32 If they make you master of the
        feast, do not exalt yourself;
    be among them as one of their
        number.
    Take care of them first and then sit
        down;
[2] when you have fulfilled all your
        duties, take your place,
    so that you may be merry along with
        them
    and receive a wreath for your
        excellent leadership.

---

[y] Other ancient authorities add *because of this*   [z] Heb Syr: Gk *at a great table*   [a] Gk *him*   [b] Heb: Gk *like a human being*   [c] Gk *reach out your hand*   [d] Heb Syr: Gk *industrious*   [e] Heb: Gk *tests the hardening of steel by dipping*

³ Speak, you who are older, for it is
    your right,
  but with accurate knowledge, and
    do not interrupt the music.
⁴ Where there is entertainment, do not
    pour out talk;
  do not display your cleverness at
    the wrong time.
⁵ A ruby seal in a setting of gold
  is a concert of music at a banquet of
    wine.
⁶ A seal of emerald in a rich setting of
    gold
  is the melody of music with good wine.

⁷ Speak, you who are young, if you are
    obliged to,
  but no more than twice, and only if
    asked.
⁸ Be brief; say much in few words;
  be as one who knows and can still
    hold his tongue.
⁹ Among the great do not act as their
    equal;
  and when another is speaking, do
    not babble.

¹⁰ Lightning travels ahead of the thunder,
  and approval goes before one who
    is modest.
¹¹ Leave in good time and do not be the
    last;
  go home quickly and do not linger.
¹² Amuse yourself there to your heart's
    content,
  but do not sin through proud speech.
¹³ But above all bless your Maker,
  who fills you with his good gifts.

The Providence of God
¹⁴ The one who seeks God[f] will accept
    his discipline,
  and those who rise early to seek
    him[g] will find favor.
¹⁵ The one who seeks the law will be
    filled with it,
  but the hypocrite will stumble at it.
¹⁶ Those who fear the Lord will form
    true judgments,
  and they will kindle righteous deeds
    like a light.
¹⁷ The sinner will shun reproof,

and will find a decision according to
    his liking.

¹⁸ A sensible person will not overlook a
    thoughtful suggestion;
  an insolent[h] and proud person will not
    be deterred by fear.[i]
¹⁹ Do nothing without deliberation,
  but when you have acted, do not
    regret it.
²⁰ Do not go on a path full of hazards,
  and do not stumble at an obstacle
    twice.[j]
²¹ Do not be overconfident on a smooth[k]
    road,
²² and give good heed to your paths.[l]
²³ Guard[m] yourself in every act,
  for this is the keeping of the
    commandments.

²⁴ The one who keeps the law preserves
    himself,[n]
  and the one who trusts the Lord
    will not suffer loss.

33

No evil will befall the one who
    fears the Lord,
  but in trials such a one will be
    rescued again and again.
² The wise will not hate the law,
  but the one who is hypocritical about
    it is like a boat in a storm.
³ The sensible person will trust in the law;
  for such a one the law is as
    dependable as a divine oracle.

⁴ Prepare what to say, and then you
    will be listened to;
  draw upon your training, and give
    your answer.
⁵ The heart of a fool is like a cart
    wheel,
  and his thoughts like a turning axle.
⁶ A mocking friend is like a stallion
  that neighs no matter who the rider is.

Differences in Nature and in Humankind
⁷ Why is one day more important than
    another,
  when all the daylight in the year is
    from the sun?
⁸ By the Lord's wisdom they were
    distinguished,

---

[f] Heb: Gk *who fears the Lord*   [g] Other ancient authorities lack *to seek him*   [h] Heb: Gk *alien*   [i] Meaning of Gk
uncertain. Other ancient authorities add *and after acting, with him, without deliberation*   [j] Heb: Gk *stumble on
stony ground*   [k] Or *an unexplored*   [l] Heb Syr: Gk *and beware of your children*   [m] Heb Syr: Gk *Trust*   [n] Heb: Gk
who believes the law heeds the commandments

and he appointed the different
seasons and festivals.
9 Some days he exalted and hallowed,
and some he made ordinary days.
10 All human beings come from the ground,
and humankind*o* was created out of
the dust.
11 In the fullness of his knowledge the
Lord distinguished them
and appointed their different ways.
12 Some he blessed and exalted,
and some he made holy and
brought near to himself;
but some he cursed and brought low,
and turned them out of their place.
13 Like clay in the hand of the potter,
to be molded as he pleases,
so all are in the hand of their Maker,
to be given whatever he decides.

14 Good is the opposite of evil,
and life the opposite of death;
so the sinner is the opposite of the
godly.
15 Look at all the works of the Most High;
they come in pairs, one the opposite
of the other.

16 Now I was the last to keep vigil;
I was like a gleaner following the
grape-pickers;
17 by the blessing of the Lord I arrived first,
and like a grape-picker I filled my
wine press.
18 Consider that I have not labored for
myself alone,
but for all who seek instruction.
19 Hear me, you who are great among
the people,
and you leaders of the congregation,
pay heed!

The Advantage of Independence
20 To son or wife, to brother or friend,
do not give power over yourself, as
long as you live;
and do not give your property to another,
in case you change your mind and
must ask for it.
21 While you are still alive and have
breath in you,
do not let anyone take your place.
22 For it is better that your children
should ask from you
than that you should look to the
hand of your children.

23 Excel in all that you do;
bring no stain upon your honor.
24 At the time when you end the days of
your life,
in the hour of death, distribute your
inheritance.

The Treatment of Slaves
25 Fodder and a stick and burdens for a
donkey;
bread and discipline and work for a
slave.
26 Set your slave to work, and you will
find rest;
leave his hands idle, and he will
seek liberty.
27 Yoke and thong will bow the neck,
and for a wicked slave there are
racks and tortures.
28 Put him to work, in order that he
may not be idle,
29 for idleness teaches much evil.
30 Set him to work, as is fitting for him,
and if he does not obey, make his
fetters heavy.
Do not be overbearing toward anyone,
and do nothing unjust.

31 If you have but one slave, treat him
like yourself,
because you have bought him with
blood.
If you have but one slave, treat him
like a brother,
for you will need him as you need
your life.
32 If you ill-treat him, and he leaves you
and runs away,
33 which way will you go to seek him?

Dreams Mean Nothing
34
The senseless have vain and false
hopes,
and dreams give wings to fools.
2 As one who catches at a shadow and
pursues the wind,
so is anyone who believes in*p* dreams.
3 What is seen in dreams is but a reflection,
the likeness of a face looking at itself.
4 From an unclean thing what can be
clean?
And from something false what can
be true?

---

o Heb: Gk *Adam*   *p* Syr: Gk *pays heed to*

5 Divinations and omens and dreams are
    unreal,
    and like a woman in labor, the
    mind has fantasies.
6 Unless they are sent by intervention
    from the Most High,
    pay no attention to them.
7 For dreams have deceived many,
    and those who put their hope in
    them have perished.
8 Without such deceptions the law will
    be fulfilled,
    and wisdom is complete in the
    mouth of the faithful.

Experience as a Teacher
9 An educated[q] person knows many
    things,
    and one with much experience knows
    what he is talking about.
10 An inexperienced person knows few
    things,
11   but he that has traveled acquires
    much cleverness.
12 I have seen many things in my travels,
    and I understand more than I can
    express.
13 I have often been in danger of death,
    but have escaped because of these
    experiences.

Fear the Lord
14 The spirit of those who fear the Lord
    will live,
15   for their hope is in him who saves
    them.
16 Those who fear the Lord will not be
    timid,
    or play the coward, for he is their
    hope.
17 Happy is the soul that fears the Lord!
18   To whom does he look? And who is
    his support?
19 The eyes of the Lord are on those
    who love him,
    a mighty shield and strong support,
    a shelter from scorching wind and a
    shade from noonday sun,
    a guard against stumbling and a
    help against falling.
20 He lifts up the soul and makes the
    eyes sparkle;
    he gives health and life and blessing.

Offering Sacrifices
21 If one sacrifices ill-gotten goods, the
    offering is blemished;[r]
22   the gifts[s] of the lawless are not
    acceptable.
23 The Most High is not pleased with the
    offerings of the ungodly,
    nor for a multitude of sacrifices does
    he forgive sins.
24 Like one who kills a son before his
    father's eyes
    is the person who offers a sacrifice
    from the property of the poor.
25 The bread of the needy is the life of
    the poor;
    whoever deprives them of it is a
    murderer.
26 To take away a neighbor's living is to
    commit murder;
27   to deprive an employee of wages is
    to shed blood.

28 When one builds and another tears
    down,
    what do they gain but hard work?
29 When one prays and another curses,
    to whose voice will the Lord listen?
30 If one washes after touching a corpse,
    and touches it again,
    what has been gained by washing?
31 So if one fasts for his sins,
    and goes again and does the same
    things,
    who will listen to his prayer?
    And what has he gained by
    humbling himself?

The Law and Sacrifices
35 The one who keeps the law makes
      many offerings;
2   one who heeds the commandments
    makes an offering of well-being.
3 The one who returns a kindness offers
    choice flour,
4   and one who gives alms sacrifices a
    thank offering.
5 To keep from wickedness is pleasing to
    the Lord,
    and to forsake unrighteousness is an
    atonement.
6 Do not appear before the Lord empty-
    handed,
7   for all that you offer is in fulfillment
    of the commandment.

---

[q] Other ancient authorities read *A traveled*   [r] Other ancient authorities read *is made in mockery*   [s] Other
ancient authorities read *mockeries*

8 The offering of the righteous enriches
      the altar,
   and its pleasing odor rises before the
      Most High.
9 The sacrifice of the righteous is
      acceptable,
   and it will never be forgotten.
10 Be generous when you worship the Lord,
   and do not stint the first fruits of
      your hands.
11 With every gift show a cheerful face,
   and dedicate your tithe with
      gladness.
12 Give to the Most High as he has given
      to you,
   and as generously as you can afford.
13 For the Lord is the one who repays,
   and he will repay you sevenfold.

Divine Justice

14 Do not offer him a bribe, for he will
      not accept it;
15   and do not rely on a dishonest sacrifice;
   for the Lord is the judge,
   and with him there is no partiality.
16 He will not show partiality to the poor;
   but he will listen to the prayer of
      one who is wronged.
17 He will not ignore the supplication of
      the orphan,
   or the widow when she pours out
      her complaint.
18 Do not the tears of the widow run
      down her cheek
19   as she cries out against the one
      who causes them to fall?
20 The one whose service is pleasing to
      the Lord will be accepted,
   and his prayer will reach to the
      clouds.
21 The prayer of the humble pierces the
      clouds,
   and it will not rest until it reaches
      its goal;
   it will not desist until the Most High
      responds
22   and does justice for the righteous,
   and executes judgment.
   Indeed, the Lord will not delay,
   and like a warrior*t* will not be patient
   until he crushes the loins of the
      unmerciful

23   and repays vengeance on the nations;
   until he destroys the multitude of the
      insolent,
   and breaks the scepters of the
      unrighteous;
24 until he repays mortals according to
      their deeds,
   and the works of all according to their
      thoughts;
25 until he judges the case of his people
   and makes them rejoice in his mercy.
26 His mercy is as welcome in time of
      distress
   as clouds of rain in time of drought.

A Prayer for God's People

36 Have mercy upon us, O God*u* of
      all,
2   and put all the nations in fear of you.
3 Lift up your hand against foreign nations
   and let them see your might.
4 As you have used us to show your
      holiness to them,
   so use them to show your glory to us.
5 Then they will know,*v* as we have known,
   that there is no God but you,
      O Lord.
6 Give new signs, and work other wonders;
7   make your hand and right arm
      glorious.
8 Rouse your anger and pour out your
      wrath;
9   destroy the adversary and wipe out
      the enemy.
10 Hasten the day, and remember the
      appointed time,*w*
   and let people recount your mighty
      deeds.
11 Let survivors be consumed in the fiery
      wrath,
   and may those who harm your
      people meet destruction.
12 Crush the heads of hostile rulers
   who say, "There is no one but
      ourselves."
13 Gather all the tribes of Jacob,*x*
16   and give them their inheritance, as
      at the beginning.
17 Have mercy, O Lord, on the people
      called by your name,
   on Israel, whom you have named*y*
      your firstborn,

---

t Heb: Gk *and with them*   *u* Heb: Gk *O Master, the God*   *v* Heb: Gk *And let them know you*   *w* Other ancient
authorities read *remember your oath*   *x* Owing to a dislocation in the Greek Mss of Sirach, the verse numbers
14 and 15 are not used in chapter 36, though no text is missing   *y* Other ancient authorities read *you have
likened to*

¹⁸ Have pity on the city of your sanctuary,ᶻ
　 Jerusalem, the place of your dwelling.ᵃ
¹⁹ Fill Zion with your majesty,ᵇ
　 and your templeᶜ with your glory.
²⁰ Bear witness to those whom you
　　created in the beginning,
　 and fulfill the prophecies spoken in
　　your name.
²¹ Reward those who wait for you
　 and let your prophets be found
　　trustworthy.
²² Hear, O Lord, the prayer of your
　　servants, according to your
　　goodwill towardᵈ your people,
　 and all who are on the earth will know
　 that you are the Lord, the God of
　　the ages.

Concerning Discrimination
²³ The stomach will take any food,
　 yet one food is better than another.
²⁴ As the palate tastes the kinds of game,
　 so an intelligent mind detects false
　　words.
²⁵ A perverse mind will cause grief,
　 but a person with experience will
　　pay him back.
²⁶ A woman will accept any man as a
　　husband,
　 but one girl is preferable to another.
²⁷ A woman's beauty lights up a man's
　　face,
　 and there is nothing he desires more.
²⁸ If kindness and humility mark her
　　speech,
　 her husband is more fortunate than
　　other men.
²⁹ He who acquires a wife gets his best
　　possession,ᵉ
　 a helper fit for him and a pillar of
　　support.ᶠ
³⁰ Where there is no fence, the property
　　will be plundered;
　 and where there is no wife, a man
　　will become a fugitive and a
　　wanderer.ᵍ
³¹ For who will trust a nimble robber
　　that skips from city to city?
　 So who will trust a man that has no
　　nest,
　 but lodges wherever night overtakes
　　him?

False Friends

37 Every friend says, "I too am a
　　friend";
　 but some friends are friends only in
　　name.
² Is it not a sorrow like that for death itself
　 when a dear friend turns into an
　　enemy?
³ O inclination to evil, why were you
　　formed
　 to cover the land with deceit?
⁴ Some companions rejoice in the
　　happiness of a friend,
　 but in time of trouble they are
　　against him.
⁵ Some companions help a friend for
　　their stomachs' sake,
　 yet in battle they will carry his shield.
⁶ Do not forget a friend during the battle,ʰ
　 and do not be unmindful of him
　　when you distribute your
　　spoils.ⁱ

Caution in Taking Advice
⁷ All counselors praise the counsel they
　　give,
　 but some give counsel in their own
　　interest.
⁸ Be wary of a counselor,
　 and learn first what is his interest,
　 for he will take thought for himself.
　 He may cast the lot against you
⁹ and tell you, "Your way is good,"
　 and then stand aside to see what
　　happens to you.
¹⁰ Do not consult the one who regards
　　you with suspicion;
　 hide your intentions from those who
　　are jealous of you.
¹¹ Do not consult with a woman about
　　her rival
　 or with a coward about war,
　 with a merchant about business
　 or with a buyer about selling,
　 with a miser about generosityʲ
　 or with the merciless about kindness,
　 with an idler about any work
　 or with a seasonal laborer about
　　completing his work,
　 with a lazy servant about a big task—
　　pay no attention to any advice they
　　give.

ᶻ Or *on your holy city*　ᵃ Heb: Gk *your rest*　ᵇ Heb Syr: Gk *the celebration of your wondrous deeds*　ᶜ Heb Syr: Gk
Lat *people*　ᵈ Heb and two Gk witnesses: Lat and most Gk witnesses read *according to the blessing of Aaron for*
ᵉ Heb: Gk *enters upon a possession*　ᶠ Heb: Gk *rest*　ᵍ Heb: Gk *wander about and sigh*　ʰ Heb: Gk *in your heart*
ⁱ Heb: Gk *him in your wealth*　ʲ Heb: Gk *gratitude*

¹² But associate with a godly person
  whom you know to be a keeper of
    the commandments,
  who is like-minded with yourself,
  and who will grieve with you if you
    fail.
¹³ And heed*k* the counsel of your own
    heart,
  for no one is more faithful to you
    than it is.
¹⁴ For our own mind sometimes keeps us
    better informed
  than seven sentinels sitting high on
    a watchtower.
¹⁵ But above all pray to the Most High
  that he may direct your way in truth.

True and False Wisdom
¹⁶ Discussion is the beginning of every
    work,
  and counsel precedes every
    undertaking.
¹⁷ The mind is the root of all conduct;
¹⁸   it sprouts four branches,*l*
  good and evil, life and death;
  and it is the tongue that continually
    rules them.
¹⁹ Some people may be clever enough to
    teach many,
  and yet be useless to themselves.
²⁰ A skillful speaker may be hated;
  he will be destitute of all food,
²¹ for the Lord has withheld the gift of
    charm,
  since he is lacking in all wisdom.
²² If a person is wise to his own
    advantage,
  the fruits of his good sense will be
    praiseworthy.*m*
²³ A wise person instructs his own people,
  and the fruits of his good sense will
    endure.
²⁴ A wise person will have praise heaped
    upon him,
  and all who see him will call him
    happy.
²⁵ The days of a person's life are
    numbered,
  but the days of Israel are without
    number.
²⁶ One who is wise among his people
    will inherit honor,*n*
  and his name will live forever.

Concerning Moderation
²⁷ My child, test yourself while you live;
  see what is bad for you and do not
    give in to it.
²⁸ For not everything is good for
    everyone,
  and no one enjoys everything.
²⁹ Do not be greedy for every delicacy,
  and do not eat without restraint;
³⁰ for overeating brings sickness,
  and gluttony leads to nausea.
³¹ Many have died of gluttony,
  but the one who guards against it
    prolongs his life.

Concerning Physicians and Health
38 Honor physicians for their
    services,
  for the Lord created them;
² for their gift of healing comes from
    the Most High,
  and they are rewarded by the king.
³ The skill of physicians makes them
    distinguished,
  and in the presence of the great
    they are admired.
⁴ The Lord created medicines out of the
    earth,
  and the sensible will not despise them.
⁵ Was not water made sweet with a tree
  in order that its*o* power might be
    known?
⁶ And he gave skill to human beings
  that he*p* might be glorified in his
    marvelous works.
⁷ By them the physician*q* heals and
    takes away pain;
⁸   the pharmacist makes a mixture
    from them.
  God's*r* works will never be finished;
  and from him health*s* spreads over
    all the earth.

⁹ My child, when you are ill, do not
    delay,
  but pray to the Lord, and he will
    heal you.
¹⁰ Give up your faults and direct your
    hands rightly,
  and cleanse your heart from all sin.
¹¹ Offer a sweet-smelling sacrifice, and a
    memorial portion of choice
    flour,

---

k Heb: Gk *establish* *l* Heb: Gk *As a clue to changes of heart four kinds of destiny appear* *m* Other ancient witnesses read *trustworthy* *n* Other ancient authorities read *confidence* *o* Or *his* *p* Or *they* *q* Heb: Gk *he* *r* Gk *His* *s* Or *peace*

and pour oil on your offering, as
much as you can afford.[t]
12 Then give the physician his place, for
the Lord created him;
do not let him leave you, for you
need him.
13 There may come a time when
recovery lies in the hands of
physicians,[u]
14 for they too pray to the Lord
that he grant them success in
diagnosis[v]
and in healing, for the sake of
preserving life.
15 He who sins against his Maker,
will be defiant toward the
physician.[w]

On Mourning for the Dead
16 My child, let your tears fall for the
dead,
and as one in great pain begin the
lament.
Lay out the body with due ceremony,
and do not neglect the burial.
17 Let your weeping be bitter and your
wailing fervent;
make your mourning worthy of the
departed,
for one day, or two, to avoid criticism;
then be comforted for your grief.
18 For grief may result in death,
and a sorrowful heart saps one's
strength.
19 When a person is taken away, sorrow
is over;
but the life of the poor weighs
down the heart.
20 Do not give your heart to grief;
drive it away, and remember your
own end.
21 Do not forget, there is no coming
back;
you do the dead[x] no good, and you
injure yourself.
22 Remember his[y] fate, for yours is like it;
yesterday it was his,[z] and today it is
yours.
23 When the dead is at rest, let his
remembrance rest too,
and be comforted for him when his
spirit has departed.

Trades and Crafts
24 The wisdom of the scribe depends on
the opportunity of leisure;
only the one who has little business
can become wise.
25 How can one become wise who
handles the plow,
and who glories in the shaft of a
goad,
who drives oxen and is occupied with
their work,
and whose talk is about bulls?
26 He sets his heart on plowing furrows,
and he is careful about fodder for
the heifers.
27 So it is with every artisan and master
artisan
who labors by night as well as by day;
those who cut the signets of seals,
each is diligent in making a great
variety;
they set their heart on painting a
lifelike image,
and they are careful to finish their
work.
28 So it is with the smith, sitting by the
anvil,
intent on his iron-work;
the breath of the fire melts his flesh,
and he struggles with the heat of
the furnace;
the sound of the hammer deafens his
ears,[a]
and his eyes are on the pattern of
the object.
He sets his heart on finishing his
handiwork,
and he is careful to complete its
decoration.
29 So it is with the potter sitting at his work
and turning the wheel with his feet;
he is always deeply concerned over his
products,
and he produces them in quantity.
30 He molds the clay with his arm
and makes it pliable with his feet;
he sets his heart to finish the glazing,
and he takes care in firing[b] the kiln.

31 All these rely on their hands,
and all are skillful in their own work.
32 Without them no city can be
inhabited,

---

[t] Heb: Lat lacks *as much as you can afford*; Meaning of Gk uncertain   [u] Gk *in their hands*   [v] Heb: Gk *rest*
[w] Heb: Gk *may he fall into the hands of the physician*   [x] Gk *him*   [y] Heb: Gk *my*   [z] Heb: Gk *mine*   [a] Cn: Gk
renews his ear   [b] Cn: Gk *cleaning*

and wherever they live, they will
not go hungry.[c]
Yet they are not sought out for the
council of the people,[d]
33 nor do they attain eminence in the
public assembly.
They do not sit in the judge's seat,
nor do they understand the
decisions of the courts;
they cannot expound discipline or
judgment,
and they are not found among the
rulers.[e]
34 But they maintain the fabric of the
world,
and their concern is for[f] the exercise
of their trade.

The Activity of the Scribe
How different the one who devotes
himself
to the study of the law of the Most High!

39 He seeks out the wisdom of all the
ancients,
and is concerned with prophecies;
2 he preserves the sayings of the famous
and penetrates the subtleties of
parables;
3 he seeks out the hidden meanings of
proverbs
and is at home with the obscurities
of parables.
4 He serves among the great
and appears before rulers;
he travels in foreign lands
and learns what is good and evil in
the human lot.
5 He sets his heart to rise early
to seek the Lord who made him,
and to petition the Most High;
he opens his mouth in prayer
and asks pardon for his sins.

6 If the great Lord is willing,
he will be filled with the spirit of
understanding;
he will pour forth words of wisdom of
his own
and give thanks to the Lord in prayer.
7 The Lord[g] will direct his counsel and
knowledge,
as he meditates on his mysteries.
8 He will show the wisdom of what he
has learned,

and will glory in the law of the
Lord's covenant.
9 Many will praise his understanding;
it will never be blotted out.
His memory will not disappear,
and his name will live through all
generations.
10 Nations will speak of his wisdom,
and the congregation will proclaim
his praise.
11 If he lives long, he will leave a name
greater than a thousand,
and if he goes to rest, it is enough[h]
for him.

A Hymn of Praise to God
12 I have more on my mind to express;
I am full like the full moon.
13 Listen to me, my faithful children, and
blossom
like a rose growing by a stream of
water.
14 Send out fragrance like incense,
and put forth blossoms like a lily.
Scatter the fragrance, and sing a
hymn of praise;
bless the Lord for all his works.
15 Ascribe majesty to his name
and give thanks to him with praise,
with songs on your lips, and with harps;
this is what you shall say in
thanksgiving:

16 "All the works of the Lord are very
good,
and whatever he commands will be
done at the appointed time.
17 No one can say, 'What is this?' or
'Why is that?'—
for at the appointed time all such
questions will be answered.
At his word the waters stood in a
heap,
and the reservoirs of water at the
word of his mouth.
18 When he commands, his every
purpose is fulfilled,
and none can limit his saving
power.
19 The works of all are before him,
and nothing can be hidden from his
eyes.
20 From the beginning to the end of time
he can see everything,

[c] Syr: Gk *and people can neither live nor walk there* [d] Most ancient authorities lack this line [e] Cn: Gk *among parables* [f] Syr: Gk *prayer is in* [g] Gk *He himself* [h] Cn: Meaning of Gk uncertain

and nothing is too marvelous for him.
21 No one can say, 'What is this?' or
'Why is that?'—
for everything has been created for
its own purpose.

22 "His blessing covers the dry land like
a river,
and drenches it like a flood.
23 But his wrath drives out the nations,
as when he turned a watered land
into salt.
24 To the faithful his ways are straight,
but full of pitfalls for the wicked.
25 From the beginning good things were
created for the good,
but for sinners good things and bad.*i*
26 The basic necessities of human life
are water and fire and iron and salt
and wheat flour and milk and honey,
the blood of the grape and oil and
clothing.
27 All these are good for the godly,
but for sinners they turn into evils.

28 "There are winds created for vengeance,
and in their anger they can dislodge
mountains;*j*
on the day of reckoning they will
pour out their strength
and calm the anger of their Maker.
29 Fire and hail and famine and pestilence,
all these have been created for
vengeance;
30 the fangs of wild animals and
scorpions and vipers,
and the sword that punishes the
ungodly with destruction.
31 They take delight in doing his bidding,
always ready for his service on earth;
and when their time comes they
never disobey his command."

32 So from the beginning I have been
convinced of all this
and have thought it out and left it
in writing:
33 All the works of the Lord are good,
and he will supply every need in its
time.
34 No one can say, "This is not as good
as that,"
for everything proves good in its
appointed time.

35 So now sing praise with all your heart
and voice,
and bless the name of the Lord.

Human Wretchedness

40 Hard work was created for
everyone,
and a heavy yoke is laid on the
children of Adam,
from the day they come forth from
their mother's womb
until the day they return to*k* the
mother of all the living.*l*
2 Perplexities and fear of heart are
theirs,
and anxious thought of the day of
their death.
3 From the one who sits on a splendid
throne
to the one who grovels in dust and
ashes,
4 from the one who wears purple and a
crown
to the one who is clothed in burlap,
5 there is anger and envy and trouble
and unrest,
and fear of death, and fury and
strife.
And when one rests upon his bed,
his sleep at night confuses his mind.
6 He gets little or no rest;
he struggles in his sleep as he did
by day.*m*
He is troubled by the visions of his
mind
like one who has escaped from the
battlefield.
7 At the moment he reaches safety he
wakes up,
astonished that his fears were
groundless.
8 To all creatures, human and animal,
but to sinners seven times more,
9 come death and bloodshed and strife
and sword,
calamities and famine and ruin and
plague.
10 All these were created for the wicked,
and on their account the flood
came.
11 All that is of earth returns to earth,
and what is from above returns
above.*n*

i Heb Lat: Gk *sinners bad things*   *j* Heb Syr: Gk *can scourge mightily*   *k* Other Gk and Lat authorities read *are buried in*   *l* Heb: Gk *of all*   *m* Arm: Meaning of Gk uncertain   *n* Heb Syr: Gk Lat *from the waters returns to the sea*

Injustice Will Not Prosper

12 All bribery and injustice will be blotted
   out,
   but good faith will last forever.
13 The wealth of the unjust will dry up
   like a river,
   and crash like a loud clap of
   thunder in a storm.
14 As a generous person has cause to
   rejoice,
   so lawbreakers will utterly fail.
15 The children of the ungodly put out
   few branches;
   they are unhealthy roots on sheer
   rock.
16 The reeds by any water or river bank
   are plucked up before any grass;
17 but kindness is like a garden of
   blessings,
   and almsgiving endures forever.

The Joys of Life

18 Wealth and wages make life sweet,*
   but better than either is finding a
   treasure.
19 Children and the building of a city
   establish one's name,
   but better than either is the one who
   finds wisdom.
   Cattle and orchards make one
   prosperous;*
   but a blameless wife is accounted
   better than either.
20 Wine and music gladden the heart,
   but the love of friends* is better
   than either.
21 The flute and the harp make sweet
   melody,
   but a pleasant voice is better than
   either.
22 The eye desires grace and beauty,
   but the green shoots of grain more
   than either.
23 A friend or companion is always
   welcome,
   but a sensible wife* is better than
   either.
24 Kindred and helpers are for a time of
   trouble,
   but almsgiving rescues better than
   either.
25 Gold and silver make one stand firm,
   but good counsel is esteemed more
   than either.

26 Riches and strength build up
   confidence,
   but the fear of the Lord is better
   than either.
   There is no want in the fear of the
   Lord,
   and with it there is no need to seek
   for help.
27 The fear of the Lord is like a garden
   of blessing,
   and covers a person better than any
   glory.

The Disgrace of Begging

28 My child, do not lead the life of a
   beggar;
   it is better to die than to beg.
29 When one looks to the table of
   another,
   one's way of life cannot be
   considered a life.
   One loses self-respect with another
   person's food,
   but one who is intelligent and well
   instructed guards against that.
30 In the mouth of the shameless begging
   is sweet,
   but it kindles a fire inside him.

Concerning Death

41 O death, how bitter is the thought
      of you
   to the one at peace among
   possessions,
   who has nothing to worry about and
   is prosperous in everything,
   and still is vigorous enough to enjoy
   food!
2 O death, how welcome is your
   sentence
   to one who is needy and failing in
   strength,
   worn down by age and anxious about
   everything;
   to one who is contrary, and has
   lost all patience!
3 Do not fear death's decree for you;
   remember those who went before
   you and those who will come
   after.
4 This is the Lord's decree for all flesh;
   why then should you reject the will
   of the Most High?

---

*Heb: Gk *Life is sweet for the self-reliant worker*   *Heb Syr: Gk lacks *but better . . . prosperous*   *Heb: Gk
wisdom   *Heb Compare Syr: Gk *wife with her husband*

Whether life lasts for ten years or a
  hundred or a thousand,
there are no questions asked in
  Hades.

The Fate of the Wicked
5 The children of sinners are abominable
  children,
  and they frequent the haunts of the
  ungodly.
6 The inheritance of the children of
  sinners will perish,
  and on their offspring will be a
  perpetual disgrace.
7 Children will blame an ungodly father,
  for they suffer disgrace because of
  him.
8 Woe to you, the ungodly,
  who have forsaken the law of the
  Most High God!
9 If you have children, calamity will be
  theirs;
  you will beget them only for
  groaning.
  When you stumble, there is lasting
  joy;^s
  and when you die, a curse is your
  lot.
10 Whatever comes from earth returns to
  earth;
  so the ungodly go from curse to
  destruction.

11 The human body is a fleeting thing,
  but a virtuous name will never be
  blotted out.^t
12 Have regard for your name, since it
  will outlive you
  longer than a thousand hoards of
  gold.
13 The days of a good life are numbered,
  but a good name lasts forever.

14 My children, be true to your training
  and be at peace;
  hidden wisdom and unseen treasure—
  of what value is either?

A Series of Contrasts
15 Better are those who hide their folly
  than those who hide their wisdom.
16 Therefore show respect for my words;

for it is not good to feel shame in
  every circumstance,
  nor is every kind of abashment to
  be approved.^u

17 Be ashamed of sexual immorality,
  before your father or mother;
  and of a lie, before a prince or a
  ruler;
18 of a crime, before a judge or
  magistrate;
  and of a breach of the law, before
  the congregation and the
  people;
  of unjust dealing, before your partner
  or your friend;
19 and of theft, in the place where you
  live.
  Be ashamed of breaking an oath or
  agreement,^v
  and of leaning on your elbow at
  meals;
  of surliness in receiving or giving,
20 and of silence, before those who
  greet you;
  of looking at a prostitute,
21 and of rejecting the appeal of a
  relative;
  of taking away someone's portion or
  gift,
  and of gazing at another man's
  wife;
22 of meddling with his servant-girl—
  and do not approach her bed;
  of abusive words, before friends—
  and do not be insulting after
  making a gift.

42 Be ashamed of repeating what you
  hear,
  and of betraying secrets.
  Then you will show proper shame,
  and will find favor with everyone.

  Of the following things do not be
  ashamed,
  and do not sin to save face:
2 Do not be ashamed of the law of the
  Most High and his covenant,
  and of rendering judgment to acquit
  the ungodly;
3 of keeping accounts with a partner or
  with traveling companions,
  and of dividing the inheritance of
  friends;

---

^sHeb: Meaning of Gk uncertain   ^tHeb: Gk *People grieve over the death of the body, but the bad name of sinners will be blotted out*   ^uHeb: Gk *and not everything is confidently esteemed by everyone*   ^vHeb: Gk *before the truth of God and the covenant*

⁴ of accuracy with scales and weights,
  and of acquiring much or little;
⁵ of profit from dealing with merchants,
  and of frequent disciplining of
    children,
  and of drawing blood from the back
    of a wicked slave.
⁶ Where there is an untrustworthy wife,
    a seal is a good thing;
  and where there are many hands,
    lock things up.
⁷ When you make a deposit, be sure it
    is counted and weighed,
  and when you give or receive, put
    it all in writing.
⁸ Do not be ashamed to correct the
    stupid or foolish
  or the aged who are guilty of
    sexual immorality.
  Then you will show your sound training,
  and will be approved by all.

Daughters and Fathers
⁹ A daughter is a secret anxiety to her
    father,
  and worry over her robs him of sleep;
  when she is young, for fear she may
    not marry,
  or if married, for fear she may be
    disliked;
¹⁰ while a virgin, for fear she may be
    seduced
  and become pregnant in her father's
    house;
  or having a husband, for fear she may
    go astray,
  or, though married, for fear she
    may be barren.
¹¹ Keep strict watch over a headstrong
    daughter,
  or she may make you a
    laughingstock to your enemies,
  a byword in the city and the assembly
    ofʷ the people,
  and put you to shame in public
    gatherings.ˣ
  See that there is no lattice in her room,
    no spot that overlooks the
      approaches to the house.ʸ
¹² Do not let her parade her beauty
    before any man,
  or spend her time among married
    women;ʷ

¹³ for from garments comes the moth,
  and from a woman comes woman's
    wickedness.
¹⁴ Better is the wickedness of a man
    than a woman who does good;
  it is woman who brings shame and
    disgrace.

The Works of God in Nature
¹⁵ I will now call to mind the works of
    the Lord,
  and will declare what I have seen.
  By the word of the Lord his works are
    made;
  and all his creatures do his will.ᶻ
¹⁶ The sun looks down on everything
    with its light,
  and the work of the Lord is full of
    his glory.
¹⁷ The Lord has not empowered even his
    holy ones
  to recount all his marvelous works,
  which the Lord the Almighty has
    established
  so that the universe may stand firm
    in his glory.
¹⁸ He searches out the abyss and the
    human heart;
  he understands their innermost secrets.
  For the Most High knows all that may
    be known;
  he sees from of old the things that
    are to come.ᵃ
¹⁹ He discloses what has been and what
    is to be,
  and he reveals the traces of hidden
    things.
²⁰ No thought escapes him,
  and nothing is hidden from him.
²¹ He has set in order the splendors of
    his wisdom;
  he is from all eternity one and the
    same.
  Nothing can be added or taken away,
  and he needs no one to be his
    counselor.
²² How desirable are all his works,
  and how sparkling they are to see!ᵇ
²³ All these things live and remain forever;
  each creature is preserved to meet a
    particular need.ᶜ
²⁴ All things come in pairs, one opposite
    the other,

ʷ Heb: Meaning of Gk uncertain   ˣ Heb: Gk *to shame before the great multitude*   ʸ Heb: Gk lacks *See . . . house*
ᶻ Syr Compare Heb: most Gk witnesses lack *and all . . . will*   ᵃ Heb: Gk *he sees the sign(s) of the age*
ᵇ Meaning of Gk uncertain   ᶜ Heb: Gk *forever for every need, and all are obedient*

and he has made nothing
    incomplete.
25 Each supplements the virtues of the
    other.
Who could ever tire of seeing his
    glory?

it is exceedingly beautiful in its
    brightness.
12 It encircles the sky with its glorious arc;
    the hands of the Most High have
    stretched it out.

The Splendor of the Sun

43 The pride of the higher realms is
    the clear vault of the sky,
as glorious to behold as the sight of
    the heavens.
2 The sun, when it appears, proclaims
    as it rises
what a marvelous instrument it is,
    the work of the Most High.
3 At noon it parches the land,
    and who can withstand its burning
    heat?
4 A man tending*d* a furnace works in
    burning heat,
but three times as hot is the sun
    scorching the mountains;
it breathes out fiery vapors,
    and its bright rays blind the eyes.
5 Great is the Lord who made it;
    at his orders it hurries on its course.

The Splendor of the Moon
6 It is the moon that marks the
    changing seasons,*e*
governing the times, their
    everlasting sign.
7 From the moon comes the sign for
    festal days,
a light that wanes when it
    completes its course.
8 The new moon, as its name suggests,
    renews itself;*f*
how marvelous it is in this change,
a beacon to the hosts on high,
shining in the vault of the heavens!

The Glory of the Stars and the Rainbow
9 The glory of the stars is the beauty of
    heaven,
a glittering array in the heights of
    the Lord.
10 On the orders of the Holy One they
    stand in their appointed places;
they never relax in their watches.
11 Look at the rainbow, and praise him
    who made it;

The Marvels of Nature
13 By his command he sends the driving
    snow
and speeds the lightnings of his
    judgment.
14 Therefore the storehouses are opened,
    and the clouds fly out like birds.
15 In his majesty he gives the clouds
    their strength,
and the hailstones are broken in
    pieces.
17aThe voice of his thunder rebukes the
    earth;
16 when he appears, the mountains shake.
At his will the south wind blows;
17b so do the storm from the north and
    the whirlwind.
He scatters the snow like birds flying
    down,
and its descent is like locusts
    alighting.
18 The eye is dazzled by the beauty of its
    whiteness,
and the mind is amazed as it falls.
19 He pours frost over the earth like salt,
    and icicles form like pointed thorns.
20 The cold north wind blows,
    and ice freezes on the water;
it settles on every pool of water,
    and the water puts it on like a
    breastplate.
21 He consumes the mountains and
    burns up the wilderness,
and withers the tender grass like fire.
22 A mist quickly heals all things;
    the falling dew gives refreshment
    from the heat.

23 By his plan he stilled the deep
    and planted islands in it.
24 Those who sail the sea tell of its
    dangers,
and we marvel at what we hear.
25 In it are strange and marvelous
    creatures,
all kinds of living things, and huge
    sea-monsters.

---

d Other ancient authorities read *blowing upon*   *e* Heb: Meaning of Gk uncertain   *f* Heb: Gk *The month is named after the moon*

²⁶ Because of him each of his messengers
  succeeds,
  and by his word all things hold
  together.

²⁷ We could say more but could never
  say enough;
  let the final word be: "He is the all."
²⁸ Where can we find the strength to
  praise him?
  For he is greater than all his works.
²⁹ Awesome is the Lord and very great,
  and marvelous is his power.
³⁰ Glorify the Lord and exalt him as
  much as you can,
  for he surpasses even that.
  When you exalt him, summon all
  your strength,
  and do not grow weary, for you
  cannot praise him enough.
³¹ Who has seen him and can describe
  him?
  Or who can extol him as he is?
³² Many things greater than these lie
  hidden,
  for I*^g* have seen but few of his works.
³³ For the Lord has made all things,
  and to the godly he has given wisdom.

Hymn in Honor of Our Ancestors*^h*

44 Let us now sing the praises of
  famous men,
  our ancestors in their generations.
² The Lord apportioned to them*ⁱ* great
  glory,
  his majesty from the beginning.
³ There were those who ruled in their
  kingdoms,
  and made a name for themselves by
  their valor;
  those who gave counsel because they
  were intelligent;
  those who spoke in prophetic oracles;
⁴ those who led the people by their
  counsels
  and by their knowledge of the
  people's lore;
  they were wise in their words of
  instruction;
⁵ those who composed musical tunes,
  or put verses in writing;
⁶ rich men endowed with resources,
  living peacefully in their homes—
⁷ all these were honored in their
  generations,

  and were the pride of their times.
⁸ Some of them have left behind a name,
  so that others declare their praise.
⁹ But of others there is no memory;
  they have perished as though they
  had never existed;
  they have become as though they had
  never been born,
  they and their children after them.
¹⁰ But these also were godly men,
  whose righteous deeds have not
  been forgotten;
¹¹ their wealth will remain with their
  descendants,
  and their inheritance with their
  children's children.*^j*
¹² Their descendants stand by the
  covenants;
  their children also, for their sake.
¹³ Their offspring will continue forever,
  and their glory will never be blotted
  out.
¹⁴ Their bodies are buried in peace,
  but their name lives on generation
  after generation.
¹⁵ The assembly declares*^k* their wisdom,
  and the congregation proclaims their
  praise.

Enoch
¹⁶ Enoch pleased the Lord and was taken
  up,
  an example of repentance to all
  generations.

Noah
¹⁷ Noah was found perfect and righteous;
  in the time of wrath he kept the
  race alive;*^l*
  therefore a remnant was left on the
  earth
  when the flood came.
¹⁸ Everlasting covenants were made with
  him
  that all flesh should never again be
  blotted out by a flood.

Abraham
¹⁹ Abraham was the great father of a
  multitude of nations,
  and no one has been found like
  him in glory.

---

^g Heb: Gk *we*   *^h* This title is included in the Gk text.   *ⁱ* Heb: Gk *created*   *^j* Heb Compare Lat Syr: Meaning of
Gk uncertain   *^k* Heb: Gk *Peoples declare*   *^l* Heb: Gk *was taken in exchange*

20 He kept the law of the Most High,
and entered into a covenant with him;
he certified the covenant in his flesh,
and when he was tested he proved
faithful.
21 Therefore the Lord*m* assured him with
an oath
that the nations would be blessed
through his offspring;
that he would make him as numerous
as the dust of the earth,
and exalt his offspring like the stars,
and give them an inheritance from sea
to sea
and from the Euphrates*n* to the ends
of the earth.

Isaac and Jacob
22 To Isaac also he gave the same
assurance
for the sake of his father Abraham.
The blessing of all people and the
covenant
23   he made to rest on the head of Jacob;
he acknowledged him with his
blessings,
and gave him his inheritance;
he divided his portions,
and distributed them among twelve
tribes.

Moses
From his descendants the Lord*m*
brought forth a godly man,
who found favor in the sight of all

45 ¹ and was beloved by God and
people,
Moses, whose memory is blessed.
2 He made him equal in glory to the
holy ones,
and made him great, to the terror
of his enemies.
3 By his words he performed swift miracles;*o*
the Lord*m* glorified him in the
presence of kings.
He gave him commandments for his
people,
and revealed to him his glory.
4 For his faithfulness and meekness he
consecrated him,
choosing him out of all humankind.
5 He allowed him to hear his voice,
and led him into the dark cloud,
and gave him the commandments face
to face,

the law of life and knowledge,
so that he might teach Jacob the
covenant,
and Israel his decrees.

Aaron
6 He exalted Aaron, a holy man like
Moses*p*
who was his brother, of the tribe of
Levi.
7 He made an everlasting covenant with
him,
and gave him the priesthood of the
people.
He blessed him with stateliness,
and put a glorious robe on him.
8 He clothed him in perfect splendor,
and strengthened him with the
symbols of authority,
the linen undergarments, the long
robe, and the ephod.
9 And he encircled him with pomegranates,
with many golden bells all around,
to send forth a sound as he walked,
to make their ringing heard in the
temple
as a reminder to his people;
10 with the sacred vestment, of gold and
violet
and purple, the work of an embroiderer;
with the oracle of judgment, Urim and
Thummim;
11   with twisted crimson, the work of an
artisan;
with precious stones engraved like seals,
in a setting of gold, the work of a
jeweler,
to commemorate in engraved letters
each of the tribes of Israel;
12 with a gold crown upon his turban,
inscribed like a seal with "Holiness,"
a distinction to be prized, the work of
an expert,
a delight to the eyes, richly adorned.
13 Before him such beautiful things did
not exist.
No outsider ever put them on,
but only his sons
and his descendants in perpetuity.
14 His sacrifices shall be wholly burned
twice every day continually.
15 Moses ordained him,
and anointed him with holy oil;
it was an everlasting covenant for him
and for his descendants as long as
the heavens endure,

m Gk *he*   *n* Syr: Heb Gk *River*   *o* Heb: Gk *caused signs to cease*   *p* Gk *him*

to minister to the Lord^q and serve as
priest
and bless his people in his name.
^16 He chose him out of all the living
to offer sacrifice to the Lord,
incense and a pleasing odor as a
memorial portion,
to make atonement for the^r people.
^17 In his commandments he gave him
authority and statutes and^s
judgments,
to teach Jacob the testimonies,
and to enlighten Israel with his law.
^18 Outsiders conspired against him,
and envied him in the wilderness,
Dathan and Abiram and their
followers
and the company of Korah, in
wrath and anger.
^19 The Lord saw it and was not pleased,
and in the heat of his anger they
were destroyed;
he performed wonders against them
to consume them in flaming fire.
^20 He added glory to Aaron
and gave him a heritage;
he allotted to him the best of the first
fruits,
and prepared bread of first fruits in
abundance;
^21 for they eat the sacrifices of the Lord,
which he gave to him and his
descendants.
^22 But in the land of the people he has
no inheritance,
and he has no portion among the
people;
for the Lord^t himself is his^u portion
and inheritance.

Phinehas
^23 Phinehas son of Eleazar ranks third in
glory
for being zealous in the fear of the
Lord,
and standing firm, when the people
turned away,
in the noble courage of his soul;
and he made atonement for Israel.
^24 Therefore a covenant of friendship was
established with him,
that he should be leader of the
sanctuary and of his people,

that he and his descendants should
have
the dignity of the priesthood forever.
^25 Just as a covenant was established
with David
son of Jesse of the tribe of Judah,
that the king's heritage passes only
from son to son,
so the heritage of Aaron is for his
descendants alone.

^26 And now bless the Lord
who has crowned you with glory.^v
May the Lord^t grant you wisdom of
mind
to judge his people with justice,
so that their prosperity may not
vanish,
and that their glory may endure
through all their generations.

Joshua and Caleb

46

Joshua son of Nun was mighty in
war,
and was the successor of Moses in
the prophetic office.
He became, as his name implies,
a great savior of God's^w elect,
to take vengeance on the enemies that
rose against them,
so that he might give Israel its
inheritance.
^2 How glorious he was when he lifted
his hands
and brandished his sword against
the cities!
^3 Who before him ever stood so firm?
For he waged the wars of the Lord.
^4 Was it not through him that the sun
stood still
and one day became as long as two?
^5 He called upon the Most High, the
Mighty One,
when enemies pressed him on every
side,
and the great Lord answered him
with hailstones of mighty power.
^6 He overwhelmed that nation in battle,
and on the slope he destroyed his
opponents,
so that the nations might know his
armament,
that he was fighting in the sight of
the Lord;

---

^q Gk *him*   ^r Other ancient authorities read *his* or *your*   ^s Heb: Gk *authority in covenants of*   ^t Gk *he*   ^u Other
ancient authorities read *your*   ^v Heb: Gk lacks *And . . . glory*   ^w Gk *his*

for he was a devoted follower of the
  Mighty One.
7 And in the days of Moses he proved
    his loyalty,
  he and Caleb son of Jephunneh:
  they opposed the congregation,^x
    restrained the people from sin,
    and stilled their wicked grumbling.
8 And these two alone were spared
    out of six hundred thousand
    infantry,
  to lead the people^y into their
    inheritance,
    the land flowing with milk and
    honey.
9 The Lord gave Caleb strength,
    which remained with him in his old
    age,
  so that he went up to the hill
    country,
    and his children obtained it for an
    inheritance,
10 so that all the Israelites might see
    how good it is to follow the Lord.

The Judges
11 The judges also, with their respective
    names,
    whose hearts did not fall into
    idolatry
  and who did not turn away from the
    Lord—
    may their memory be blessed!
12 May their bones send forth new life
    from where they lie,
    and may the names of those who
    have been honored
    live again in their children!

13 Samuel was beloved by his Lord;
    a prophet of the Lord, he established
    the kingdom
    and anointed rulers over his people.
14 By the law of the Lord he judged the
    congregation,
    and the Lord watched over Jacob.
15 By his faithfulness he was proved to
    be a prophet,
    and by his words he became known
    as a trustworthy seer.
16 He called upon the Lord, the Mighty
    One,
    when his enemies pressed him on
    every side,

and he offered in sacrifice a suckling
    lamb.
17 Then the Lord thundered from heaven,
    and made his voice heard with a
    mighty sound;
18 he subdued the leaders of the enemy^z
    and all the rulers of the Philistines.
19 Before the time of his eternal sleep,
    Samuel^a bore witness before the
    Lord and his anointed:
  "No property, not so much as a pair
    of shoes,
    have I taken from anyone!"
  And no one accused him.
20 Even after he had fallen asleep, he
    prophesied
    and made known to the king his
    death,
  and lifted up his voice from the
    ground
  in prophecy, to blot out the
    wickedness of the people.

Nathan
47 After him Nathan rose up
        to prophesy in the days of
        David.

David
2 As the fat is set apart from the
    offering of well-being,
  so David was set apart from the
    Israelites.
3 He played with lions as though they
    were young goats,
    and with bears as though they were
    lambs of the flock.
4 In his youth did he not kill a giant,
    and take away the people's disgrace,
  when he whirled the stone in the
    sling
    and struck down the boasting
    Goliath?
5 For he called on the Lord, the Most
    High,
    and he gave strength to his right
    arm
  to strike down a mighty warrior,
    and to exalt the power^b of his
    people.
6 So they glorified him for the tens of
    thousands he conquered,
    and praised him for the blessings

---

^x Other ancient authorities read *the enemy*   ^y Gk *them*   ^z Heb: Gk *leaders of the people of Tyre*   ^a Gk *he*   ^b Gk
horn

bestowed by the Lord,
    when the glorious diadem was given
        to him.
7 For he wiped out his enemies on
        every side,
    and annihilated his adversaries the
        Philistines;
    he crushed their power[c] to our own
        day.
8 In all that he did he gave thanks
    to the Holy One, the Most High,
        proclaiming his glory;
    he sang praise with all his heart,
    and he loved his Maker.
9 He placed singers before the altar,
    to make sweet melody with their
        voices.[d]
10 He gave beauty to the festivals,
    and arranged their times throughout
        the year,[e]
    while they praised God's[f] holy name,
    and the sanctuary resounded from
        early morning.
11 The Lord took away his sins,
    and exalted his power[c] forever;
    he gave him a covenant of kingship
    and a glorious throne in Israel.

Solomon
12 After him a wise son rose up
    who because of him lived in
        security:[g]
13 Solomon reigned in an age of peace,
    because God made all his borders
        tranquil,
    so that he might build a house in his
        name
    and provide a sanctuary to stand
        forever.
14 How wise you were when you were
        young!
    You overflowed like the Nile[h] with
        understanding.
15 Your influence spread throughout the
        earth,
    and you filled it with proverbs
        having deep meaning.
16 Your fame reached to far-off islands,
    and you were loved for your
        peaceful reign.
17 Your songs, proverbs, and parables,
    and the answers you gave
        astounded the nations.

18 In the name of the Lord God,
    who is called the God of Israel,
    you gathered gold like tin
    and amassed silver like lead.
19 But you brought in women to lie at
        your side,
    and through your body you were
        brought into subjection.
20 You stained your honor,
    and defiled your family line,
    so that you brought wrath upon your
        children,
    and they were grieved[i] at your folly,
21 because the sovereignty was divided
    and a rebel kingdom arose out of
        Ephraim.
22 But the Lord will never give up his
        mercy,
    or cause any of his works to perish;
    he will never blot out the descendants
        of his chosen one,
    or destroy the family line of him
        who loved him.
So he gave a remnant to Jacob,
    and to David a root from his own
        family.

Rehoboam and Jeroboam
23 Solomon rested with his ancestors,
    and left behind him one of his sons,
    broad in[j] folly and lacking in sense,
    Rehoboam, whose policy drove the
        people to revolt.
Then Jeroboam son of Nebat led Israel
        into sin
    and started Ephraim on its sinful
        ways.
24 Their sins increased more and more,
    until they were exiled from their land.
25 For they sought out every kind of
        wickedness,
    until vengeance came upon them.

Elijah

48 Then Elijah arose, a prophet like
    fire,
    and his word burned like a torch.
2 He brought a famine upon them,
    and by his zeal he made them few
        in number.
3 By the word of the Lord he shut up
        the heavens,

---

[c] Gk *horn*   [d] Other ancient authorities add *and daily they sing his praises*   [e] Gk *to completion*   [f] Gk *his*
[g] Heb: Gk *in a broad place*   [h] Heb: Gk *a river*   [i] Other ancient authorities read *I was grieved*   [j] Heb (with a play on the name Rehoboam) Syr: Gk *the people's*

and also three times brought down
fire.
4 How glorious you were, Elijah, in your
wondrous deeds!
Whose glory is equal to yours?
5 You raised a corpse from death
and from Hades, by the word of the
Most High.
6 You sent kings down to destruction,
and famous men, from their sickbeds.
7 You heard rebuke at Sinai
and judgments of vengeance at Horeb.
8 You anointed kings to inflict
retribution,
and prophets to succeed you.[k]
9 You were taken up by a whirlwind of
fire,
in a chariot with horses of fire.
10 At the appointed time, it is written,
you are destined[l]
to calm the wrath of God before it
breaks out in fury,
to turn the hearts of parents to their
children,
and to restore the tribes of Jacob.
11 Happy are those who saw you
and were adorned[m] with your love!
For we also shall surely live.[n]

Elisha

12 When Elijah was enveloped in the
whirlwind,
Elisha was filled with his spirit.
He performed twice as many signs,
and marvels with every utterance of
his mouth.[o]
Never in his lifetime did he tremble
before any ruler,
nor could anyone intimidate him at
all.
13 Nothing was too hard for him,
and when he was dead, his body
prophesied.
14 In his life he did wonders,
and in death his deeds were marvelous.

15 Despite all this the people did not repent,
nor did they forsake their sins,
until they were carried off as plunder
from their land,
and were scattered over all the earth.
The people were left very few in
number,
but with a ruler from the house of
David.
16 Some of them did what was right,
but others sinned more and more.

Hezekiah

17 Hezekiah fortified his city,
and brought water into its midst;
he tunneled the rock with iron tools,
and built cisterns for the water.
18 In his days Sennacherib invaded the
country;
he sent his commander[p] and departed;
he shook his fist against Zion,
and made great boasts in his
arrogance.
19 Then their hearts were shaken and
their hands trembled,
and they were in anguish, like
women in labor.
20 But they called upon the Lord who is
merciful,
spreading out their hands toward
him.
The Holy One quickly heard them
from heaven,
and delivered them through Isaiah.
21 The Lord[q] struck down the camp of
the Assyrians,
and his angel wiped them out.
22 For Hezekiah did what was pleasing to
the Lord,
and he kept firmly to the ways of
his ancestor David,
as he was commanded by the prophet
Isaiah,
who was great and trustworthy in
his visions.

Isaiah

23 In Isaiah's[r] days the sun went
backward,
and he prolonged the life of the
king.
24 By his dauntless spirit he saw the
future,
and comforted the mourners in
Zion.
25 He revealed what was to occur to the
end of time,
and the hidden things before they
happened.

[k] Heb: Gk *him* [l] Heb: Gk *are for reproofs* [m] Other ancient authorities read *and have died* [n] Text and meaning of Gk uncertain [o] Heb: Gk lacks *He performed . . . mouth* [p] Other ancient authorities add *from Lachish* [q] Gk *He* [r] Gk *his*

Josiah and Other Worthies

49 The name[s] of Josiah is like blended incense
prepared by the skill of the perfumer;
his memory[t] is as sweet as honey to every mouth,
and like music at a banquet of wine.
2 He did what was right by reforming the people,
and removing the wicked abominations.
3 He kept his heart fixed on the Lord;
in lawless times he made godliness prevail.

4 Except for David and Hezekiah and Josiah,
all of them were great sinners,
for they abandoned the law of the Most High;
the kings of Judah came to an end.
5 They[u] gave their power to others,
and their glory to a foreign nation,
6 who set fire to the chosen city of the sanctuary,
and made its streets desolate,
as Jeremiah had foretold.[v]
7 For they had mistreated him,
who even in the womb had been consecrated a prophet,
to pluck up and ruin and destroy,
and likewise to build and to plant.

8 It was Ezekiel who saw the vision of glory,
which God[w] showed him above the chariot of the cherubim.
9 For God[x] also mentioned Job
who held fast to all the ways of justice.[y]
10 May the bones of the Twelve Prophets send forth new life from where they lie,
for they comforted the people of Jacob
and delivered them with confident hope.

11 How shall we magnify Zerubbabel?
He was like a signet ring on the right hand,
12 and so was Jeshua son of Jozadak;

in their days they built the house
and raised a temple[z] holy to the Lord,
destined for everlasting glory.
13 The memory of Nehemiah also is lasting;
he raised our fallen walls,
and set up gates and bars,
and rebuilt our ruined houses.

Retrospect
14 Few have[a] ever been created on earth like Enoch,
for he was taken up from the earth.
15 Nor was anyone ever born like Joseph;[b]
even his bones were cared for.
16 Shem and Seth and Enosh were honored,[c]
but above every other created living being was Adam.

Simon Son of Onias

50 The leader of his brothers and the pride of his people[d]
was the high priest, Simon son of Onias,
who in his life repaired the house,
and in his time fortified the temple.
2 He laid the foundations for the high double walls,
the high retaining walls for the temple enclosure.
3 In his days a water cistern was dug,[e]
a reservoir like the sea in circumference.
4 He considered how to save his people from ruin,
and fortified the city against siege.
5 How glorious he was, surrounded by the people,
as he came out of the house of the curtain.
6 Like the morning star among the clouds,
like the full moon at the festal season;[e]
7 like the sun shining on the temple of the Most High,
like the rainbow gleaming in splendid clouds;
8 like roses in the days of first fruits,

---

[s] Heb: Gk *memory* [t] Heb: Gk *it* [u] Heb *He* [v] Gk *by the hand of Jeremiah* [w] Gk *He* [x] Gk *he* [y] Heb Compare
Syr: Meaning of Gk uncertain [z] Other ancient authorities read *people* [a] Heb Syr: Gk *No one has* [b] Heb Syr:
Gk adds *the leader of his brothers, the support of the people* [c] Heb: Gk *Shem and Seth were honored by people*
[d] Heb Syr: Gk lacks this line. Compare 49.15 [e] Heb: Meaning of Gk uncertain

like lilies by a spring of water,
like a green shoot on Lebanon on a
summer day;
9 like fire and incense in the censer,
like a vessel of hammered gold
studded with all kinds of precious
stones;
10 like an olive tree laden with fruit,
and like a cypress towering in the
clouds.
11 When he put on his glorious robe
and clothed himself in perfect
splendor,
when he went up to the holy altar,
he made the court of the sanctuary
glorious.

12 When he received the portions from
the hands of the priests,
as he stood by the hearth of the altar
with a garland of brothers around him,
he was like a young cedar on Lebanon
surrounded by the trunks of palm
trees.
13 All the sons of Aaron in their splendor
held the Lord's offering in their hands
before the whole congregation of Israel.
14 Finishing the service at the altars,*
and arranging the offering to the
Most High, the Almighty,
15 he held out his hand for the cup
and poured a drink offering of the
blood of the grape;
he poured it out at the foot of the altar,
a pleasing odor to the Most High,
the king of all.
16 Then the sons of Aaron shouted;
they blew their trumpets of
hammered metal;
they sounded a mighty fanfare
as a reminder before the Most High.
17 Then all the people together quickly
fell to the ground on their faces
to worship their Lord,
the Almighty, God Most High.

18 Then the singers praised him with
their voices
in sweet and full-toned melody.*
19 And the people of the Lord Most High
offered

their prayers before the Merciful One,
until the order of worship of the Lord
was ended,
and they completed his ritual.
20 Then Simon* came down and raised
his hands
over the whole congregation of
Israelites,
to pronounce the blessing of the Lord
with his lips,
and to glory in his name;
21 and they bowed down in worship a
second time,
to receive the blessing from the
Most High.

A Benediction
22 And now bless the God of all,
who everywhere works great wonders,
who fosters our growth from birth,
and deals with us according to his
mercy.
23 May he give us* gladness of heart,
and may there be peace in our* days
in Israel, as in the days of old.
24 May he entrust to us his mercy,
and may he deliver us in our* days!

Epilogue
25 Two nations my soul detests,
and the third is not even a people:
26 Those who live in Seir,* and the
Philistines,
and the foolish people that live in
Shechem.

27 Instruction in understanding and
knowledge
I have written in this book,
Jesus son of Eleazar son of Sirach* of
Jerusalem,
whose mind poured forth wisdom.
28 Happy are those who concern
themselves with these things,
and those who lay them to heart
will become wise.
29 For if they put them into practice,
they will be equal to anything,
for the fear* of the Lord is their path.

---

*Other ancient authorities read *altar*   *Other ancient authorities read *in sweet melody throughout the house*
*Gk *he*   *Other ancient authorities read *you*   *Other ancient authorities read *your*   *Other ancient
authorities read *his*   *Heb Compare Lat: Gk *on the mountain of Samaria*   *Heb: Meaning of Gk uncertain
*Heb: Other ancient authorities read *light*

PRAYER OF JESUS SON OF SIRACH[o]

51

I give you thanks, O Lord and King,
and praise you, O God my Savior.
I give thanks to your name,

2 for you have been my protector and helper
and have delivered me from destruction
and from the trap laid by a slanderous tongue,
from lips that fabricate lies.
In the face of my adversaries
you have been my helper ³and delivered me,
in the greatness of your mercy and of your name,
from grinding teeth about to devour me,
from the hand of those seeking my life,
from the many troubles I endured,

4 from choking fire on every side,
and from the midst of fire that I had not kindled,

5 from the deep belly of Hades,
from an unclean tongue and lying words—

6 the slander of an unrighteous tongue to the king.
My soul drew near to death,
and my life was on the brink of Hades below.

7 They surrounded me on every side,
and there was no one to help me;
I looked for human assistance,
and there was none.

8 Then I remembered your mercy, O Lord,
and your kindness[p] from of old,
for you rescue those who wait for you
and save them from the hand of their enemies.

9 And I sent up my prayer from the earth,
and begged for rescue from death.

10 I cried out, "Lord, you are my Father;[q]
do not forsake me in the days of trouble,
when there is no help against the proud.

11 I will praise your name continually,
and will sing hymns of thanksgiving."
My prayer was heard,

12 for you saved me from destruction

and rescued me in time of trouble.
For this reason I thank you and praise you,
and I bless the name of the Lord.

———

Heb adds:

*Give thanks to the LORD, for he is good,
for his mercy endures forever;*

*Give thanks to the God of praises,
for his mercy endures forever;*

*Give thanks to the guardian of Israel,
for his mercy endures forever;*

*Give thanks to him who formed all things,
for his mercy endures forever;*

*Give thanks to the redeemer of Israel,
for his mercy endures forever;*

*Give thanks to him who gathers the dispersed of Israel,
for his mercy endures forever;*

*Give thanks to him who rebuilt his city and his sanctuary,
for his mercy endures forever;*

*Give thanks to him who makes a horn to sprout for the house of David,
for his mercy endures forever;*

*Give thanks to him who has chosen the sons of Zadok to be priests,
for his mercy endures forever;*

*Give thanks to the shield of Abraham,
for his mercy endures forever;*

*Give thanks to the rock of Isaac,
for his mercy endures forever;*

*Give thanks to the mighty one of Jacob,
for his mercy endures forever;*

*Give thanks to him who has chosen Zion,
for his mercy endures forever;*

*Give thanks to the King of the kings of kings,
for his mercy endures forever;*

---

[o] This title is included in the Gk text. [p] Other ancient authorities read *work* [q] Heb: Gk *the Father of my lord*

He has raised up a horn for his people,
   praise for all his loyal ones.

For the children of Israel, the people close
   to him.
Praise the Lord!

Autobiographical Poem on Wisdom
¹³ While I was still young, before I went
   on my travels,
   I sought wisdom openly in my prayer.
¹⁴ Before the temple I asked for her,
   and I will search for her until the end.

¹⁵ From the first blossom to the ripening
   grape
   my heart delighted in her;
my foot walked on the straight path;
   from my youth I followed her steps.

¹⁶ I inclined my ear a little and received
   her,
   and I found for myself much
   instruction.
¹⁷ I made progress in her;
   to him who gives wisdom I will
   give glory.

¹⁸ For I resolved to live according to
   wisdom,ʳ
   and I was zealous for the good,
   and I shall never be disappointed.
¹⁹ My soul grappled with wisdom,ʳ
   and in my conduct I was strict;ˢ

I spread out my hands to the heavens,
   and lamented my ignorance of her.
²⁰ I directed my soul to her,
   and in purity I found her.

With her I gained understanding from
   the first;
   therefore I will never be forsaken.
²¹ My heart was stirred to seek her;
   therefore I have gained a prize
   possession.
²² The Lord gave me my tongue as a
   reward,
   and I will praise him with it.

²³ Draw near to me, you who are
   uneducated,
   and lodge in the house of
   instruction.
²⁴ Why do you say you are lacking in
   these things,ᵗ
   and why do you endure such great
   thirst?
²⁵ I opened my mouth and said,
   Acquire wisdomᵘ for yourselves
   without money.

²⁶ Put your neck under herᵛ yoke,
   and let your souls receive
   instruction;
   it is to be found close by.

²⁷ See with your own eyes that I have
   labored but little
   and found for myself much serenity.
²⁸ Hear but a little of my instruction,
   and through me you will acquire
   silver and gold.ʷ

²⁹ May your soul rejoice in God'sˣ mercy,
   and may you never be ashamed to
   praise him.
³⁰ Do your work in good time,
   and in his own time Godʸ will give
   you your reward.

ʳ Gk *her*   ˢ Meaning of Gk uncertain   ᵗ Cn Compare Heb Syr: Meaning of Gk uncertain   ᵘ Heb: Gk lacks
wisdom   ᵛ Heb: other ancient authorities read *the*   ʷ Syr Compare Heb: Gk *Get instruction with a large sum of*
silver, and you will gain by it much gold.   ˣ Gk *his*   ʸ Gk *he*

BARUCH

Baruch and the Jews in Babylon

1 These are the words of the book that Baruch son of Neriah son of Mahseiah son of Zedekiah son of Hasadiah son of Hilkiah wrote in Babylon, [2]in the fifth year, on the seventh day of the month, at the time when the Chaldeans took Jerusalem and burned it with fire.

3 Baruch read the words of this book to Jeconiah son of Jehoiakim, king of Judah, and to all the people who came to hear the book, [4]and to the nobles and the princes, and to the elders, and to all the people, small and great, all who lived in Babylon by the river Sud.

5 Then they wept, and fasted, and prayed before the Lord; [6]they collected as much money as each could give, [7]and sent it to Jerusalem to the high priest[a] Jehoiakim son of Hilkiah son of Shallum, and to the priests, and to all the people who were present with him in Jerusalem. [8]At the same time, on the tenth day of Sivan, Baruch[b] took the vessels of the house of the Lord, which had been carried away from the temple, to return them to the land of Judah—the silver vessels that Zedekiah son of Josiah, king of Judah, had made, [9]after King Nebuchadnezzar of Babylon had carried away from Jerusalem Jeconiah and the princes and the prisoners and the nobles and the people of the land, and brought them to Babylon.

A Letter to Jerusalem

10 They said: Here we send you money; so buy with the money burnt offerings and sin offerings and incense, and prepare a grain offering, and offer them on the altar of the Lord our God; [11]and pray for the life of King Nebuchadnezzar of Babylon, and for the life of his son Belshazzar, so that their days on earth may be like the days of heaven. [12]The Lord will give us strength, and light to our eyes; we shall live under the protection[c] of King Nebuchadnezzar of Babylon, and under the protection of his son Belshazzar, and we shall serve them many days and find favor in their sight. [13]Pray also for us to the Lord our God, for we have sinned against the Lord our God, and to this day the anger of the Lord and his wrath have not turned away from us.

[14]And you shall read aloud this scroll that we are sending you, to make your confession in the house of the Lord on the days of the festivals and at appointed seasons.

Confession of Sins

15 And you shall say: The Lord our God is in the right, but there is open shame on us today, on the people of Judah, on the inhabitants of Jerusalem, [16]and on our kings, our rulers, our priests, our prophets, and our ancestors, [17]because we have sinned before the Lord. [18]We have disobeyed him, and have not heeded the voice of the Lord our God, to walk in the statutes of the Lord that he set before us. [19]From the time when the Lord brought our ancestors out of the land of Egypt until today, we have been disobedient to the Lord our God, and we have been negligent, in not heeding his voice. [20]So to this day there have clung to us the calamities and the curse that the Lord declared through his servant Moses at the time when he brought our ancestors out of the land of Egypt to give to us a land flowing with milk and honey. [21]We did not listen to the voice of the Lord our God in all the words of the prophets whom he sent to us, [22]but all of us followed the intent of our own wicked hearts by serving other gods and doing what is evil in the sight of the Lord our God.

2 So the Lord carried out the threat he spoke against us: against our judges who ruled Israel, and against our kings and our rulers and the people of Israel and Judah. [2]Under the whole heaven there has not been done the like of what he has done in Jerusalem, in accordance with the threats that were[d] written in the law of Moses. [3]Some of us ate the flesh of their sons and others the flesh of their daughters. [4]He made them subject to all the kingdoms around us, to be an object of scorn and a desolation among all the surrounding peoples, where the Lord has scattered them. [5]They were brought down and not raised up, because our nation[e] sinned against the Lord our God, in not heeding his voice.

6 The Lord our God is in the right, but there is open shame on us and our ancestors this very day. [7]All those calamities with

---

a Gk *the priest*   *b* Gk *he*   *c* Gk *in the shadow*   *d* Gk *in accordance with what is*   *e* Gk *because we* which the Lord threatened us have come upon us. ⁸Yet we have not entreated the favor of the Lord by turning away, each of us, from the thoughts of our wicked hearts. ⁹And the Lord has kept the calamities ready, and the Lord has brought them upon us, for the Lord is just in all the works that he has commanded us to do. ¹⁰Yet we have not obeyed his voice, to walk in the statutes of the Lord that he set before us.

Prayer for Deliverance

11 And now, O Lord God of Israel, who brought your people out of the land of Egypt with a mighty hand and with signs and wonders and with great power and outstretched arm, and made yourself a name that continues to this day, ¹²we have sinned, we have been ungodly, we have done wrong, O Lord our God, against all your ordinances. ¹³Let your anger turn away from us, for we are left, few in number, among the nations where you have scattered us. ¹⁴Hear, O Lord, our prayer and our supplication, and for your own sake deliver us, and grant us favor in the sight of those who have carried us into exile; ¹⁵so that all the earth may know that you are the Lord our God, for Israel and his descendants are called by your name.

16 O Lord, look down from your holy dwelling, and consider us. Incline your ear, O Lord, and hear; ¹⁷open your eyes, O Lord, and see, for the dead who are in Hades, whose spirit has been taken from their bodies, will not ascribe glory or justice to the Lord; ¹⁸but the person who is deeply grieved, who walks bowed and feeble, with failing eyes and famished soul, will declare your glory and righteousness, O Lord.

19 For it is not because of any righteous deeds of our ancestors or our kings that we bring before you our prayer for mercy, O Lord our God. ²⁰For you have sent your anger and your wrath upon us, as you declared by your servants the prophets, saying: ²¹Thus says the Lord: Bend your shoulders and serve the king of Babylon, and you will remain in the land that I gave to your ancestors. ²²But if you will not obey the voice of the Lord and will not serve the king of Babylon, ²³I will make to cease from the towns of Judah and from the region around Jerusalem the voice of mirth and the voice of gladness, the voice of the bride-

groom and the voice of the bride, and the whole land will be a desolation without inhabitants.

24 But we did not obey your voice, to serve the king of Babylon; and you have carried out your threats, which you spoke by your servants the prophets, that the bones of our kings and the bones of our ancestors would be brought out of their resting place; ²⁵and indeed they have been thrown out to the heat of day and the frost of night. They perished in great misery, by famine and sword and pestilence. ²⁶And the house that is called by your name you have made as it is today, because of the wickedness of the house of Israel and the house of Judah.

God's Promise Recalled

27 Yet you have dealt with us, O Lord our God, in all your kindness and in all your great compassion, ²⁸as you spoke by your servant Moses on the day when you commanded him to write your law in the presence of the people of Israel, saying, ²⁹"If you will not obey my voice, this very great multitude will surely turn into a small number among the nations, where I will scatter them. ³⁰For I know that they will not obey me, for they are a stiff-necked people. But in the land of their exile they will come to themselves ³¹and know that I am the Lord their God. I will give them a heart that obeys and ears that hear; ³²they will praise me in the land of their exile, and will remember my name ³³and turn from their stubbornness and their wicked deeds; for they will remember the ways of their ancestors, who sinned before the Lord. ³⁴I will bring them again into the land that I swore to give to their ancestors, to Abraham, Isaac, and Jacob, and they will rule over it; and I will increase them, and they will not be diminished. ³⁵I will make an everlasting covenant with them to be their God and they shall be my people; and I will never again remove my people Israel from the land that I have given them."

3 O Lord Almighty, God of Israel, the soul in anguish and the wearied spirit cry out to you. ²Hear, O Lord, and have mercy, for we have sinned before you. ³For you are enthroned forever, and we are perishing forever. ⁴O Lord Almighty, God of Israel, hear now the prayer of the people*ᶠ*

ᶠ Gk dead

of Israel, the children of those who sinned before you, who did not heed the voice of the Lord their God, so that calamities have clung to us. ⁵Do not remember the iniquities of our ancestors, but in this crisis remember your power and your name. ⁶For you are the Lord our God, and it is you, O Lord, whom we will praise. ⁷For you have put the fear of you in our hearts so that we would call upon your name; and we will praise you in our exile, for we have put away from our hearts all the iniquity of our ancestors who sinned against you. ⁸See, we are today in our exile where you have scattered us, to be reproached and cursed and punished for all the iniquities of our ancestors, who forsook the Lord our God.

In Praise of Wisdom

9 Hear the commandments of life,
    O Israel;
  give ear, and learn wisdom!
¹⁰ Why is it, O Israel, why is it that you
    are in the land of your
    enemies,
  that you are growing old in a
    foreign country,
  that you are defiled with the dead,
¹¹   that you are counted among those
    in Hades?
¹² You have forsaken the fountain of
    wisdom.
¹³ If you had walked in the way of God,
    you would be living in peace
    forever.
¹⁴ Learn where there is wisdom,
    where there is strength,
    where there is understanding,
  so that you may at the same time
    discern
    where there is length of days, and
    life,
    where there is light for the eyes,
    and peace.

¹⁵ Who has found her place?
    And who has entered her
    storehouses?
¹⁶ Where are the rulers of the nations,
    and those who lorded it over the
    animals on earth;
¹⁷ those who made sport of the birds of
    the air,
    and who hoarded up silver and gold
    in which people trust,

    and there is no end to their getting;
¹⁸ those who schemed to get silver, and
    were anxious,
    but there is no trace of their works?
¹⁹ They have vanished and gone down
    to Hades,
    and others have arisen in their
    place.

²⁰ Later generations have seen the light
    of day,
    and have lived upon the earth;
  but they have not learned the way to
    knowledge,
    nor understood her paths,
    nor laid hold of her.
²¹ Their descendants have strayed far
    from her*ᵍ* way.
²² She has not been heard of in Canaan,
    or seen in Teman;
²³ the descendants of Hagar, who seek
    for understanding on the earth,
    the merchants of Merran and
    Teman,
    the story-tellers and the seekers for
    understanding,
  have not learned the way to wisdom,
    or given thought to her paths.

²⁴ O Israel, how great is the house of
    God,
    how vast the territory that he
    possesses!
²⁵ It is great and has no bounds;
    it is high and immeasurable.
²⁶ The giants were born there, who were
    famous of old,
    great in stature, expert in war.
²⁷ God did not choose them,
    or give them the way to knowledge;
²⁸ so they perished because they had no
    wisdom,
    they perished through their folly.

²⁹ Who has gone up into heaven, and
    taken her,
    and brought her down from the
    clouds?
³⁰ Who has gone over the sea, and
    found her,
    and will buy her for pure gold?
³¹ No one knows the way to her,
    or is concerned about the path to
    her.
³² But the one who knows all things
    knows her,

*ᵍ Other ancient authorities read *their*

he found her by his understanding.
The one who prepared the earth for
all time
filled it with four-footed creatures;
³³ the one who sends forth the light, and
it goes;
he called it, and it obeyed him,
trembling;
³⁴ the stars shone in their watches, and
were glad;
he called them, and they said, "Here
we are!"
They shone with gladness for him
who made them.
³⁵ This is our God;
no other can be compared to him.
³⁶ He found the whole way to
knowledge,
and gave her to his servant Jacob
and to Israel, whom he loved.
³⁷ Afterward she appeared on earth
and lived with humankind.

4 She is the book of the commandments
of God,
the law that endures forever.
All who hold her fast will live,
and those who forsake her will die.
² Turn, O Jacob, and take her;
walk toward the shining of her light.
³ Do not give your glory to another,
or your advantages to an alien people.
⁴ Happy are we, O Israel,
for we know what is pleasing to God.

Encouragement for Israel
⁵ Take courage, my people,
who perpetuate Israel's name!
⁶ It was not for destruction
that you were sold to the nations,
but you were handed over to your enemies
because you angered God.
⁷ For you provoked the one who made you
by sacrificing to demons and not to
God.
⁸ You forgot the everlasting God, who
brought you up,
and you grieved Jerusalem, who
reared you.
⁹ For she saw the wrath that came
upon you from God,
and she said:
Listen, you neighbors of Zion,
God has brought great sorrow upon
me;

¹⁰ for I have seen the exile of my sons
and daughters,
which the Everlasting brought upon
them.
¹¹ With joy I nurtured them,
but I sent them away with weeping
and sorrow.
¹² Let no one rejoice over me, a widow
and bereaved of many;
I was left desolate because of the sins
of my children,
because they turned away from the
law of God.
¹³ They had no regard for his statutes;
they did not walk in the ways of
God's commandments,
or tread the paths his righteousness
showed them.
¹⁴ Let the neighbors of Zion come;
remember the capture of my sons
and daughters,
which the Everlasting brought upon
them.
¹⁵ For he brought a distant nation
against them,
a nation ruthless and of a strange
language,
which had no respect for the aged
and no pity for a child.
¹⁶ They led away the widow's beloved sons,
and bereaved the lonely woman of
her daughters.

¹⁷ But I, how can I help you?
¹⁸ For he who brought these calamities
upon you
will deliver you from the hand of
your enemies.
¹⁹ Go, my children, go;
for I have been left desolate.
²⁰ I have taken off the robe of peace
and put on sackcloth for my
supplication;
I will cry to the Everlasting all my
days.

²¹ Take courage, my children, cry to God,
and he will deliver you from the
power and hand of the enemy.
²² For I have put my hope in the
Everlasting to save you,
and joy has come to me from the
Holy One,
because of the mercy that will soon
come to you
from your everlasting savior.^h

^h Or from the Everlasting, your savior

²³ For I sent you out with sorrow and
weeping,
but God will give you back to me
with joy and gladness forever.
²⁴ For as the neighbors of Zion have
now seen your capture,
so they soon will see your salvation
by God,
which will come to you with great glory
and with the splendor of the
Everlasting.
²⁵ My children, endure with patience the
wrath that has come upon you
from God.
Your enemy has overtaken you,
but you will soon see their destruction
and will tread upon their necks.
²⁶ My pampered children have traveled
rough roads;
they were taken away like a flock
carried off by the enemy.

²⁷ Take courage, my children, and cry to
God,
for you will be remembered by the one
who brought this upon you.
²⁸ For just as you were disposed to go
astray from God,
return with tenfold zeal to seek him.
²⁹ For the one who brought these
calamities upon you
will bring you everlasting joy with
your salvation.

Jerusalem Is Assured of Help
³⁰ Take courage, O Jerusalem,
for the one who named you will
comfort you.
³¹ Wretched will be those who mistreated
you
and who rejoiced at your fall.
³² Wretched will be the cities that your
children served as slaves;
wretched will be the city that
received your offspring.
³³ For just as she rejoiced at your fall
and was glad for your ruin,
so she will be grieved at her own
desolation.
³⁴ I will take away her pride in her
great population,
and her insolence will be turned to
grief.
³⁵ For fire will come upon her from the
Everlasting for many days,

and for a long time she will be
inhabited by demons.

³⁶ Look toward the east, O Jerusalem,
and see the joy that is coming to
you from God.
³⁷ Look, your children are coming, whom
you sent away;
they are coming, gathered from east
and west,
at the word of the Holy One,
rejoicing in the glory of God.

5 Take off the garment of your sorrow
and affliction, O Jerusalem,
and put on forever the beauty of
the glory from God.
² Put on the robe of the righteousness
that comes from God;
put on your head the diadem of the
glory of the Everlasting;
³ for God will show your splendor
everywhere under heaven.
⁴ For God will give you evermore the
name,
"Righteous Peace, Godly Glory."

⁵ Arise, O Jerusalem, stand upon the
height;
look toward the east,
and see your children gathered from
west and east
at the word of the Holy One,
rejoicing that God has remembered
them.
⁶ For they went out from you on foot,
led away by their enemies;
but God will bring them back to you,
carried in glory, as on a royal
throne.
⁷ For God has ordered that every high
mountain and the everlasting
hills be made low
and the valleys filled up, to make
level ground,
so that Israel may walk safely in
the glory of God.
⁸ The woods and every fragrant tree
have shaded Israel at God's
command.
⁹ For God will lead Israel with joy,
in the light of his glory,
with the mercy and righteousness
that come from him.

THE LETTER OF JEREMIAH

6 [a] A copy of a letter that Jeremiah sent to those who were to be taken to Babylon as exiles by the king of the Babylonians, to give them the message that God had commanded him.

The People Face a Long Captivity

2 Because of the sins that you have committed before God, you will be taken to Babylon as exiles by Nebuchadnezzar, king of the Babylonians. [3]Therefore when you have come to Babylon you will remain there for many years, for a long time, up to seven generations; after that I will bring you away from there in peace. [4]Now in Babylon you will see gods made of silver and gold and wood, which people carry on their shoulders, and which cause the heathen to fear. [5]So beware of becoming at all like the foreigners or of letting fear for these gods[b] possess you [6]when you see the multitude before and behind them worshiping them. But say in your heart, "It is you, O Lord, whom we must worship." [7]For my angel is with you, and he is watching over your lives.

The Helplessness of Idols

8 Their tongues are smoothed by the carpenter, and they themselves are overlaid with gold and silver; but they are false and cannot speak. [9]People[c] take gold and make crowns for the heads of their gods, as they might for a girl who loves ornaments. [10]Sometimes the priests secretly take gold and silver from their gods and spend it on themselves, [11]or even give some of it to the prostitutes on the terrace. They deck their gods[d] out with garments like human beings—these gods of silver and gold and wood [12]that cannot save themselves from rust and corrosion. When they have been dressed in purple robes, [13]their faces are wiped because of the dust from the temple, which is thick upon them. [14]One of them holds a scepter, like a district judge, but is unable to destroy anyone who offends it. [15]Another has a dagger in its right hand, and an ax, but cannot defend itself from war and robbers. [16]From this it is evident that they are not gods; so do not fear them.

17 For just as someone's dish is useless when it is broken, [18]so are their gods when they have been set up in the temples. Their eyes are full of the dust raised by the feet of those who enter. And just as the gates are shut on every side against anyone who has offended a king, as though under sentence of death, so the priests make their temples secure with doors and locks and bars, in order that they may not be plundered by robbers. [19]They light more lamps for them than they light for themselves, though their gods[e] can see none of them. [20]They are[f] just like a beam of the temple, but their hearts, it is said, are eaten away when crawling creatures from the earth devour them and their robes. They do not notice [21]when their faces have been blackened by the smoke of the temple. [22]Bats, swallows, and birds alight on their bodies and heads; and so do cats. [23]From this you will know that they are not gods; so do not fear them.

24 As for the gold that they wear for beauty—it[g] will not shine unless someone wipes off the tarnish; for even when they were being cast, they did not feel it. [25]They are bought without regard to cost, but there is no breath in them. [26]Having no feet, they are carried on the shoulders of others, revealing to humankind their worthlessness. And those who serve them are put to shame [27]because, if any of these gods falls[h] to the ground, they themselves must pick it up. If anyone sets it upright, it cannot move itself; and if it is tipped over, it cannot straighten itself. Gifts are placed before them just as before the dead. [28]The priests sell the sacrifices that are offered to these gods[i] and use the money themselves. Likewise their wives preserve some of the meat[j] with salt, but give none to the poor or helpless. [29]Sacrifices to them may even be touched by women in their periods or at childbirth. Since you know by these things that they are not gods, do not fear them.

30 For how can they be called gods?

---

[a] The King James Version (like the Latin Vulgate) prints The Letter of Jeremiah as Chapter 6 of the Book of Baruch, and the chapter and verse numbers are here retained. In the Greek Septuagint, the Letter is separated from Baruch by the Book of Lamentations. [b] Gk *for them* [c] Gk *They* [d] Gk *them* [e] Gk *they* [f] Gk *It is* [g] Lat Syr: Gk *they* [h] Gk *if they fall* [i] Gk *to them* [j] Gk *of them*

Women serve meals for gods of silver and gold and wood; [31]and in their temples the priests sit with their clothes torn, their heads and beards shaved, and their heads uncovered. [32]They howl and shout before their gods as some do at a funeral banquet. [33]The priests take some of the clothing of their gods[k] to clothe their wives and children. [34]Whether one does evil to them or good, they will not be able to repay it. They cannot set up a king or depose one. [35]Likewise they are not able to give either wealth or money; if one makes a vow to them and does not keep it, they will not require it. [36]They cannot save anyone from death or rescue the weak from the strong. [37]They cannot restore sight to the blind; they cannot rescue one who is in distress. [38]They cannot take pity on a widow or do good to an orphan. [39]These things that are made of wood and overlaid with gold and silver are like stones from the mountain, and those who serve them will be put to shame. [40]Why then must anyone think that they are gods, or call them gods?

The Foolishness of Worshiping Idols

Besides, even the Chaldeans themselves dishonor them; for when they see someone who cannot speak, they bring Bel and pray that the mute may speak, as though Bel[l] were able to understand! [41]Yet they themselves cannot perceive this and abandon them, for they have no sense. [42]And the women, with cords around them, sit along the passageways, burning bran for incense. [43]When one of them is led off by one of the passers-by and is taken to bed by him, she derides the woman next to her, because she was not as attractive as herself and her cord was not broken. [44]Whatever is done for these idols[m] is false. Why then must anyone think that they are gods, or call them gods?

45 They are made by carpenters and goldsmiths; they can be nothing but what the artisans wish them to be. [46]Those who make them will certainly not live very long themselves; [47]how then can the things that are made by them be gods? They have left only lies and reproach for those who come after. [48]For when war or calamity comes upon them, the priests consult together as to where they can hide themselves and their gods.[m] [49]How then can one fail to see that these are not gods, for they cannot

save themselves from war or calamity? [50]Since they are made of wood and overlaid with gold and silver, it will afterward be known that they are false. [51]It will be manifest to all the nations and kings that they are not gods but the work of human hands, and that there is no work of God in them. [52]Who then can fail to know that they are not gods?[n]

53 For they cannot set up a king over a country or give rain to people. [54]They cannot judge their own cause or deliver one who is wronged, for they have no power; [55]they are like crows between heaven and earth. When fire breaks out in a temple of wooden gods overlaid with gold or silver, their priests will flee and escape, but the gods[o] will be burned up like timbers. [56]Besides, they can offer no resistance to king or enemy. Why then must anyone admit or think that they are gods?

57 Gods made of wood and overlaid with silver and gold are unable to save themselves from thieves or robbers. [58]Anyone who can will strip them of their gold and silver and of the robes they wear, and go off with this booty, and they will not be able to help themselves. [59]So it is better to be a king who shows his courage, or a household utensil that serves its owner's need, than to be these false gods; better even the door of a house that protects its contents, than these false gods; better also a wooden pillar in a palace, than these false gods.

60 For sun and moon and stars are bright, and when sent to do a service, they are obedient. [61]So also the lightning, when it flashes, is widely seen; and the wind likewise blows in every land. [62]When God commands the clouds to go over the whole world, they carry out his command. [63]And the fire sent from above to consume mountains and woods does what it is ordered. But these idols[p] are not to be compared with them in appearance or power. [64]Therefore one must not think that they are gods, nor call them gods, for they are not able either to decide a case or to do good to anyone. [65]Since you know then that they are not gods, do not fear them.

66 They can neither curse nor bless kings; [67]they cannot show signs in the heavens for the nations, or shine like the sun or give light like the moon. [68]The wild animals are better than they are, for they can flee to shelter and help themselves. [69]So we have

---

[k] Gk *some of their clothing*   [l] Gk *he*   [m] Gk *them*   [n] Meaning of Gk uncertain   [o] Gk *they*   [p] Gk *these things*

no evidence whatever that they are gods; therefore do not fear them.

70 Like a scarecrow in a cucumber bed, which guards nothing, so are their gods of wood, overlaid with gold and silver. [71]In the same way, their gods of wood, overlaid with gold and silver, are like a thornbush in a garden on which every bird perches; or like a corpse thrown out in the darkness. [72]From the purple and linen[q] that rot upon them you will know that they are not gods; and they will finally be consumed themselves, and be a reproach in the land. [73]Better, therefore, is someone upright who has no idols; such a person will be far above reproach.

[q] Cn: Gk *marble*, Syr *silk*

THE PRAYER OF

AZARIAH

AND THE SONG OF THE THREE JEWS

(Additions to Daniel, inserted between 3.23 and 3.24)

The Prayer of Azariah in the Furnace
1 They[a] walked around in the midst of the flames, singing hymns to God and blessing the Lord. [2]Then Azariah stood still in the fire and prayed aloud:
[3] "Blessed are you, O Lord, God of our
   ancestors, and worthy of praise;
   and glorious is your name forever!
[4] For you are just in all you have done;
   all your works are true and your
     ways right,
   and all your judgments are true.
[5] You have executed true judgments in
   all you have brought upon us
   and upon Jerusalem, the holy city of
     our ancestors;
   by a true judgment you have
     brought all this upon us
     because of our sins.
[6] For we have sinned and broken your
   law in turning away from you;
   in all matters we have sinned
     grievously.
[7] We have not obeyed your
   commandments,
   we have not kept them or done

   what you have commanded us
     for our own good.
[8] So all that you have brought upon us,
   and all that you have done to us,
   you have done by a true judgment.
[9] You have handed us over to our enemies,
   lawless and hateful rebels,
   and to an unjust king, the most
     wicked in all the world.
[10] And now we cannot open our mouths;
   we, your servants who worship you,
     have become a shame and a
     reproach.
[11] For your name's sake do not give us
     up forever,
   and do not annul your covenant.
[12] Do not withdraw your mercy from us,
   for the sake of Abraham your beloved
   and for the sake of your servant
     Isaac
   and Israel your holy one,
[13] to whom you promised
   to multiply their descendants like
     the stars of heaven
   and like the sand on the shore of
     the sea.
[14] For we, O Lord, have become fewer
     than any other nation,
   and are brought low this day in all
     the world because of our sins.

[a] That is, Hananiah, Mishael, and Azariah (Dan 2.17), the original names of Shadrach, Meshach, and Abednego (Dan 1.6–7)

¹⁵ In our day we have no ruler, or
     prophet, or leader,
   no burnt offering, or sacrifice, or
     oblation, or incense,
   no place to make an offering before
     you and to find mercy.
¹⁶ Yet with a contrite heart and a
     humble spirit may we be
     accepted,
¹⁷ as though it were with burnt
     offerings of rams and bulls,
   or with tens of thousands of fat
     lambs;
   such may our sacrifice be in your
     sight today,
   and may we unreservedly follow
     you,ᵇ
   for no shame will come to those
     who trust in you.
¹⁸ And now with all our heart we follow
     you;
   we fear you and seek your presence.
¹⁹ Do not put us to shame,
   but deal with us in your patience
   and in your abundant mercy.
²⁰ Deliver us in accordance with your
     marvelous works,
   and bring glory to your name,
     O Lord.
²¹ Let all who do harm to your servants
     be put to shame;
   let them be disgraced and deprived
     of all power,
   and let their strength be broken.
²² Let them know that you alone are the
     Lord God,
   glorious over the whole world."

The Song of the Three Jews

23 Now the king's servants who threw
them in kept stoking the furnace with
naphtha, pitch, tow, and brushwood.
²⁴And the flames poured out above the furnace forty-nine cubits, ²⁵and spread out
and burned those Chaldeans who were
caught near the furnace. ²⁶But the angel of
the Lord came down into the furnace to be
with Azariah and his companions, and
drove the fiery flame out of the furnace,
²⁷and made the inside of the furnace as
though a moist wind were whistling
through it. The fire did not touch them at
all and caused them no pain or distress.
    28 Then the three with one voice praised

and glorified and blessed God in the furnace:
²⁹ "Blessed are you, O Lord, God of our
     ancestors,
   and to be praised and highly exalted
     forever;
³⁰ And blessed is your glorious, holy name,
   and to be highly praised and highly
     exalted forever.
³¹ Blessed are you in the temple of your
     holy glory,
   and to be extolled and highly
     glorified forever.
³² Blessed are you who look into the
     depths from your throne on the
     cherubim,
   and to be praised and highly exalted
     forever.
³³ Blessed are you on the throne of your
     kingdom,
   and to be extolled and highly
     exalted forever.
³⁴ Blessed are you in the firmament of
     heaven,
   and to be sung and glorified forever.

³⁵ "Bless the Lord, all you works of the
     Lord;
   sing praise to him and highly exalt
     him forever.
³⁶ Bless the Lord, you heavens;
   sing praise to him and highly exalt
     him forever.
³⁷ Bless the Lord, you angels of the Lord;
   sing praise to him and highly exalt
     him forever.
³⁸ Bless the Lord, all you waters above
     the heavens;
   sing praise to him and highly exalt
     him forever.
³⁹ Bless the Lord, all you powers of the
     Lord;
   sing praise to him and highly exalt
     him forever.
⁴⁰ Bless the Lord, sun and moon;
   sing praise to him and highly exalt
     him forever.
⁴¹ Bless the Lord, stars of heaven;
   sing praise to him and highly exalt
     him forever.

⁴² "Bless the Lord, all rain and dew;
   sing praise to him and highly exalt
     him forever.
⁴³ Bless the Lord, all you winds;
   sing praise to him and highly exalt
     him forever.

ᵇ Meaning of Gk uncertain

122

44 Bless the Lord, fire and heat;
  sing praise to him and highly exalt
    him forever.
45 Bless the Lord, winter cold and
    summer heat;
  sing praise to him and highly exalt
    him forever.
46 Bless the Lord, dews and falling snow;
  sing praise to him and highly exalt
    him forever.
47 Bless the Lord, nights and days;
  sing praise to him and highly exalt
    him forever.
48 Bless the Lord, light and darkness;
  sing praise to him and highly exalt
    him forever.
49 Bless the Lord, ice and cold;
  sing praise to him and highly exalt
    him forever.
50 Bless the Lord, frosts and snows;
  sing praise to him and highly exalt
    him forever.
51 Bless the Lord, lightnings and clouds;
  sing praise to him and highly exalt
    him forever.

52 "Let the earth bless the Lord;
  let it sing praise to him and highly
    exalt him forever.
53 Bless the Lord, mountains and hills;
  sing praise to him and highly exalt
    him forever.
54 Bless the Lord, all that grows in the
    ground;
  sing praise to him and highly exalt
    him forever.
55 Bless the Lord, seas and rivers;
  sing praise to him and highly exalt
    him forever.
56 Bless the Lord, you springs;
  sing praise to him and highly exalt
    him forever.
57 Bless the Lord, you whales and all
    that swim in the waters;
  sing praise to him and highly exalt
    him forever.

58 Bless the Lord, all birds of the air;
  sing praise to him and highly exalt
    him forever.
59 Bless the Lord, all wild animals and cattle;
  sing praise to him and highly exalt
    him forever.

60 "Bless the Lord, all people on earth;
  sing praise to him and highly exalt
    him forever.
61 Bless the Lord, O Israel;
  sing praise to him and highly exalt
    him forever.
62 Bless the Lord, you priests of the Lord;
  sing praise to him and highly exalt
    him forever.
63 Bless the Lord, you servants of the Lord;
  sing praise to him and highly exalt
    him forever.
64 Bless the Lord, spirits and souls of the
    righteous;
  sing praise to him and highly exalt
    him forever.
65 Bless the Lord, you who are holy and
    humble in heart;
  sing praise to him and highly exalt
    him forever.

66 "Bless the Lord, Hananiah, Azariah,
    and Mishael;
  sing praise to him and highly exalt
    him forever.
  For he has rescued us from Hades and
    saved us from the power^c of
    death,
  and delivered us from the midst of
    the burning fiery furnace;
  from the midst of the fire he has
    delivered us.
67 Give thanks to the Lord, for he is good,
  for his mercy endures forever.
68 All who worship the Lord, bless the
    God of gods,
  sing praise to him and give thanks
    to him,
  for his mercy endures forever."

^{c} Gk *hand*

123

SUSANNA

(Chapter 13 of the Greek Version of Daniel)

Susanna's Beauty Attracts Two Elders

1 There was a man living in Babylon whose name was Joakim. [2]He married the daughter of Hilkiah, named Susanna, a very beautiful woman and one who feared the Lord. [3]Her parents were righteous, and had trained their daughter according to the law of Moses. [4]Joakim was very rich, and had a fine garden adjoining his house; the Jews used to come to him because he was the most honored of them all.

5 That year two elders from the people were appointed as judges. Concerning them the Lord had said: "Wickedness came forth from Babylon, from elders who were judges, who were supposed to govern the people." [6]These men were frequently at Joakim's house, and all who had a case to be tried came to them there.

7 When the people left at noon, Susanna would go into her husband's garden to walk. [8]Every day the two elders used to see her, going in and walking about, and they began to lust for her. [9]They suppressed their consciences and turned away their eyes from looking to Heaven or remembering their duty to administer justice. [10]Both were overwhelmed with passion for her, but they did not tell each other of their distress, [11]for they were ashamed to disclose their lustful desire to seduce her. [12]Day after day they watched eagerly to see her.

13 One day they said to each other, "Let us go home, for it is time for lunch." So they both left and parted from each other. [14]But turning back, they met again; and when each pressed the other for the reason, they confessed their lust. Then together they arranged for a time when they could find her alone.

The Elders Attempt to Seduce Susanna

15 Once, while they were watching for an opportune day, she went in as before with only two maids, and wished to bathe in the garden, for it was a hot day. [16]No one was there except the two elders, who had hidden themselves and were watching her. [17]She said to her maids, "Bring me olive oil and ointments, and shut the garden doors

so that I can bathe." [18]They did as she told them: they shut the doors of the garden and went out by the side doors to bring what they had been commanded; they did not see the elders, because they were hiding.

19 When the maids had gone out, the two elders got up and ran to her. [20]They said, "Look, the garden doors are shut, and no one can see us. We are burning with desire for you; so give your consent, and lie with us. [21]If you refuse, we will testify against you that a young man was with you, and this was why you sent your maids away."

22 Susanna groaned and said, "I am completely trapped. For if I do this, it will mean death for me; if I do not, I cannot escape your hands. [23]I choose not to do it; I will fall into your hands, rather than sin in the sight of the Lord."

24 Then Susanna cried out with a loud voice, and the two elders shouted against her. [25]And one of them ran and opened the garden doors. [26]When the people in the house heard the shouting in the garden, they rushed in at the side door to see what had happened to her. [27]And when the elders told their story, the servants felt very much ashamed, for nothing like this had ever been said about Susanna.

The Elders Testify against Susanna

28 The next day, when the people gathered at the house of her husband Joakim, the two elders came, full of their wicked plot to have Susanna put to death. In the presence of the people they said, [29]"Send for Susanna daughter of Hilkiah, the wife of Joakim." [30]So they sent for her. And she came with her parents, her children, and all her relatives.

31 Now Susanna was a woman of great refinement and beautiful in appearance. [32]As she was veiled, the scoundrels ordered her to be unveiled, so that they might feast their eyes on her beauty. [33]Those who were with her and all who saw her were weeping.

34 Then the two elders stood up before the people and laid their hands on her head. [35]Through her tears she looked up toward

Heaven, for her heart trusted in the Lord. [36]The elders said, "While we were walking in the garden alone, this woman came in with two maids, shut the garden doors, and dismissed the maids. [37]Then a young man, who was hiding there, came to her and lay with her. [38]We were in a corner of the garden, and when we saw this wickedness we ran to them. [39]Although we saw them embracing, we could not hold the man, because he was stronger than we, and he opened the doors and got away. [40]We did, however, seize this woman and asked who the young man was, [41]but she would not tell us. These things we testify."

Because they were elders of the people and judges, the assembly believed them and condemned her to death.

42 Then Susanna cried out with a loud voice, and said, "O eternal God, you know what is secret and are aware of all things before they come to be; [43]you know that these men have given false evidence against me. And now I am to die, though I have done none of the wicked things that they have charged against me!"

44 The Lord heard her cry. [45]Just as she was being led off to execution, God stirred up the holy spirit of a young lad named Daniel, [46]and he shouted with a loud voice, "I want no part in shedding this woman's blood!"

Daniel Rescues Susanna

47 All the people turned to him and asked, "What is this you are saying?" [48]Taking his stand among them he said, "Are you such fools, O Israelites, as to condemn a daughter of Israel without examination and without learning the facts? [49]Return to court, for these men have given false evidence against her."

50 So all the people hurried back. And the rest of the[a] elders said to him, "Come, sit among us and inform us, for God has given you the standing of an elder." [51]Daniel said to them, "Separate them far from each other, and I will examine them."

52 When they were separated from each other, he summoned one of them and said to him, "You old relic of wicked days, your sins have now come home, which you have committed in the past, [53]pronouncing unjust judgments, condemning the innocent and acquitting the guilty, though the Lord said, 'You shall not put an innocent and righteous person to death.' [54]Now then, if you really saw this woman, tell me this: Under what tree did you see them being intimate with each other?" He answered, "Under a mastic tree."[b] [55]And Daniel said, "Very well! This lie has cost you your head, for the angel of God has received the sentence from God and will immediately cut[b] you in two."

56 Then, putting him to one side, he ordered them to bring the other. And he said to him, "You offspring of Canaan and not of Judah, beauty has beguiled you and lust has perverted your heart. [57]This is how you have been treating the daughters of Israel, and they were intimate with you through fear; but a daughter of Judah would not tolerate your wickedness. [58]Now then, tell me: Under what tree did you catch them being intimate with each other?" He answered, "Under an evergreen oak."[c] [59]Daniel said to him, "Very well! This lie has cost you also your head, for the angel of God is waiting with his sword to split[c] you in two, so as to destroy you both."

60 Then the whole assembly raised a great shout and blessed God, who saves those who hope in him. [61]And they took action against the two elders, because out of their own mouths Daniel had convicted them of bearing false witness; they did to them as they had wickedly planned to do to their neighbor. [62]Acting in accordance with the law of Moses, they put them to death. Thus innocent blood was spared that day.

63 Hilkiah and his wife praised God for their daughter Susanna, and so did her husband Joakim and all her relatives, because she was found innocent of a shameful deed. [64]And from that day onward Daniel had a great reputation among the people.

---

[a] Gk lacks *rest of the* [b] The Greek words for *mastic tree* and *cut* are similar, thus forming an ironic wordplay
[c] The Greek words for *evergreen oak* and *split* are similar, thus forming an ironic wordplay

BEL AND THE DRAGON

(Chapter 14 of the Greek Version of Daniel)

Daniel and the Priests of Bel

1 When King Astyages was laid to rest with his ancestors, Cyrus the Persian succeeded to his kingdom. [2]Daniel was a companion of the king, and was the most honored of all his Friends.

3 Now the Babylonians had an idol called Bel, and every day they provided for it twelve bushels of choice flour and forty sheep and six measures[a] of wine. [4]The king revered it and went every day to worship it. But Daniel worshiped his own God. So the king said to him, "Why do you not worship Bel?" [5]He answered, "Because I do not revere idols made with hands, but the living God, who created heaven and earth and has dominion over all living creatures."

6 The king said to him, "Do you not think that Bel is a living god? Do you not see how much he eats and drinks every day?" [7]And Daniel laughed, and said, "Do not be deceived, O king, for this thing is only clay inside and bronze outside, and it never ate or drank anything."

8 Then the king was angry and called the priests of Bel[b] and said to them, "If you do not tell me who is eating these provisions, you shall die. [9]But if you prove that Bel is eating them, Daniel shall die, because he has spoken blasphemy against Bel." Daniel said to the king, "Let it be done as you have said."

10 Now there were seventy priests of Bel, besides their wives and children. So the king went with Daniel into the temple of Bel. [11]The priests of Bel said, "See, we are now going outside; you yourself, O king, set out the food and prepare the wine, and shut the door and seal it with your signet. [12]When you return in the morning, if you do not find that Bel has eaten it all, we will die; otherwise Daniel will, who is telling lies about us." [13]They were unconcerned, for beneath the table they had made a hidden entrance, through which they used to go in regularly and consume the provisions. [14]After they had gone out, the king set out the food for Bel. Then Daniel ordered his servants to bring ashes, and they scattered them throughout the whole temple in the presence of the king alone. Then they went out, shut the door and sealed it with the king's signet, and departed. [15]During the night the priests came as usual, with their wives and children, and they ate and drank everything.

16 Early in the morning the king rose and came, and Daniel with him. [17]The king said, "Are the seals unbroken, Daniel?" He answered, "They are unbroken, O king." [18]As soon as the doors were opened, the king looked at the table, and shouted in a loud voice, "You are great, O Bel, and in you there is no deceit at all!"

19 But Daniel laughed and restrained the king from going in. "Look at the floor," he said, "and notice whose footprints these are." [20]The king said, "I see the footprints of men and women and children." [21]Then the king was enraged, and he arrested the priests and their wives and children. They showed him the secret doors through which they used to enter to consume what was on the table. [22]Therefore the king put them to death, and gave Bel over to Daniel, who destroyed it and its temple.

Daniel Kills the Dragon

23 Now in that place[c] there was a great dragon, which the Babylonians revered. [24]The king said to Daniel, "You cannot deny that this is a living god; so worship him." [25]Daniel said, "I worship the Lord my God, for he is the living God. [26]But give me permission, O king, and I will kill the dragon without sword or club." The king said, "I give you permission."

27 Then Daniel took pitch, fat, and hair, and boiled them together and made cakes, which he fed to the dragon. The dragon ate them, and burst open. Then Daniel said, "See what you have been worshiping!"

28 When the Babylonians heard about it, they were very indignant and conspired against the king, saying, "The king has become a Jew; he has destroyed Bel, and killed the dragon, and slaughtered the priests." [29]Going to the king, they said, "Hand

---

[a] A little more than fifty gallons   [b] Gk *his priests*   [c] Other ancient authorities lack *in that place*

Daniel over to us, or else we will kill you and your household." [30]The king saw that they were pressing him hard, and under compulsion he handed Daniel over to them.

Daniel in the Lions' Den

31 They threw Daniel into the lions' den, and he was there for six days. [32]There were seven lions in the den, and every day they had been given two human bodies and two sheep; but now they were given nothing, so that they would devour Daniel. [33]Now the prophet Habakkuk was in Judea; he had made a stew and had broken bread into a bowl, and was going into the field to take it to the reapers. [34]But the angel of the Lord said to Habakkuk, "Take the food that you have to Babylon, to Daniel, in the lions' den." [35]Habakkuk said, "Sir, I have never seen Babylon, and I

know nothing about the den." [36]Then the angel of the Lord took him by the crown of his head and carried him by his hair; with the speed of the wind[d] he set him down in Babylon, right over the den.

37 Then Habakkuk shouted, "Daniel, Daniel! Take the food that God has sent you." [38]Daniel said, "You have remembered me, O God, and have not forsaken those who love you." [39]So Daniel got up and ate. And the angel of God immediately returned Habakkuk to his own place.

40 On the seventh day the king came to mourn for Daniel. When he came to the den he looked in, and there sat Daniel! [41]The king shouted with a loud voice, "You are great, O Lord, the God of Daniel, and there is no other besides you!" [42]Then he pulled Daniel[e] out, and threw into the den those who had attempted his destruction, and they were instantly eaten before his eyes.

[d] Or by the power of his spirit   *[e] Gk him*

1 MACCABEES

Alexander the Great

1 After Alexander son of Philip, the Macedonian, who came from the land of Kittim, had defeated[a] King Darius of the Persians and the Medes, he succeeded him as king. (He had previously become king of Greece.) [2]He fought many battles, conquered strongholds, and put to death the kings of the earth. [3]He advanced to the ends of the earth, and plundered many nations. When the earth became quiet before him, he was exalted, and his heart was lifted up. [4]He gathered a very strong army and ruled over countries, nations, and princes, and they became tributary to him.

5 After this he fell sick and perceived that he was dying. [6]So he summoned his most honored officers, who had been brought up with him from youth, and divided his kingdom among them while he

was still alive. [7]And after Alexander had reigned twelve years, he died.

8 Then his officers began to rule, each in his own place. [9]They all put on crowns after his death, and so did their descendants after them for many years; and they caused many evils on the earth.

Antiochus Epiphanes and Renegade Jews

10 From them came forth a sinful root, Antiochus Epiphanes, son of King Antiochus; he had been a hostage in Rome. He began to reign in the one hundred thirty-seventh year of the kingdom of the Greeks.[b]

11 In those days certain renegades came out from Israel and misled many, saying, "Let us go and make a covenant with the Gentiles around us, for since we separated from them many disasters have come upon

[a] Gk adds and he defeated   *[b] 175 B.C.*

us." ¹²This proposal pleased them, ¹³and some of the people eagerly went to the king, who authorized them to observe the ordinances of the Gentiles. ¹⁴So they built a gymnasium in Jerusalem, according to Gentile custom, ¹⁵and removed the marks of circumcision, and abandoned the holy covenant. They joined with the Gentiles and sold themselves to do evil.

Antiochus in Egypt

16 When Antiochus saw that his kingdom was established, he determined to become king of the land of Egypt, in order that he might reign over both kingdoms. ¹⁷So he invaded Egypt with a strong force, with chariots and elephants and cavalry and with a large fleet. ¹⁸He engaged King Ptolemy of Egypt in battle, and Ptolemy turned and fled before him, and many were wounded and fell. ¹⁹They captured the fortified cities in the land of Egypt, and he plundered the land of Egypt.

Persecution of the Jews

20 After subduing Egypt, Antiochus returned in the one hundred forty-third year.ᶜ He went up against Israel and came to Jerusalem with a strong force. ²¹He arrogantly entered the sanctuary and took the golden altar, the lampstand for the light, and all its utensils. ²²He took also the table for the bread of the Presence, the cups for drink offerings, the bowls, the golden censers, the curtain, the crowns, and the gold decoration on the front of the temple; he stripped it all off. ²³He took the silver and the gold, and the costly vessels; he took also the hidden treasures that he found. ²⁴Taking them all, he went into his own land.

He shed much blood,
    and spoke with great arrogance.
²⁵ Israel mourned deeply in every
        community,
²⁶   rulers and elders groaned,
    young women and young men became
        faint,
    the beauty of the women faded.
²⁷ Every bridegroom took up the lament;
    she who sat in the bridal chamber
        was mourning.
²⁸ Even the land trembled for its inhabitants,
    and all the house of Jacob was
        clothed with shame.

The Occupation of Jerusalem

29 Two years later the king sent to the cities of Judah a chief collector of tribute, and he came to Jerusalem with a large force. ³⁰Deceitfully he spoke peaceable words to them, and they believed him; but he suddenly fell upon the city, dealt it a severe blow, and destroyed many people of Israel. ³¹He plundered the city, burned it with fire, and tore down its houses and its surrounding walls. ³²They took captive the women and children, and seized the livestock. ³³Then they fortified the city of David with a great strong wall and strong towers, and it became their citadel. ³⁴They stationed there a sinful people, men who were renegades. These strengthened their position; ³⁵they stored up arms and food, and collecting the spoils of Jerusalem they stored them there, and became a great menace,

³⁶ for the citadelᵈ became an ambush
        against the sanctuary,
    an evil adversary of Israel at all times.
³⁷ On every side of the sanctuary they
        shed innocent blood;
    they even defiled the sanctuary.
³⁸ Because of them the residents of
        Jerusalem fled;
    she became a dwelling of strangers;
    she became strange to her offspring,
    and her children forsook her.
³⁹ Her sanctuary became desolate like a
        desert;
    her feasts were turned into mourning,
    her sabbaths into a reproach,
    her honor into contempt.
⁴⁰ Her dishonor now grew as great as
        her glory;
    her exaltation was turned into
        mourning.

Installation of Gentile Cults

41 Then the king wrote to his whole kingdom that all should be one people, ⁴²and that all should give up their particular customs. ⁴³All the Gentiles accepted the command of the king. Many even from Israel gladly adopted his religion; they sacrificed to idols and profaned the sabbath. ⁴⁴And the king sent letters by messengers to Jerusalem and the towns of Judah; he directed them to follow customs strange to the land, ⁴⁵to forbid burnt offerings and sacrifices and drink offerings in the sanctuary, to profane sabbaths and festivals, ⁴⁶to

defile the sanctuary and the priests, [47]to build altars and sacred precincts and shrines for idols, to sacrifice swine and other unclean animals, [48]and to leave their sons uncircumcised. They were to make themselves abominable by everything unclean and profane, [49]so that they would forget the law and change all the ordinances. [50]He added,[e] "And whoever does not obey the command of the king shall die."

51 In such words he wrote to his whole kingdom. He appointed inspectors over all the people and commanded the towns of Judah to offer sacrifice, town by town. [52]Many of the people, everyone who forsook the law, joined them, and they did evil in the land; [53]they drove Israel into hiding in every place of refuge they had.

54 Now on the fifteenth day of Chislev, in the one hundred forty-fifth year,[f] they erected a desolating sacrilege on the altar of burnt offering. They also built altars in the surrounding towns of Judah, [55]and offered incense at the doors of the houses and in the streets. [56]The books of the law that they found they tore to pieces and burned with fire. [57]Anyone found possessing the book of the covenant, or anyone who adhered to the law, was condemned to death by decree of the king. [58]They kept using violence against Israel, against those who were found month after month in the towns. [59]On the twenty-fifth day of the month they offered sacrifice on the altar that was on top of the altar of burnt offering. [60]According to the decree, they put to death the women who had their children circumcised, [61]and their families and those who circumcised them; and they hung the infants from their mothers' necks.

62 But many in Israel stood firm and were resolved in their hearts not to eat unclean food. [63]They chose to die rather than to be defiled by food or to profane the holy covenant; and they did die. [64]Very great wrath came upon Israel.

Mattathias and His Sons

2 In those days Mattathias son of John son of Simeon, a priest of the family of Joarib, moved from Jerusalem and settled in Modein. [2]He had five sons, John surnamed Gaddi, [3]Simon called Thassi, [4]Judas called Maccabeus, [5]Eleazar called Avaran,

and Jonathan called Apphus. [6]He saw the blasphemies being committed in Judah and Jerusalem, [7]and said,

"Alas! Why was I born to see this,
    the ruin of my people, the ruin of
        the holy city,
    and to live there when it was given
        over to the enemy,
    the sanctuary given over to aliens?
[8] Her temple has become like a person
        without honor;[g]
[9]   her glorious vessels have been
        carried into exile.
    Her infants have been killed in her
        streets,
    her youths by the sword of the foe.
[10] What nation has not inherited her
        palaces[h]
    and has not seized her spoils?
[11] All her adornment has been taken
        away;
    no longer free, she has become a
        slave.
[12] And see, our holy place, our beauty,
    and our glory have been laid waste;
    the Gentiles have profaned them.
[13]   Why should we live any longer?"

14 Then Mattathias and his sons tore their clothes, put on sackcloth, and mourned greatly.

Pagan Worship Refused

15 The king's officers who were enforcing the apostasy came to the town of Modein to make them offer sacrifice. [16]Many from Israel came to them; and Mattathias and his sons were assembled. [17]Then the king's officers spoke to Mattathias as follows: "You are a leader, honored and great in this town, and supported by sons and brothers. [18]Now be the first to come and do what the king commands, as all the Gentiles and the people of Judah and those that are left in Jerusalem have done. Then you and your sons will be numbered among the Friends of the king, and you and your sons will be honored with silver and gold and many gifts."

19 But Mattathias answered and said in a loud voice: "Even if all the nations that live under the rule of the king obey him, and have chosen to obey his commandments, everyone of them abandoning the religion of their ancestors, [20]I and my sons

---

[e] Gk lacks *He added*   [f] 167 B.C.   [g] Meaning of Gk uncertain   [h] Other ancient authorities read *has not had a part in her kingdom*

and my brothers will continue to live by the covenant of our ancestors. [21]Far be it from us to desert the law and the ordinances. [22]We will not obey the king's words by turning aside from our religion to the right hand or to the left."

23 When he had finished speaking these words, a Jew came forward in the sight of all to offer sacrifice on the altar in Modein, according to the king's command. [24]When Mattathias saw it, he burned with zeal and his heart was stirred. He gave vent to righteous anger; he ran and killed him on the altar. [25]At the same time he killed the king's officer who was forcing them to sacrifice, and he tore down the altar. [26]Thus he burned with zeal for the law, just as Phinehas did against Zimri son of Salu.

27 Then Mattathias cried out in the town with a loud voice, saying: "Let every one who is zealous for the law and supports the covenant come out with me!" [28]Then he and his sons fled to the hills and left all that they had in the town.

29 At that time many who were seeking righteousness and justice went down to the wilderness to live there, [30]they, their sons, their wives, and their livestock, because troubles pressed heavily upon them. [31]And it was reported to the king's officers, and to the troops in Jerusalem the city of David, that those who had rejected the king's command had gone down to the hiding places in the wilderness. [32]Many pursued them, and overtook them; they encamped opposite them and prepared for battle against them on the sabbath day. [33]They said to them, "Enough of this! Come out and do what the king commands, and you will live." [34]But they said, "We will not come out, nor will we do what the king commands and so profane the sabbath day." [35]Then the enemy[i] quickly attacked them. [36]But they did not answer them or hurl a stone at them or block up their hiding places, [37]for they said, "Let us all die in our innocence; heaven and earth testify for us that you are killing us unjustly." [38]So they attacked them on the sabbath, and they died, with their wives and children and livestock, to the number of a thousand persons.

39 When Mattathias and his friends learned of it, they mourned for them deeply. [40]And all said to their neighbors: "If we all do as our kindred have done and

refuse to fight with the Gentiles for our lives and for our ordinances, they will quickly destroy us from the earth." [41]So they made this decision that day: "Let us fight against anyone who comes to attack us on the sabbath day; let us not all die as our kindred died in their hiding places."

Counter-Attack

42 Then there united with them a company of Hasideans, mighty warriors of Israel, all who offered themselves willingly for the law. [43]And all who became fugitives to escape their troubles joined them and reinforced them. [44]They organized an army, and struck down sinners in their anger and renegades in their wrath; the survivors fled to the Gentiles for safety. [45]And Mattathias and his friends went around and tore down the altars; [46]they forcibly circumcised all the uncircumcised boys that they found within the borders of Israel. [47]They hunted down the arrogant, and the work prospered in their hands. [48]They rescued the law out of the hands of the Gentiles and kings, and they never let the sinner gain the upper hand.

The Last Words of Mattathias

49 Now the days drew near for Mattathias to die, and he said to his sons: "Arrogance and scorn have now become strong; it is a time of ruin and furious anger. [50]Now, my children, show zeal for the law, and give your lives for the covenant of our ancestors.

51 "Remember the deeds of the ancestors, which they did in their generations; and you will receive great honor and an everlasting name. [52]Was not Abraham found faithful when tested, and it was reckoned to him as righteousness? [53]Joseph in the time of his distress kept the commandment, and became lord of Egypt. [54]Phinehas our ancestor, because he was deeply zealous, received the covenant of everlasting priesthood. [55]Joshua, because he fulfilled the command, became a judge in Israel. [56]Caleb because he testified in the assembly, received an inheritance in the land. [57]David, because he was merciful, inherited the throne of the kingdom forever. [58]Elijah, because of great zeal for the law, was taken up into heaven. [59]Hananiah, Azariah, and Mishael believed and were saved from the flame. [60]Daniel,

i Gk they

because of his innocence, was delivered from the mouth of the lions.

61 "And so observe, from generation to generation, that none of those who put their trust in him will lack strength. ⁶²Do not fear the words of sinners, for their splendor will turn into dung and worms. ⁶³Today they will be exalted, but tomorrow they will not be found, because they will have returned to the dust, and their plans will have perished. ⁶⁴My children, be courageous and grow strong in the law, for by it you will gain honor.

65 "Here is your brother Simeon who, I know, is wise in counsel; always listen to him; he shall be your father. ⁶⁶Judas Maccabeus has been a mighty warrior from his youth; he shall command the army for you and fight the battle against the peoples.ʲ ⁶⁷You shall rally around you all who observe the law, and avenge the wrong done to your people. ⁶⁸Pay back the Gentiles in full, and obey the commands of the law."

69 Then he blessed them, and was gathered to his ancestors. ⁷⁰He died in the one hundred forty-sixth yearᵏ and was buried in the tomb of his ancestors at Modein. And all Israel mourned for him with great lamentation.

The Early Victories of Judas

3 Then his son Judas, who was called Maccabeus, took command in his place. ²All his brothers and all who had joined his father helped him; they gladly fought for Israel.

³ He extended the glory of his people.
  Like a giant he put on his
    breastplate;
  he bound on his armor of war and
    waged battles,
  protecting the camp by his sword.
⁴ He was like a lion in his deeds,
  like a lion's cub roaring for prey.
⁵ He searched out and pursued those
    who broke the law;
  he burned those who troubled his
    people.
⁶ Lawbreakers shrank back for fear of him;
  all the evildoers were confounded;
  and deliverance prospered by his
    hand.
⁷ He embittered many kings,
  but he made Jacob glad by his
    deeds,

and his memory is blessed forever.
⁸ He went through the cities of Judah;
  he destroyed the ungodly out of the
    land;ˡ
  thus he turned away wrath from
    Israel.
⁹ He was renowned to the ends of the
    earth;
  he gathered in those who were
    perishing.

10 Apollonius now gathered together Gentiles and a large force from Samaria to fight against Israel. ¹¹When Judas learned of it, he went out to meet him, and he defeated and killed him. Many were wounded and fell, and the rest fled. ¹²Then they seized their spoils; and Judas took the sword of Apollonius, and used it in battle the rest of his life.

13 When Seron, the commander of the Syrian army, heard that Judas had gathered a large company, including a body of faithful soldiers who stayed with him and went out to battle, ¹⁴he said, "I will make a name for myself and win honor in the kingdom. I will make war on Judas and his companions, who scorn the king's command." ¹⁵Once again a strong army of godless men went up with him to help him, to take vengeance on the Israelites.

16 When he approached the ascent of Beth-horon, Judas went out to meet him with a small company. ¹⁷But when they saw the army coming to meet them, they said to Judas, "How can we, few as we are, fight against so great and so strong a multitude? And we are faint, for we have eaten nothing today." ¹⁸Judas replied, "It is easy for many to be hemmed in by few, for in the sight of Heaven there is no difference between saving by many or by few. ¹⁹It is not on the size of the army that victory in battle depends, but strength comes from Heaven. ²⁰They come against us in great insolence and lawlessness to destroy us and our wives and our children, and to despoil us; ²¹but we fight for our lives and our laws. ²²He himself will crush them before us; as for you, do not be afraid of them."

23 When he finished speaking, he rushed suddenly against Seron and his army, and they were crushed before him. ²⁴They pursued themᵐ down the descent of Beth-horon to the plain; eight hundred of them fell, and the rest fled into the land of the Philistines. ²⁵Then Judas and his brothers began to be

ʲOr *of the people*   ᵏ166 B.C.   ˡGk *it*   ᵐOther ancient authorities read *him* feared, and terror fell on the Gentiles all around them. [26]His fame reached the king, and the Gentiles talked of the battles of Judas.

The Policy of Antiochus

27 When King Antiochus heard these reports, he was greatly angered; and he sent and gathered all the forces of his kingdom, a very strong army. [28]He opened his coffers and gave a year's pay to his forces, and ordered them to be ready for any need. [29]Then he saw that the money in the treasury was exhausted, and that the revenues from the country were small because of the dissension and disaster that he had caused in the land by abolishing the laws that had existed from the earliest days. [30]He feared that he might not have such funds as he had before for his expenses and for the gifts that he used to give more lavishly than preceding kings. [31]He was greatly perplexed in mind; then he determined to go to Persia and collect the revenues from those regions and raise a large fund.

32 He left Lysias, a distinguished man of royal lineage, in charge of the king's affairs from the river Euphrates to the borders of Egypt. [33]Lysias was also to take care of his son Antiochus until he returned. [34]And he turned over to Lysias[n] half of his forces and the elephants, and gave him orders about all that he wanted done. As for the residents of Judea and Jerusalem, [35]Lysias was to send a force against them to wipe out and destroy the strength of Israel and the remnant of Jerusalem; he was to banish the memory of them from the place, [36]settle aliens in all their territory, and distribute their land by lot. [37]Then the king took the remaining half of his forces and left Antioch his capital in the one hundred and forty-seventh year.[o] He crossed the Euphrates river and went through the upper provinces.

Preparations for Battle

38 Lysias chose Ptolemy son of Dorymenes, and Nicanor and Gorgias, able men among the Friends of the king, [39]and sent with them forty thousand infantry and seven thousand cavalry to go into the land of Judah and destroy it, as the king had commanded. [40]So they set out with their entire force, and when they arrived they encamped near Emmaus in the plain. [41]When the traders of the region heard what was said to them, they took silver and gold in immense amounts, and fetters,[p] and went to the camp to get the Israelites for slaves. And forces from Syria and the land of the Philistines joined with them.

42 Now Judas and his brothers saw that misfortunes had increased and that the forces were encamped in their territory. They also learned what the king had commanded to do to the people to cause their final destruction. [43]But they said to one another, "Let us restore the ruins of our people, and fight for our people and the sanctuary." [44]So the congregation assembled to be ready for battle, and to pray and ask for mercy and compassion.

[45] Jerusalem was uninhabited like a
> wilderness;
> not one of her children went in or out.
> The sanctuary was trampled down,
> and aliens held the citadel;
> it was a lodging place for the Gentiles.
> Joy was taken from Jacob;
> the flute and the harp ceased to play.

46 Then they gathered together and went to Mizpah, opposite Jerusalem, because Israel formerly had a place of prayer in Mizpah. [47]They fasted that day, put on sackcloth and sprinkled ashes on their heads, and tore their clothes. [48]And they opened the book of the law to inquire into those matters about which the Gentiles consulted the likenesses of their gods. [49]They also brought the vestments of the priesthood and the first fruits and the tithes, and they stirred up the nazirites[q] who had completed their days; [50]and they cried aloud to Heaven, saying,
> "What shall we do with these?
> Where shall we take them?
[51] Your sanctuary is trampled down and
> profaned,
> and your priests mourn in
> humiliation.
[52] Here the Gentiles are assembled
> against us to destroy us;
> you know what they plot against us.
[53] How will we be able to withstand them,
> if you do not help us?"

54 Then they sounded the trumpets and gave a loud shout. [55]After this Judas appointed leaders of the people, in charge of thousands and hundreds and fifties and tens. [56]Those who were building houses, or were about to be married, or were planting

---

[n] Gk *him*   [o] 165 B.C.   [p] Syr: Gk Mss, Vg *slaves*   [q] That is *those separated* or *those consecrated*

a vineyard, or were fainthearted, he told to go home again, according to the law. [57]Then the army marched out and encamped to the south of Emmaus.

58 And Judas said, "Arm yourselves and be courageous. Be ready early in the morning to fight with these Gentiles who have assembled against us to destroy us and our sanctuary. [59]It is better for us to die in battle than to see the misfortunes of our nation and of the sanctuary. [60]But as his will in heaven may be, so shall he do."

The Battle at Emmaus

4 Now Gorgias took five thousand infantry and one thousand picked cavalry, and this division moved out by night [2]to fall upon the camp of the Jews and attack them suddenly. Men from the citadel were his guides. [3]But Judas heard of it, he and his warriors moved out to attack the king's force in Emmaus [4]while the division was still absent from the camp. [5]When Gorgias entered the camp of Judas by night, he found no one there, so he looked for them in the hills, because he said, "These men are running away from us."

6 At daybreak Judas appeared in the plain with three thousand men, but they did not have armor and swords such as they desired. [7]And they saw the camp of the Gentiles, strong and fortified, with cavalry all around it; and these men were trained in war. [8]But Judas said to those who were with him, "Do not fear their numbers or be afraid when they charge. [9]Remember how our ancestors were saved at the Red Sea, when Pharaoh with his forces pursued them. [10]And now, let us cry to Heaven, to see whether he will favor us and remember his covenant with our ancestors and crush this army before us today. [11]Then all the Gentiles will know that there is one who redeems and saves Israel."

12 When the foreigners looked up and saw them coming against them, [13]they went out from their camp to battle. Then the men with Judas blew their trumpets [14]and engaged in battle. The Gentiles were crushed, and fled into the plain, [15]and all those in the rear fell by the sword. They pursued them to Gazara, and to the plains of Idumea, and to Azotus and Jamnia; and three thousand of them fell. [16]Then Judas and his force turned back from pursuing

them, [17]and he said to the people, "Do not be greedy for plunder, for there is a battle before us; [18]Gorgias and his force are near us in the hills. But stand now against our enemies and fight them, and afterward seize the plunder boldly."

19 Just as Judas was finishing this speech, a detachment appeared, coming out of the hills. [20]They saw that their army[r] had been put to flight, and that the Jews[r] were burning the camp, for the smoke that was seen showed what had happened. [21]When they perceived this, they were greatly frightened, and when they also saw the army of Judas drawn up in the plain for battle, [22]they all fled into the land of the Philistines. [23]Then Judas returned to plunder the camp, and they seized a great amount of gold and silver, and cloth dyed blue and sea purple, and great riches. [24]On their return they sang hymns and praises to Heaven—"For he is good, for his mercy endures forever." [25]Thus Israel had a great deliverance that day.

First Campaign of Lysias

26 Those of the foreigners who escaped went and reported to Lysias all that had happened. [27]When he heard it, he was perplexed and discouraged, for things had not happened to Israel as he had intended, nor had they turned out as the king had ordered. [28]But the next year he mustered sixty thousand picked infantry and five thousand cavalry to subdue them. [29]They came into Idumea and encamped at Bethzur, and Judas met them with ten thousand men.

30 When he saw that their army was strong, he prayed, saying, "Blessed are you, O Savior of Israel, who crushed the attack of the mighty warrior by the hand of your servant David, and gave the camp of the Philistines into the hands of Jonathan son of Saul, and of the man who carried his armor. [31]Hem in this army by the hand of your people Israel, and let them be ashamed of their troops and their cavalry. [32]Fill them with cowardice; melt the boldness of their strength; let them tremble in their destruction. [33]Strike them down with the sword of those who love you, and let all who know your name praise you with hymns."

34 Then both sides attacked, and there fell of the army of Lysias five thousand men;

---

[r] Gk *they*

they fell in action.^{s} ^{35}When Lysias saw the rout of his troops and observed the boldness that inspired those of Judas, and how ready they were either to live or to die nobly, he withdrew to Antioch and enlisted mercenaries in order to invade Judea again with an even larger army.

Cleansing and Dedication of the Temple

36 Then Judas and his brothers said, "See, our enemies are crushed; let us go up to cleanse the sanctuary and dedicate it." ^{37}So all the army assembled and went up to Mount Zion. ^{38}There they saw the sanctuary desolate, the altar profaned, and the gates burned. In the courts they saw bushes sprung up as in a thicket, or as on one of the mountains. They saw also the chambers of the priests in ruins. ^{39}Then they tore their clothes and mourned with great lamentation; they sprinkled themselves with ashes ^{40}and fell face down on the ground. And when the signal was given with the trumpets, they cried out to Heaven.

41 Then Judas detailed men to fight against those in the citadel until he had cleansed the sanctuary. ^{42}He chose blameless priests devoted to the law, ^{43}and they cleansed the sanctuary and removed the defiled stones to an unclean place. ^{44}They deliberated what to do about the altar of burnt offering, which had been profaned. ^{45}And they thought it best to tear it down, so that it would not be a lasting shame to them that the Gentiles had defiled it. So they tore down the altar, ^{46}and stored the stones in a convenient place on the temple hill until a prophet should come to tell what to do with them. ^{47}Then they took unhewn^t stones, as the law directs, and built a new altar like the former one. ^{48}They also rebuilt the sanctuary and the interior of the temple, and consecrated the courts. ^{49}They made new holy vessels, and brought the lampstand, the altar of incense, and the table into the temple. ^{50}Then they offered incense on the altar and lit the lamps on the lampstand, and these gave light in the temple. ^{51}They placed the bread on the table and hung up the curtains. Thus they finished all the work they had undertaken.

52 Early in the morning on the twenty-fifth day of the ninth month, which is the month of Chislev, in the one hundred forty-eighth year,^{u} ^{53}they rose and offered sacri-

fice, as the law directs, on the new altar of burnt offering that they had built. ^{54}At the very season and on the very day that the Gentiles had profaned it, it was dedicated with songs and harps and lutes and cymbals. ^{55}All the people fell on their faces and worshiped and blessed Heaven, who had prospered them. ^{56}So they celebrated the dedication of the altar for eight days, and joyfully offered burnt offerings; they offered a sacrifice of well-being and a thanksgiving offering. ^{57}They decorated the front of the temple with golden crowns and small shields; they restored the gates and the chambers for the priests, and fitted them with doors. ^{58}There was very great joy among the people, and the disgrace brought by the Gentiles was removed.

59 Then Judas and his brothers and all the assembly of Israel determined that every year at that season the days of dedication of the altar should be observed with joy and gladness for eight days, beginning with the twenty-fifth day of the month of Chislev.

60 At that time they fortified Mount Zion with high walls and strong towers all around, to keep the Gentiles from coming and trampling them down as they had done before. ^{61}Judas^v stationed a garrison there to guard it; he also fortified Beth-zur to guard it, so that the people might have a stronghold that faced Idumea.

Wars with Neighboring Peoples

5 When the Gentiles all around heard that the altar had been rebuilt and the sanctuary dedicated as it was before, they became very angry, ^{2}and they determined to destroy the descendants of Jacob who lived among them. So they began to kill and destroy among the people. ^{3}But Judas made war on the descendants of Esau in Idumea, at Akrabattene, because they kept lying in wait for Israel. He dealt them a heavy blow and humbled them and despoiled them. ^{4}He also remembered the wickedness of the sons of Baean, who were a trap and a snare to the people and ambushed them on the highways. ^{5}They were shut up by him in their^w towers; and he encamped against them, vowed their complete destruction, and burned with fire their towers and all who were in them. ^{6}Then he crossed over to attack the Ammonites, where he found a strong band and many people,

---

^{s} Or *and some fell on the opposite side* ^{t} Gk *whole* ^{u} 164 B.C. ^{v} Gk *He* ^{w} Gk *her*

with Timothy as their leader. [7]He engaged in many battles with them, and they were crushed before him; he struck them down. [8]He also took Jazer and its villages; then he returned to Judea.

Liberation of Galilean Jews

9 Now the Gentiles in Gilead gathered together against the Israelites who lived in their territory, and planned to destroy them. But they fled to the stronghold of Dathema, [10]and sent to Judas and his brothers a letter that said, "The Gentiles around us have gathered together to destroy us. [11]They are preparing to come and capture the stronghold to which we have fled, and Timothy is leading their forces. [12]Now then, come and rescue us from their hands, for many of us have fallen, [13]and all our kindred who were in the land of Tob have been killed; the enemy[x] have captured their wives and children and goods, and have destroyed about a thousand persons there."

14 While the letter was still being read, other messengers, with their garments torn, came from Galilee and made a similar report; [15]they said that the people of Ptolemais and Tyre and Sidon, and all Galilee of the Gentiles,[y] had gathered together against them "to annihilate us." [16]When Judas and the people heard these messages, a great assembly was called to determine what they should do for their kindred who were in distress and were being attacked by enemies.[z] [17]Then Judas said to his brother Simon, "Choose your men and go and rescue your kindred in Galilee; Jonathan my brother and I will go to Gilead." [18]But he left Joseph, son of Zechariah, and Azariah, a leader of the people, with the rest of the forces, in Judea to guard it; [19]and he gave them this command, "Take charge of this people, but do not engage in battle with the Gentiles until we return." [20]Then three thousand men were assigned to Simon to go to Galilee, and eight thousand to Judas for Gilead.

21 So Simon went to Galilee and fought many battles against the Gentiles, and the Gentiles were crushed before him. [22]He pursued them to the gate of Ptolemais; as many as three thousand of the Gentiles fell, and he despoiled them. [23]Then he took the Jews[a] of Galilee and Arbatta, with their wives and children, and all they possessed, and led them to Judea with great rejoicing.

Judas and Jonathan in Gilead

24 Judas Maccabeus and his brother Jonathan crossed the Jordan and made three days' journey into the wilderness. [25]They encountered the Nabateans, who met them peaceably and told them all that had happened to their kindred in Gilead: [26]"Many of them have been shut up in Bozrah and Bosor, in Alema and Chaspho, Maked and Carnaim"—all these towns were strong and large— [27]"and some have been shut up in the other towns of Gilead; the enemy[x] are getting ready to attack the strongholds tomorrow and capture and destroy all these people in a single day."

28 Then Judas and his army quickly turned back by the wilderness road to Bozrah; and he took the town, and killed every male by the edge of the sword; then he seized all its spoils and burned it with fire. [29]He left the place at night, and they went all the way to the stronghold of Dathema.[b] [30]At dawn they looked out and saw a large company, which could not be counted, carrying ladders and engines of war to capture the stronghold, and attacking the Jews within.[c] [31]So Judas saw that the battle had begun and that the cry of the town went up to Heaven, with trumpets and loud shouts, [32]and he said to the men of his forces, "Fight today for your kindred!" [33]Then he came up behind them in three companies, who sounded their trumpets and cried aloud in prayer. [34]And when the army of Timothy realized that it was Maccabeus, they fled before him, and he dealt them a heavy blow. As many as eight thousand of them fell that day.

35 Next he turned aside to Maapha,[d] and fought against it and took it; and killed every male in it, plundered it, and burned it with fire. [36]From there he marched on and took Chaspho, Maked, and Bosor, and the other towns of Gilead.

37 After these things Timothy gathered another army and encamped opposite Raphon, on the other side of the stream. [38]Judas sent men to spy out the camp, and they reported to him, "All the Gentiles around us have gathered to him; it is a very large force. [39]They also have hired Arabs to help them, and they are encamped across the stream, ready to come and fight against you." And Judas went to meet them.

40 Now as Judas and his army drew

---

[x] Gk *they*   [y] Gk *aliens*   [z] Gk *them*   [a] Gk *those*   [b] Gk lacks *of Dathema*. See verse 9   [c] Gk *and they were attacking them*   [d] Other ancient authorities read *Alema*

near to the stream of water, Timothy said to the officers of his forces, "If he crosses over to us first, we will not be able to resist him, for he will surely defeat us. ⁴¹But if he shows fear and camps on the other side of the river, we will cross over to him and defeat him." ⁴²When Judas approached the stream of water, he stationed the officers*ᵉ* of the army at the stream and gave them this command, "Permit no one to encamp, but make them all enter the battle." ⁴³Then he crossed over against them first, and the whole army followed him. All the Gentiles were defeated before him, and they threw away their arms and fled into the sacred precincts at Carnaim. ⁴⁴But he took the town and burned the sacred precincts with fire, together with all who were in them. Thus Carnaim was conquered; they could stand before Judas no longer.

The Return to Jerusalem

45 Then Judas gathered together all the Israelites in Gilead, the small and the great, with their wives and children and goods, a very large company, to go to the land of Judah. ⁴⁶So they came to Ephron. This was a large and very strong town on the road, and they could not go around it to the right or to the left; they had to go through it. ⁴⁷But the people of the town shut them out and blocked up the gates with stones.

48 Judas sent them this friendly message, "Let us pass through your land to get to our land. No one will do you harm; we will simply pass by on foot." But they refused to open to him. ⁴⁹Then Judas ordered proclamation to be made to the army that all should encamp where they were. ⁵⁰So the men of the forces encamped, and he fought against the town all that day and all the night, and the town was delivered into his hands. ⁵¹He destroyed every male by the edge of the sword, and razed and plundered the town. Then he passed through the town over the bodies of the dead.

52 Then they crossed the Jordan into the large plain before Beth-shan. ⁵³Judas kept rallying the laggards and encouraging the people all the way until he came to the land of Judah. ⁵⁴So they went up to Mount Zion with joy and gladness, and offered burnt offerings, because they had returned in safety; not one of them had fallen.

Joseph and Azariah Defeated

55 Now while Judas and Jonathan were in Gilead and their*ᶠ* brother Simon was in Galilee before Ptolemais, ⁵⁶Joseph son of Zechariah, and Azariah, the commanders of the forces, heard of their brave deeds and of the heroic war they had fought. ⁵⁷So they said, "Let us also make a name for ourselves; let us go and make war on the Gentiles around us." ⁵⁸So they issued orders to the men of the forces that were with them and marched against Jamnia. ⁵⁹Gorgias and his men came out of the town to meet them in battle. ⁶⁰Then Joseph and Azariah were routed, and were pursued to the borders of Judea; as many as two thousand of the people of Israel fell that day. ⁶¹Thus the people suffered a great rout because, thinking to do a brave deed, they did not listen to Judas and his brothers. ⁶²But they did not belong to the family of those men through whom deliverance was given to Israel.

63 The man Judas and his brothers were greatly honored in all Israel and among all the Gentiles, wherever their name was heard. ⁶⁴People gathered to them and praised them.

Success at Hebron and Philistia

65 Then Judas and his brothers went out and fought the descendants of Esau in the land to the south. He struck Hebron and its villages and tore down its strongholds and burned its towers on all sides. ⁶⁶Then he marched off to go into the land of the Philistines, and passed through Marisa.*ᵍ* ⁶⁷On that day some priests, who wished to do a brave deed, fell in battle, for they went out to battle unwisely. ⁶⁸But Judas turned aside to Azotus in the land of the Philistines; he tore down their altars, and the carved images of their gods he burned with fire; he plundered the towns and returned to the land of Judah.

The Last Days of Antiochus Epiphanes

6 King Antiochus was going through the upper provinces when he heard that Elymais in Persia was a city famed for its wealth in silver and gold. ²Its temple was very rich, containing golden shields, breastplates, and weapons left there by Alexander son of Philip, the Macedonian king who first reigned over the Greeks. ³So he came and

tried to take the city and plunder it, but he could not because his plan had become known to the citizens [4]and they withstood him in battle. So he fled and in great disappointment left there to return to Babylon.

5 Then someone came to him in Persia and reported that the armies that had gone into the land of Judah had been routed; [6]that Lysias had gone first with a strong force, but had turned and fled before the Jews;[h] that the Jews[i] had grown strong from the arms, supplies, and abundant spoils that they had taken from the armies they had cut down; [7]that they had torn down the abomination that he had erected on the altar in Jerusalem; and that they had surrounded the sanctuary with high walls as before, and also Beth-zur, his town.

8 When the king heard this news, he was astounded and badly shaken. He took to his bed and became sick from disappointment, because things had not turned out for him as he had planned. [9]He lay there for many days, because deep disappointment continually gripped him, and he realized that he was dying. [10]So he called all his Friends and said to them, "Sleep has departed from my eyes and I am downhearted with worry. [11]I said to myself, 'To what distress I have come! And into what a great flood I now am plunged! For I was kind and beloved in my power.' [12]But now I remember the wrong I did in Jerusalem. I seized all its vessels of silver and gold, and I sent to destroy the inhabitants of Judah without good reason. [13]I know that it is because of this that these misfortunes have come upon me; here I am, perishing of bitter disappointment in a strange land."

14 Then he called for Philip, one of his Friends, and made him ruler over all his kingdom. [15]He gave him the crown and his robe and the signet, so that he might guide his son Antiochus and bring him up to be king. [16]Thus King Antiochus died there in the one hundred forty-ninth year.[j] [17]When Lysias learned that the king was dead, he set up Antiochus the king's[k] son to reign. Lysias[l] had brought him up from boyhood; he named him Eupator.

Renewed Attacks from Syria

18 Meanwhile the garrison in the citadel kept hemming Israel in around the sanctu-

ary. They were trying in every way to harm them and strengthen the Gentiles. [19]Judas therefore resolved to destroy them, and assembled all the people to besiege them. [20]They gathered together and besieged the citadel[m] in the one hundred fiftieth year;[n] and he built siege towers and other engines of war. [21]But some of the garrison escaped from the siege and some of the ungodly Israelites joined them. [22]They went to the king and said, "How long will you fail to do justice and to avenge our kindred? [23]We were happy to serve your father, to live by what he said, and to follow his commands. [24]For this reason the sons of our people besieged the citadel[o] and became hostile to us; moreover, they have put to death as many of us as they have caught, and they have seized our inheritances. [25]It is not against us alone that they have stretched out their hands; they have also attacked all the lands on their borders. [26]And see, today they have encamped against the citadel in Jerusalem to take it; they have fortified both the sanctuary and Beth-zur; [27]unless you quickly prevent them, they will do still greater things, and you will not be able to stop them."

28 The king was enraged when he heard this. He assembled all his Friends, the commanders of his forces and those in authority.[p] [29]Mercenary forces also came to him from other kingdoms and from islands of the seas. [30]The number of his forces was one hundred thousand foot soldiers, twenty thousand horsemen, and thirty-two elephants accustomed to war. [31]They came through Idumea and encamped against Beth-zur, and for many days they fought and built engines of war; but the Jews[i] sallied out and burned these with fire, and fought courageously.

The Battle at Beth-zechariah

32 Then Judas marched away from the citadel and encamped at Beth-zechariah, opposite the camp of the king. [33]Early in the morning the king set out and took his army by a forced march along the road to Beth-zechariah, and his troops made ready for battle and sounded their trumpets. [34]They offered the elephants the juice of grapes and mulberries, to arouse them for battle. [35]They distributed the animals among the

[h] Gk them   [i] Gk they   [j] 163 B.C.   [k] Gk his   [l] Gk He   [m] Gk it   [n] 162 B.C.   [o] Meaning of Gk uncertain   [p] Gk those over the reins

phalanxes; with each elephant they stationed a thousand men armed with coats of mail, and with brass helmets on their heads; and five hundred picked horsemen were assigned to each beast. [36]These took their position beforehand wherever the animal was; wherever it went, they went with it, and they never left it. [37]On the elephants[q] were wooden towers, strong and covered; they were fastened on each animal by special harness, and on each were four[r] armed men who fought from there, and also its Indian driver. [38]The rest of the cavalry were stationed on either side, on the two flanks of the army, to harass the enemy while being themselves protected by the phalanxes. [39]When the sun shone on the shields of gold and brass, the hills were ablaze with them and gleamed like flaming torches.

40 Now a part of the king's army was spread out on the high hills, and some troops were on the plain, and they advanced steadily and in good order. [41]All who heard the noise made by their multitude, by the marching of the multitude and the clanking of their arms, trembled, for the army was very large and strong. [42]But Judas and his army advanced to the battle, and six hundred of the king's army fell. [43]Now Eleazar, called Avaran, saw that one of the animals was equipped with royal armor. It was taller than all the others, and he supposed that the king was on it. [44]So he gave his life to save his people and to win for himself an everlasting name. [45]He courageously ran into the midst of the phalanx to reach it; he killed men right and left, and they parted before him on both sides. [46]He got under the elephant, stabbed it from beneath, and killed it; but it fell to the ground upon him and he died. [47]When the Jews[s] saw the royal might and the fierce attack of the forces, they turned away in flight.

The Siege of the Temple

48 The soldiers of the king's army went up to Jerusalem against them, and the king encamped in Judea and at Mount Zion. [49]He made peace with the people of Bethzur, and they evacuated the town because they had no provisions there to withstand a siege, since it was a sabbatical year for the land. [50]So the king took Beth-zur and

stationed a guard there to hold it. [51]Then he encamped before the sanctuary for many days. He set up siege towers, engines of war to throw fire and stones, machines to shoot arrows, and catapults. [52]The Jews[s] also made engines of war to match theirs, and fought for many days. [53]But they had no food in storage,[t] because it was the seventh year; those who had found safety in Judea from the Gentiles had consumed the last of the stores. [54]Only a few men were left in the sanctuary; the rest scattered to their own homes, for the famine proved too much for them.

Syria Offers Terms

55 Then Lysias heard that Philip, whom King Antiochus while still living had appointed to bring up his son Antiochus to be king, [56]had returned from Persia and Media with the forces that had gone with the king, and that he was trying to seize control of the government. [57]So he quickly gave orders to withdraw, and said to the king, to the commanders of the forces, and to the troops, "Daily we grow weaker, our food supply is scant, the place against which we are fighting is strong, and the affairs of the kingdom press urgently on us. [58]Now then let us come to terms with these people, and make peace with them and with all their nation. [59]Let us agree to let them live by their laws as they did before; for it was on account of their laws that we abolished that they became angry and did all these things."

60 The speech pleased the king and the commanders, and he sent to the Jews[q] an offer of peace, and they accepted it. [61]So the king and the commanders gave them their oath. On these conditions the Jews[s] evacuated the stronghold. [62]But when the king entered Mount Zion and saw what a strong fortress the place was, he broke the oath he had sworn and gave orders to tear down the wall all around. [63]Then he set off in haste and returned to Antioch. He found Philip in control of the city, but he fought against him, and took the city by force.

Expedition of Bacchides and Alcimus

7 In the one hundred fifty-first year[u] Demetrius son of Seleucus set out from Rome, sailed with a few men to a town by

---

[q] Gk *them*   [r] Cn: Some authorities read *thirty*; others *thirty-two*   [s] Gk *they*   [t] Other ancient authorities read *in the sanctuary*   [u] 161 B.C.

the sea, and there began to reign. ²As he was entering the royal palace of his ancestors, the army seized Antiochus and Lysias to bring them to him. ³But when this act became known to him, he said, "Do not let me see their faces!" ⁴So the army killed them, and Demetrius took his seat on the throne of his kingdom.

5 Then there came to him all the renegade and godless men of Israel; they were led by Alcimus, who wanted to be high priest. ⁶They brought to the king this accusation against the people: "Judas and his brothers have destroyed all your Friends, and have driven us out of our land. ⁷Now then send a man whom you trust; let him go and see all the ruin that Judas' has brought on us and on the land of the king, and let him punish them and all who help them."

8 So the king chose Bacchides, one of the king's Friends, governor of the province Beyond the River; he was a great man in the kingdom and was faithful to the king. ⁹He sent him, and with him he sent the ungodly Alcimus, whom he made high priest; and he commanded him to take vengeance on the Israelites. ¹⁰So they marched away and came with a large force into the land of Judah; and he sent messengers to Judas and his brothers with peaceable but treacherous words. ¹¹But they paid no attention to their words, for they saw that they had come with a large force.

12 Then a group of scribes appeared in a body before Alcimus and Bacchides to ask for just terms. ¹³The Hasideans were first among the Israelites to seek peace from them, ¹⁴for they said, "A priest of the line of Aaron has come with the army, and he will not harm us." ¹⁵Alcimusʷ spoke peaceable words to them and swore this oath to them, "We will not seek to injure you or your friends." ¹⁶So they trusted him; but he seized sixty of them and killed them in one day, in accordance with the word that was written,

¹⁷ "The flesh of your faithful ones and
          their blood
     they poured out all around Jerusalem,
     and there was no one to bury them."

¹⁸Then the fear and dread of them fell on all the people, for they said, "There is no truth or justice in them, for they have violated the agreement and the oath that they swore."

19 Then Bacchides withdrew from Jerusalem and encamped in Beth-zaith. And he sent and seized many of the men who had deserted to him,ˣ and some of the people, and killed them and threw them into a great pit. ²⁰He placed Alcimus in charge of the country and left with him a force to help him; then Bacchides went back to the king.

21 Alcimus struggled to maintain his high priesthood, ²²and all who were troubling their people joined him. They gained control of the land of Judah and did great damage in Israel. ²³And Judas saw all the wrongs that Alcimus and those with him had done among the Israelites; it was more than the Gentiles had done. ²⁴So Judasᵛ went out into all the surrounding parts of Judea, taking vengeance on those who had deserted and preventing those in the cityʸ from going out into the country. ²⁵When Alcimus saw that Judas and those with him had grown strong, and realized that he could not withstand them, he returned to the king and brought malicious charges against them.

Nicanor in Judea

26 Then the king sent Nicanor, one of his honored princes, who hated and detested Israel, and he commanded him to destroy the people. ²⁷So Nicanor came to Jerusalem with a large force, and treacherously sent to Judas and his brothers this peaceable message, ²⁸"Let there be no fighting between you and me; I shall come with a few men to see you face to face in peace."

29 So he came to Judas, and they greeted one another peaceably; but the enemy were preparing to kidnap Judas. ³⁰It became known to Judas that Nicanorᵛ had come to him with treacherous intent, and he was afraid of him and would not meet him again. ³¹When Nicanor learned that his plan had been disclosed, he went out to meet Judas in battle near Caphar-salama. ³²About five hundred of the army of Nicanor fell, and the restᶻ fled into the city of David.

Nicanor Threatens the Temple

33 After these events Nicanor went up to Mount Zion. Some of the priests from the sanctuary and some of the elders of the people came out to greet him peaceably and

ᵛ Gk *he*   ʷ Gk *He*   ˣ Or *many of his men who had deserted*   ʸ Gk *and they were prevented*   ᶻ Gk *they*

to show him the burnt offering that was being offered for the king. [34]But he mocked them and derided them and defiled them and spoke arrogantly, [35]and in anger he swore this oath, "Unless Judas and his army are delivered into my hands this time, then if I return safely I will burn up this house." And he went out in great anger. [36]At this the priests went in and stood before the altar and the temple; they wept and said,

[37] "You chose this house to be called by
your name,
and to be for your people a house
of prayer and supplication.
[38] Take vengeance on this man and on
his army,
and let them fall by the sword;
remember their blasphemies,
and let them live no longer."

The Death of Nicanor

39 Now Nicanor went out from Jerusalem and encamped in Beth-horon, and the Syrian army joined him. [40]Judas encamped in Adasa with three thousand men. Then Judas prayed and said, [41]"When the messengers from the king spoke blasphemy, your angel went out and struck down one hundred eighty-five thousand of the Assyrians.[a] [42]So also crush this army before us today; let the rest learn that Nicanor[b] has spoken wickedly against the sanctuary, and judge him according to this wickedness."

43 So the armies met in battle on the thirteenth day of the month of Adar. The army of Nicanor was crushed, and he himself was the first to fall in the battle. [44]When his army saw that Nicanor had fallen, they threw down their arms and fled. [45]The Jews[c] pursued them a day's journey, from Adasa as far as Gazara, and as they followed they kept sounding the battle call on the trumpets. [46]People came out of all the surrounding villages of Judea, and they outflanked the enemy[d] and drove them back to their pursuers,[e] so that they all fell by the sword; not even one of them was left. [47]Then the Jews[c] seized the spoils and the plunder; they cut off Nicanor's head and the right hand that he had so arrogantly stretched out, and brought them and displayed them just outside Jerusalem. [48]The people rejoiced greatly and celebrated that day as a day of great gladness. [49]They decreed that this day should be celebrated each year on the thirteenth day of Adar. [50]So the land of Judah had rest for a few days.

A Eulogy of the Romans

8 Now Judas heard of the fame of the Romans, that they were very strong and were well-disposed toward all who made an alliance with them, that they pledged friendship to those who came to them, [2]and that they were very strong. He had been told of their wars and of the brave deeds that they were doing among the Gauls, how they had defeated them and forced them to pay tribute, [3]and what they had done in the land of Spain to get control of the silver and gold mines there, [4]and how they had gained control of the whole region by their planning and patience, even though the place was far distant from them. They also subdued the kings who came against them from the ends of the earth, until they crushed them and inflicted great disaster on them; the rest paid them tribute every year. [5]They had crushed in battle and conquered Philip, and King Perseus of the Macedonians,[f] and the others who rose up against them. [6]They also had defeated Antiochus the Great, king of Asia, who went to fight against them with one hundred twenty elephants and with cavalry and chariots and a very large army. He was crushed by them; [7]they took him alive and decreed that he and those who would reign after him should pay a heavy tribute and give hostages and surrender some of their best provinces, [8]the countries of India, Media, and Lydia. These they took from him and gave to King Eumenes. [9]The Greeks planned to come and destroy them, [10]but this became known to them, and they sent a general against the Greeks[d] and attacked them. Many of them were wounded and fell, and the Romans[c] took captive their wives and children; they plundered them, conquered the land, tore down their strongholds, and enslaved them to this day. [11]The remaining kingdoms and islands, as many as ever opposed them, they destroyed and enslaved; [12]but with their friends and those who rely on them they have kept friendship. They have subdued kings far and near, and as many as have heard of their fame have feared them. [13]Those whom they wish to help and to make kings, they make kings, and those whom they wish

[a] Gk *of them*   [b] Gk *he*   [c] Gk *they*   [d] Gk *them*   [e] Gk *these*   [f] Or *Kittim*

they depose; and they have been greatly exalted. ¹⁴Yet for all this not one of them has put on a crown or worn purple as a mark of pride, ¹⁵but they have built for themselves a senate chamber, and every day three hundred twenty senators constantly deliberate concerning the people, to govern them well. ¹⁶They trust one man each year to rule over them and to control all their land; they all heed the one man, and there is no envy or jealousy among them.

An Alliance with Rome

17 So Judas chose Eupolemus son of John son of Accos, and Jason son of Eleazar, and sent them to Rome to establish friendship and alliance, ¹⁸and to free themselves from the yoke; for they saw that the kingdom of the Greeks was enslaving Israel completely. ¹⁹They went to Rome, a very long journey; and they entered the senate chamber and spoke as follows: ²⁰"Judas, who is also called Maccabeus, and his brothers and the people of the Jews have sent us to you to establish alliance and peace with you, so that we may be enrolled as your allies and friends." ²¹The proposal pleased them, ²²and this is a copy of the letter that they wrote in reply, on bronze tablets, and sent to Jerusalem to remain with them there as a memorial of peace and alliance:

23 "May all go well with the Romans and with the nation of the Jews at sea and on land forever, and may sword and enemy be far from them. ²⁴If war comes first to Rome or to any of their allies in all their dominion, ²⁵the nation of the Jews shall act as their allies wholeheartedly, as the occasion may indicate to them. ²⁶To the enemy that makes war they shall not give or supply grain, arms, money, or ships, just as Rome has decided; and they shall keep their obligations without receiving any return. ²⁷In the same way, if war comes first to the nation of the Jews, the Romans shall willingly act as their allies, as the occasion may indicate to them. ²⁸And to their enemies there shall not be given grain, arms, money, or ships, just as Rome has decided; and they shall keep these obligations and do so without deceit. ²⁹Thus on these terms the Romans make a treaty with the Jewish people. ³⁰If after these terms are in effect both parties shall determine to add or delete any-

thing, they shall do so at their discretion, and any addition or deletion that they may make shall be valid.

31 "Concerning the wrongs that King Demetrius is doing to them, we have written to him as follows, 'Why have you made your yoke heavy on our friends and allies the Jews? ³²If now they appeal again for help against you, we will defend their rights and fight you on sea and on land.'"

Bacchides Returns to Judea

9 When Demetrius heard that Nicanor and his army had fallen in battle, he sent Bacchides and Alcimus into the land of Judah a second time, and with them the right wing of the army. ²They went by the road that leads to Gilgal and encamped against Mesaloth in Arbela, and they took it and killed many people. ³In the first month of the one hundred fifty-second year*ᵍ* they encamped against Jerusalem; ⁴then they marched off and went to Berea with twenty thousand foot soldiers and two thousand cavalry.

5 Now Judas was encamped in Elasa, and with him were three thousand picked men. ⁶When they saw the huge number of the enemy forces, they were greatly frightened, and many slipped away from the camp, until no more than eight hundred of them were left.

7 When Judas saw that his army had slipped away and the battle was imminent, he was crushed in spirit, for he had no time to assemble them. ⁸He became faint, but he said to those who were left, "Let us get up and go against our enemies. We may have the strength to fight them." ⁹But they tried to dissuade him, saying, "We do not have the strength. Let us rather save our own lives now, and let us come back with our kindred and fight them; we are too few." ¹⁰But Judas said, "Far be it from us to do such a thing as to flee from them. If our time has come, let us die bravely for our kindred, and leave no cause to question our honor."

The Last Battle of Judas

11 Then the army of Bacchides*ʰ* marched out from the camp and took its stand for the encounter. The cavalry was divided into two companies, and the slingers and the

---

ᵍ 160 B.C.   *ʰ* Gk lacks *of Bacchides*

archers went ahead of the army, as did all the chief warriors. [12]Bacchides was on the right wing. Flanked by the two companies, the phalanx advanced to the sound of the trumpets; and the men with Judas also blew their trumpets. [13]The earth was shaken by the noise of the armies, and the battle raged from morning until evening.

14 Judas saw that Bacchides and the strength of his army were on the right; then all the stouthearted men went with him, [15]and they crushed the right wing, and he pursued them as far as Mount Azotus. [16]When those on the left wing saw that the right wing was crushed, they turned and followed close behind Judas and his men. [17]The battle became desperate, and many on both sides were wounded and fell. [18]Judas also fell, and the rest fled.

19 Then Jonathan and Simon took their brother Judas and buried him in the tomb of their ancestors at Modein, [20]and wept for him. All Israel made great lamentation for him; they mourned many days and said,
[21] "How is the mighty fallen,
    the savior of Israel!"
[22]Now the rest of the acts of Judas, and his wars and the brave deeds that he did, and his greatness, have not been recorded, but they were very many.

Jonathan Succeeds Judas

23 After the death of Judas, the renegades emerged in all parts of Israel; all the wrongdoers reappeared. [24]In those days a very great famine occurred, and the country went over to their side. [25]Bacchides chose the godless and put them in charge of the country. [26]They made inquiry and searched for the friends of Judas, and brought them to Bacchides, who took vengeance on them and made sport of them. [27]So there was great distress in Israel, such as had not been since the time that prophets ceased to appear among them.

28 Then all the friends of Judas assembled and said to Jonathan, [29]"Since the death of your brother Judas there has been no one like him to go against our enemies and Bacchides, and to deal with those of our nation who hate us. [30]Now therefore we have chosen you today to take his place as our ruler and leader, to fight our battle." [31]So Jonathan accepted the leadership at that time in place of his brother Judas.

The Campaigns of Jonathan

32 When Bacchides learned of this, he tried to kill him. [33]But Jonathan and his brother Simon and all who were with him heard of it, and they fled into the wilderness of Tekoa and camped by the water of the pool of Asphar. [34]Bacchides found this out on the sabbath day, and he with all his army crossed the Jordan.

35 So Jonathan[i] sent his brother as leader of the multitude and begged the Nabateans, who were his friends, for permission to store with them the great amount of baggage that they had. [36]But the family of Jambri from Medeba came out and seized John and all that he had, and left with it.

37 After these things it was reported to Jonathan and his brother Simon, "The family of Jambri are celebrating a great wedding, and are conducting the bride, a daughter of one of the great nobles of Canaan, from Nadabath with a large escort." [38]Remembering how their brother John had been killed, they went up and hid under cover of the mountain. [39]They looked out and saw a tumultuous procession with a great amount of baggage; and the bridegroom came out with his friends and his brothers to meet them with tambourines and musicians and many weapons. [40]Then they rushed on them from the ambush and began killing them. Many were wounded and fell, and the rest fled to the mountain; and the Jews[j] took all their goods. [41]So the wedding was turned into mourning and the voice of their musicians into a funeral dirge. [42]After they had fully avenged the blood of their brother, they returned to the marshes of the Jordan.

43 When Bacchides heard of this, he came with a large force on the sabbath day to the banks of the Jordan. [44]And Jonathan said to those with him, "Let us get up now and fight for our lives, for today things are not as they were before. [45]For look! the battle is in front of us and behind us; the water of the Jordan is on this side and on that, with marsh and thicket; there is no place to turn. [46]Cry out now to Heaven that you may be delivered from the hands of our enemies." [47]So the battle began, and Jonathan stretched out his hand to strike Bacchides, but he eluded him and went to the rear. [48]Then Jonathan and the men with him leaped into the Jordan and swam across to the other side, and the enemy[j] did

[i] Gk he [j] Gk they

142

not cross the Jordan to attack them. [49]And about one thousand of Bacchides' men fell that day.

Bacchides Builds Fortifications

50 Then Bacchides[k] returned to Jerusalem and built strong cities in Judea: the fortress in Jericho, and Emmaus, and Beth-horon, and Bethel, and Timnath, and[l] Pharathon, and Tephon, with high walls and gates and bars. [51]And he placed garrisons in them to harass Israel. [52]He also fortified the town of Beth-zur, and Gazara, and the citadel, and in them he put troops and stores of food. [53]And he took the sons of the leading men of the land as hostages and put them under guard in the citadel at Jerusalem.

54 In the one hundred and fifty-third year,[m] in the second month, Alcimus gave orders to tear down the wall of the inner court of the sanctuary. He tore down the work of the prophets! [55]But he only began to tear it down, for at that time Alcimus was stricken and his work was hindered; his mouth was stopped and he was paralyzed, so that he could no longer say a word or give commands concerning his house. [56]And Alcimus died at that time in great agony. [57]When Bacchides saw that Alcimus was dead, he returned to the king, and the land of Judah had rest for two years.

The End of the War

58 Then all the lawless plotted and said, "See! Jonathan and his men are living in quiet and confidence. So now let us bring Bacchides back, and he will capture them all in one night." [59]And they went and consulted with him. [60]He started to come with a large force, and secretly sent letters to all his allies in Judea, telling them to seize Jonathan and his men; but they were unable to do it, because their plan became known. [61]And Jonathan's men[n] seized about fifty of the men of the country who were leaders in this treachery, and killed them.

62 Then Jonathan with his men, and Simon, withdrew to Bethbasi in the wilderness; he rebuilt the parts of it that had been demolished, and they fortified it. [63]When Bacchides learned of this, he assembled all his forces, and sent orders to the men of Judea. [64]Then he came and encamped against Bethbasi; he fought against it for many days and made machines of war.

65 But Jonathan left his brother Simon in the town, while he went out into the country; and he went with only a few men. [66]He struck down Odomera and his kindred and the people of Phasiron in their tents. [67]Then he[o] began to attack and went into battle with his forces; and Simon and his men sallied out from the town and set fire to the machines of war. [68]They fought with Bacchides, and he was crushed by them. They pressed him very hard, for his plan and his expedition had been in vain. [69]So he was very angry at the renegades who had counseled him to come into the country, and he killed many of them. Then he decided to go back to his own land.

70 When Jonathan learned of this, he sent ambassadors to him to make peace with him and obtain release of the captives. [71]He agreed, and did as he said; and he swore to Jonathan[p] that he would not try to harm him as long as he lived. [72]He restored to him the captives whom he had taken previously from the land of Judah; then he turned and went back to his own land, and did not come again into their territory. [73]Thus the sword ceased from Israel. Jonathan settled in Michmash and began to judge the people; and he destroyed the godless out of Israel.

Revolt of Alexander Epiphanes

10 In the one hundred sixtieth year[q] Alexander Epiphanes, son of Antiochus, landed and occupied Ptolemais. They welcomed him, and there he began to reign. [2]When King Demetrius heard of it, he assembled a very large army and marched out to meet him in battle. [3]Demetrius sent Jonathan a letter in peaceable words to honor him; [4]for he said to himself, "Let us act first to make peace with him[r] before he makes peace with Alexander against us, [5]for he will remember all the wrongs that we did to him and to his brothers and his nation." [6]So Demetrius[k] gave him authority to recruit troops, to equip them with arms, and to become his ally; and he commanded that the hostages in the citadel should be released to him.

7 Then Jonathan came to Jerusalem and

[k] Gk he   [l] Some authorities omit *and*   [m] 159 B.C.   [n] Gk *they*   [o] Other ancient authorities read *they*   [p] Gk *him*   [q] 152 B.C.   [r] Gk *them*

read the letter in the hearing of all the people and of those in the citadel. ⁸They were greatly alarmed when they heard that the king had given him authority to recruit troops. ⁹But those in the citadel released the hostages to Jonathan, and he returned them to their parents.

10 And Jonathan took up residence in Jerusalem and began to rebuild and restore the city. ¹¹He directed those who were doing the work to build the walls and encircle Mount Zion with squared stones, for better fortification; and they did so.

12 Then the foreigners who were in the strongholds that Bacchides had built fled; ¹³all of them left their places and went back to their own lands. ¹⁴Only in Beth-zur did some remain who had forsaken the law and the commandments, for it served as a place of refuge.

15 Now King Alexander heard of all the promises that Demetrius had sent to Jonathan, and he heard of the battles that Jonathan⁵ and his brothers had fought, of the brave deeds that they had done, and of the troubles that they had endured. ¹⁶So he said, "Shall we find another such man? Come now, we will make him our friend and ally." ¹⁷And he wrote a letter and sent it to him, in the following words:

Jonathan Becomes High Priest

18 "King Alexander to his brother Jonathan, greetings. ¹⁹We have heard about you, that you are a mighty warrior and worthy to be our friend. ²⁰And so we have appointed you today to be the high priest of your nation; you are to be called the king's Friend and you are to take our side and keep friendship with us." He also sent him a purple robe and a golden crown.

21 So Jonathan put on the sacred vestments in the seventh month of the one hundred sixtieth year,ᵗ at the festival of booths,ᵘ and he recruited troops and equipped them with arms in abundance. ²²When Demetrius heard of these things he was distressed and said, ²³"What is this that we have done? Alexander has gotten ahead of us in forming a friendship with the Jews to strengthen himself. ²⁴I also will write them words of encouragement and promise them honor and gifts, so that I may have their help." ²⁵So he sent a message to them in the following words:

A Letter from Demetrius to Jonathan

"King Demetrius to the nation of the Jews, greetings. ²⁶Since you have kept your agreement with us and have continued your friendship with us, and have not sided with our enemies, we have heard of it and rejoiced. ²⁷Now continue still to keep faith with us, and we will repay you with good for what you do for us. ²⁸We will grant you many immunities and give you gifts.

29 "I now free you and exempt all the Jews from payment of tribute and salt tax and crown levies, ³⁰and instead of collecting the third of the grain and the half of the fruit of the trees that I should receive, I release them from this day and henceforth. I will not collect them from the land of Judah or from the three districts added to it from Samaria and Galilee, from this day and for all time. ³¹Jerusalem and its environs, its tithes and its revenues, shall be holy and free from tax. ³²I release also my control of the citadel in Jerusalem and give it to the high priest, so that he may station in it men of his own choice to guard it. ³³And everyone of the Jews taken as a captive from the land of Judah into any part of my kingdom, I set free without payment; and let all officials cancel also the taxes on their livestock.

34 "All the festivals and sabbaths and new moons and appointed days, and the three days before a festival and the three after a festival—let them all be days of immunity and release for all the Jews who are in my kingdom. ³⁵No one shall have authority to exact anything from them or annoy any of them about any matter.

36 "Let Jews be enrolled in the king's forces to the number of thirty thousand men, and let the maintenance be given them that is due to all the forces of the king. ³⁷Let some of them be stationed in the great strongholds of the king, and let some of them be put in positions of trust in the kingdom. Let their officers and leaders be of their own number, and let them live by their own laws, just as the king has commanded in the land of Judah.

38 "As for the three districts that have been added to Judea from the country of Samaria, let them be annexed to Judea so that they may be considered to be under one ruler and obey no other authority than the high priest. ³⁹Ptolemais and the land adjoining it I have given as a gift to the

---

ˢ Gk *he*   ᵗ 152 B.C.   ᵘ Or *tabernacles*

sanctuary in Jerusalem, to meet the necessary expenses of the sanctuary. [40]I also grant fifteen thousand shekels of silver yearly out of the king's revenues from appropriate places. [41]And all the additional funds that the government officials have not paid as they did in the first years,[v] they shall give from now on for the service of the temple.[w] [42]Moreover, the five thousand shekels of silver that my officials[x] have received every year from the income of the services of the temple, this too is canceled, because it belongs to the priests who minister there. [43]And all who take refuge at the temple in Jerusalem, or in any of its precincts, because they owe money to the king or are in debt, let them be released and receive back all their property in my kingdom.

44 "Let the cost of rebuilding and restoring the structures of the sanctuary be paid from the revenues of the king. [45]And let the cost of rebuilding the walls of Jerusalem and fortifying it all around, and the cost of rebuilding the walls in Judea, also be paid from the revenues of the king."

Death of Demetrius

46 When Jonathan and the people heard these words, they did not believe or accept them, because they remembered the great wrongs that Demetrius[y] had done in Israel and how much he had oppressed them. [47]They favored Alexander, because he had been the first to speak peaceable words to them, and they remained his allies all his days.

48 Now King Alexander assembled large forces and encamped opposite Demetrius. [49]The two kings met in battle, and the army of Demetrius fled, and Alexander[z] pursued him and defeated them. [50]He pressed the battle strongly until the sun set, and on that day Demetrius fell.

Treaty of Ptolemy and Alexander

51 Then Alexander sent ambassadors to Ptolemy king of Egypt with the following message: [52]"Since I have returned to my kingdom and have taken my seat on the throne of my ancestors, and established my rule—for I crushed Demetrius and gained control of our country; [53]I met him in battle, and he and his army were crushed by us, and we have taken our seat on the throne of his kingdom—[54]now therefore let us establish friendship with one another; give me now your daughter as my wife, and I will become your son-in-law, and will make gifts to you and to her in keeping with your position."

55 Ptolemy the king replied and said, "Happy was the day on which you returned to the land of your ancestors and took your seat on the throne of their kingdom. [56]And now I will do for you as you wrote, but meet me at Ptolemais, so that we may see one another, and I will become your father-in-law, as you have said."

57 So Ptolemy set out from Egypt, he and his daughter Cleopatra, and came to Ptolemais in the one hundred sixty-second year.[a] [58]King Alexander met him, and Ptolemy[y] gave him his daughter Cleopatra in marriage, and celebrated her wedding at Ptolemais with great pomp, as kings do.

59 Then King Alexander wrote to Jonathan to come and meet him. [60]So he went with pomp to Ptolemais and met the two kings; he gave them and their Friends silver and gold and many gifts, and found favor with them. [61]A group of malcontents from Israel, renegades, gathered together against him to accuse him; but the king paid no attention to them. [62]The king gave orders to take off Jonathan's garments and to clothe him in purple, and they did so. [63]The king also seated him at his side; and he said to his officers, "Go out with him into the middle of the city and proclaim that no one is to bring charges against him about any matter, and let no one annoy him for any reason." [64]When his accusers saw the honor that was paid him, in accord with the proclamation, and saw him clothed in purple, they all fled. [65]Thus the king honored him and enrolled him among his chief[b] Friends, and made him general and governor of the province. [66]And Jonathan returned to Jerusalem in peace and gladness.

Apollonius Is Defeated by Jonathan

67 In the one hundred sixty-fifth year[c] Demetrius son of Demetrius came from Crete to the land of his ancestors. [68]When King Alexander heard of it, he was greatly distressed and returned to Antioch. [69]And Demetrius appointed Apollonius the governor

---

[v] Meaning of Gk uncertain   [w] Gk *house*   [x] Gk *they*   [y] Gk *he*   [z] Other ancient authorities read *Alexander fled, and Demetrius*   [a] 150 B.C.   [b] Gk *first*   [c] 147 B.C.

of Coelesyria, and he assembled a large force and encamped against Jamnia. Then he sent the following message to the high priest Jonathan:

70 "You are the only one to rise up against us, and I have fallen into ridicule and disgrace because of you. Why do you assume authority against us in the hill country? [71]If you now have confidence in your forces, come down to the plain to meet us, and let us match strength with each other there, for I have with me the power of the cities. [72]Ask and learn who I am and who the others are that are helping us. People will tell you that you cannot stand before us, for your ancestors were twice put to flight in their own land. [73]And now you will not be able to withstand my cavalry and such an army in the plain, where there is no stone or pebble, or place to flee."

74 When Jonathan heard the words of Apollonius, his spirit was aroused. He chose ten thousand men and set out from Jerusalem, and his brother Simon met him to help him. [75]He encamped before Joppa, but the people of the city closed its gates, for Apollonius had a garrison in Joppa. [76]So they fought against it, and the people of the city became afraid and opened the gates, and Jonathan gained possession of Joppa.

77 When Apollonius heard of it, he mustered three thousand cavalry and a large army, and went to Azotus as though he were going farther. At the same time he advanced into the plain, for he had a large troop of cavalry and put confidence in it. [78]Jonathan[d] pursued him to Azotus, and the armies engaged in battle. [79]Now Apollonius had secretly left a thousand cavalry behind them. [80]Jonathan learned that there was an ambush behind him, for they surrounded his army and shot arrows at his men from early morning until late afternoon. [81]But his men stood fast, as Jonathan had commanded, and the enemy's[e] horses grew tired.

82 Then Simon brought forward his force and engaged the phalanx in battle (for the cavalry was exhausted); they were overwhelmed by him and fled, [83]and the cavalry was dispersed in the plain. They fled to Azotus and entered Beth-dagon, the temple of their idol, for safety. [84]But Jonathan burned Azotus and the surrounding towns and plundered them; and the temple of Dagon, and those who had taken refuge in it, he burned with fire. [85]The number of those who fell by the sword, with those burned alive, came to eight thousand.

86 Then Jonathan left there and encamped against Askalon, and the people of the city came out to meet him with great pomp.

87 He and those with him then returned to Jerusalem with a large amount of booty. [88]When King Alexander heard of these things, he honored Jonathan still more; [89]and he sent to him a golden buckle, such as it is the custom to give to the King's Kinsmen. He also gave him Ekron and all its environs as his possession.

Ptolemy Invades Syria

11 Then the king of Egypt gathered great forces, like the sand by the seashore, and many ships; and he tried to get possession of Alexander's kingdom by trickery and add it to his own kingdom. [2]He set out for Syria with peaceable words, and the people of the towns opened their gates to him and went to meet him, for King Alexander had commanded them to meet him, since he was Alexander's[f] father-in-law. [3]But when Ptolemy entered the towns he stationed forces as a garrison in each town.

4 When he[g] approached Azotus, they showed him the burnt-out temple of Dagon, and Azotus and its suburbs destroyed, and the corpses lying about, and the charred bodies of those whom Jonathan[d] had burned in the war, for they had piled them in heaps along his route. [5]They also told the king what Jonathan had done, to throw blame on him; but the king kept silent. [6]Jonathan met the king at Joppa with pomp, and they greeted one another and spent the night there. [7]And Jonathan went with the king as far as the river called Eleutherus; then he returned to Jerusalem.

8 So King Ptolemy gained control of the coastal cities as far as Seleucia by the sea, and he kept devising wicked designs against Alexander. [9]He sent envoys to King Demetrius, saying, "Come, let us make a covenant with each other, and I will give you in marriage my daughter who was Alexander's wife, and you shall reign over your father's kingdom. [10]I now regret that I gave him my daughter, for he has tried to kill me." [11]He threw blame on Alexander[h] because he coveted his kingdom. [12]So he

---

[d] Gk *he*   [e] Gk *their*   [f] Gk *his*   [g] Other ancient authorities read *they*   [h] Gk *him*

146

took his daughter away from him and gave her to Demetrius. He was estranged from Alexander, and their enmity became manifest. 13 Then Ptolemy entered Antioch and put on the crown of Asia. Thus he put two crowns on his head, the crown of Egypt and that of Asia. [14]Now King Alexander was in Cilicia at that time, because the people of that region were in revolt. [15]When Alexander heard of it, he came against him in battle. Ptolemy marched out and met him with a strong force, and put him to flight. [16]So Alexander fled into Arabia to find protection there, and King Ptolemy was triumphant. [17]Zabdiel the Arab cut off the head of Alexander and sent it to Ptolemy. [18]But King Ptolemy died three days later, and his troops in the strongholds were killed by the inhabitants of the strongholds. [19]So Demetrius became king in the one hundred sixty-seventh year.[i]

Jonathan's Diplomacy

20 In those days Jonathan assembled the Judeans to attack the citadel in Jerusalem, and he built many engines of war to use against it. [21]But certain renegades who hated their nation went to the king and reported to him that Jonathan was besieging the citadel. [22]When he heard this he was angry, and as soon as he heard it he set out and came to Ptolemais; and he wrote Jonathan not to continue the siege, but to meet him for a conference at Ptolemais as quickly as possible.

23 When Jonathan heard this, he gave orders to continue the siege. He chose some of the elders of Israel and some of the priests, and put himself in danger, [24]for he went to the king at Ptolemais, taking silver and gold and clothing and numerous other gifts. And he won his favor. [25]Although certain renegades of his nation kept making complaints against him, [26]the king treated him as his predecessors had treated him; he exalted him in the presence of all his Friends. [27]He confirmed him in the high priesthood and in as many other honors as he had formerly had, and caused him to be reckoned among his chief[j] Friends. [28]Then Jonathan asked the king to free Judea and the three districts of Samaria[k] from tribute, and promised him three hundred talents.

[29]The king consented, and wrote a letter to Jonathan about all these things; its contents were as follows:

30 "King Demetrius to his brother Jonathan and to the nation of the Jews, greetings. [31]This copy of the letter that we wrote concerning you to our kinsman Lasthenes we have written to you also, so that you may know what it says. [32]'King Demetrius to his father Lasthenes, greetings. [33]We have determined to do good to the nation of the Jews, who are our friends and fulfill their obligations to us, because of the goodwill they show toward us. [34]We have confirmed as their possession both the territory of Judea and the three districts of Aphairema and Lydda and Rathamin; the latter, with all the region bordering them, were added to Judea from Samaria. To all those who offer sacrifice in Jerusalem we have granted release from[l] the royal taxes that the king formerly received from them each year, from the crops of the land and the fruit of the trees. [35]And the other payments henceforth due to us of the tithes, and the taxes due to us, and the salt pits and the crown taxes due to us—from all these we shall grant them release. [36]And not one of these grants shall be canceled from this time on forever. [37]Now therefore take care to make a copy of this, and let it be given to Jonathan and put up in a conspicuous place on the holy mountain.' "

The Intrigue of Trypho

38 When King Demetrius saw that the land was quiet before him and that there was no opposition to him, he dismissed all his troops, all of them to their own homes, except the foreign troops that he had recruited from the islands of the nations. So all the troops who had served under his predecessors hated him. [39]A certain Trypho had formerly been one of Alexander's supporters; he saw that all the troops were grumbling against Demetrius. So he went to Imalkue the Arab, who was bringing up Antiochus, the young son of Alexander, [40]and insistently urged him to hand Antiochus[m] over to him, to become king in place of his father. He also reported to Imalkue[m] what Demetrius had done and told of the hatred that the troops of Demetrius[n] had for him; and he stayed there many days.

[i] 145 B.C.   [j] Gk first   [k] Cn: Gk the three districts and Samaria   [l] Or Samaria, for all those who offer sacrifice in Jerusalem, in place of   [m] Gk him   [n] Gk his troops

41 Now Jonathan sent to King Demetrius the request that he remove the troops of the citadel from Jerusalem, and the troops in the strongholds; for they kept fighting against Israel. [42]And Demetrius sent this message back to Jonathan: "Not only will I do these things for you and your nation, but I will confer great honor on you and your nation, if I find an opportunity. [43]Now then you will do well to send me men who will help me, for all my troops have revolted." [44]So Jonathan sent three thousand stalwart men to him at Antioch, and when they came to the king, the king rejoiced at their arrival.

45 Then the people of the city assembled within the city, to the number of a hundred and twenty thousand, and they wanted to kill the king. [46]But the king fled into the palace. Then the people of the city seized the main streets of the city and began to fight. [47]So the king called the Jews to his aid, and they all rallied around him and then spread out through the city; and they killed on that day about one hundred thousand. [48]They set fire to the city and seized a large amount of spoil on that day, and saved the king. [49]When the people of the city saw that the Jews had gained control of the city as they pleased, their courage failed and they cried out to the king with this entreaty: [50]"Grant us peace, and make the Jews stop fighting against us and our city." [51]And they threw down their arms and made peace. So the Jews gained glory in the sight of the king and of all the people in his kingdom, and they returned to Jerusalem with a large amount of spoil.

52 So King Demetrius sat on the throne of his kingdom, and the land was quiet before him. [53]But he broke his word about all that he had promised; he became estranged from Jonathan and did not repay the favors that Jonathan[o] had done him, but treated him very harshly.

Trypho Seizes Power

54 After this Trypho returned, and with him the young boy Antiochus who began to reign and put on the crown. [55]All the troops that Demetrius had discharged gathered around him; they fought against Demetrius,[p] and he fled and was routed. [56]Trypho captured the elephants[q] and gained control of Antioch. [57]Then the young Antiochus wrote to Jonathan, say-

ing, "I confirm you in the high priesthood and set you over the four districts and make you one of the king's Friends." [58]He also sent him gold plates and a table service, and granted him the right to drink from gold cups and dress in purple and wear a gold buckle. [59]He appointed Jonathan's[r] brother Simon governor from the Ladder of Tyre to the borders of Egypt.

Campaigns of Jonathan and Simon

60 Then Jonathan set out and traveled beyond the river and among the towns, and all the army of Syria gathered to him as allies. When he came to Askalon, the people of the city met him and paid him honor. [61]From there he went to Gaza, but the people of Gaza shut him out. So he besieged it and burned its suburbs with fire and plundered them. [62]Then the people of Gaza pleaded with Jonathan, and he made peace with them, and took the sons of their rulers as hostages and sent them to Jerusalem. And he passed through the country as far as Damascus.

63 Then Jonathan heard that the officers of Demetrius had come to Kadesh in Galilee with a large army, intending to remove him from office. [64]He went to meet them, but left his brother Simon in the country. [65]Simon encamped before Beth-zur and fought against it for many days and hemmed it in. [66]Then they asked him to grant them terms of peace, and he did so. He removed them from there, took possession of the town, and set a garrison over it.

67 Jonathan and his army encamped by the waters of Gennesaret. Early in the morning they marched to the plain of Hazor, [68]and there in the plain the army of the foreigners met him; they had set an ambush against him in the mountains, but they themselves met him face to face. [69]Then the men in ambush emerged from their places and joined battle. [70]All the men with Jonathan fled; not one of them was left except Mattathias son of Absalom and Judas son of Chalphi, commanders of the forces of the army. [71]Jonathan tore his clothes, put dust on his head, and prayed. [72]Then he turned back to the battle against the enemy[s] and routed them, and they fled. [73]When his men who were fleeing saw this, they returned to him and joined him in the pursuit as far as Kadesh, to their camp, and

o Gk *he*　　*p* Gk *him*　　*q* Gk *animals*　　*r* Gk *his*　　*s* Gk *them* there they encamped. ⁷⁴As many as three thousand of the foreigners fell that day. And Jonathan returned to Jerusalem.

Alliances with Rome and Sparta

12 Now when Jonathan saw that the time was favorable for him, he chose men and sent them to Rome to confirm and renew the friendship with them. ²He also sent letters to the same effect to the Spartans and to other places. ³So they went to Rome and entered the senate chamber and said, "The high priest Jonathan and the Jewish nation have sent us to renew the former friendship and alliance with them." ⁴And the Romans*ᵗ* gave them letters to the people in every place, asking them to provide for the envoys*ᵘ* safe conduct to the land of Judah.

5 This is a copy of the letter that Jonathan wrote to the Spartans: ⁶"The high priest Jonathan, the senate of the nation, the priests, and the rest of the Jewish people to their brothers the Spartans, greetings. ⁷Already in time past a letter was sent to the high priest Onias from Arius,*ᵛ* who was king among you, stating that you are our brothers, as the appended copy shows. ⁸Onias welcomed the envoy with honor, and received the letter, which contained a clear declaration of alliance and friendship. ⁹Therefore, though we have no need of these things, since we have as encouragement the holy books that are in our hands, ¹⁰we have undertaken to send to renew our family ties and friendship with you, so that we may not become estranged from you, for considerable time has passed since you sent your letter to us. ¹¹We therefore remember you constantly on every occasion, both at our festivals and on other appropriate days, at the sacrifices that we offer and in our prayers, as it is right and proper to remember brothers. ¹²And we rejoice in your glory. ¹³But as for ourselves, many trials and many wars have encircled us; the kings around us have waged war against us. ¹⁴We were unwilling to annoy you and our other allies and friends with these wars, ¹⁵for we have the help that comes from Heaven for our aid, and so we were delivered from our enemies, and our enemies were humbled. ¹⁶We therefore have chosen Numenius son of Antiochus and Antipater son of Jason, and have sent them to Rome

to renew our former friendship and alliance with them. ¹⁷We have commanded them to go also to you and greet you and deliver to you this letter from us concerning the renewal of our family ties. ¹⁸And now please send us a reply to this."

19 This is a copy of the letter that they sent to Onias: ²⁰"King Arius of the Spartans, to the high priest Onias, greetings. ²¹It has been found in writing concerning the Spartans and the Jews that they are brothers and are of the family of Abraham. ²²And now that we have learned this, please write us concerning your welfare; ²³we on our part write to you that your livestock and your property belong to us, and ours belong to you. We therefore command that our envoys*ᵗ* report to you accordingly."

Further Campaigns of Jonathan and Simon

24 Now Jonathan heard that the commanders of Demetrius had returned, with a larger force than before, to wage war against him. ²⁵So he marched away from Jerusalem and met them in the region of Hamath, for he gave them no opportunity to invade his own country. ²⁶He sent spies to their camp, and they returned and reported to him that the enemy*ᵗ* were being drawn up in formation to attack the Jews*ᵘ* by night. ²⁷So when the sun had set, Jonathan commanded his troops to be alert and to keep their arms at hand so as to be ready all night for battle, and he stationed outposts around the camp. ²⁸When the enemy heard that Jonathan and his troops were prepared for battle, they were afraid and were terrified at heart; so they kindled fires in their camp and withdrew.*ʷ* ²⁹But Jonathan and his troops did not know it until morning, for they saw the fires burning. ³⁰Then Jonathan pursued them, but he did not overtake them, for they had crossed the Eleutherus river. ³¹So Jonathan turned aside against the Arabs who are called Zabadeans, and he crushed them and plundered them. ³²Then he broke camp and went to Damascus, and marched through all that region.

33 Simon also went out and marched through the country as far as Askalon and the neighboring strongholds. He turned aside to Joppa and took it by surprise, ³⁴for he had heard that they were ready to hand over the stronghold to those whom Demetrius had sent. And he stationed a garrison there to guard it.

ᵗ Gk *they*   *ᵘ* Gk *them*   *ᵛ* Vg Compare verse 20: Gk *Darius*   *ʷ* Other ancient authorities omit *and withdrew*

35 When Jonathan returned he convened the elders of the people and planned with them to build strongholds in Judea, [36]to build the walls of Jerusalem still higher, and to erect a high barrier between the citadel and the city to separate it from the city, in order to isolate it so that its garrison[x] could neither buy nor sell. [37]So they gathered together to rebuild the city; part of the wall on the valley to the east had fallen, and he repaired the section called Chaphenatha. [38]Simon also built Adida in the Shephelah; he fortified it and installed gates with bolts.

Trypho Captures Jonathan

39 Then Trypho attempted to become king in Asia and put on the crown, and to raise his hand against King Antiochus. [40]He feared that Jonathan might not permit him to do so, but might make war on him, so he kept seeking to seize and kill him, and he marched out and came to Beth-shan. [41]Jonathan went out to meet him with forty thousand picked warriors, and he came to Beth-shan. [42]When Trypho saw that he had come with a large army, he was afraid to raise his hand against him. [43]So he received him with honor and commended him to all his Friends, and he gave him gifts and commanded his Friends and his troops to obey him as they would himself. [44]Then he said to Jonathan, "Why have you put all these people to so much trouble when we are not at war? [45]Dismiss them now to their homes and choose for yourself a few men to stay with you, and come with me to Ptolemais. I will hand it over to you as well as the other strongholds and the remaining troops and all the officials, and will turn around and go home. For that is why I am here."

46 Jonathan[y] trusted him and did as he said; he sent away the troops, and they returned to the land of Judah. [47]He kept with himself three thousand men, two thousand of whom he left in Galilee, while one thousand accompanied him. [48]But when Jonathan entered Ptolemais, the people of Ptolemais closed the gates and seized him, and they killed with the sword all who had entered with him.

49 Then Trypho sent troops and cavalry into Galilee and the Great Plain to destroy all Jonathan's soldiers. [50]But they realized that Jonathan had been seized and had perished along with his men, and they encouraged one another and kept marching in close formation, ready for battle. [51]When their pursuers saw that they would fight for their lives, they turned back. [52]So they all reached the land of Judah safely, and they mourned for Jonathan and his companions and were in great fear; and all Israel mourned deeply. [53]All the nations around them tried to destroy them, for they said, "They have no leader or helper. Now therefore let us make war on them and blot out the memory of them from humankind."

Simon Takes Command

13 Simon heard that Trypho had assembled a large army to invade the land of Judah and destroy it, [2]and he saw that the people were trembling with fear. So he went up to Jerusalem, and gathering the people together [3]he encouraged them, saying to them, "You yourselves know what great things my brothers and I and the house of my father have done for the laws and the sanctuary; you know also the wars and the difficulties that my brothers and I have seen. [4]By reason of this all my brothers have perished for the sake of Israel, and I alone am left. [5]And now, far be it from me to spare my life in any time of distress, for I am not better than my brothers. [6]But I will avenge my nation and the sanctuary and your wives and children, for all the nations have gathered together out of hatred to destroy us."

7 The spirit of the people was rekindled when they heard these words, [8]and they answered in a loud voice, "You are our leader in place of Judas and your brother Jonathan. [9]Fight our battles, and all that you say to us we will do." [10]So he assembled all the warriors and hurried to complete the walls of Jerusalem, and he fortified it on every side. [11]He sent Jonathan son of Absalom to Joppa, and with him a considerable army; he drove out its occupants and remained there.

Deceit and Treachery of Trypho

12 Then Trypho left Ptolemais with a large army to invade the land of Judah, and Jonathan was with him under guard. [13]Simon encamped in Adida, facing the plain. [14]Trypho learned that Simon had risen up

x Gk *they*   *y* Gk *he*

in place of his brother Jonathan, and that he was about to join battle with him, so he sent envoys to him and said, [15]"It is for the money that your brother Jonathan owed the royal treasury, in connection with the offices he held, that we are detaining him. [16]Send now one hundred talents of silver and two of his sons as hostages, so that when released he will not revolt against us, and we will release him."

17 Simon knew that they were speaking deceitfully to him, but he sent to get the money and the sons, so that he would not arouse great hostility among the people, who might say, [18]"It was because Simon[z] did not send him the money and the sons, that Jonathan[a] perished." [19]So he sent the sons and the hundred talents, but Trypho[a] broke his word and did not release Jonathan.

20 After this Trypho came to invade the country and destroy it, and he circled around by the way to Adora. But Simon and his army kept marching along opposite him to every place he went. [21]Now the men in the citadel kept sending envoys to Trypho urging him to come to them by way of the wilderness and to send them food. [22]So Trypho got all his cavalry ready to go, but that night a very heavy snow fell, and he did not go because of the snow. He marched off and went into the land of Gilead. [23]When he approached Baskama, he killed Jonathan, and he was buried there. [24]Then Trypho turned and went back to his own land.

Jonathan's Tomb

25 Simon sent and took the bones of his brother Jonathan, and buried him in Modein, the city of his ancestors. [26]All Israel bewailed him with great lamentation, and mourned for him many days. [27]And Simon built a monument over the tomb of his father and his brothers; he made it high so that it might be seen, with polished stone at the front and back. [28]He also erected seven pyramids, opposite one another, for his father and mother and four brothers. [29]For the pyramids[b] he devised an elaborate setting, erecting about them great columns, and on the columns he put suits of armor for a permanent memorial, and beside the suits of armor he carved ships, so that they could be seen by all who sail the sea. [30]This is the tomb that he built in Modein; it remains to this day.

Judea Gains Independence

31 Trypho dealt treacherously with the young King Antiochus; he killed him [32]and became king in his place, putting on the crown of Asia; and he brought great calamity on the land. [33]But Simon built up the strongholds of Judea and walled them all around, with high towers and great walls and gates and bolts, and he stored food in the strongholds. [34]Simon also chose emissaries and sent them to King Demetrius with a request to grant relief to the country, for all that Trypho did was to plunder. [35]King Demetrius sent him a favorable reply to this request, and wrote him a letter as follows, [36]"King Demetrius to Simon, the high priest and friend of kings, and to the elders and nation of the Jews, greetings. [37]We have received the gold crown and the palm branch that you[c] sent, and we are ready to make a general peace with you and to write to our officials to grant you release from tribute. [38]All the grants that we have made to you remain valid, and let the strongholds that you have built be your possession. [39]We pardon any errors and offenses committed to this day, and cancel the crown tax that you owe; and whatever other tax has been collected in Jerusalem shall be collected no longer. [40]And if any of you are qualified to be enrolled in our bodyguard,[d] let them be enrolled, and let there be peace between us."

41 In the one hundred seventieth year[e] the yoke of the Gentiles was removed from Israel, [42]and the people began to write in their documents and contracts, "In the first year of Simon the great high priest and commander and leader of the Jews."

The Capture of Gazara by Simon

43 In those days Simon[a] encamped against Gazara[f] and surrounded it with troops. He made a siege engine, brought it up to the city, and battered and captured one tower. [44]The men in the siege engine leaped out into the city, and a great tumult arose in the city. [45]The men in the city, with their wives and children, went up on the wall with their clothes torn, and they cried out with a loud voice, asking Simon to make peace with them; [46]they said, "Do not treat us according to our wicked acts but according to your mercy." [47]So Simon

[z] Gk *I*   [a] Gk *he*   [b] Gk *For these*   [c] The word *you* in verses 37–40 is plural   [d] Or *court*   [e] 142 B.C.   [f] Cn: Gk *Gaza*

reached an agreement with them and stopped fighting against them. But he expelled them from the city and cleansed the houses in which the idols were located, and then entered it with hymns and praise. ⁴⁸He removed all uncleanness from it, and settled in it those who observed the law. He also strengthened its fortifications and built in it a house for himself.

Simon Regains the Citadel at Jerusalem

49 Those who were in the citadel at Jerusalem were prevented from going in and out to buy and sell in the country. So they were very hungry, and many of them perished from famine. ⁵⁰Then they cried to Simon to make peace with them, and he did so. But he expelled them from there and cleansed the citadel from its pollutions. ⁵¹On the twenty-third day of the second month, in the one hundred seventy-first year,ᵍ the Jewsʰ entered it with praise and palm branches, and with harps and cymbals and stringed instruments, and with hymns and songs, because a great enemy had been crushed and removed from Israel. ⁵²Simonⁱ decreed that every year they should celebrate this day with rejoicing. He strengthened the fortifications of the temple hill alongside the citadel, and he and his men lived there. ⁵³Simon saw that his son John had reached manhood, and so he made him commander of all the forces; and he lived at Gazara.

Capture of Demetrius

14 In the one hundred seventy-second yearʲ King Demetrius assembled his forces and marched into Media to obtain help, so that he could make war against Trypho. ²When King Arsaces of Persia and Media heard that Demetrius had invaded his territory, he sent one of his generals to take him alive. ³The generalⁱ went and defeated the army of Demetrius, and seized him and took him to Arsaces, who put him under guard.

Eulogy of Simon

⁴ The landᵏ had rest all the days of Simon.
  He sought the good of his nation;
  his rule was pleasing to them,

as was the honor shown him, all
  his days.
⁵ To crown all his honors he took Joppa
  for a harbor,
  and opened a way to the isles of
  the sea.
⁶ He extended the borders of his nation,
  and gained full control of the country.
⁷ He gathered a host of captives;
  he ruled over Gazara and Beth-zur
  and the citadel,
  and he removed its uncleanness from it;
  and there was none to oppose him.
⁸ They tilled their land in peace;
  the ground gave its increase,
  and the trees of the plains their fruit.
⁹ Old men sat in the streets;
  they all talked together of good things,
  and the youths put on splendid
  military attire.
¹⁰ He supplied the towns with food,
  and furnished them with the means
  of defense,
  until his renown spread to the ends
  of the earth.
¹¹ He established peace in the land,
  and Israel rejoiced with great joy.
¹² All the people sat under their own
  vines and fig trees,
  and there was none to make them
  afraid.
¹³ No one was left in the land to fight them,
  and the kings were crushed in those
  days.
¹⁴ He gave help to all the humble among
  his people;
  he sought out the law,
  and did away with all the renegades
  and outlaws.
¹⁵ He made the sanctuary glorious,
  and added to the vessels of the
  sanctuary.

Diplomacy with Rome and Sparta

16 It was heard in Rome, and as far away as Sparta, that Jonathan had died, and they were deeply grieved. ¹⁷When they heard that his brother Simon had become high priest in his stead, and that he was ruling over the country and the towns in it, ¹⁸they wrote to him on bronze tablets to renew with him the friendship and alliance that they had established with his brothers Judas and Jonathan. ¹⁹And these were read before the assembly in Jerusalem.

ᵍ 141 B.C.   ʰ Gk *they*   ⁱ Gk *He*   ʲ 140 B.C.   ᵏ Other ancient authorities add *of Judah*

20 This is a copy of the letter that the Spartans sent:

"The rulers and the city of the Spartans to the high priest Simon and to the elders and the priests and the rest of the Jewish people, our brothers, greetings. ²¹The envoys who were sent to our people have told us about your glory and honor, and we rejoiced at their coming. ²²We have recorded what they said in our public decrees, as follows, 'Numenius son of Antiochus and Antipater son of Jason, envoys of the Jews, have come to us to renew their friendship with us. ²³It has pleased our people to receive these men with honor and to put a copy of their words in the public archives, so that the people of the Spartans may have a record of them. And they have sent a copy of this to the high priest Simon.' "

24 After this Simon sent Numenius to Rome with a large gold shield weighing one thousand minas, to confirm the alliance with the Romans.*l*

Official Honors for Simon

25 When the people heard these things they said, "How shall we thank Simon and his sons? ²⁶For he and his brothers and the house of his father have stood firm; they have fought and repulsed Israel's enemies and established its freedom." ²⁷So they made a record on bronze tablets and put it on pillars on Mount Zion.

This is a copy of what they wrote: "On the eighteenth day of Elul, in the one hundred seventy-second year,*m* which is the third year of the great high priest Simon, ²⁸in Asaramel,*n* in the great assembly of the priests and the people and the rulers of the nation and the elders of the country, the following was proclaimed to us:

29 "Since wars often occurred in the country, Simon son of Mattathias, a priest of the sons*o* of Joarib, and his brothers, exposed themselves to danger and resisted the enemies of their nation, in order that their sanctuary and the law might be preserved; and they brought great glory to their nation. ³⁰Jonathan rallied the*p* nation, became their high priest, and was gathered to his people. ³¹When their enemies decided to invade their country and lay hands on their sanctuary, ³²then Simon rose up and

fought for his nation. He spent great sums of his own money; he armed the soldiers of his nation and paid them wages. ³³He fortified the towns of Judea, and Beth-zur on the borders of Judea, where formerly the arms of the enemy had been stored, and he placed there a garrison of Jews. ³⁴He also fortified Joppa, which is by the sea, and Gazara, which is on the borders of Azotus, where the enemy formerly lived. He settled Jews there, and provided in those towns*l* whatever was necessary for their restoration.

35 "The people saw Simon's faithfulness*q* and the glory that he had resolved to win for his nation, and they made him their leader and high priest, because he had done all these things and because of the justice and loyalty that he had maintained toward his nation. He sought in every way to exalt his people. ³⁶In his days things prospered in his hands, so that the Gentiles were put out of the*p* country, as were also those in the city of David in Jerusalem, who had built themselves a citadel from which they used to sally forth and defile the environs of the sanctuary, doing great damage to its purity. ³⁷He settled Jews in it and fortified it for the safety of the country and of the city, and built the walls of Jerusalem higher.

38 "In view of these things King Demetrius confirmed him in the high priesthood, ³⁹made him one of his Friends, and paid him high honors. ⁴⁰For he had heard that the Jews were addressed by the Romans as friends and allies and brothers, and that the Romans*r* had received the envoys of Simon with honor.

41 "The Jews and their priests have resolved that Simon should be their leader and high priest forever, until a trustworthy prophet should arise, ⁴²and that he should be governor over them and that he should take charge of the sanctuary and appoint officials over its tasks and over the country and the weapons and the strongholds, and that he should take charge of the sanctuary, ⁴³and that he should be obeyed by all, and that all contracts in the country should be written in his name, and that he should be clothed in purple and wear gold.

44 "None of the people or priests shall be permitted to nullify any of these decisions or to oppose what he says, or to convene an

---

l Gk *them*   *m* 140 B.C.   *n* This word resembles the Hebrew words for *the court of the people of God* or *the prince of the people of God*   *o* Meaning of Gk uncertain   *p* Gk *their*   *q* Other ancient authorities read *conduct*   *r* Gk *they*

assembly in the country without his permission, or to be clothed in purple or put on a gold buckle. ⁴⁵Whoever acts contrary to these decisions or rejects any of them shall be liable to punishment."

46 All the people agreed to grant Simon the right to act in accordance with these decisions. ⁴⁷So Simon accepted and agreed to be high priest, to be commander and ethnarch of the Jews and priests, and to be protector of them all.^s ⁴⁸And they gave orders to inscribe this decree on bronze tablets, to put them up in a conspicuous place in the precincts of the sanctuary, ⁴⁹and to deposit copies of them in the treasury, so that Simon and his sons might have them.

Letter of Antiochus VII

15 Antiochus, son of King Demetrius, sent a letter from the islands of the sea to Simon, the priest and ethnarch of the Jews, and to all the nation; ²its contents were as follows: "King Antiochus to Simon the high priest and ethnarch and to the nation of the Jews, greetings. ³Whereas certain scoundrels have gained control of the kingdom of our ancestors, and I intend to lay claim to the kingdom so that I may restore it as it formerly was, and have recruited a host of mercenary troops and have equipped warships, ⁴and intend to make a landing in the country so that I may proceed against those who have destroyed our country and those who have devastated many cities in my kingdom, ⁵now therefore I confirm to you all the tax remissions that the kings before me have granted you, and a release from all the other payments from which they have released you. ⁶I permit you to mint your own coinage as money for your country, ⁷and I grant freedom to Jerusalem and the sanctuary. All the weapons that you have prepared and the strongholds that you have built and now hold shall remain yours. ⁸Every debt you owe to the royal treasury and any such future debts shall be canceled for you from henceforth and for all time. ⁹When we gain control of our kingdom, we will bestow great honor on you and your nation and the temple, so that your glory will become manifest in all the earth."

10 In the one hundred seventy-fourth year^t Antiochus set out and invaded the land of his ancestors. All the troops rallied

to him, so that there were only a few with Trypho. ¹¹Antiochus pursued him, and Trypho^u came in his flight to Dor, which is by the sea; ¹²for he knew that troubles had converged on him, and his troops had deserted him. ¹³So Antiochus encamped against Dor, and with him were one hundred twenty thousand warriors and eight thousand cavalry. ¹⁴He surrounded the town, and the ships joined battle from the sea; he pressed the town hard from land and sea, and permitted no one to leave or enter it.

Rome Supports the Jews

15 Then Numenius and his companions arrived from Rome, with letters to the kings and countries, in which the following was written: ¹⁶"Lucius, consul of the Romans, to King Ptolemy, greetings. ¹⁷The envoys of the Jews have come to us as our friends and allies to renew our ancient friendship and alliance. They had been sent by the high priest Simon and by the Jewish people ¹⁸and have brought a gold shield weighing one thousand minas. ¹⁹We therefore have decided to write to the kings and countries that they should not seek their harm or make war against them and their cities and their country, or make alliance with those who war against them. ²⁰And it has seemed good to us to accept the shield from them. ²¹Therefore if any scoundrels have fled to you from their country, hand them over to the high priest Simon, so that he may punish them according to their law."

22 The consul^v wrote the same thing to King Demetrius and to Attalus and Ariarathes and Arsaces, ²³and to all the countries, and to Sampsames,^w and to the Spartans, and to Delos, and to Myndos, and to Sicyon, and to Caria, and to Samos, and to Pamphylia, and to Lycia, and to Halicarnassus, and to Rhodes, and to Phaselis, and to Cos, and to Side, and to Aradus and Gortyna and Cnidus and Cyprus and Cyrene. ²⁴They also sent a copy of these things to the high priest Simon.

Antiochus VII Threatens Simon

25 King Antiochus besieged Dor for the second time, continually throwing his forces against it and making engines of war; and he shut Trypho up and kept him from going out or in. ²⁶And Simon sent to Antiochus^x

two thousand picked troops, to fight for him, and silver and gold and a large amount of military equipment. ²⁷But he refused to receive them, and broke all the agreements he formerly had made with Simon, and became estranged from him. ²⁸He sent to him Athenobius, one of his Friends, to confer with him, saying, "You hold control of Joppa and Gazara and the citadel in Jerusalem; they are cities of my kingdom. ²⁹You have devastated their territory, you have done great damage in the land, and you have taken possession of many places in my kingdom. ³⁰Now then, hand over the cities that you have seized and the tribute money of the places that you have conquered outside the borders of Judea; ³¹or else pay me five hundred talents of silver for the destruction that you have caused and five hundred talents more for the tribute money of the cities. Otherwise we will come and make war on you."

32 So Athenobius, the king's Friend, came to Jerusalem, and when he saw the splendor of Simon, and the sideboard with its gold and silver plate, and his great magnificence, he was amazed. When he reported to him the king's message, ³³Simon said to him in reply: "We have neither taken foreign land nor seized foreign property, but only the inheritance of our ancestors, which at one time had been unjustly taken by our enemies. ³⁴Now that we have the opportunity, we are firmly holding the inheritance of our ancestors. ³⁵As for Joppa and Gazara, which you demand, they were causing great damage among the people and to our land; for them we will give you one hundred talents."

Athenobius*ᵘ* did not answer him a word, ³⁶but returned in wrath to the king and reported to him these words, and also the splendor of Simon and all that he had seen. And the king was very angry.

Victory over Cendebeus

37 Meanwhile Trypho embarked on a ship and escaped to Orthosia. ³⁸Then the king made Cendebeus commander-in-chief of the coastal country, and gave him troops of infantry and cavalry. ³⁹He commanded him to encamp against Judea, to build up Kedron and fortify its gates, and to make war on the people; but the king pursued Trypho. ⁴⁰So Cendebeus came to Jamnia

and began to provoke the people and invade Judea and take the people captive and kill them. ⁴¹He built up Kedron and stationed horsemen and troops there, so that they might go out and make raids along the highways of Judea, as the king had ordered him.

16 John went up from Gazara and reported to his father Simon what Cendebeus had done. ²And Simon called in his two eldest sons Judas and John, and said to them: "My brothers and I and my father's house have fought the wars of Israel from our youth until this day, and things have prospered in our hands so that we have delivered Israel many times. ³But now I have grown old, and you by Heaven's*ᶻ* mercy are mature in years. Take my place and my brother's, and go out and fight for our nation, and may the help that comes from Heaven be with you."

4 So John*ᵃ* chose out of the country twenty thousand warriors and cavalry, and they marched against Cendebeus and camped for the night in Modein. ⁵Early in the morning they started out and marched into the plain, where a large force of infantry and cavalry was coming to meet them; and a stream lay between them. ⁶Then he and his army lined up against them. He saw that the soldiers were afraid to cross the stream, so he crossed over first; and when his troops saw him, they crossed over after him. ⁷Then he divided the army and placed the cavalry in the center of the infantry, for the cavalry of the enemy were very numerous. ⁸They sounded the trumpets, and Cendebeus and his army were put to flight; many of them fell wounded and the rest fled into the stronghold. ⁹At that time Judas the brother of John was wounded, but John pursued them until Cendebeus*ᵇ* reached Kedron, which he had built. ¹⁰They also fled into the towers that were in the fields of Azotus, and John*ᵇ* burned it with fire, and about two thousand of them fell. He then returned to Judea safely.

Murder of Simon and His Sons

11 Now Ptolemy son of Abubus had been appointed governor over the plain of Jericho; he had a large store of silver and gold, ¹²for he was son-in-law of the high priest. ¹³His heart was lifted up; he determined to get control of the country, and made treacherous

plans against Simon and his sons, to do away with them. [14]Now Simon was visiting the towns of the country and attending to their needs, and he went down to Jericho with his sons Mattathias and Judas, in the one hundred seventy-seventh year,[c] in the eleventh month, which is the month of Shebat. [15]The son of Abubus received them treacherously in the little stronghold called Dok, which he had built; he gave them a great banquet, and hid men there. [16]When Simon and his sons were drunk, Ptolemy and his men rose up, took their weapons, rushed in against Simon in the banquet hall and killed him and his two sons, as well as some of his servants. [17]So he committed an act of great treachery and returned evil for good.

John Succeeds Simon

18 Then Ptolemy wrote a report about these things and sent it to the king, asking him to send troops to aid him and to turn over to him the towns and the country. [19]He sent other troops to Gazara to do away with John; he sent letters to the captains asking them to come to him so that he might give them silver and gold and gifts; [20]and he sent other troops to take possession of Jerusalem and the temple hill. [21]But someone ran ahead and reported to John at Gazara that his father and brothers had perished, and that "he has sent men to kill you also." [22]When he heard this, he was greatly shocked; he seized the men who came to destroy him and killed them, for he had found out that they were seeking to destroy him.

23 The rest of the acts of John and his wars and the brave deeds that he did, and the building of the walls that he completed, and his achievements, [24]are written in the annals of his high priesthood, from the time that he became high priest after his father.

[c] 134 B.C.

2 MACCABEES

A Letter to the Jews in Egypt

1 The Jews in Jerusalem and those in the land of Judea,

To their Jewish kindred in Egypt,

Greetings and true peace.

2 May God do good to you, and may he remember his covenant with Abraham and Isaac and Jacob, his faithful servants. [3]May he give you all a heart to worship him and to do his will with a strong heart and a willing spirit. [4]May he open your heart to his law and his commandments, and may he bring peace. [5]May he hear your prayers and be reconciled to you, and may he not forsake you in time of evil. [6]We are now praying for you here.

7 In the reign of Demetrius, in the one hundred sixty-ninth year,[a] we Jews wrote to you, in the critical distress that came upon us in those years after Jason and his company revolted from the holy land and the kingdom [8]and burned the gate and shed innocent blood. We prayed to the Lord and were heard, and we offered sacrifice and grain offering, and we lit the lamps and set out the loaves. [9]And now see that you keep the festival of booths in the month of Chislev, in the one hundred eighty-eighth year.[b]

A Letter to Aristobulus

10 The people of Jerusalem and of Judea and the senate and Judas,

To Aristobulus, who is of the family of the anointed priests, teacher of King Ptolemy, and to the Jews in Egypt,

Greetings and good health.

11 Having been saved by God out of grave dangers we thank him greatly for taking our side against the king,[c] [12]for he drove out those who fought against the holy city. [13]When the leader reached Persia

[a] 143 B.C. [b] 124 B.C. [c] Cn: Gk *as those who array themselves against a king*

with a force that seemed irresistible, they were cut to pieces in the temple of Nanea by a deception employed by the priests of the goddess[d] Nanea. [14]On the pretext of intending to marry her, Antiochus came to the place together with his Friends, to secure most of its treasures as a dowry. [15]When the priests of the temple of Nanea had set out the treasures and Antiochus had come with a few men inside the wall of the sacred precinct, they closed the temple as soon as he entered it. [16]Opening a secret door in the ceiling, they threw stones and struck down the leader and his men; they dismembered them and cut off their heads and threw them to the people outside. [17]Blessed in every way be our God, who has brought judgment on those who have behaved impiously.

Fire Consumes Nehemiah's Sacrifice

18 Since on the twenty-fifth day of Chislev we shall celebrate the purification of the temple, we thought it necessary to notify you, in order that you also may celebrate the festival of booths and the festival of the fire given when Nehemiah, who built the temple and the altar, offered sacrifices. [19]For when our ancestors were being led captive to Persia, the pious priests of that time took some of the fire of the altar and secretly hid it in the hollow of a dry cistern, where they took such precautions that the place was unknown to anyone. [20]But after many years had passed, when it pleased God, Nehemiah, having been commissioned by the king of Persia, sent the descendants of the priests who had hidden the fire to get it. And when they reported to us that they had not found fire but only a thick liquid, he ordered them to dip it out and bring it. [21]When the materials for the sacrifices were presented, Nehemiah ordered the priests to sprinkle the liquid on the wood and on the things laid upon it. [22]When this had been done and some time had passed, and when the sun, which had been clouded over, shone out, a great fire blazed up, so that all marveled. [23]And while the sacrifice was being consumed, the priests offered prayer—the priests and everyone. Jonathan led, and the rest responded, as did Nehemiah. [24]The prayer was to this effect:

"O Lord, Lord God, Creator of all things, you are awe-inspiring and strong and just

and merciful, you alone are king and are kind, [25]you alone are bountiful, you alone are just and almighty and eternal. You rescue Israel from every evil; you chose the ancestors and consecrated them. [26]Accept this sacrifice on behalf of all your people Israel and preserve your portion and make it holy. [27]Gather together our scattered people, set free those who are slaves among the Gentiles, look on those who are rejected and despised, and let the Gentiles know that you are our God. [28]Punish those who oppress and are insolent with pride. [29]Plant your people in your holy place, as Moses promised."

30 Then the priests sang the hymns. [31]After the materials of the sacrifice had been consumed, Nehemiah ordered that the liquid that was left should be poured on large stones. [32]When this was done, a flame blazed up; but when the light from the altar shone back, it went out. [33]When this matter became known, and it was reported to the king of the Persians that, in the place where the exiled priests had hidden the fire, the liquid had appeared with which Nehemiah and his associates had burned the materials of the sacrifice, [34]the king investigated the matter, and enclosed the place and made it sacred. [35]And with those persons whom the king favored, he exchanged many excellent gifts. [36]Nehemiah and his associates called this "nephthar," which means purification, but by most people it is called naphtha.[e]

Jeremiah Hides the Tent, Ark, and Altar

2 One finds in the records that the prophet Jeremiah ordered those who were being deported to take some of the fire, as has been mentioned, [2]and that the prophet, after giving them the law, instructed those who were being deported not to forget the commandments of the Lord, or to be led astray in their thoughts on seeing the gold and silver statues and their adornment. [3]And with other similar words he exhorted them that the law should not depart from their hearts.

4 It was also in the same document that the prophet, having received an oracle, ordered that the tent and the ark should follow with him, and that he went out to the mountain where Moses had gone up and had seen the inheritance of God. [5]Jeremiah came and found a cave-dwelling,

[d] Gk lacks *the goddess*   *[e]* Gk *nephthai*

and he brought there the tent and the ark and the altar of incense; then he sealed up the entrance. [6]Some of those who followed him came up intending to mark the way, but could not find it. [7]When Jeremiah learned of it, he rebuked them and declared: "The place shall remain unknown until God gathers his people together again and shows his mercy. [8]Then the Lord will disclose these things, and the glory of the Lord and the cloud will appear, as they were shown in the case of Moses, and as Solomon asked that the place should be specially consecrated."

9 It was also made clear that being possessed of wisdom Solomon[f] offered sacrifice for the dedication and completion of the temple. [10]Just as Moses prayed to the Lord, and fire came down from heaven and consumed the sacrifices, so also Solomon prayed, and the fire came down and consumed the whole burnt offerings. [11]And Moses said, "They were consumed because the sin offering had not been eaten." [12]Likewise Solomon also kept the eight days.

13 The same things are reported in the records and in the memoirs of Nehemiah, and also that he founded a library and collected the books about the kings and prophets, and the writings of David, and letters of kings about votive offerings. [14]In the same way Judas also collected all the books that had been lost on account of the war that had come upon us, and they are in our possession. [15]So if you have need of them, send people to get them for you.

16 Since, therefore, we are about to celebrate the purification, we write to you. Will you therefore please keep the days? [17]It is God who has saved all his people, and has returned the inheritance to all, and the kingship and the priesthood and the consecration, [18]as he promised through the law. We have hope in God that he will soon have mercy on us and will gather us from everywhere under heaven into his holy place, for he has rescued us from great evils and has purified the place.

The Compiler's Preface

19 The story of Judas Maccabeus and his brothers, and the purification of the great temple, and the dedication of the altar, [20]and further the wars against Antiochus Epiphanes and his son Eupator, [21]and the

appearances that came from heaven to those who fought bravely for Judaism, so that though few in number they seized the whole land and pursued the barbarian hordes, [22]and regained possession of the temple famous throughout the world, and liberated the city, and re-established the laws that were about to be abolished, while the Lord with great kindness became gracious to them— [23]all this, which has been set forth by Jason of Cyrene in five volumes, we shall attempt to condense into a single book. [24]For considering the flood of statistics involved and the difficulty there is for those who wish to enter upon the narratives of history because of the mass of material, [25]we have aimed to please those who wish to read, to make it easy for those who are inclined to memorize, and to profit all readers. [26]For us who have undertaken the toil of abbreviating, it is no light matter but calls for sweat and loss of sleep, [27]just as it is not easy for one who prepares a banquet and seeks the benefit of others. Nevertheless, to secure the gratitude of many we will gladly endure the uncomfortable toil, [28]leaving the responsibility for exact details to the compiler, while devoting our effort to arriving at the outlines of the condensation. [29]For as the master builder of a new house must be concerned with the whole construction, while the one who undertakes its painting and decoration has to consider only what is suitable for its adornment, such in my judgment is the case with us. [30]It is the duty of the original historian to occupy the ground, to discuss matters from every side, and to take trouble with details, [31]but the one who recasts the narrative should be allowed to strive for brevity of expression and to forego exhaustive treatment. [32]At this point therefore let us begin our narrative, without adding any more to what has already been said; for it would be foolish to lengthen the preface while cutting short the history itself.

Arrival of Heliodorus in Jerusalem

3 While the holy city was inhabited in unbroken peace and the laws were strictly observed because of the piety of the high priest Onias and his hatred of wickedness, [2]it came about that the kings themselves honored the place and glorified the temple with the finest presents, [3]even to the

[f] Gk *he*

extent that King Seleucus of Asia defrayed from his own revenues all the expenses connected with the service of the sacrifices. 4 But a man named Simon, of the tribe of Benjamin, who had been made captain of the temple, had a disagreement with the high priest about the administration of the city market. ⁵Since he could not prevail over Onias, he went to Apollonius of Tarsus,ᵍ who at that time was governor of Coelesyria and Phoenicia, ⁶and reported to him that the treasury in Jerusalem was full of untold sums of money, so that the amount of the funds could not be reckoned, and that they did not belong to the account of the sacrifices, but that it was possible for them to fall under the control of the king. ⁷When Apollonius met the king, he told him of the money about which he had been informed. The kingʰ chose Heliodorus, who was in charge of his affairs, and sent him with commands to effect the removal of the reported wealth. ⁸Heliodorus at once set out on his journey, ostensibly to make a tour of inspection of the cities of Coelesyria and Phoenicia, but in fact to carry out the king's purpose.

9 When he had arrived at Jerusalem and had been kindly welcomed by the high priest ofⁱ the city, he told about the disclosure that had been made and stated why he had come, and he inquired whether this really was the situation. ¹⁰The high priest explained that there were some deposits belonging to widows and orphans, ¹¹and also some money of Hyrcanus son of Tobias, a man of very prominent position, and that it totaled in all four hundred talents of silver and two hundred of gold. To such an extent the impious Simon had misrepresented the facts. ¹²And he said that it was utterly impossible that wrong should be done to those people who had trusted in the holiness of the place and in the sanctity and inviolability of the temple that is honored throughout the whole world.

Heliodorus Plans to Rob the Temple

13 But Heliodorus, because of the orders he had from the king, said that this money must in any case be confiscated for the king's treasury. ¹⁴So he set a day and went in to direct the inspection of these funds. There was no little distress throughout the whole city. ¹⁵The priests prostrated themselves before the altar in their priestly vestments and called toward heaven upon him who had given the law about deposits, that he should keep them safe for those who had deposited them. ¹⁶To see the appearance of the high priest was to be wounded at heart, for his face and the change in his color disclosed the anguish of his soul. ¹⁷For terror and bodily trembling had come over the man, which plainly showed to those who looked at him the pain lodged in his heart. ¹⁸People also hurried out of their houses in crowds to make a general supplication because the holy place was about to be brought into dishonor. ¹⁹Women, girded with sackcloth under their breasts, thronged the streets. Some of the young women who were kept indoors ran together to the gates, and some to the walls, while others peered out of the windows. ²⁰And holding up their hands to heaven, they all made supplication. ²¹There was something pitiable in the prostration of the whole populace and the anxiety of the high priest in his great anguish.

The Lord Protects His Temple

22 While they were calling upon the Almighty Lord that he would keep what had been entrusted safe and secure for those who had entrusted it, ²³Heliodorus went on with what had been decided. ²⁴But when he arrived at the treasury with his bodyguard, then and there the Sovereign of spirits and of all authority caused so great a manifestation that all who had been so bold as to accompany him were astounded by the power of God, and became faint with terror. ²⁵For there appeared to them a magnificently caparisoned horse, with a rider of frightening mien; it rushed furiously at Heliodorus and struck at him with its front hoofs. Its rider was seen to have armor and weapons of gold. ²⁶Two young men also appeared to him, remarkably strong, gloriously beautiful and splendidly dressed, who stood on either side of him and flogged him continuously, inflicting many blows on him. ²⁷When he suddenly fell to the ground and deep darkness came over him, his men took him up, put him on a stretcher, ²⁸and carried him away—this man who had just entered the aforesaid treasury with a great retinue and all his bodyguard but was now unable to help himself. They recognized clearly the sovereign power of God.

ᵍ Gk *Apollonius son of Tharseas* ʰ Gk *He* ⁱ Other ancient authorities read *and*

Onias Prays for Heliodorus

29 While he lay prostrate, speechless because of the divine intervention and deprived of any hope of recovery, ³⁰they praised the Lord who had acted marvelously for his own place. And the temple, which a little while before was full of fear and disturbance, was filled with joy and gladness, now that the Almighty Lord had appeared.

31 Some of Heliodorus's friends quickly begged Onias to call upon the Most High to grant life to one who was lying quite at his last breath. ³²So the high priest, fearing that the king might get the notion that some foul play had been perpetrated by the Jews with regard to Heliodorus, offered sacrifice for the man's recovery. ³³While the high priest was making an atonement, the same young men appeared again to Heliodorus dressed in the same clothing, and they stood and said, "Be very grateful to the high priest Onias, since for his sake the Lord has granted you your life. ³⁴And see that you, who have been flogged by heaven, report to all people the majestic power of God." Having said this they vanished.

The Conversion of Heliodorus

35 Then Heliodorus offered sacrifice to the Lord and made very great vows to the Savior of his life, and having bidden Onias farewell, he marched off with his forces to the king. ³⁶He bore testimony to all concerning the deeds of the supreme God, which he had seen with his own eyes. ³⁷When the king asked Heliodorus what sort of person would be suitable to send on another mission to Jerusalem, he replied, ³⁸"If you have any enemy or plotter against your government, send him there, for you will get him back thoroughly flogged, if he survives at all; for there is certainly some power of God about the place. ³⁹For he who has his dwelling in heaven watches over that place himself and brings it aid, and he strikes and destroys those who come to do it injury." ⁴⁰This was the outcome of the episode of Heliodorus and the protection of the treasury.

Simon Accuses Onias

4 The previously mentioned Simon, who had informed about the money against[j] his own country, slandered Onias, saying that it was he who had incited Heliodorus

and had been the real cause of the misfortune. ²He dared to designate as a plotter against the government the man who was the benefactor of the city, the protector of his compatriots, and a zealot for the laws. ³When his hatred progressed to such a degree that even murders were committed by one of Simon's approved agents, ⁴Onias recognized that the rivalry was serious and that Apollonius son of Menestheus,[k] and governor of Coelesyria and Phoenicia, was intensifying the malice of Simon. ⁵So he appealed to the king, not accusing his compatriots but having in view the welfare, both public and private, of all the people. ⁶For he saw that without the king's attention public affairs could not again reach a peaceful settlement, and that Simon would not stop his folly.

Jason's Reforms

7 When Seleucus died and Antiochus, who was called Epiphanes, succeeded to the kingdom, Jason the brother of Onias obtained the high priesthood by corruption, ⁸promising the king at an interview[l] three hundred sixty talents of silver, and from another source of revenue eighty talents. ⁹In addition to this he promised to pay one hundred fifty more if permission were given to establish by his authority a gymnasium and a body of youth for it, and to enroll the people of Jerusalem as citizens of Antioch. ¹⁰When the king assented and Jason[m] came to office, he at once shifted his compatriots over to the Greek way of life.

11 He set aside the existing royal concessions to the Jews, secured through John the father of Eupolemus, who went on his mission to establish friendship and alliance with the Romans; and he destroyed the lawful ways of living and introduced new customs contrary to the law. ¹²He took delight in establishing a gymnasium right under the citadel, and he induced the noblest of the young men to wear the Greek hat. ¹³There was such an extreme of Hellenization and increase in the adoption of foreign ways because of the surpassing wickedness of Jason, who was ungodly and no true[n] high priest, ¹⁴that the priests were no longer intent upon their service at the altar. Despising the sanctuary and neglecting the sacrifices, they hurried to take part in the unlawful proceedings in the wrestling

j Gk *and*   *k* Vg Compare verse 21: Meaning of Gk uncertain   *l* Or *by a petition*   *m* Gk *he*   *n* Gk lacks *true*

arena after the signal for the discus-throwing, [15]disdaining the honors prized by their ancestors and putting the highest value upon Greek forms of prestige. [16]For this reason heavy disaster overtook them, and those whose ways of living they admired and wished to imitate completely became their enemies and punished them. [17]It is no light thing to show irreverence to the divine laws—a fact that later events will make clear.

Jason Introduces Greek Customs

18 When the quadrennial games were being held at Tyre and the king was present, [19]the vile Jason sent envoys, chosen as being Antiochian citizens from Jerusalem, to carry three hundred silver drachmas for the sacrifice to Hercules. Those who carried the money, however, thought best not to use it for sacrifice, because that was inappropriate, but to expend it for another purpose. [20]So this money was intended by the sender for the sacrifice to Hercules, but by the decision of its carriers it was applied to the construction of triremes.

21 When Apollonius son of Menestheus was sent to Egypt for the coronation[o] of Philometor as king, Antiochus learned that Philometor[p] had become hostile to his government, and he took measures for his own security. Therefore upon arriving at Joppa he proceeded to Jerusalem. [22]He was welcomed magnificently by Jason and the city, and ushered in with a blaze of torches and with shouts. Then he marched his army into Phoenicia.

Menelaus Becomes High Priest

23 After a period of three years Jason sent Menelaus, the brother of the previously mentioned Simon, to carry the money to the king and to complete the records of essential business. [24]But he, when presented to the king, extolled him with an air of authority, and secured the high priesthood for himself, outbidding Jason by three hundred talents of silver. [25]After receiving the king's orders he returned, possessing no qualification for the high priesthood, but having the hot temper of a cruel tyrant and the rage of a savage wild beast. [26]So Jason, who after supplanting his own brother was supplanted by another man, was driven as

a fugitive into the land of Ammon. [27]Although Menelaus continued to hold the office, he did not pay regularly any of the money promised to the king. [28]When Sostratus the captain of the citadel kept requesting payment—for the collection of the revenue was his responsibility—the two of them were summoned by the king on account of this issue. [29]Menelaus left his own brother Lysimachus as deputy in the high priesthood, while Sostratus left Crates, the commander of the Cyprian troops.

The Murder of Onias

30 While such was the state of affairs, it happened that the people of Tarsus and of Mallus revolted because their cities had been given as a present to Antiochis, the king's concubine. [31]So the king went hurriedly to settle the trouble, leaving Andronicus, a man of high rank, to act as his deputy. [32]But Menelaus, thinking he had obtained a suitable opportunity, stole some of the gold vessels of the temple and gave them to Andronicus; other vessels, as it happened, he had sold to Tyre and the neighboring cities. [33]When Onias became fully aware of these acts, he publicly exposed them, having first withdrawn to a place of sanctuary at Daphne near Antioch. [34]Therefore Menelaus, taking Andronicus aside, urged him to kill Onias. Andronicus[q] came to Onias, and resorting to treachery, offered him sworn pledges and gave him his right hand; he persuaded him, though still suspicious, to come out from the place of sanctuary; then, with no regard for justice, he immediately put him out of the way.

Andronicus Is Punished

35 For this reason not only Jews, but many also of other nations, were grieved and displeased at the unjust murder of the man. [36]When the king returned from the region of Cilicia, the Jews in the city[r] appealed to him with regard to the unreasonable murder of Onias, and the Greeks shared their hatred of the crime. [37]Therefore Antiochus was grieved at heart and filled with pity, and wept because of the moderation and good conduct of the deceased. [38]Inflamed with anger, he immediately stripped off the purple robe from Andronicus, tore off his clothes, and led him around the whole

---

[o] Meaning of Gk uncertain   [p] Gk *he*   [q] Gk *He*   [r] Or *in each city*

city to that very place where he had committed the outrage against Onias, and there he dispatched the bloodthirsty fellow. The Lord thus repaid him with the punishment he deserved.

Unpopularity of Lysimachus and Menelaus

39 When many acts of sacrilege had been committed in the city by Lysimachus with the connivance of Menelaus, and when report of them had spread abroad, the populace gathered against Lysimachus, because many of the gold vessels had already been stolen. ⁴⁰Since the crowds were becoming aroused and filled with anger, Lysimachus armed about three thousand men and launched an unjust attack, under the leadership of a certain Auranus, a man advanced in years and no less advanced in folly. ⁴¹But when the Jewsˢ became aware that Lysimachus was attacking them, some picked up stones, some blocks of wood, and others took handfuls of the ashes that were lying around, and threw them in wild confusion at Lysimachus and his men. ⁴²As a result, they wounded many of them, and killed some, and put all the rest to flight; the temple robber himself they killed close by the treasury.

43 Charges were brought against Menelaus about this incident. ⁴⁴When the king came to Tyre, three men sent by the senate presented the case before him. ⁴⁵But Menelaus, already as good as beaten, promised a substantial bribe to Ptolemy son of Dorymenes to win over the king. ⁴⁶Therefore Ptolemy, taking the king aside into a colonnade as if for refreshment, induced the king to change his mind. ⁴⁷Menelaus, the cause of all the trouble, he acquitted of the charges against him, while he sentenced to death those unfortunate men, who would have been freed uncondemned if they had pleaded even before Scythians. ⁴⁸And so those who had spoken for the city and the villagesᵗ and the holy vessels quickly suffered the unjust penalty. ⁴⁹Therefore even the Tyrians, showing their hatred of the crime, provided magnificently for their funeral. ⁵⁰But Menelaus, because of the greed of those in power, remained in office, growing in wickedness, having become the chief plotter against his compatriots.

Jason Tries to Regain Control

5 About this time Antiochus made his second invasion of Egypt. ²And it happened that, for almost forty days, there appeared over all the city golden-clad cavalry charging through the air, in companies fully armed with lances and drawn swords— ³troops of cavalry drawn up, attacks and counterattacks made on this side and on that, brandishing of shields, massing of spears, hurling of missiles, the flash of golden trappings, and armor of all kinds. ⁴Therefore everyone prayed that the apparition might prove to have been a good omen.

5 When a false rumor arose that Antiochus was dead, Jason took no fewer than a thousand men and suddenly made an assault on the city. When the troops on the wall had been forced back and at last the city was being taken, Menelaus took refuge in the citadel. ⁶But Jason kept relentlessly slaughtering his compatriots, not realizing that success at the cost of one's kindred is the greatest misfortune, but imagining that he was setting up trophies of victory over enemies and not over compatriots. ⁷He did not, however, gain control of the government; in the end he got only disgrace from his conspiracy, and fled again into the country of the Ammonites. ⁸Finally he met a miserable end. Accusedᵘ before Aretas the ruler of the Arabs, fleeing from city to city, pursued by everyone, hated as a rebel against the laws, and abhorred as the executioner of his country and his compatriots, he was cast ashore in Egypt. ⁹There he who had driven many from their own country into exile died in exile, having embarked to go to the Lacedaemonians in hope of finding protection because of their kinship. ¹⁰He who had cast out many to lie unburied had no one to mourn for him; he had no funeral of any sort and no place in the tomb of his ancestors.

11 When news of what had happened reached the king, he took it to mean that Judea was in revolt. So, raging inwardly, he left Egypt and took the city by storm. ¹²He commanded his soldiers to cut down relentlessly everyone they met and to kill those who went into their houses. ¹³Then there was massacre of young and old, destruction of boys, women, and children, and slaughter of young girls and infants. ¹⁴Within the

ˢ Gk *they*   ᵗ Other ancient authorities read *the people*   ᵘ Cn: Gk *Imprisoned* total of three days eighty thousand were destroyed, forty thousand in hand-to-hand fighting, and as many were sold into slavery as were killed.

Pillage of the Temple

15 Not content with this, Antiochus[v] dared to enter the most holy temple in all the world, guided by Menelaus, who had become a traitor both to the laws and to his country. [16]He took the holy vessels with his polluted hands, and swept away with profane hands the votive offerings that other kings had made to enhance the glory and honor of the place. [17]Antiochus was elated in spirit, and did not perceive that the Lord was angered for a little while because of the sins of those who lived in the city, and that this was the reason he was disregarding the holy place. [18]But if it had not happened that they were involved in many sins, this man would have been flogged and turned back from his rash act as soon as he came forward, just as Heliodorus had been, whom King Seleucus sent to inspect the treasury. [19]But the Lord did not choose the nation for the sake of the holy place, but the place for the sake of the nation. [20]Therefore the place itself shared in the misfortunes that befell the nation and afterward participated in its benefits; and what was forsaken in the wrath of the Almighty was restored again in all its glory when the great Lord became reconciled.

21 So Antiochus carried off eighteen hundred talents from the temple, and hurried away to Antioch, thinking in his arrogance that he could sail on the land and walk on the sea, because his mind was elated. [22]He left governors to oppress the people: at Jerusalem, Philip, by birth a Phrygian and in character more barbarous than the man who appointed him; [23]and at Gerizim, Andronicus; and besides these Menelaus, who lorded it over his compatriots worse than the others did. In his malice toward the Jewish citizens,[w] [24]Antiochus[v] sent Apollonius, the captain of the Mysians, with an army of twenty-two thousand, and commanded him to kill all the grown men and to sell the women and boys as slaves. [25]When this man arrived in Jerusalem, he pretended to be peaceably disposed and waited until the holy sabbath

day; then, finding the Jews not at work, he ordered his troops to parade under arms. [26]He put to the sword all those who came out to see them, then rushed into the city with his armed warriors and killed great numbers of people.

27 But Judas Maccabeus, with about nine others, got away to the wilderness, and kept himself and his companions alive in the mountains as wild animals do; they continued to live on what grew wild, so that they might not share in the defilement.

The Suppression of Judaism

6 Not long after this, the king sent an Athenian[x] senator[y] to compel the Jews to forsake the laws of their ancestors and no longer to live by the laws of God; [2]also to pollute the temple in Jerusalem and to call it the temple of Olympian Zeus, and to call the one in Gerizim the temple of Zeus-the-Friend-of-Strangers, as did the people who lived in that place.

3 Harsh and utterly grievous was the onslaught of evil. [4]For the temple was filled with debauchery and reveling by the Gentiles, who dallied with prostitutes and had intercourse with women within the sacred precincts, and besides brought in things for sacrifice that were unfit. [5]The altar was covered with abominable offerings that were forbidden by the laws. [6]People could neither keep the sabbath, nor observe the festivals of their ancestors, nor so much as confess themselves to be Jews.

7 On the monthly celebration of the king's birthday, the Jews[z] were taken, under bitter constraint, to partake of the sacrifices; and when a festival of Dionysus was celebrated, they were compelled to wear wreaths of ivy and to walk in the procession in honor of Dionysus. [8]At the suggestion of the people of Ptolemais[a] a decree was issued to the neighboring Greek cities that they should adopt the same policy toward the Jews and make them partake of the sacrifices, [9]and should kill those who did not choose to change over to Greek customs. One could see, therefore, the misery that had come upon them. [10]For example, two women were brought in for having circumcised their children. They publicly paraded them around the city, with their babies hanging at their breasts, and then hurled them down headlong from

---

[v] Gk *he*   [w] Or *worse than the others did in his malice toward the Jewish citizens*   [x] Other ancient authorities read *Antiochian*   [y] Or *Geron an Athenian*   [z] Gk *they*   [a] Cn: Gk *suggestion of the Ptolemies* (or *of Ptolemy*)

the wall. [11]Others who had assembled in the caves nearby, in order to observe the seventh day secretly, were betrayed to Philip and were all burned together, because their piety kept them from defending themselves, in view of their regard for that most holy day.

Providential Significance of the Persecution

12 Now I urge those who read this book not to be depressed by such calamities, but to recognize that these punishments were designed not to destroy but to discipline our people. [13]In fact, it is a sign of great kindness not to let the impious alone for long, but to punish them immediately. [14]For in the case of the other nations the Lord waits patiently to punish them until they have reached the full measure of their sins; but he does not deal in this way with us, [15]in order that he may not take vengeance on us afterward when our sins have reached their height. [16]Therefore he never withdraws his mercy from us. Although he disciplines us with calamities, he does not forsake his own people. [17]Let what we have said serve as a reminder; we must go on briefly with the story.

The Martyrdom of Eleazar

18 Eleazar, one of the scribes in high position, a man now advanced in age and of noble presence, was being forced to open his mouth to eat swine's flesh. [19]But he, welcoming death with honor rather than life with pollution, went up to the rack of his own accord, spitting out the flesh, [20]as all ought to go who have the courage to refuse things that it is not right to taste, even for the natural love of life.

21 Those who were in charge of that unlawful sacrifice took the man aside because of their long acquaintance with him, and privately urged him to bring meat of his own providing, proper for him to use, and to pretend that he was eating the flesh of the sacrificial meal that had been commanded by the king, [22]so that by doing this he might be saved from death, and be treated kindly on account of his old friendship with them. [23]But making a high resolve, worthy of his years and the dignity of his old age and the gray hairs that he had reached with distinction and his excel-

lent life even from childhood, and moreover according to the holy God-given law, he declared himself quickly, telling them to send him to Hades.

24 "Such pretense is not worthy of our time of life," he said, "for many of the young might suppose that Eleazar in his ninetieth year had gone over to an alien religion, [25]and through my pretense, for the sake of living a brief moment longer, they would be led astray because of me, while I defile and disgrace my old age. [26]Even if for the present I would avoid the punishment of mortals, yet whether I live or die I will not escape the hands of the Almighty. [27]Therefore, by bravely giving up my life now, I will show myself worthy of my old age [28]and leave to the young a noble example of how to die a good death willingly and nobly for the revered and holy laws."

When he had said this, he went[b] at once to the rack. [29]Those who a little before had acted toward him with goodwill now changed to ill will, because the words he had uttered were in their opinion sheer madness.[c] [30]When he was about to die under the blows, he groaned aloud and said: "It is clear to the Lord in his holy knowledge that, though I might have been saved from death, I am enduring terrible sufferings in my body under this beating, but in my soul I am glad to suffer these things because I fear him."

31 So in this way he died, leaving in his death an example of nobility and a memorial of courage, not only to the young but to the great body of his nation.

The Martyrdom of Seven Brothers

7 It happened also that seven brothers and their mother were arrested and were being compelled by the king, under torture with whips and thongs, to partake of unlawful swine's flesh. [2]One of them, acting as their spokesman, said, "What do you intend to ask and learn from us? For we are ready to die rather than transgress the laws of our ancestors."

3 The king fell into a rage, and gave orders to have pans and caldrons heated. [4]These were heated immediately, and he commanded that the tongue of their spokesman be cut out and that they scalp him and cut off his hands and feet, while the rest of the brothers and the mother looked on.

[5]When he was utterly helpless, the king[d] ordered them to take him to the fire, still breathing, and to fry him in a pan. The smoke from the pan spread widely, but the brothers[e] and their mother encouraged one another to die nobly, saying, [6]"The Lord God is watching over us and in truth has compassion on us, as Moses declared in his song that bore witness against the people to their faces, when he said, 'And he will have compassion on his servants.'"[f]

7 After the first brother had died in this way, they brought forward the second for their sport. They tore off the skin of his head with the hair, and asked him, "Will you eat rather than have your body punished limb by limb?" [8]He replied in the language of his ancestors and said to them, "No." Therefore he in turn underwent tortures as the first brother had done. [9]And when he was at his last breath, he said, "You accursed wretch, you dismiss us from this present life, but the King of the universe will raise us up to an everlasting renewal of life, because we have died for his laws."

10 After him, the third was the victim of their sport. When it was demanded, he quickly put out his tongue and courageously stretched forth his hands, [11]and said nobly, "I got these from Heaven, and because of his laws I disdain them, and from him I hope to get them back again." [12]As a result the king himself and those with him were astonished at the young man's spirit, for he regarded his sufferings as nothing.

13 After he too had died, they maltreated and tortured the fourth in the same way. [14]When he was near death, he said, "One cannot but choose to die at the hands of mortals and to cherish the hope God gives of being raised again by him. But for you there will be no resurrection to life!"

15 Next they brought forward the fifth and maltreated him. [16]But he looked at the king,[g] and said, "Because you have authority among mortals, though you also are mortal, you do what you please. But do not think that God has forsaken our people. [17]Keep on, and see how his mighty power will torture you and your descendants!"

18 After him they brought forward the sixth. And when he was about to die, he said, "Do not deceive yourself in vain. For we are suffering these things on our own account, because of our sins against our own God. Therefore[h] astounding things have happened. [19]But do not think that you will go unpunished for having tried to fight against God!"

20 The mother was especially admirable and worthy of honorable memory. Although she saw her seven sons perish within a single day, she bore it with good courage because of her hope in the Lord. [21]She encouraged each of them in the language of their ancestors. Filled with a noble spirit, she reinforced her woman's reasoning with a man's courage, and said to them, [22]"I do not know how you came into being in my womb. It was not I who gave you life and breath, nor I who set in order the elements within each of you. [23]Therefore the Creator of the world, who shaped the beginning of humankind and devised the origin of all things, will in his mercy give life and breath back to you again, since you now forget yourselves for the sake of his laws."

24 Antiochus felt that he was being treated with contempt, and he was suspicious of her reproachful tone. The youngest brother being still alive, Antiochus[d] not only appealed to him in words, but promised with oaths that he would make him rich and enviable if he would turn from the ways of his ancestors, and that he would take him for his Friend and entrust him with public affairs. [25]Since the young man would not listen to him at all, the king called the mother to him and urged her to advise the youth to save himself. [26]After much urging on his part, she undertook to persuade her son. [27]But, leaning close to him, she spoke in their native language as follows, deriding the cruel tyrant: "My son, have pity on me. I carried you nine months in my womb, and nursed you for three years, and have reared you and brought you up to this point in your life, and have taken care of you.[i] [28]I beg you, my child, to look at the heaven and the earth and see everything that is in them, and recognize that God did not make them out of things that existed.[j] And in the same way the human race came into being. [29]Do not fear this butcher, but prove worthy of your brothers. Accept death, so that in God's mercy I may get you back again along with your brothers."

[d] Gk *he*   [e] Gk *they*   [f] Gk *slaves*   [g] Gk *at him*   [h] Lat: Other ancient authorities lack *Therefore*   [i] Or *have borne the burden of your education*   [j] Or *God made them out of things that did not exist*

30 While she was still speaking, the young man said, "What are you[k] waiting for? I will not obey the king's command, but I obey the command of the law that was given to our ancestors through Moses. [31]But you,[l] who have contrived all sorts of evil against the Hebrews, will certainly not escape the hands of God. [32]For we are suffering because of our own sins. [33]And if our living Lord is angry for a little while, to rebuke and discipline us, he will again be reconciled with his own servants.[m] [34]But you, unholy wretch, you most defiled of all mortals, do not be elated in vain and puffed up by uncertain hopes, when you raise your hand against the children of heaven. [35]You have not yet escaped the judgment of the almighty, all-seeing God. [36]For our brothers after enduring a brief suffering have drunk[n] of ever-flowing life, under God's covenant; but you, by the judgment of God, will receive just punishment for your arrogance. [37]I, like my brothers, give up body and life for the laws of our ancestors, appealing to God to show mercy soon to our nation and by trials and plagues to make you confess that he alone is God, [38]and through me and my brothers to bring to an end the wrath of the Almighty that has justly fallen on our whole nation."

39 The king fell into a rage, and handled him worse than the others, being exasperated at his scorn. [40]So he died in his integrity, putting his whole trust in the Lord.

41 Last of all, the mother died, after her sons.

42 Let this be enough, then, about the eating of sacrifices and the extreme tortures.

The Revolt of Judas Maccabeus

8 Meanwhile Judas, who was also called Maccabeus, and his companions secretly entered the villages and summoned their kindred and enlisted those who had continued in the Jewish faith, and so they gathered about six thousand. [2]They implored the Lord to look upon the people who were oppressed by all; and to have pity on the temple that had been profaned by the godless; [3]to have mercy on the city that was being destroyed and about to be leveled to the ground; to hearken to the blood that cried out to him; [4]to remember also the lawless destruction of the innocent babies and

the blasphemies committed against his name; and to show his hatred of evil.

5 As soon as Maccabeus got his army organized, the Gentiles could not withstand him, for the wrath of the Lord had turned to mercy. [6]Coming without warning, he would set fire to towns and villages. He captured strategic positions and put to flight not a few of the enemy. [7]He found the nights most advantageous for such attacks. And talk of his valor spread everywhere.

8 When Philip saw that the man was gaining ground little by little, and that he was pushing ahead with more frequent successes, he wrote to Ptolemy, the governor of Coelesyria and Phoenicia, to come to the aid of the king's government. [9]Then Ptolemy[o] promptly appointed Nicanor son of Patroclus, one of the king's chief[p] Friends, and sent him, in command of no fewer than twenty thousand Gentiles of all nations, to wipe out the whole race of Judea. He associated with him Gorgias, a general and a man of experience in military service. [10]Nicanor determined to make up for the king the tribute due to the Romans, two thousand talents, by selling the captured Jews into slavery. [11]So he immediately sent to the towns on the seacoast, inviting them to buy Jewish slaves and promising to hand over ninety slaves for a talent, not expecting the judgment from the Almighty that was about to overtake him.

Preparation for Battle

12 Word came to Judas concerning Nicanor's invasion; and when he told his companions of the arrival of the army, [13]those who were cowardly and distrustful of God's justice ran off and got away. [14]Others sold all their remaining property, and at the same time implored the Lord to rescue those who had been sold by the ungodly Nicanor before he ever met them, [15]if not for their own sake, then for the sake of the covenants made with their ancestors, and because he had called them by his holy and glorious name. [16]But Maccabeus gathered his forces together, to the number six thousand, and exhorted them not to be frightened by the enemy and not to fear the great multitude of Gentiles who were wickedly coming against them, but to fight nobly, [17]keeping before their eyes the lawless out-

---

[k] The Gk here for *you* is plural   [l] The Gk here for *you* is singular   [m] Gk *slaves*   [n] Cn: Gk *fallen*   [o] Gk *he*
[p] Gk *one of the first*

rage that the Gentiles[q] had committed against the holy place, and the torture of the derided city, and besides, the overthrow of their ancestral way of life. [18]"For they trust to arms and acts of daring," he said, "but we trust in the Almighty God, who is able with a single nod to strike down those who are coming against us, and even, if necessary, the whole world."

19 Moreover, he told them of the occasions when help came to their ancestors; how, in the time of Sennacherib, when one hundred eighty-five thousand perished, [20]and the time of the battle against the Galatians that took place in Babylonia, when eight thousand Jews[r] fought along with four thousand Macedonians; yet when the Macedonians were hard pressed, the eight thousand, by the help that came to them from heaven, destroyed one hundred twenty thousand Galatians[s] and took a great amount of booty.

Judas Defeats Nicanor

21 With these words he filled them with courage and made them ready to die for their laws and their country; then he divided his army into four parts. [22]He appointed his brothers also, Simon and Joseph and Jonathan, each to command a division, putting fifteen hundred men under each. [23]Besides, he appointed Eleazar to read aloud[t] from the holy book, and gave the watchword, "The help of God"; then, leading the first division himself, he joined battle with Nicanor.

24 With the Almighty as their ally, they killed more than nine thousand of the enemy, and wounded and disabled most of Nicanor's army, and forced them all to flee. [25]They captured the money of those who had come to buy them as slaves. After pursuing them for some distance, they were obliged to return because the hour was late. [26]It was the day before the sabbath, and for that reason they did not continue their pursuit. [27]When they had collected the arms of the enemy and stripped them of their spoils, they kept the sabbath, giving great praise and thanks to the Lord, who had preserved them for that day and allotted it to them as the beginning of mercy. [28]After the sabbath they gave some of the spoils to those who had been tortured and

to the widows and orphans, and distributed the rest among themselves and their children. [29]When they had done this, they made common supplication and implored the merciful Lord to be wholly reconciled with his servants.[u]

Judas Defeats Timothy and Bacchides

30 In encounters with the forces of Timothy and Bacchides they killed more than twenty thousand of them and got possession of some exceedingly high strongholds, and they divided a very large amount of plunder, giving to those who had been tortured and to the orphans and widows, and also to the aged, shares equal to their own. [31]They collected the arms of the enemy,[v] and carefully stored all of them in strategic places; the rest of the spoils they carried to Jerusalem. [32]They killed the commander of Timothy's forces, a most wicked man, and one who had greatly troubled the Jews. [33]While they were celebrating the victory in the city of their ancestors, they burned those who had set fire to the sacred gates, Callisthenes and some others, who had fled into one little house; so these received the proper reward for their impiety.[t]

34 The thrice-accursed Nicanor, who had brought the thousand merchants to buy the Jews, [35]having been humbled with the help of the Lord by opponents whom he regarded as of the least account, took off his splendid uniform and made his way alone like a runaway slave across the country until he reached Antioch, having succeeded chiefly in the destruction of his own army! [36]So he who had undertaken to secure tribute for the Romans by the capture of the people of Jerusalem proclaimed that the Jews had a Defender, and that therefore the Jews were invulnerable, because they followed the laws ordained by him.

The Last Campaign of Antiochus Epiphanes

9 About that time, as it happened, Antiochus had retreated in disorder from the region of Persia. [2]He had entered the city called Persepolis and attempted to rob the temples and control the city. Therefore the people rushed to the rescue with arms, and Antiochus and his army were defeated,[w] with the result that Antiochus

[q] Gk *they*   [r] Gk lacks *Jews*   [s] Gk lacks *Galatians*   [t] Meaning of Gk uncertain   [u] Gk *slaves*   [v] Gk *their arms*
[w] Gk *they were defeated*

167

was put to flight by the inhabitants and beat a shameful retreat. [3]While he was in Ecbatana, news came to him of what had happened to Nicanor and the forces of Timothy. [4]Transported with rage, he conceived the idea of turning upon the Jews the injury done by those who had put him to flight; so he ordered his charioteer to drive without stopping until he completed the journey. But the judgment of heaven rode with him! For in his arrogance he said, "When I get there I will make Jerusalem a cemetery of Jews."

5 But the all-seeing Lord, the God of Israel, struck him with an incurable and invisible blow. As soon as he stopped speaking he was seized with a pain in his bowels, for which there was no relief, and with sharp internal tortures— [6]and that very justly, for he had tortured the bowels of others with many and strange inflictions. [7]Yet he did not in any way stop his insolence, but was even more filled with arrogance, breathing fire in his rage against the Jews, and giving orders to drive even faster. And so it came about that he fell out of his chariot as it was rushing along, and the fall was so hard as to torture every limb of his body. [8]Thus he who only a little while before had thought in his superhuman arrogance that he could command the waves of the sea, and had imagined that he could weigh the high mountains in a balance, was brought down to earth and carried in a litter, making the power of God manifest to all. [9]And so the ungodly man's body swarmed with worms, and while he was still living in anguish and pain, his flesh rotted away, and because of the stench the whole army felt revulsion at his decay. [10]Because of his intolerable stench no one was able to carry the man who a little while before had thought that he could touch the stars of heaven. [11]Then it was that, broken in spirit, he began to lose much of his arrogance and to come to his senses under the scourge of God, for he was tortured with pain every moment. [12]And when he could not endure his own stench, he uttered these words, "It is right to be subject to God; mortals should not think that they are equal to God."[x]

Antiochus Makes a Promise to God

13 Then the abominable fellow made a vow to the Lord, who would no longer have mercy on him, stating [14]that the holy city, which he was hurrying to level to the ground and to make a cemetery, he was now declaring to be free; [15]and the Jews, whom he had not considered worth burying but had planned to throw out with their children for the wild animals and for the birds to eat, he would make, all of them, equal to citizens of Athens; [16]and the holy sanctuary, which he had formerly plundered, he would adorn with the finest offerings; and all the holy vessels he would give back, many times over; and the expenses incurred for the sacrifices he would provide from his own revenues; [17]and in addition to all this he also would become a Jew and would visit every inhabited place to proclaim the power of God. [18]But when his sufferings did not in any way abate, for the judgment of God had justly come upon him, he gave up all hope for himself and wrote to the Jews the following letter, in the form of a supplication. This was its content:

Antiochus's Letter and Death

19 "To his worthy Jewish citizens, Antiochus their king and general sends hearty greetings and good wishes for their health and prosperity. [20]If you and your children are well and your affairs are as you wish, I am glad. As my hope is in heaven, [21]I remember with affection your esteem and goodwill. On my way back from the region of Persia I suffered an annoying illness, and I have deemed it necessary to take thought for the general security of all. [22]I do not despair of my condition, for I have good hope of recovering from my illness, [23]but I observed that my father, on the occasions when he made expeditions into the upper country, appointed his successor, [24]so that, if anything unexpected happened or any unwelcome news came, the people throughout the realm would not be troubled, for they would know to whom the government was left. [25]Moreover, I understand how the princes along the borders and the neighbors of my kingdom keep watching for opportunities and waiting to see what will happen. So I have appointed my son Antiochus to be king, whom I have often entrusted and commended to most of you when I hurried off to the upper provinces; and I have written to him what is written here. [26]I therefore urge and beg you

---

[x] Or *not think thoughts proper only to God*

to remember the public and private services rendered to you and to maintain your present goodwill, each of you, toward me and my son. [27]For I am sure that he will follow my policy and will treat you with moderation and kindness."

28 So the murderer and blasphemer, having endured the more intense suffering, such as he had inflicted on others, came to the end of his life by a most pitiable fate, among the mountains in a strange land. [29]And Philip, one of his courtiers, took his body home; then, fearing the son of Antiochus, he withdrew to Ptolemy Philometor in Egypt.

Purification of the Temple

10 Now Maccabeus and his followers, the Lord leading them on, recovered the temple and the city; [2]they tore down the altars that had been built in the public square by the foreigners, and also destroyed the sacred precincts. [3]They purified the sanctuary, and made another altar of sacrifice; then, striking fire out of flint, they offered sacrifices, after a lapse of two years, and they offered incense and lighted lamps and set out the bread of the Presence. [4]When they had done this, they fell prostrate and implored the Lord that they might never again fall into such misfortunes, but that, if they should ever sin, they might be disciplined by him with forbearance and not be handed over to blasphemous and barbarous nations. [5]It happened that on the same day on which the sanctuary had been profaned by the foreigners, the purification of the sanctuary took place, that is, on the twenty-fifth day of the same month, which was Chislev. [6]They celebrated it for eight days with rejoicing, in the manner of the festival of booths, remembering how not long before, during the festival of booths, they had been wandering in the mountains and caves like wild animals. [7]Therefore, carrying ivy-wreathed wands and beautiful branches and also fronds of palm, they offered hymns of thanksgiving to him who had given success to the purifying of his own holy place. [8]They decreed by public edict, ratified by vote, that the whole nation of the Jews should observe these days every year.

9 Such then was the end of Antiochus, who was called Epiphanes.

Accession of Antiochus Eupator

10 Now we will tell what took place under Antiochus Eupator, who was the son of that ungodly man, and will give a brief summary of the principal calamities of the wars. [11]This man, when he succeeded to the kingdom, appointed one Lysias to have charge of the government and to be chief governor of Coelesyria and Phoenicia. [12]Ptolemy, who was called Macron, took the lead in showing justice to the Jews because of the wrong that had been done to them, and attempted to maintain peaceful relations with them. [13]As a result he was accused before Eupator by the king's Friends. He heard himself called a traitor at every turn, because he had abandoned Cyprus, which Philometor had entrusted to him, and had gone over to Antiochus Epiphanes. Unable to command the respect due his office,[*y*] he took poison and ended his life.

Campaign in Idumea

14 When Gorgias became governor of the region, he maintained a force of mercenaries, and at every turn kept attacking the Jews. [15]Besides this, the Idumeans, who had control of important strongholds, were harassing the Jews; they received those who were banished from Jerusalem, and endeavored to keep up the war. [16]But Maccabeus and his forces, after making solemn supplication and imploring God to fight on their side, rushed to the strongholds of the Idumeans. [17]Attacking them vigorously, they gained possession of the places, and beat off all who fought upon the wall, and slaughtered those whom they encountered, killing no fewer than twenty thousand.

18 When at least nine thousand took refuge in two very strong towers well equipped to withstand a siege, [19]Maccabeus left Simon and Joseph, and also Zacchaeus and his troops, a force sufficient to besiege them; and he himself set off for places where he was more urgently needed. [20]But those with Simon, who were money-hungry, were bribed by some of those who were in the towers, and on receiving seventy thousand drachmas let some of them slip away. [21]When word of what had happened came to Maccabeus, he gathered the leaders of the people, and accused these men of having sold their kindred for money by setting

[*y*] Cn: Meaning of Gk uncertain

their enemies free to fight against them. ²²Then he killed these men who had turned traitor, and immediately captured the two towers. ²³Having success at arms in everything he undertook, he destroyed more than twenty thousand in the two strongholds.

Judas Defeats Timothy

24 Now Timothy, who had been defeated by the Jews before, gathered a tremendous force of mercenaries and collected the cavalry from Asia in no small number. He came on, intending to take Judea by storm. ²⁵As he drew near, Maccabeus and his men sprinkled dust on their heads and girded their loins with sackcloth, in supplication to God. ²⁶Falling upon the steps before the altar, they implored him to be gracious to them and to be an enemy to their enemies and an adversary to their adversaries, as the law declares. ²⁷And rising from their prayer they took up their arms and advanced a considerable distance from the city; and when they came near the enemy they halted. ²⁸Just as dawn was breaking, the two armies joined battle, the one having as pledge of success and victory not only their valor but also their reliance on the Lord, while the other made rage their leader in the fight.

29 When the battle became fierce, there appeared to the enemy from heaven five resplendent men on horses with golden bridles, and they were leading the Jews. ³⁰Two of them took Maccabeus between them, and shielding him with their own armor and weapons, they kept him from being wounded. They showered arrows and thunderbolts on the enemy, so that, confused and blinded, they were thrown into disorder and cut to pieces. ³¹Twenty thousand five hundred were slaughtered, besides six hundred cavalry.

32 Timothy himself fled to a stronghold called Gazara, especially well garrisoned, where Chaereas was commander. ³³Then Maccabeus and his men were glad, and they besieged the fort for four days. ³⁴The men within, relying on the strength of the place, kept blaspheming terribly and uttering wicked words. ³⁵But at dawn of the fifth day, twenty young men in the army of Maccabeus, fired with anger because of the blasphemies, bravely stormed the wall and with savage fury cut down everyone they

met. ³⁶Others who came up in the same way wheeled around against the defenders and set fire to the towers; they kindled fires and burned the blasphemers alive. Others broke open the gates and let in the rest of the force, and they occupied the city. ³⁷They killed Timothy, who was hiding in a cistern, and his brother Chaereas, and Apollophanes. ³⁸When they had accomplished these things, with hymns and thanksgivings they blessed the Lord who shows great kindness to Israel and gives them the victory.

Lysias Besieges Beth-zur

11 Very soon after this, Lysias, the king's guardian and kinsman, who was in charge of the government, being vexed at what had happened, ²gathered about eighty thousand infantry and all his cavalry and came against the Jews. He intended to make the city a home for Greeks, ³and to levy tribute on the temple as he did on the sacred places of the other nations, and to put up the high priesthood for sale every year. ⁴He took no account whatever of the power of God, but was elated with his ten thousands of infantry, and his thousands of cavalry, and his eighty elephants. ⁵Invading Judea, he approached Beth-zur, which was a fortified place about five stadia^z from Jerusalem, and pressed it hard.

6 When Maccabeus and his men got word that Lysias^a was besieging the strongholds, they and all the people, with lamentations and tears, prayed the Lord to send a good angel to save Israel. ⁷Maccabeus himself was the first to take up arms, and he urged the others to risk their lives with him to aid their kindred. Then they eagerly rushed off together. ⁸And there, while they were still near Jerusalem, a horseman appeared at their head, clothed in white and brandishing weapons of gold. ⁹And together they all praised the merciful God, and were strengthened in heart, ready to assail not only humans but the wildest animals or walls of iron. ¹⁰They advanced in battle order, having their heavenly ally, for the Lord had mercy on them. ¹¹They hurled themselves like lions against the enemy, and laid low eleven thousand of them and sixteen hundred cavalry, and forced all the rest to flee. ¹²Most of them got away stripped and wounded, and Lysias himself escaped by disgraceful flight.

^z Meaning of Gk uncertain   ^a Gk *he*

Lysias Makes Peace with the Jews

13 As he was not without intelligence, he pondered over the defeat that had befallen him, and realized that the Hebrews were invincible because the mighty God fought on their side. So he sent to them ¹⁴and persuaded them to settle everything on just terms, promising that he would persuade the king, constraining him to be their friend.^b ¹⁵Maccabeus, having regard for the common good, agreed to all that Lysias urged. For the king granted every request in behalf of the Jews which Maccabeus delivered to Lysias in writing. 16 The letter written to the Jews by Lysias was to this effect:

"Lysias to the people of the Jews, greetings. ¹⁷John and Absalom, who were sent by you, have delivered your signed communication and have asked about the matters indicated in it. ¹⁸I have informed the king of everything that needed to be brought before him, and he has agreed to what was possible. ¹⁹If you will maintain your goodwill toward the government, I will endeavor in the future to help promote your welfare. ²⁰And concerning such matters and their details, I have ordered these men and my representatives to confer with you. ²¹Farewell. The one hundred forty-eighth year,^c Dioscorinthius twenty-fourth."

22 The king's letter ran thus:

"King Antiochus to his brother Lysias, greetings. ²³Now that our father has gone on to the gods, we desire that the subjects of the kingdom be undisturbed in caring for their own affairs. ²⁴We have heard that the Jews do not consent to our father's change to Greek customs, but prefer their own way of living and ask that their own customs be allowed them. ²⁵Accordingly, since we choose that this nation also should be free from disturbance, our decision is that their temple be restored to them and that they shall live according to the customs of their ancestors. ²⁶You will do well, therefore, to send word to them and give them pledges of friendship, so that they may know our policy and be of good cheer and go on happily in the conduct of their own affairs."

27 To the nation the king's letter was as follows:

"King Antiochus to the senate of the Jews and to the other Jews, greetings. ²⁸If you are well, it is as we desire. We also are in good health. ²⁹Menelaus has informed us

that you wish to return home and look after your own affairs. ³⁰Therefore those who go home by the thirtieth of Xanthicus will have our pledge of friendship and full permission ³¹for the Jews to enjoy their own food and laws, just as formerly, and none of them shall be molested in any way for what may have been done in ignorance. ³²And I have also sent Menelaus to encourage you. ³³Farewell. The one hundred forty-eighth year,^c Xanthicus fifteenth."

34 The Romans also sent them a letter, which read thus:

"Quintus Memmius and Titus Manius, envoys of the Romans, to the people of the Jews, greetings. ³⁵With regard to what Lysias the kinsman of the king has granted you, we also give consent. ³⁶But as to the matters that he decided are to be referred to the king, as soon as you have considered them, send some one promptly so that we may make proposals appropriate for you. For we are on our way to Antioch. ³⁷Therefore make haste and send messengers so that we may have your judgment. ³⁸Farewell. The one hundred forty-eighth year,^c Xanthicus fifteenth."

Incidents at Joppa and Jamnia

12 When this agreement had been reached, Lysias returned to the king, and the Jews went about their farming.

2 But some of the governors in various places, Timothy and Apollonius son of Gennaeus, as well as Hieronymus and Demophon, and in addition to these Nicanor the governor of Cyprus, would not let them live quietly and in peace. ³And the people of Joppa did so ungodly a deed as this: they invited the Jews who lived among them to embark, with their wives and children, on boats that they had provided, as though there were no ill will to the Jews;^d ⁴and this was done by public vote of the city. When they accepted, because they wished to live peaceably and suspected nothing, the people of Joppa^e took them out to sea and drowned them, at least two hundred. ⁵When Judas heard of the cruelty visited on his compatriots, he gave orders to his men ⁶and, calling upon God, the righteous judge, attacked the murderers of his kindred. He set fire to the harbor by night, burned the boats, and massacred those who had taken

^b Meaning of Gk uncertain   ^c 164 B.C.   ^d Gk *to them*   ^e Gk *they*

refuge there. [7]Then, because the city's gates were closed, he withdrew, intending to come again and root out the whole community of Joppa. [8]But learning that the people in Jamnia meant in the same way to wipe out the Jews who were living among them, [9]he attacked the Jamnites by night and set fire to the harbor and the fleet, so that the glow of the light was seen in Jerusalem, thirty miles[f] distant.

The Campaign in Gilead

10 When they had gone more than a mile[g] from there, on their march against Timothy, at least five thousand Arabs with five hundred cavalry attacked them. [11]After a hard fight, Judas and his companions, with God's help, were victorious. The defeated nomads begged Judas to grant them pledges of friendship, promising to give him livestock and to help his people[h] in all other ways. [12]Judas, realizing that they might indeed be useful in many ways, agreed to make peace with them; and after receiving his pledges they went back to their tents.

13 He also attacked a certain town that was strongly fortified with earthworks[i] and walls, and inhabited by all sorts of Gentiles. Its name was Caspin. [14]Those who were within, relying on the strength of the walls and on their supply of provisions, behaved most insolently toward Judas and his men, railing at them and even blaspheming and saying unholy things. [15]But Judas and his men, calling upon the great Sovereign of the world, who without battering rams or engines of war overthrew Jericho in the days of Joshua, rushed furiously upon the walls. [16]They took the town by the will of God, and slaughtered untold numbers, so that the adjoining lake, a quarter of a mile[j] wide, appeared to be running over with blood.

Judas Defeats Timothy's Army

17 When they had gone ninety-five miles[k] from there, they came to Charax, to the Jews who are called Toubiani. [18]They did not find Timothy in that region, for he had by then left there without accomplishing anything, though in one place he had left a very strong garrison. [19]Dositheus and Sosipater, who were captains under

Maccabeus, marched out and destroyed those whom Timothy had left in the stronghold, more than ten thousand men. [20]But Maccabeus arranged his army in divisions, set men[h] in command of the divisions, and hurried after Timothy, who had with him one hundred twenty thousand infantry and two thousand five hundred cavalry. [21]When Timothy learned of the approach of Judas, he sent off the women and the children and also the baggage to a place called Carnaim; for that place was hard to besiege and difficult of access because of the narrowness of all the approaches. [22]But when Judas's first division appeared, terror and fear came over the enemy at the manifestation to them of him who sees all things. In their flight they rushed headlong in every direction, so that often they were injured by their own men and pierced by the points of their own swords. [23]Judas pressed the pursuit with the utmost vigor, putting the sinners to the sword, and destroyed as many as thirty thousand.

24 Timothy himself fell into the hands of Dositheus and Sosipater and their men. With great guile he begged them to let him go in safety, because he held the parents of most of them, and the brothers of some, to whom no consideration would be shown. [25]And when with many words he had confirmed his solemn promise to restore them unharmed, they let him go, for the sake of saving their kindred.

Judas Wins Other Victories

26 Then Judas[l] marched against Carnaim and the temple of Atargatis, and slaughtered twenty-five thousand people. [27]After the rout and destruction of these, he marched also against Ephron, a fortified town where Lysias lived with multitudes of people of all nationalities.[i] Stalwart young men took their stand before the walls and made a vigorous defense; and great stores of war engines and missiles were there. [28]But the Jews[m] called upon the Sovereign who with power shatters the might of his enemies, and they got the town into their hands, and killed as many as twenty-five thousand of those who were in it.

29 Setting out from there, they hastened to Scythopolis, which is seventy-five miles[n] from Jerusalem. [30]But when the Jews who

---

[f] Gk *two hundred forty stadia*   [g] Gk *nine stadia*   [h] Gk *them*   [i] Meaning of Gk uncertain   [j] Gk *two stadia*
[k] Gk *seven hundred fifty stadia*   [l] Gk *he*   [m] Gk *they*   [n] Gk *six hundred stadia*

lived there bore witness to the goodwill that the people of Scythopolis had shown them and their kind treatment of them in times of misfortune, [31]they thanked them and exhorted them to be well disposed to their race in the future also. Then they went up to Jerusalem, as the festival of weeks was close at hand.

Judas Defeats Gorgias

32 After the festival called Pentecost, they hurried against Gorgias, the governor of Idumea, [33]who came out with three thousand infantry and four hundred cavalry. [34]When they joined battle, it happened that a few of the Jews fell. [35]But a certain Dositheus, one of Bacenor's men, who was on horseback and was a strong man, caught hold of Gorgias, and grasping his cloak was dragging him off by main strength, wishing to take the accursed man alive, when one of the Thracian cavalry bore down on him and cut off his arm; so Gorgias escaped and reached Marisa.

36 As Esdris and his men had been fighting for a long time and were weary, Judas called upon the Lord to show himself their ally and leader in the battle. [37]In the language of their ancestors he raised the battle cry, with hymns; then he charged against Gorgias's troops when they were not expecting it, and put them to flight.

Prayers for Those Killed in Battle

38 Then Judas assembled his army and went to the city of Adullam. As the seventh day was coming on, they purified themselves according to the custom, and kept the sabbath there.

39 On the next day, as had now become necessary, Judas and his men went to take up the bodies of the fallen and to bring them back to lie with their kindred in the sepulchres of their ancestors. [40]Then under the tunic of each one of the dead they found sacred tokens of the idols of Jamnia, which the law forbids the Jews to wear. And it became clear to all that this was the reason these men had fallen. [41]So they all blessed the ways of the Lord, the righteous judge, who reveals the things that are hidden; [42]and they turned to supplication, praying that the sin that had been committed might

be wholly blotted out. The noble Judas exhorted the people to keep themselves free from sin, for they had seen with their own eyes what had happened as the result of the sin of those who had fallen. [43]He also took up a collection, man by man, to the amount of two thousand drachmas of silver, and sent it to Jerusalem to provide for a sin offering. In doing this he acted very well and honorably, taking account of the resurrection. [44]For if he were not expecting that those who had fallen would rise again, it would have been superfluous and foolish to pray for the dead. [45]But if he was looking to the splendid reward that is laid up for those who fall asleep in godliness, it was a holy and pious thought. Therefore he made atonement for the dead, so that they might be delivered from their sin.

Menelaus Is Put to Death

13 In the one hundred forty-ninth year[o] word came to Judas and his men that Antiochus Eupator was coming with a great army against Judea, [2]and with him Lysias, his guardian, who had charge of the government. Each of them had a Greek force of one hundred ten thousand infantry, five thousand three hundred cavalry, twenty-two elephants, and three hundred chariots armed with scythes.

3 Menelaus also joined them and with utter hypocrisy urged Antiochus on, not for the sake of his country's welfare, but because he thought that he would be established in office. [4]But the King of kings aroused the anger of Antiochus against the scoundrel; and when Lysias informed him that this man was to blame for all the trouble, he ordered them to take him to Beroea and to put him to death by the method that is customary in that place. [5]For there is a tower there, fifty cubits high, full of ashes, and it has a rim running around it that on all sides inclines precipitously into the ashes. [6]There they all push to destruction anyone guilty of sacrilege or notorious for other crimes. [7]By such a fate it came about that Menelaus the lawbreaker died, without even burial in the earth. [8]And this was eminently just; because he had committed many sins against the altar whose fire and ashes were holy, he met his death in ashes.

A Battle Near the City of Modein

9 The king with barbarous arrogance was coming to show the Jews things far worse than those that had been done[p] in his father's time. [10]But when Judas heard of this, he ordered the people to call upon the Lord day and night, now if ever to help those who were on the point of being deprived of the law and their country and the holy temple, [11]and not to let the people who had just begun to revive fall into the hands of the blasphemous Gentiles. [12]When they had all joined in the same petition and had implored the merciful Lord with weeping and fasting and lying prostrate for three days without ceasing, Judas exhorted them and ordered them to stand ready.

13 After consulting privately with the elders, he determined to march out and decide the matter by the help of God before the king's army could enter Judea and get possession of the city. [14]So, committing the decision to the Creator of the world and exhorting his troops to fight bravely to the death for the laws, temple, city, country, and commonwealth, he pitched his camp near Modein. [15]He gave his troops the watchword, "God's victory," and with a picked force of the bravest young men, he attacked the king's pavilion at night and killed as many as two thousand men in the camp. He stabbed[q] the leading elephant and its rider. [16]In the end they filled the camp with terror and confusion and withdrew in triumph. [17]This happened, just as day was dawning, because the Lord's help protected him.

Antiochus Makes a Treaty with the Jews

18 The king, having had a taste of the daring of the Jews, tried strategy in attacking their positions. [19]He advanced against Beth-zur, a strong fortress of the Jews, was turned back, attacked again,[r] and was defeated. [20]Judas sent in to the garrison whatever was necessary. [21]But Rhodocus, a man from the ranks of the Jews, gave secret information to the enemy; he was sought for, caught, and put in prison. [22]The king negotiated a second time with the people in Beth-zur, gave pledges, received theirs, withdrew, attacked Judas and his men, was defeated; [23]he got word that Philip, who had been left in charge of the government, had

revolted in Antioch; he was dismayed, called in the Jews, yielded and swore to observe all their rights, settled with them and offered sacrifice, honored the sanctuary and showed generosity to the holy place. [24]He received Maccabeus, left Hegemonides as governor from Ptolemais to Gerar, [25]and went to Ptolemais. The people of Ptolemais were indignant over the treaty; in fact they were so angry that they wanted to annul its terms.[q] [26]Lysias took the public platform, made the best possible defense, convinced them, appeased them, gained their goodwill, and set out for Antioch. This is how the king's attack and withdrawal turned out.

Alcimus Speaks against Judas

14 Three years later, word came to Judas and his men that Demetrius son of Seleucus had sailed into the harbor of Tripolis with a strong army and a fleet, [2]and had taken possession of the country, having made away with Antiochus and his guardian Lysias.

3 Now a certain Alcimus, who had formerly been high priest but had willfully defiled himself in the times of separation,[s] realized that there was no way for him to be safe or to have access again to the holy altar, [4]and went to King Demetrius about the one hundred fifty-first year,[t] presenting to him a crown of gold and a palm, and besides these some of the customary olive branches from the temple. During that day he kept quiet. [5]But he found an opportunity that furthered his mad purpose when he was invited by Demetrius to a meeting of the council and was asked about the attitude and intentions of the Jews. He answered:

6 "Those of the Jews who are called Hasideans, whose leader is Judas Maccabeus, are keeping up war and stirring up sedition, and will not let the kingdom attain tranquility. [7]Therefore I have laid aside my ancestral glory—I mean the high priesthood—and have now come here, [8]first because I am genuinely concerned for the interests of the king, and second because I have regard also for my compatriots. For through the folly of those whom I have mentioned our whole nation is now in no small misfortune. [9]Since you are acquainted, O king, with the details of this matter, may

---

[p] Or *the worst of the things that had been done*   [q] Meaning of Gk uncertain   [r] Or *faltered*   [s] Other ancient authorities read *of mixing*   [t] 161 B.C.

it please you to take thought for our country and our hard-pressed nation with the gracious kindness that you show to all. [10]For as long as Judas lives, it is impossible for the government to find peace." [11]When he had said this, the rest of the king's Friends,[u] who were hostile to Judas, quickly inflamed Demetrius still more. [12]He immediately chose Nicanor, who had been in command of the elephants, appointed him governor of Judea, and sent him off [13]with orders to kill Judas and scatter his troops, and to install Alcimus as high priest of the great[v] temple. [14]And the Gentiles throughout Judea, who had fled before[w] Judas, flocked to join Nicanor, thinking that the misfortunes and calamities of the Jews would mean prosperity for themselves.

Nicanor Makes Friends with Judas

15 When the Jews[x] heard of Nicanor's coming and the gathering of the Gentiles, they sprinkled dust on their heads and prayed to him who established his own people forever and always upholds his own heritage by manifesting himself. [16]At the command of the leader, they[y] set out from there immediately and engaged them in battle at a village called Dessau.[w] [17]Simon, the brother of Judas, had encountered Nicanor, but had been temporarily[z] checked because of the sudden consternation created by the enemy.

18 Nevertheless Nicanor, hearing of the valor of Judas and his troops and their courage in battle for their country, shrank from deciding the issue by bloodshed. [19]Therefore he sent Posidonius, Theodotus, and Mattathias to give and receive pledges of friendship. [20]When the terms had been fully considered, and the leader had informed the people, and it had appeared that they were of one mind, they agreed to the covenant. [21]The leaders[a] set a day on which to meet by themselves. A chariot came forward from each army; seats of honor were set in place; [22]Judas posted armed men in readiness at key places to prevent sudden treachery on the part of the enemy; so they duly held the consultation.

23 Nicanor stayed on in Jerusalem and did nothing out of the way, but dismissed the flocks of people that had gathered. [24]And he kept Judas always in his presence; he was warmly attached to the man. [25]He

urged him to marry and have children; so Judas[y] married, settled down, and shared the common life.

Nicanor Turns against Judas

26 But when Alcimus noticed their goodwill for one another, he took the covenant that had been made and went to Demetrius. He told him that Nicanor was disloyal to the government, since he had appointed that conspirator against the kingdom, Judas, to be his successor. [27]The king became excited and, provoked by the false accusations of that depraved man, wrote to Nicanor, stating that he was displeased with the covenant and commanding him to send Maccabeus to Antioch as a prisoner without delay.

28 When this message came to Nicanor, he was troubled and grieved that he had to annul their agreement when the man had done no wrong. [29]Since it was not possible to oppose the king, he watched for an opportunity to accomplish this by a stratagem. [30]But Maccabeus, noticing that Nicanor was more austere in his dealings with him and was meeting him more rudely than had been his custom, concluded that this austerity did not spring from the best motives. So he gathered not a few of his men, and went into hiding from Nicanor. [31]When the latter became aware that he had been cleverly outwitted by the man, he went to the great[b] and holy temple while the priests were offering the customary sacrifices, and commanded them to hand the man over. [32]When they declared on oath that they did not know where the man was whom he wanted, [33]he stretched out his right hand toward the sanctuary, and swore this oath: "If you do not hand Judas over to me as a prisoner, I will level this shrine of God to the ground and tear down the altar, and build here a splendid temple to Dionysus."

34 Having said this, he went away. Then the priests stretched out their hands toward heaven and called upon the constant Defender of our nation, in these words: [35]"O Lord of all, though you have need of nothing, you were pleased that there should be a temple for your habitation among us; [36]so now, O holy One, Lord of all holiness, keep undefiled forever this house that has been so recently purified."

[u] Gk *of the Friends* [v] Gk *greatest* [w] Meaning of Gk uncertain [x] Gk *they* [y] Gk *he* [z] Other ancient authorities read *slowly* [a] Gk *They* [b] Gk *greatest*

Razis Dies for His Country

37 A certain Razis, one of the elders of Jerusalem, was denounced to Nicanor as a man who loved his compatriots and was very well thought of and for his goodwill was called father of the Jews. [38]In former times, when there was no mingling with the Gentiles, he had been accused of Judaism, and he had most zealously risked body and life for Judaism. [39]Nicanor, wishing to exhibit the enmity that he had for the Jews, sent more than five hundred soldiers to arrest him; [40]for he thought that by arresting[c] him he would do them an injury. [41]When the troops were about to capture the tower and were forcing the door of the courtyard, they ordered that fire be brought and the doors burned. Being surrounded, Razis[d] fell upon his own sword, [42]preferring to die nobly rather than to fall into the hands of sinners and suffer outrages unworthy of his noble birth. [43]But in the heat of the struggle he did not hit exactly, and the crowd was now rushing in through the doors. He courageously ran up on the wall, and bravely threw himself down into the crowd. [44]But as they quickly drew back, a space opened and he fell in the middle of the empty space. [45]Still alive and aflame with anger, he rose, and though his blood gushed forth and his wounds were severe he ran through the crowd; and standing upon a steep rock, [46]with his blood now completely drained from him, he tore out his entrails, took them in both hands and hurled them at the crowd, calling upon the Lord of life and spirit to give them back to him again. This was the manner of his death.

Nicanor's Arrogance

15 When Nicanor heard that Judas and his troops were in the region of Samaria, he made plans to attack them with complete safety on the day of rest. [2]When the Jews who were compelled to follow him said, "Do not destroy so savagely and barbarously, but show respect for the day that he who sees all things has honored and hallowed above other days," [3]the thrice-accursed wretch asked if there were a sovereign in heaven who had commanded the keeping of the sabbath day. [4]When they declared, "It is the living Lord himself, the Sovereign in heaven, who ordered us to observe the seventh day," [5]he replied, "But I am a sovereign also, on earth, and I command you to take up arms and finish the king's business." Nevertheless, he did not succeed in carrying out his abominable design.

Judas Prepares the Jews for Battle

6 This Nicanor in his utter boastfulness and arrogance had determined to erect a public monument of victory over Judas and his forces. [7]But Maccabeus did not cease to trust with all confidence that he would get help from the Lord. [8]He exhorted his troops not to fear the attack of the Gentiles, but to keep in mind the former times when help had come to them from heaven, and so to look for the victory that the Almighty would give them. [9]Encouraging them from the law and the prophets, and reminding them also of the struggles they had won, he made them the more eager. [10]When he had aroused their courage, he issued his orders, at the same time pointing out the perfidy of the Gentiles and their violation of oaths. [11]He armed each of them not so much with confidence in shields and spears as with the inspiration of brave words, and he cheered them all by relating a dream, a sort of vision,[e] which was worthy of belief.

12 What he saw was this: Onias, who had been high priest, a noble and good man, of modest bearing and gentle manner, one who spoke fittingly and had been trained from childhood in all that belongs to excellence, was praying with outstretched hands for the whole body of the Jews. [13]Then in the same fashion another appeared, distinguished by his gray hair and dignity, and of marvelous majesty and authority. [14]And Onias spoke, saying, "This is a man who loves the family of Israel and prays much for the people and the holy city—Jeremiah, the prophet of God." [15]Jeremiah stretched out his right hand and gave to Judas a golden sword, and as he gave it he addressed him thus: [16]"Take this holy sword, a gift from God, with which you will strike down your adversaries."

17 Encouraged by the words of Judas, so noble and so effective in arousing valor and awaking courage in the souls of the young, they determined not to carry on a campaign[e] but to attack bravely, and to decide the matter by fighting hand to hand with all courage, because the city and the sanctuary

---

[c] Meaning of Gk uncertain   [d] Gk *he*   [e] Or *to remain in camp*

and the temple were in danger. [18]Their concern for wives and children, and also for brothers and sisters[f] and relatives, lay upon them less heavily; their greatest and first fear was for the consecrated sanctuary. [19]And those who had to remain in the city were in no little distress, being anxious over the encounter in the open country.

The Defeat and Death of Nicanor

20 When all were now looking forward to the coming issue, and the enemy was already close at hand with their army drawn up for battle, the elephants[g] strategically stationed and the cavalry deployed on the flanks, [21]Maccabeus, observing the masses that were in front of him and the varied supply of arms and the savagery of the elephants, stretched out his hands toward heaven and called upon the Lord who works wonders; for he knew that it is not by arms, but as the Lord[h] decides, that he gains the victory for those who deserve it. [22]He called upon him in these words: "O Lord, you sent your angel in the time of King Hezekiah of Judea, and he killed fully one hundred eighty-five thousand in the camp of Sennacherib. [23]So now, O Sovereign of the heavens, send a good angel to spread terror and trembling before us. [24]By the might of your arm may these blasphemers who come against your holy people be struck down." With these words he ended his prayer.

25 Nicanor and his troops advanced with trumpets and battle songs, [26]but Judas and his troops met the enemy in battle with invocations to God and prayers. [27]So, fighting with their hands and praying to God in their hearts, they laid low at least thirty-five thousand, and were greatly gladdened by God's manifestation.

28 When the action was over and they were returning with joy, they recognized Nicanor, lying dead, in full armor. [29]Then there was shouting and tumult, and they blessed the Sovereign Lord in the language of their ancestors. [30]Then the man who was ever in body and soul the defender of his people, the man who maintained his youthful goodwill toward his compatriots, ordered them to cut off Nicanor's head and arm and carry them to Jerusalem. [31]When he arrived there and had called his compatriots together and stationed the priests before the altar, he sent for those who were in the citadel. [32]He showed them the vile Nicanor's head and that profane man's arm, which had been boastfully stretched out against the holy house of the Almighty. [33]He cut out the tongue of the ungodly Nicanor and said that he would feed it piecemeal to the birds and would hang up these rewards of his folly opposite the sanctuary. [34]And they all, looking to heaven, blessed the Lord who had manifested himself, saying, "Blessed is he who has kept his own place undefiled!" [35]Judas[i] hung Nicanor's head from the citadel, a clear and conspicuous sign to everyone of the help of the Lord. [36]And they all decreed by public vote never to let this day go unobserved, but to celebrate the thirteenth day of the twelfth month—which is called Adar in the Aramaic language—the day before Mordecai's day.

37 This, then, is how matters turned out with Nicanor, and from that time the city has been in the possession of the Hebrews. So I will here end my story.

The Compiler's Epilogue

38 If it is well told and to the point, that is what I myself desired; if it is poorly done and mediocre, that was the best I could do. [39]For just as it is harmful to drink wine alone, or, again, to drink water alone, while wine mixed with water is sweet and delicious and enhances one's enjoyment, so also the style of the story delights the ears of those who read the work. And here will be the end.

---

[f] Gk *for brothers*   [g] Gk *animals*   [h] Gk *he*   [i] Gk *He*

177

(b) The books from 1 Esdras through 3 Maccabees are recognized as Deuterocanonical Scripture by the Greek and the Russian Orthodox Churches. They are not so recognized by the Roman Catholic Church, but 1 Esdras and the Prayer of Manasseh (together with 2 Esdras) are placed in an appendix to the Latin Vulgate Bible.

1 ESDRAS

Josiah Celebrates the Passover

1 Josiah kept the passover to his Lord in Jerusalem; he killed the passover lamb on the fourteenth day of the first month, [2]having placed the priests according to their divisions, arrayed in their vestments, in the temple of the Lord. [3]He told the Levites, the temple servants of Israel, that they should sanctify themselves to the Lord and put the holy ark of the Lord in the house that King Solomon, son of David, had built; [4]and he said, "You need no longer carry it on your shoulders. Now worship the Lord your God and serve his people Israel; prepare yourselves by your families and kindred, [5]in accordance with the directions of King David of Israel and the magnificence of his son Solomon. Stand in order in the temple according to the groupings of the ancestral houses of you Levites, who minister before your kindred the people of Israel, [6]and kill the passover lamb and prepare the sacrifices for your kindred, and keep the passover according to the commandment of the Lord that was given to Moses."

7 To the people who were present Josiah gave thirty thousand lambs and kids, and three thousand calves; these were given from the king's possessions, as he promised, to the people and the priests and Levites. [8]Hilkiah, Zechariah, and Jehiel,[a] the chief officers of the temple, gave to the priests for the passover two thousand six hundred sheep and three hundred calves. [9]And Jeconiah and Shemaiah and his brother Nethanel, and Hashabiah and Ochiel and Joram, captains over thousands, gave the Levites for the passover five thousand sheep and seven hundred calves.

10 This is what took place. The priests and the Levites, having the unleavened bread, stood in proper order according to kindred [11]and the grouping of the ancestral houses, before the people, to make the offering to the Lord as it is written in the book of Moses; this they did in the morning. [12]They roasted the passover lamb with fire, as required; and they boiled the sacrifices in bronze pots and caldrons, with a pleasing odor, [13]and carried them to all the people. Afterward they prepared the passover for

themselves and for their kindred the priests, the sons of Aaron, [14]because the priests were offering the fat until nightfall; so the Levites prepared it for themselves and for their kindred the priests, the sons of Aaron. [15]The temple singers, the sons of Asaph, were in their place according to the arrangement made by David, and also Asaph, Zechariah, and Eddinus, who represented the king. [16]The gatekeepers were at each gate; no one needed to interrupt his daily duties, for their kindred the Levites prepared the passover for them.

17 So the things that had to do with the sacrifices to the Lord were accomplished that day: the passover was kept [18]and the sacrifices were offered on the altar of the Lord, according to the command of King Josiah. [19]And the people of Israel who were present at that time kept the passover and the festival of unleavened bread seven days. [20]No passover like it had been kept in Israel since the times of the prophet Samuel; [21]none of the kings of Israel had kept such a passover as was kept by Josiah and the priests and Levites and the people of Judah and all of Israel who were living in Jerusalem. [22]In the eighteenth year of the reign of Josiah this passover was kept.

The End of Josiah's Reign

23 And the deeds of Josiah were upright in the sight of the Lord, for his heart was full of godliness. [24]In ancient times the events of his reign have been recorded— concerning those who sinned and acted wickedly toward the Lord beyond any other people or kingdom, and how they grieved the Lord[b] deeply, so that the words of the Lord fell upon Israel.

25 After all these acts of Josiah, it happened that Pharaoh, king of Egypt, went to make war at Carchemish on the Euphrates, and Josiah went out against him. [26]And the king of Egypt sent word to him saying, "What have we to do with each other, O king of Judea? [27]I was not sent against you by the Lord God, for my war is at the Euphrates. And now the Lord is with me! The Lord is with me, urging me on! Stand aside, and do not oppose the Lord."

[a] Gk Esyelus   [b] Gk him

28 Josiah, however, did not turn back to his chariot, but tried to fight with him, and did not heed the words of the prophet Jeremiah from the mouth of the Lord. ²⁹He joined battle with him in the plain of Megiddo, and the commanders came down against King Josiah. ³⁰The king said to his servants, "Take me away from the battle, for I am very weak." And immediately his servants took him out of the line of battle. ³¹He got into his second chariot; and after he was brought back to Jerusalem he died, and was buried in the tomb of his ancestors.

32 In all Judea they mourned for Josiah. The prophet Jeremiah lamented for Josiah, and the principal men, with the women,^c have made lamentation for him to this day; it was ordained that this should always be done throughout the whole nation of Israel. ³³These things are written in the book of the histories of the kings of Judea; and every one of the acts of Josiah, and his splendor, and his understanding of the law of the Lord, and the things that he had done before, and these that are now told, are recorded in the book of the kings of Israel and Judah.

The Last Kings of Judah

34 The men of the nation took Jeconiah^d son of Josiah, who was twenty-three years old, and made him king in succession to his father Josiah. ³⁵He reigned three months in Judah and Jerusalem. Then the king of Egypt deposed him from reigning in Jerusalem, ³⁶and fined the nation one hundred talents of silver and one talent of gold. ³⁷The king of Egypt made his brother Jehoiakim king of Judea and Jerusalem. ³⁸Jehoiakim put the nobles in prison, and seized his brother Zarius and brought him back from Egypt.

39 Jehoiakim was twenty-five years old when he began to reign in Judea and Jerusalem; he did what was evil in the sight of the Lord. ⁴⁰King Nebuchadnezzar of Babylon came up against him; he bound him with a chain of bronze and took him away to Babylon. ⁴¹Nebuchadnezzar also took some holy vessels of the Lord, and carried them away, and stored them in his temple in Babylon. ⁴²But the things that are reported about Jehoiakim,^e and his uncleanness and impiety, are written in the annals of the kings.

43 His son Jehoiachin^f became king in his place; when he was made king he was eighteen years old, ⁴⁴and he reigned three months and ten days in Jerusalem. He did what was evil in the sight of the Lord. ⁴⁵A year later Nebuchadnezzar sent and removed him to Babylon, with the holy vessels of the Lord, ⁴⁶and made Zedekiah king of Judea and Jerusalem.

The Fall of Jerusalem

Zedekiah was twenty-one years old, and he reigned eleven years. ⁴⁷He also did what was evil in the sight of the Lord, and did not heed the words that were spoken by the prophet Jeremiah from the mouth of the Lord. ⁴⁸Although King Nebuchadnezzar had made him swear by the name of the Lord, he broke his oath and rebelled; he stiffened his neck and hardened his heart and transgressed the laws of the Lord, the God of Israel. ⁴⁹Even the leaders of the people and of the priests committed many acts of sacrilege and lawlessness beyond all the unclean deeds of all the nations, and polluted the temple of the Lord in Jerusalem— the temple that God had made holy. ⁵⁰The God of their ancestors sent his messenger to call them back, because he would have spared them and his dwelling place. ⁵¹But they mocked his messengers, and whenever the Lord spoke, they scoffed at his prophets, ⁵²until in his anger against his people because of their ungodly acts he gave command to bring against them the kings of the Chaldeans. ⁵³These killed their young men with the sword around their holy temple, and did not spare young man or young woman,^g old man or child, for he gave them all into their hands. ⁵⁴They took all the holy vessels of the Lord, great and small, the treasure chests of the Lord, and the royal stores, and carried them away to Babylon. ⁵⁵They burned the house of the Lord, broke down the walls of Jerusalem, burned their towers with fire, ⁵⁶and utterly destroyed all its glorious things. The survivors he led away to Babylon with the sword, ⁵⁷and they were servants to him and to his sons until the Persians began to reign, in fulfillment of the word of the Lord by the mouth of Jeremiah, ⁵⁸saying, "Until the land has enjoyed its sabbaths, it shall keep sabbath all the time of its desolation until the completion of seventy years."

^c Or *their wives*   ^d 2 Kings 23.30; 2 Chr 36.1 *Jehoahaz*   ^e Gk *him*   ^f Gk *Jehoiakim*   ^g Gk *virgin*

Cyrus Permits the Exiles to Return

2 In the first year of Cyrus as king of the Persians, so that the word of the Lord by the mouth of Jeremiah might be accomplished— ²the Lord stirred up the spirit of King Cyrus of the Persians, and he made a proclamation throughout all his kingdom and also put it in writing:

3 "Thus says Cyrus king of the Persians: The Lord of Israel, the Lord Most High, made me king of the world, ⁴and he has commanded me to build him a house at Jerusalem, which is in Judea. ⁵If any of you, therefore, are of his people, may your Lord be with you; go up to Jerusalem, which is in Judea, and build the house of the Lord of Israel—he is the Lord who dwells in Jerusalem—⁶and let each of you, wherever you may live, be helped by the people of your place with gold and silver, ⁷with gifts and with horses and cattle, besides the other things added as votive offerings for the temple of the Lord that is in Jerusalem."

8 Then arose the heads of families of the tribes of Judah and Benjamin, and the priests and the Levites, and all whose spirit the Lord had stirred to go up to build the house in Jerusalem for the Lord; ⁹their neighbors helped them with everything, with silver and gold, with horses and cattle, and with a very great number of votive offerings from many whose hearts were stirred.

10 King Cyrus also brought out the holy vessels of the Lord that Nebuchadnezzar had carried away from Jerusalem and stored in his temple of idols. ¹¹When King Cyrus of the Persians brought these out, he gave them to Mithridates, his treasurer, ¹²and by him they were given to Sheshbazzar,ʰ the governor of Judea. ¹³The number of these was: one thousand gold cups, one thousand silver cups, twenty-nine silver censers, thirty gold bowls, two thousand four hundred ten silver bowls, and one thousand other vessels. ¹⁴All the vessels were handed over, gold and silver, five thousand four hundred sixty-nine, ¹⁵and they were carried back by Sheshbazzar with the returning exiles from Babylon to Jerusalem.

Opposition to Rebuilding Jerusalem

16 In the time of King Artaxerxes of the Persians, Bishlam, Mithridates, Tabeel, Rehum, Beltethmus, the scribe Shimshai, and the rest of their associates, living in Samaria and other places, wrote him the following letter, against those who were living in Judea and Jerusalem:

17 "To King Artaxerxes our lord, your servants the recorder Rehum and the scribe Shimshai and the other members of their council, and the judges in Coelesyria and Phoenicia: ¹⁸Let it now be known to our lord the king that the Jews who came up from you to us have gone to Jerusalem and are building that rebellious and wicked city, repairing its market places and walls and laying the foundations for a temple. ¹⁹Now if this city is built and the walls finished, they will not only refuse to pay tribute but will even resist kings. ²⁰Since the building of the temple is now going on, we think it best not to neglect such a matter, ²¹but to speak to our lord the king, in order that, if it seems good to you, search may be made in the records of your ancestors. ²²You will find in the annals what has been written about them, and will learn that this city was rebellious, troubling both kings and other cities, ²³and that the Jews were rebels and kept setting up blockades in it from of old. That is why this city was laid waste. ²⁴Therefore we now make known to you, O lord and king, that if this city is built and its walls finished, you will no longer have access to Coelesyria and Phoenicia."

25 Then the king, in reply to the recorder Rehum, Beltethmus, the scribe Shimshai, and the others associated with them and living in Samaria and Syria and Phoenicia, wrote as follows:

26 "I have read the letter that you sent me. So I ordered search to be made, and it has been found that this city from of old has fought against kings, ²⁷that the people in it were given to rebellion and war, and that mighty and cruel kings ruled in Jerusalem and exacted tribute from Coelesyria and Phoenicia. ²⁸Therefore I have now issued orders to prevent these people from building the city and to take care that nothing more be done ²⁹and that such wicked proceedings go no further to the annoyance of kings."

30 Then, when the letter from King Artaxerxes was read, Rehum and the scribe Shimshai and their associates went quickly to Jerusalem, with cavalry and a large number of armed troops, and began to hinder the builders. And the building of the temple in Jerusalem stopped until the second year of the reign of King Darius of the Persians.

ʰ Gk *Sanabassaros*

The Debate of the Three Bodyguards

3 Now King Darius gave a great banquet for all that were under him, all that were born in his house, and all the nobles of Media and Persia, ²and all the satraps and generals and governors that were under him in the hundred twenty-seven satrapies from India to Ethiopia. ³They ate and drank, and when they were satisfied they went away, and King Darius went to his bedroom; he went to sleep, but woke up again.

4 Then the three young men of the bodyguard, who kept guard over the person of the king, said to one another, ⁵"Let each of us state what one thing is strongest; and to the one whose statement seems wisest, King Darius will give rich gifts and great honors of victory. ⁶He shall be clothed in purple, and drink from gold cups, and sleep on a gold bed,ⁱ and have a chariot with gold bridles, and a turban of fine linen, and a necklace around his neck; ⁷and because of his wisdom he shall sit next to Darius and shall be called Kinsman of Darius."

8 Then each wrote his own statement, and they sealed them and put them under the pillow of King Darius, ⁹and said, "When the king wakes, they will give him the writing; and to the one whose statement the king and the three nobles of Persia judge to be wisest the victory shall be given according to what is written." ¹⁰The first wrote, "Wine is strongest." ¹¹The second wrote, "The king is strongest." ¹²The third wrote, "Women are strongest, but above all things truth is victor."ʲ

13 When the king awoke, they took the writing and gave it to him, and he read it. ¹⁴Then he sent and summoned all the nobles of Persia and Media and the satraps and generals and governors and prefects, ¹⁵and he took his seat in the council chamber, and the writing was read in their presence. ¹⁶He said, "Call the young men, and they shall explain their statements." So they were summoned, and came in. ¹⁷They said to them, "Explain to us what you have written."

The Speech about Wine

Then the first, who had spoken of the strength of wine, began and said: ¹⁸"Gentlemen, how is wine the strongest? It leads astray the minds of all who drink it. ¹⁹It makes equal the mind of the king and the orphan, of the slave and the free, of the poor and the rich. ²⁰It turns every thought to feasting and mirth, and forgets all sorrow and debt. ²¹It makes all hearts feel rich, forgets kings and satraps, and makes everyone talk in millions.ᵏ ²²When people drink they forget to be friendly with friends and kindred, and before long they draw their swords. ²³And when they recover from the wine, they do not remember what they have done. ²⁴Gentlemen, is not wine the strongest, since it forces people to do these things?" When he had said this, he stopped speaking.

The Speech about the King

4 Then the second, who had spoken of the strength of the king, began to speak: ²"Gentlemen, are not men strongest, who rule over land and sea and all that is in them? ³But the king is stronger; he is their lord and master, and whatever he says to them they obey. ⁴If he tells them to make war on one another, they do it; and if he sends them out against the enemy, they go, and conquer mountains, walls, and towers. ⁵They kill and are killed, and do not disobey the king's command; if they win the victory, they bring everything to the king—whatever spoil they take and everything else. ⁶Likewise those who do not serve in the army or make war but till the soil; whenever they sow and reap, they bring some to the king; and they compel one another to pay taxes to the king. ⁷And yet he is only one man! If he tells them to kill, they kill; if he tells them to release, they release; ⁸if he tells them to attack, they attack; if he tells them to lay waste, they lay waste; if he tells them to build, they build; ⁹if he tells them to cut down, they cut down; if he tells them to plant, they plant. ¹⁰All his people and his armies obey him. Furthermore, he reclines, he eats and drinks and sleeps, ¹¹but they keep watch around him, and no one may go away to attend to his own affairs, nor do they disobey him. ¹²Gentlemen, why is not the king the strongest, since he is to be obeyed in this fashion?" And he stopped speaking.

The Speech about Women

13 Then the third, who had spoken of women and truth (and this was Zerubbabel),

---

ⁱ Gk *on gold*   ʲ Or *but truth is victor over all things*   ᵏ Gk *talents* began to speak: [14]"Gentlemen, is not the king great, and are not men many, and is not wine strong? Who is it, then, that rules them, or has the mastery over them? Is it not women? [15]Women gave birth to the king and to every people that rules over sea and land. [16]From women they came; and women brought up the very men who plant the vineyards from which comes wine. [17]Women make men's clothes; they bring men glory; men cannot exist without women. [18]If men gather gold and silver or any other beautiful thing, and then see a woman lovely in appearance and beauty, [19]they let all those things go, and gape at her, and with open mouths stare at her, and all prefer her to gold or silver or any other beautiful thing. [20]A man leaves his own father, who brought him up, and his own country, and clings to his wife. [21]With his wife he ends his days, with no thought of his father or his mother or his country. [22]Therefore you must realize that women rule over you!

"Do you not labor and toil, and bring everything and give it to women? [23]A man takes his sword, and goes out to travel and rob and steal and to sail the sea and rivers; [24]he faces lions, and he walks in darkness, and when he steals and robs and plunders, he brings it back to the woman he loves. [25]A man loves his wife more than his father or his mother. [26]Many men have lost their minds because of women, and have become slaves because of them. [27]Many have perished, or stumbled, or sinned because of women. [28]And now do you not believe me?

"Is not the king great in his power? Do not all lands fear to touch him? [29]Yet I have seen him with Apame, the king's concubine, the daughter of the illustrious Bartacus; she would sit at the king's right hand [30]and take the crown from the king's head and put it on her own, and slap the king with her left hand. [31]At this the king would gaze at her with mouth agape. If she smiles at him, he laughs; if she loses her temper with him, he flatters her, so that she may be reconciled to him. [32]Gentlemen, why are not women strong, since they do such things?"

The Speech about Truth

33 Then the king and the nobles looked at one another; and he began to speak about truth: [34]"Gentlemen, are not women strong? The earth is vast, and heaven is high, and the sun is swift in its course, for it makes the circuit of the heavens and returns to its place in one day. [35]Is not the one who does these things great? But truth is great, and stronger than all things. [36]The whole earth calls upon truth, and heaven blesses it. All God's works[l] quake and tremble, and with him there is nothing unrighteous. [37]Wine is unrighteous, the king is unrighteous, women are unrighteous, all human beings are unrighteous, all their works are unrighteous, and all such things. There is no truth in them and in their unrighteousness they will perish. [38]But truth endures and is strong forever, and lives and prevails forever and ever. [39]With it there is no partiality or preference, but it does what is righteous instead of anything that is unrighteous or wicked. Everyone approves its deeds, [40]and there is nothing unrighteous in its judgment. To it belongs the strength and the kingship and the power and the majesty of all the ages. Blessed be the God of truth!" [41]When he stopped speaking, all the people shouted and said, "Great is truth, and strongest of all!"

Zerubbabel's Reward

42 Then the king said to him, "Ask what you wish, even beyond what is written, and we will give it to you, for you have been found to be the wisest. You shall sit next to me, and be called my Kinsman." [43]Then he said to the king, "Remember the vow that you made on the day when you became king, to build Jerusalem, [44]and to send back all the vessels that were taken from Jerusalem, which Cyrus set apart when he began[m] to destroy Babylon, and vowed to send them back there. [45]You also vowed to build the temple, which the Edomites burned when Judea was laid waste by the Chaldeans. [46]And now, O lord the king, this is what I ask and request of you, and this befits your greatness. I pray therefore that you fulfill the vow whose fulfillment you vowed to the King of heaven with your own lips."

47 Then King Darius got up and kissed him, and wrote letters for him to all the treasurers and governors and generals and satraps, that they should give safe conduct to him and to all who were going up with him to build Jerusalem. [48]And he wrote

---

[l] Gk *All the works*   [m] Cn: Gk *vowed*

letters to all the governors in Coelesyria and Phoenicia and to those in Lebanon, to bring cedar timber from Lebanon to Jerusalem, and to help him build the city. ⁴⁹He wrote in behalf of all the Jews who were going up from his kingdom to Judea, in the interest of their freedom, that no officer or satrap or governor or treasurer should forcibly enter their doors; ⁵⁰that all the country that they would occupy should be theirs without tribute; that the Idumeans should give up the villages of the Jews that they held; ⁵¹that twenty talents a year should be given for the building of the temple until it was completed, ⁵²and an additional ten talents a year for burnt offerings to be offered on the altar every day, in accordance with the commandment to make seventeen offerings; ⁵³and that all who came from Babylonia to build the city should have their freedom, they and their children and all the priests who came. ⁵⁴He wrote also concerning their support and the priests' vestments in which*ⁿ* they were to minister. ⁵⁵He wrote that the support for the Levites should be provided until the day when the temple would be finished and Jerusalem built. ⁵⁶He wrote that land and wages should be provided for all who guarded the city. ⁵⁷And he sent back from Babylon all the vessels that Cyrus had set apart; everything that Cyrus had ordered to be done, he also commanded to be done and to be sent to Jerusalem.

Zerubbabel's Prayer

58 When the young man went out, he lifted up his face to heaven toward Jerusalem, and praised the King of heaven, saying, ⁵⁹"From you comes the victory; from you comes wisdom, and yours is the glory. I am your servant. ⁶⁰Blessed are you, who have given me wisdom; I give you thanks, O Lord of our ancestors."

61 So he took the letters, and went to Babylon and told this to all his kindred. ⁶²And they praised the God of their ancestors, because he had given them release and permission ⁶³to go up and build Jerusalem and the temple that is called by his name; and they feasted, with music and rejoicing, for seven days.

List of the Returning Exiles

5 After this the heads of ancestral houses were chosen to go up, according to their tribes, with their wives and sons and daughters, and their male and female servants, and their livestock. ²And Darius sent with them a thousand cavalry to take them back to Jerusalem in safety, with the music of drums and flutes; ³all their kindred were making merry. And he made them go up with them.

4 These are the names of the men who went up, according to their ancestral houses in the tribes, over their groups: ⁵the priests, the descendants of Phinehas son of Aaron; Jeshua son of Jozadak son of Seraiah and Joakim son of Zerubbabel son of Shealtiel, of the house of David, of the lineage of Phares, of the tribe of Judah, ⁶who spoke wise words before King Darius of the Persians, in the second year of his reign, in the month of Nisan, the first month.

7 These are the Judeans who came up out of their sojourn in exile, whom King Nebuchadnezzar of Babylon had carried away to Babylon ⁸and who returned to Jerusalem and the rest of Judea, each to his own town. They came with Zerubbabel and Jeshua, Nehemiah, Seraiah, Resaiah, Eneneus, Mordecai, Beelsarus, Aspharasus, Reeliah, Rehum, and Baanah, their leaders.

9 The number of those of the nation and their leaders: the descendants of Parosh, two thousand one hundred seventy-two. The descendants of Shephatiah, four hundred seventy-two. ¹⁰The descendants of Arah, seven hundred fifty-six. ¹¹The descendants of Pahath-moab, of the descendants of Jeshua and Joab, two thousand eight hundred twelve. ¹²The descendants of Elam, one thousand two hundred fifty-four. The descendants of Zattu, nine hundred forty-five. The descendants of Chorbe, seven hundred five. The descendants of Bani, six hundred forty-eight. ¹³The descendants of Bebai, six hundred twenty-three. The descendants of Azgad, one thousand three hundred twenty-two. ¹⁴The descendants of Adonikam, six hundred sixty-seven. The descendants of Bigvai, two thousand sixty-six. The descendants of Adin, four hundred fifty-four. ¹⁵The descendants of Ater, namely of Hezekiah, ninety-two. The descendants of Kilan and Azetas, sixty-seven. The descendants of Azaru, four hundred thirty-two. ¹⁶The descendants of Annias, one hundred one. The descendants of Arom. The descendants of Bezai, three hundred twenty-three. The descendants of Arsiphurith, one hundred twelve. ¹⁷The descendants of Baiterus, three

---

ⁿ Gk *in what priestly vestments*

thousand five. The descendants of Beth-lomon, one hundred twenty-three. [18]Those from Netophah, fifty-five. Those from Anathoth, one hundred fifty-eight. Those from Bethasmoth, forty-two. [19]Those from Kiriatharim, twenty-five. Those from Chephirah and Beeroth, seven hundred forty-three. [20]The Chadiasans and Ammidians, four hundred twenty-two. Those from Kirama and Geba, six hundred twenty-one. [21]Those from Macalon, one hundred twenty-two. Those from Betolio, fifty-two. The descendants of Niphish, one hundred fifty-six. [22]The descendants of the other Calamolalus and Ono, seven hundred twenty-five. The descendants of Jerechus, three hundred forty-five. [23]The descendants of Senaah, three thousand three hundred thirty.

24 The priests: the descendants of Jedaiah son of Jeshua, of the descendants of Anasib, nine hundred seventy-two. The descendants of Immer, one thousand and fifty-two. [25]The descendants of Pashhur, one thousand two hundred forty-seven. The descendants of Charme, one thousand seventeen.

26 The Levites: the descendants of Jeshua and Kadmiel and Bannas and Sudias, seventy-four. [27]The temple singers: the descendants of Asaph, one hundred twenty-eight. [28]The gatekeepers: the descendants of Shallum, the descendants of Ater, the descendants of Talmon, the descendants of Akkub, the descendants of Hatita, the descendants of Shobai, in all one hundred thirty-nine.

29 The temple servants: the descendants of Esau, the descendants of Hasupha, the descendants of Tabbaoth, the descendants of Keros, the descendants of Sua, the descendants of Padon, the descendants of Lebanah, the descendants of Hagabah, [30]the descendants of Akkub, the descendants of Uthai, the descendants of Ketab, the descendants of Hagab, the descendants of Subai, the descendants of Hana, the descendants of Cathua, the descendants of Geddur, [31]the descendants of Jairus, the descendants of Daisan, the descendants of Noeba, the descendants of Chezib, the descendants of Gazera, the descendants of Uzza, the descendants of Phinoe, the descendants of Hasrah, the descendants of Basthai, the descendants of Asnah, the descendants of Maani, the descendants of Nephisim, the descendants of Acuph,[o] the descendants of Hakupha, the descendants

of Asur, the descendants of Pharakim, the descendants of Bazluth, [32]the descendants of Mehida, the descendants of Cutha, the descendants of Charea, the descendants of Barkos, the descendants of Serar, the descendants of Temah, the descendants of Neziah, the descendants of Hatipha.

33 The descendants of Solomon's servants: the descendants of Assaphioth, the descendants of Peruda, the descendants of Jaalah, the descendants of Lozon, the descendants of Isdael, the descendants of Shephatiah, [34]the descendants of Agia, the descendants of Pochereth-hazzebaim, the descendants of Sarothie, the descendants of Masiah, the descendants of Gas, the descendants of Addus, the descendants of Subas, the descendants of Apherra, the descendants of Barodis, the descendants of Shaphat, the descendants of Allon.

35 All the temple servants and the descendants of Solomon's servants were three hundred seventy-two.

36 The following are those who came up from Tel-melah and Tel-harsha, under the leadership of Cherub, Addan, and Immer, [37]though they could not prove by their ancestral houses or lineage that they belonged to Israel: the descendants of Delaiah son of Tobiah, and the descendants of Nekoda, six hundred fifty-two.

38 Of the priests the following had assumed the priesthood but were not found registered: the descendants of Habaiah, the descendants of Hakkoz, and the descendants of Jaddus who had married Agia, one of the daughters of Barzillai, and was called by his name. [39]When a search was made in the register and the genealogy of these men was not found, they were excluded from serving as priests. [40]And Nehemiah and Attharias[p] told them not to share in the holy things until a high priest should appear wearing Urim and Thummim.[q]

41 All those of Israel, twelve or more years of age, besides male and female servants, were forty-two thousand three hundred sixty; [42]their male and female servants were seven thousand three hundred thirty-seven; there were two hundred forty-five musicians and singers. [43]There were four hundred thirty-five camels, and seven thousand thirty-six horses, two hundred forty-five mules, and five thousand five hundred twenty-five donkeys.

44 Some of the heads of families, when

---

[o] Other ancient authorities read *Acub* or *Acum*   [p] Or *the governor*   [q] Gk *Manifestation and Truth*

they came to the temple of God that is in Jerusalem, vowed that, to the best of their ability, they would erect the house on its site, ⁴⁵and that they would give to the sacred treasury for the work a thousand minas of gold, five thousand minas of silver, and one hundred priests' vestments.

46 The priests, the Levites, and some of the people*ʳ* settled in Jerusalem and its vicinity; and the temple singers, the gate-keepers, and all Israel in their towns.

Worship Begins Again

47 When the seventh month came, and the Israelites were all in their own homes, they gathered with a single purpose in the square before the first gate toward the east. ⁴⁸Then Jeshua son of Jozadak, with his fellow priests, and Zerubbabel son of Shealtiel, with his kinsmen, took their places and prepared the altar of the God of Israel, ⁴⁹to offer burnt offerings upon it, in accordance with the directions in the book of Moses the man of God. ⁵⁰And some joined them from the other peoples of the land. And they erected the altar in its place, for all the peoples of the land were hostile to them and were stronger than they; and they offered sacrifices at the proper times and burnt offerings to the Lord morning and evening. ⁵¹They kept the festival of booths, as it is commanded in the law, and offered the proper sacrifices every day, ⁵²and thereafter the regular offerings and sacrifices on sabbaths and at new moons and at all the consecrated feasts. ⁵³And all who had made any vow to God began to offer sacrifices to God, from the new moon of the seventh month, though the temple of God was not yet built. ⁵⁴They gave money to the masons and the carpenters, and food and drink ⁵⁵and carts*ˢ* to the Sidonians and the Tyrians, to bring cedar logs from Lebanon and convey them in rafts to the harbor of Joppa, according to the decree that they had in writing from King Cyrus of the Persians.

The Foundations of the Temple Laid

56 In the second year after their coming to the temple of God in Jerusalem, in the second month, Zerubbabel son of Shealtiel and Jeshua son of Jozadak made a beginning, together with their kindred and the levitical priests and all who had come back to Jerusalem from exile; ⁵⁷and they laid the foundation of the temple of God on the new moon of the second month in the second year after they came to Judea and Jerusalem. ⁵⁸They appointed the Levites who were twenty or more years of age to have charge of the work of the Lord. And Jeshua arose, and his sons and kindred and his brother Kadmiel and the sons of Jeshua Emadabun and the sons of Joda son of Iliadun, with their sons and kindred, all the Levites, pressing forward the work on the house of God with a single purpose.

So the builders built the temple of the Lord. ⁵⁹And the priests stood arrayed in their vestments, with musical instruments and trumpets, and the Levites, the sons of Asaph, with cymbals, ⁶⁰praising the Lord and blessing him, according to the directions of King David of Israel; ⁶¹they sang hymns, giving thanks to the Lord, "For his goodness and his glory are forever upon all Israel." ⁶²And all the people sounded trumpets and shouted with a great shout, praising the Lord for the erection of the house of the Lord. ⁶³Some of the levitical priests and heads of ancestral houses, old men who had seen the former house, came to the building of this one with outcries and loud weeping, ⁶⁴while many came with trumpets and a joyful noise, ⁶⁵so that the people could not hear the trumpets because of the weeping of the people.

For the multitude sounded the trumpets loudly, so that the sound was heard far away; ⁶⁶and when the enemies of the tribe of Judah and Benjamin heard it, they came to find out what the sound of the trumpets meant. ⁶⁷They learned that those who had returned from exile were building the temple for the Lord God of Israel. ⁶⁸So they approached Zerubbabel and Jeshua and the heads of the ancestral houses and said to them, "We will build with you. ⁶⁹For we obey your Lord just as you do and we have been sacrificing to him ever since the days of King Esar-haddon*ᵗ* of the Assyrians, who brought us here." ⁷⁰But Zerubbabel and Jeshua and the heads of the ancestral houses in Israel said to them, "You have nothing to do with us in building the house for the Lord our God, ⁷¹for we alone will build it for the Lord of Israel, as Cyrus, the king of the Persians, has commanded us." ⁷²But the peoples of the land pressed hard*ˢ* upon those in Judea, cut off their supplies, and hindered

---

ʳ Or those who were of the people   *ˢ Meaning of Gk uncertain*   *ᵗ Gk Asbasareth*

their building; [73]and by plots and demagoguery and uprisings they prevented the completion of the building as long as King Cyrus lived. They were kept from building for two years, until the reign of Darius.

Work on the Temple Begins Again

6 Now in the second year of the reign of Darius, the prophets Haggai and Zechariah son of Iddo prophesied to the Jews who were in Judea and Jerusalem; they prophesied to them in the name of the Lord God of Israel. [2]Then Zerubbabel son of Shealtiel and Jeshua son of Jozadak began to build the house of the Lord that is in Jerusalem, with the help of the prophets of the Lord who were with them.

3 At the same time Sisinnes the governor of Syria and Phoenicia and Sathrabuzanes and their associates came to them and said, [4]"By whose order are you building this house and this roof and finishing all the other things? And who are the builders that are finishing these things?" [5]Yet the elders of the Jews were dealt with kindly, for the providence of the Lord was over the captives; [6]they were not prevented from building until word could be sent to Darius concerning them and a report made.

7 A copy of the letter that Sisinnes the governor of Syria and Phoenicia, and Sathrabuzanes, and their associates the local rulers in Syria and Phoenicia, wrote and sent to Darius:

8 "To King Darius, greetings. Let it be fully known to our lord the king that, when we went to the country of Judea and entered the city of Jerusalem, we found the elders of the Jews, who had been in exile, [9]building in the city of Jerusalem a great new house for the Lord, of hewn stone, with costly timber laid in the walls. [10]These operations are going on rapidly, and the work is prospering in their hands and being completed with all splendor and care. [11]Then we asked these elders, 'At whose command are you building this house and laying the foundations of this structure?' [12]In order that we might inform you in writing who the leaders are, we questioned them and asked them for a list of the names of those who are at their head. [13]They answered us, 'We are the servants of the Lord who created the heaven and the earth. [14]The house was built many years ago by a king of Israel who was great and strong, and it was finished. [15]But when our ancestors sinned against the Lord of Israel who is in heaven, and provoked him, he gave them over into the hands of King Nebuchadnezzar of Babylon, king of the Chaldeans; [16]and they pulled down the house, and burned it, and carried the people away captive to Babylon. [17]But in the first year that Cyrus reigned over the country of Babylonia, King Cyrus wrote that this house should be rebuilt. [18]And the holy vessels of gold and of silver, which Nebuchadnezzar had taken out of the house in Jerusalem and stored in his own temple, these King Cyrus took out again from the temple in Babylon, and they were delivered to Zerubbabel and Sheshbazzar[u] the governor [19]with the command that he should take all these vessels back and put them in the temple at Jerusalem, and that this temple of the Lord should be rebuilt on its site. [20]Then this Sheshbazzar, after coming here, laid the foundations of the house of the Lord that is in Jerusalem. Although it has been in process of construction from that time until now, it has not yet reached completion.' [21]Now therefore, O king, if it seems wise to do so, let search be made in the royal archives of our lord[v] the king that are in Babylon; [22]if it is found that the building of the house of the Lord in Jerusalem was done with the consent of King Cyrus, and if it is approved by our lord the king, let him send us directions concerning these things."

Official Permission Granted

23 Then Darius commanded that search be made in the royal archives that were deposited in Babylon. And in Ecbatana, the fortress that is in the country of Media, a scroll[w] was found in which this was recorded: [24]"In the first year of the reign of King Cyrus, he ordered the building of the house of the Lord in Jerusalem, where they sacrifice with perpetual fire; [25]its height to be sixty cubits and its width sixty cubits, with three courses of hewn stone and one course of new native timber; the cost to be paid from the treasury of King Cyrus; [26]and that the holy vessels of the house of the Lord, both of gold and of silver, which Nebuchadnezzar took out of the house in Jerusalem and carried away to Babylon, should be restored to the house in Jerusa-

---

[u] Gk *Sanabassarus*   [v] Other ancient authorities read *of Cyrus*   [w] Other authorities read *passage*

lem, to be placed where they had been."

27 So Darius[x] commanded Sisinnes the governor of Syria and Phoenicia, and Sathrabuzanes, and their associates, and those who were appointed as local rulers in Syria and Phoenicia, to keep away from the place, and to permit Zerubbabel, the servant of the Lord and governor of Judea, and the elders of the Jews to build this house of the Lord on its site. [28]"And I command that it be built completely, and that full effort be made to help those who have returned from the exile of Judea, until the house of the Lord is finished; [29]and that out of the tribute of Coelesyria and Phoenicia a portion be scrupulously given to these men, that is, to Zerubbabel the governor, for sacrifices to the Lord, for bulls and rams and lambs, [30]and likewise wheat and salt and wine and oil, regularly every year, without quibbling, for daily use as the priests in Jerusalem may indicate, [31]in order that libations may be made to the Most High God for the king and his children, and prayers be offered for their lives."

32 He commanded that if anyone should transgress or nullify any of the things herein written,[y] a beam should be taken out of the house of the perpetrator, who then should be impaled upon it, and all property forfeited to the king.

33 "Therefore may the Lord, whose name is there called upon, destroy every king and nation that shall stretch out their hands to hinder or damage that house of the Lord in Jerusalem.

34 "I, King Darius, have decreed that it be done with all diligence as here prescribed."

The Temple Is Dedicated

7 Then Sisinnes the governor of Coelesyria and Phoenicia, and Sathrabuzanes, and their associates, following the orders of King Darius, [2]supervised the holy work with very great care, assisting the elders of the Jews and the chief officers of the temple. [3]The holy work prospered, while the prophets Haggai and Zechariah prophesied; [4]and they completed it by the command of the Lord God of Israel. So with the consent of Cyrus and Darius and Artaxerxes, kings of the Persians, [5]the holy house was finished by the twenty-third day

of the month of Adar, in the sixth year of King Darius. [6]And the people of Israel, the priests, the Levites, and the rest of those who returned from exile who joined them, did according to what was written in the book of Moses. [7]They offered at the dedication of the temple of the Lord one hundred bulls, two hundred rams, four hundred lambs, [8]and twelve male goats for the sin of all Israel, according to the number of the twelve leaders of the tribes of Israel; [9]and the priests and the Levites stood arrayed in their vestments, according to kindred, for the services of the Lord God of Israel in accordance with the book of Moses; and the gatekeepers were at each gate.

The Passover

10 The people of Israel who came from exile kept the passover on the fourteenth day of the first month, after the priests and the Levites were purified together. [11]Not all of the returned captives were purified, but the Levites were all purified together,[z] [12]and they sacrificed the passover lamb for all the returned captives and for their kindred the priests and for themselves. [13]The people of Israel who had returned from exile ate it, all those who had separated themselves from the abominations of the peoples of the land and sought the Lord. [14]They also kept the festival of unleavened bread seven days, rejoicing before the Lord, [15]because he had changed the will of the king of the Assyrians concerning them, to strengthen their hands for the service of the Lord God of Israel.

Ezra Arrives in Jerusalem

8 After these things, when Artaxerxes, the king of the Persians, was reigning, Ezra came, the son of Seraiah, son of Azariah, son of Hilkiah, son of Shallum, [2]son of Zadok, son of Ahitub, son of Amariah, son of Uzzi, son of Bukki, son of Abishua, son of Phineas, son of Eleazar, son of Aaron the high[a] priest. [3]This Ezra came up from Babylon as a scribe skilled in the law of Moses, which was given by the God of Israel; [4]and the king showed him honor, for he found favor before the king[b] in all his requests. [5]There came up with him to Jerusalem some of the people of Israel and some of the priests and Levites and temple singers and gatekeepers and

---

[x] Gk *he* [y] Other authorities read *stated above* or *added in writing* [z] Meaning of Gk uncertain [a] Gk *the first*
[b] Gk *him*

temple servants, [6]in the seventh year of the reign of Artaxerxes, in the fifth month (this was the king's seventh year); for they left Babylon on the new moon of the first month and arrived in Jerusalem on the new moon of the fifth month, by the prosperous journey that the Lord gave them.[c] [7]For Ezra possessed great knowledge, so that he omitted nothing from the law of the Lord or the commandments, but taught all Israel all the ordinances and judgments.

The King's Mandate

8 The following is a copy of the written commission from King Artaxerxes that was delivered to Ezra the priest and reader of the law of the Lord: [9] "King Artaxerxes to Ezra the priest and reader of the law of the Lord, greeting. [10]In accordance with my gracious decision, I have given orders that those of the Jewish nation and of the priests and Levites and others in our realm, those who freely choose to do so, may go with you to Jerusalem. [11]Let as many as are so disposed, therefore, leave with you, just as I and the seven Friends who are my counselors have decided, [12]in order to look into matters in Judea and Jerusalem, in accordance with what is in the law of the Lord, [13]and to carry to Jerusalem the gifts for the Lord of Israel that I and my Friends have vowed, and to collect for the Lord in Jerusalem all the gold and silver that may be found in the country of Babylonia, [14]together with what is given by the nation for the temple of their Lord that is in Jerusalem, both gold and silver for bulls and rams and lambs and what goes with them, [15]so as to offer sacrifices on the altar of their Lord that is in Jerusalem. [16]Whatever you and your kindred are minded to do with the gold and silver, perform it in accordance with the will of your God; [17]deliver the holy vessels of the Lord that are given you for the use of the temple of your God that is in Jerusalem. [18]And whatever else occurs to you as necessary for the temple of your God, you may provide out of the royal treasury.

19 "I, King Artaxerxes, have commanded the treasurers of Syria and Phoenicia that whatever Ezra the priest and reader of the law of the Most High God sends for, they shall take care to give him, [20]up to a hundred talents of silver, and likewise up to a hundred cors of wheat, a hundred baths of wine, and salt in abundance. [21]Let all things prescribed in the law of God be scrupulously fulfilled for the Most High God, so that wrath may not come upon the kingdom of the king and his sons. [22]You are also informed that no tribute or any other tax is to be laid on any of the priests or Levites or temple singers or gatekeepers or temple servants or persons employed in this temple, and that no one has authority to impose any tax on them.

23 "And you, Ezra, according to the wisdom of God, appoint judges and justices to judge all those who know the law of your God, throughout all Syria and Phoenicia; and you shall teach it to those who do not know it. [24]All who transgress the law of your God or the law of the kingdom shall be strictly punished, whether by death or some other punishment, either fine or imprisonment."

Ezra Praises God

25 Then Ezra the scribe said,[d] "Blessed be the Lord alone, who put this into the heart of the king, to glorify his house that is in Jerusalem, [26]and who honored me in the sight of the king and his counselors and all his Friends and nobles. [27]I was encouraged by the help of the Lord my God, and I gathered men from Israel to go up with me."

The Leaders Who Returned

28 These are the leaders, according to their ancestral houses and their groups, who went up with me from Babylon, in the reign of King Artaxerxes: [29]Of the descendants of Phineas, Gershom. Of the descendants of Ithamar, Gamael. Of the descendants of David, Hattush son of Shecaniah. [30]Of the descendants of Parosh, Zechariah, and with him a hundred fifty men enrolled. [31]Of the descendants of Pahath-moab, Eliehoenai son of Zerahiah, and with him two hundred men. [32]Of the descendants of Zattu, Shecaniah son of Jahaziel, and with him three hundred men. Of the descendants of Adin, Obed son of Jonathan, and with him two hundred fifty men. [33]Of the descendants of Elam, Jeshaiah son of Gotholiah, and with him seventy men. [34]Of the descendants of Shephatiah, Zeraiah son of

---

[c] Other authorities add *for him* or *upon him*   [d] Other ancient authorities lack *Then Ezra the scribe said*

Michael, and with him seventy men. ³⁵Of the descendants of Joab, Obadiah son of Jehiel, and with him two hundred twelve men. ³⁶Of the descendants of Bani, Shelomith son of Josiphiah, and with him a hundred sixty men. ³⁷Of the descendants of Bebai, Zechariah son of Bebai, and with him twenty-eight men. ³⁸Of the descendants of Azgad, Johanan son of Hakkatan, and with him a hundred ten men. ³⁹Of the descendants of Adonikam, the last ones, their names being Eliphelet, Jeuel, and Shemaiah, and with them seventy men. ⁴⁰Of the descendants of Bigvai, Uthai son of Istalcurus, and with him seventy men.

41 I assembled them at the river called Theras, and we encamped there three days, and I inspected them. ⁴²When I found there none of the descendants of the priests or of the Levites, ⁴³I sent word to Eliezar, Iduel, Maasmas, ⁴⁴Elnathan, Shemaiah, Jarib, Nathan, Elnathan, Zechariah, and Meshullam, who were leaders and men of understanding; ⁴⁵I told them to go to Iddo, who was the leading man at the place of the treasury, ⁴⁶and ordered them to tell Iddo and his kindred and the treasurers at that place to send us men to serve as priests in the house of our Lord. ⁴⁷And by the mighty hand of our Lord they brought us competent men of the descendants of Mahli son of Levi, son of Israel, namely Sherebiah*ᵉ* with his descendants and kinsmen, eighteen; ⁴⁸also Hashabiah and Annunus and his brother Jeshaiah, of the descendants of Hananiah, and their descendants, twenty men; ⁴⁹and of the temple servants, whom David and the leaders had given for the service of the Levites, two hundred twenty temple servants; the list of all their names was reported.

Ezra Proclaims a Fast

50 There I proclaimed a fast for the young men before our Lord, to seek from him a prosperous journey for ourselves and for our children and the livestock that were with us. ⁵¹For I was ashamed to ask the king for foot soldiers and cavalry and an escort to keep us safe from our adversaries; ⁵²for we had said to the king, "The power of our Lord will be with those who seek him, and will support them in every way." ⁵³And again we prayed to our Lord about these things, and we found him very merciful.

The Gifts for the Temple

54 Then I set apart twelve of the leaders of the priests, Sherebiah and Hashabiah, and ten of their kinsmen with them; ⁵⁵and I weighed out to them the silver and the gold and the holy vessels of the house of our Lord, which the king himself and his counselors and the nobles and all Israel had given. ⁵⁶I weighed and gave to them six hundred fifty talents of silver, and silver vessels worth a hundred talents, and a hundred talents of gold, ⁵⁷and twenty golden bowls, and twelve bronze vessels of fine bronze that glittered like gold. ⁵⁸And I said to them, "You are holy to the Lord, and the vessels are holy, and the silver and the gold are vowed to the Lord, the Lord of our ancestors. ⁵⁹Be watchful and on guard until you deliver them to the leaders of the priests and the Levites, and to the heads of the ancestral houses of Israel, in Jerusalem, in the chambers of the house of our Lord." ⁶⁰So the priests and the Levites who took the silver and the gold and the vessels that had been in Jerusalem carried them to the temple of the Lord.

The Return to Jerusalem

61 We left the river Theras on the twelfth day of the first month; and we arrived in Jerusalem by the mighty hand of our Lord, which was upon us; he delivered us from every enemy on the way, and so we came to Jerusalem. ⁶²When we had been there three days, the silver and the gold were weighed and delivered in the house of our Lord to the priest Meremoth son of Uriah; ⁶³with him was Eleazar son of Phinehas, and with them were Jozabad son of Jeshua and Moeth son of Binnui,*ᶠ* the Levites. ⁶⁴The whole was counted and weighed, and the weight of everything was recorded at that very time. ⁶⁵And those who had returned from exile offered sacrifices to the Lord, the God of Israel, twelve bulls for all Israel, ⁶⁶seventy-two lambs, and as a thank offering twelve male goats—all as a sacrifice to the Lord. ⁶⁷They delivered the king's orders to the royal stewards and to the governors of Coelesyria and Phoenicia; and these officials*ᵍ* honored the people and the temple of the Lord.

ᵉ Gk *Asbebias*   *ᶠ* Gk *Sabannus*   *ᵍ* Gk *they*

Ezra's Prayer

68 After these things had been done, the leaders came to me and said, ⁶⁹"The people of Israel and the rulers and the priests and the Levites have not put away from themselves the alien peoples of the land and their pollutions, the Canaanites, the Hittites, the Perizzites, the Jebusites, the Moabites, the Egyptians, and the Edomites. ⁷⁰For they and their descendants have married the daughters of these people,ʰ and the holy race has been mixed with the alien peoples of the land; and from the beginning of this matter the leaders and the nobles have been sharing in this iniquity."

71 As soon as I heard these things I tore my garments and my holy mantle, and pulled out hair from my head and beard, and sat down in anxiety and grief. ⁷²And all who were ever moved atⁱ the word of the Lord of Israel gathered around me, as I mourned over this iniquity, and I sat grief-stricken until the evening sacrifice. ⁷³Then I rose from my fast, with my garments and my holy mantle torn, and kneeling down and stretching out my hands to the Lord ⁷⁴I said,

"O Lord, I am ashamed and confused before your face. ⁷⁵For our sins have risen higher than our heads, and our mistakes have mounted up to heaven ⁷⁶from the times of our ancestors, and we are in great sin to this day. ⁷⁷Because of our sins and the sins of our ancestors, we with our kindred and our kings and our priests were given over to the kings of the earth, to the sword and exile and plundering, in shame until this day. ⁷⁸And now in some measure mercy has come to us from you, O Lord, to leave to us a root and a name in your holy place, ⁷⁹and to uncover a light for us in the house of the Lord our God, and to give us food in the time of our servitude. ⁸⁰Even in our bondage we were not forsaken by our Lord, but he brought us into favor with the kings of the Persians, so that they have given us food ⁸¹and glorified the temple of our Lord, and raised Zion from desolation, to give us a stronghold in Judea and Jerusalem.

82 "And now, O Lord, what shall we say, when we have these things? For we have transgressed your commandments, which you gave by your servants the prophets, saying, ⁸³"The land that you are entering to take possession of is a land polluted with the pollution of the aliens of the land, and they have filled it with their uncleanness. ⁸⁴Therefore do not give your daughters in marriage to their descendants, and do not take their daughters for your descendants; ⁸⁵do not seek ever to have peace with them, so that you may be strong and eat the good things of the land and leave it for an inheritance to your children forever.' ⁸⁶And all that has happened to us has come about because of our evil deeds and our great sins. For you, O Lord, lifted the burden of our sins ⁸⁷and gave us such a root as this; but we turned back again to transgress your law by mixing with the uncleanness of the peoples of the land. ⁸⁸Were you not angry enough with us to destroy us without leaving a root or seed or name? ⁸⁹O Lord of Israel, you are faithful; for we are left as a root to this day. ⁹⁰See, we are now before you in our iniquities; for we can no longer stand in your presence because of these things."

The Plan for Ending Mixed Marriages

91 While Ezra was praying and making his confession, weeping and lying on the ground before the temple, there gathered around him a very great crowd of men and women and youths from Jerusalem; for there was great weeping among the multitude. ⁹²Then Shecaniah son of Jehiel, one of the men of Israel, called out, and said to Ezra, "We have sinned against the Lord, and have married foreign women from the peoples of the land; but even now there is hope for Israel. ⁹³Let us take an oath to the Lord about this, that we will put away all our foreign wives, with their children, ⁹⁴as seems good to you and to all who obey the law of the Lord. ⁹⁵Rise upʲ and take action, for it is your task, and we are with you to take strong measures." ⁹⁶Then Ezra rose up and made the leaders of the priests and Levites of all Israel swear that they would do this. And they swore to it.

The Expulsion of Foreign Wives

9 Then Ezra set out and went from the court of the temple to the chamber of Jehohanan son of Eliashib, ²and spent the night there; and he did not eat bread or drink water, for he was mourning over the

---

ʰ Gk *their daughters*   ⁱ Or *zealous for*   ʲ Other ancient authorities read *as seems good to you." And all who obeyed the law of the Lord rose and said to Ezra,* ⁹⁵*"Rise up*

great iniquities of the multitude. ³And a proclamation was made throughout Judea and Jerusalem to all who had returned from exile that they should assemble at Jerusalem, ⁴and that if any did not meet there within two or three days, in accordance with the decision of the ruling elders, their livestock would be seized for sacrifice and the men themselves*ᵏ* expelled from the multitude of those who had returned from the captivity.

5 Then the men of the tribe of Judah and Benjamin assembled at Jerusalem within three days; this was the ninth month, on the twentieth day of the month. ⁶All the multitude sat in the open square before the temple, shivering because of the bad weather that prevailed. ⁷Then Ezra stood up and said to them, "You have broken the law and married foreign women, and so have increased the sin of Israel. ⁸Now make confession and give glory to the Lord the God of our ancestors, ⁹and do his will; separate yourselves from the peoples of the land and from your foreign wives."

10 Then all the multitude shouted and said with a loud voice, "We will do as you have said. ¹¹But the multitude is great and it is winter, and we are not able to stand in the open air. This is not a work we can do in one day or two, for we have sinned too much in these things. ¹²So let the leaders of the multitude stay, and let all those in our settlements who have foreign wives come at the time appointed, ¹³with the elders and judges of each place, until we are freed from the wrath of the Lord over this matter."

14 Jonathan son of Asahel and Jahzeiah son of Tikvah*ˡ* undertook the matter on these terms, and Meshullam and Levi and Shabbethai served with them as judges. ¹⁵And those who had returned from exile acted in accordance with all this.

16 Ezra the priest chose for himself the leading men of their ancestral houses, all of them by name; and on the new moon of the tenth month they began their sessions to investigate the matter. ¹⁷And the cases of the men who had foreign wives were brought to an end by the new moon of the first month.

18 Of the priests, those who were brought in and found to have foreign wives were: ¹⁹of the descendants of Jeshua son of Jozadak and his kindred, Maaseiah, Eliezar,

Jarib, and Jodan. ²⁰They pledged themselves to put away their wives, and to offer rams in expiation of their error. ²¹Of the descendants of Immer: Hanani and Zebadiah and Maaseiah and Shemaiah and Jehiel and Azariah. ²²Of the descendants of Pashhur: Elioenai, Maaseiah, Ishmael, and Nathanael, and Gedaliah, and Salthas.

23 And of the Levites: Jozabad and Shimei and Kelaiah, who was Kelita, and Pethahiah and Judah and Jonah. ²⁴Of the temple singers: Eliashib and Zaccur.*ᵐ* ²⁵Of the gatekeepers: Shallum and Telem.*ⁿ*

26 Of Israel: of the descendants of Parosh: Ramiah, Izziah, Malchijah, Mijamin, and Eleazar, and Asibias, and Benaiah. ²⁷Of the descendants of Elam: Mattaniah and Zechariah, Jezrielus and Abdi, and Jeremoth and Elijah. ²⁸Of the descendants of Zamoth: Eliadas, Eliashib, Othoniah, Jeremoth, and Zabad and Zerdaiah. ²⁹Of the descendants of Bebai: Jehohanan and Hananiah and Zabbai and Emathis. ³⁰Of the descendants of Mani: Olamus, Mamuchus, Adaiah, Jashub, and Sheal and Jeremoth. ³¹Of the descendants of Addi: Naathus and Moossias, Laccunus and Naidus, and Bescaspasmys and Sesthel, and Belnuus and Manasseas. ³²Of the descendants of Annan, Elionas and Asaias and Melchias and Sabbaias and Simon Chosamaeus. ³³Of the descendants of Hashum: Mattenai and Mattattah and Zabad and Eliphelet and Manasseh and Shimei. ³⁴Of the descendants of Bani: Jeremai, Momdius, Maerus, Joel, Mamdai and Bedeiah and Vaniah, Carabasion and Eliashib and Mamitanemus, Eliasis, Binnui, Elialis, Shimei, Shelemiah, Nethaniah. Of the descendants of Ezora: Shashai, Azarel, Azael, Samatus, Zambris, Joseph. ³⁵Of the descendants of Nooma: Mazitias, Zabad, Iddo, Joel, Benaiah. ³⁶All these had married foreign women, and they put them away together with their children.

Ezra Reads the Law to the People

37 The priests and the Levites and the Israelites settled in Jerusalem and in the country. On the new moon of the seventh month, when the people of Israel were in their settlements, ³⁸the whole multitude gathered with one accord in the open square before the east gate of the temple; ³⁹they told Ezra the chief priest and reader to bring the law of Moses that had been given by the

ᵏ Gk he himself   ˡ Gk Thocanos   ᵐ Gk Bacchurus   ⁿ Gk Tolbanes

Lord God of Israel. ⁴⁰So Ezra the chief priest brought the law, for all the multitude, men and women, and all the priests to hear the law, on the new moon of the seventh month. ⁴¹He read aloud in the open square before the gate of the temple from early morning until midday, in the presence of both men and women; and all the multitude gave attention to the law. ⁴²Ezra the priest and reader of the law stood on the wooden platform that had been prepared; ⁴³and beside him stood Mattathiah, Shema, Ananias, Azariah, Uriah, Hezekiah, and Baalsamus on his right, ⁴⁴and on his left Pedaiah, Mishael, Malchijah, Lothasubus, Nabariah, and Zechariah. ⁴⁵Then Ezra took up the book of the law in the sight of the multitude, for he had the place of honor in the presence of all. ⁴⁶When he opened the law, they all stood erect. And Ezra blessed the Lord God Most High, the God of hosts, the Almighty, ⁴⁷and the multitude answered, "Amen." They lifted up their hands, and fell to the ground and worshiped the Lord.

⁴⁸Jeshua and Anniuth and Sherebiah, Jadinus, Akkub, Shabbethai, Hodiah, Maiannas and Kelita, Azariah and Jozabad, Hanan, Pelaiah, the Levites, taught the law of the Lord,° at the same time explaining what was read.

49 Then Attharates^p said to Ezra the chief priest and reader, and to the Levites who were teaching the multitude, and to all, ⁵⁰"This day is holy to the Lord"—now they were all weeping as they heard the law— ⁵¹"so go your way, eat the fat and drink the sweet, and send portions to those who have none; ⁵²for the day is holy to the Lord; and do not be sorrowful, for the Lord will exalt you." ⁵³The Levites commanded all the people, saying, "This day is holy; do not be sorrowful." ⁵⁴Then they all went their way, to eat and drink and enjoy themselves, and to give portions to those who had none, and to make great rejoicing; ⁵⁵because they were inspired by the words which they had been taught. And they came together.^q

° Other ancient authorities add *and read the law of the Lord to the multitude*   ^p Or *the governor*   ^q The Greek text ends abruptly: compare Neh 8.13

THE PRAYER OF MANASSEH

Ascription of Praise
1   O Lord Almighty,
     God of our ancestors,
     of Abraham and Isaac and Jacob
     and of their righteous offspring;
2   you who made heaven and earth
     with all their order;
3   who shackled the sea by your word of
          command,
     who confined the deep
     and sealed it with your terrible and
          glorious name;
4   at whom all things shudder,
     and tremble before your power,
5   for your glorious splendor cannot be borne,
     and the wrath of your threat to
          sinners is unendurable;
6   yet immeasurable and unsearchable
     is your promised mercy,
7   for you are the Lord Most High,

of great compassion, long-suffering,
     and very merciful,
     and you relent at human suffering.
     O Lord, according to your great
          goodness
     you have promised repentance and
          forgiveness
     to those who have sinned against you,
     and in the multitude of your mercies
     you have appointed repentance for
          sinners,
     so that they may be saved.^a
8   Therefore you, O Lord, God of the
          righteous,
     have not appointed repentance for the
          righteous,
     for Abraham and Isaac and Jacob,
          who did not sin against you,
     but you have appointed repentance for
          me, who am a sinner.

^a Other ancient authorities lack *O Lord, according . . . be saved*

Confession of Sins

9 For the sins I have committed are
   more in number than the sand
   of the sea;
   my transgressions are multiplied,
       O Lord, they are multiplied!
   I am not worthy to look up and see
       the height of heaven
   because of the multitude of my
       iniquities.
10 I am weighted down with many an
       iron fetter,
   so that I am rejected[b] because of my
           sins,
   and I have no relief;
   for I have provoked your wrath
   and have done what is evil in your
       sight,
   setting up abominations and
       multiplying offenses.

Supplication for Pardon

11 And now I bend the knee of my heart,

imploring you for your kindness.
12 I have sinned, O Lord, I have sinned,
    and I acknowledge my transgressions.
13 I earnestly implore you,
    forgive me, O Lord, forgive me!
    Do not destroy me with my
        transgressions!
    Do not be angry with me forever or
        store up evil for me;
    do not condemn me to the depths of
        the earth.
    For you, O Lord, are the God of those
        who repent,
14 and in me you will manifest your
        goodness;
    for, unworthy as I am, you will save
        me according to your great
        mercy,
15 and I will praise you continually all
        the days of my life.
    For all the host of heaven sings your
        praise,
    and yours is the glory forever. Amen.

---

[b] Other ancient authorities read *so that I cannot lift up my head*

PSALM 151

This psalm is ascribed to David as his own composition (though it is outside the number[a]), after he had fought in single combat with Goliath.

1 I was small among my brothers,
    and the youngest in my father's house;
  I tended my father's sheep.

2 My hands made a harp;
    my fingers fashioned a lyre.

3 And who will tell my Lord?
    The Lord himself; it is he who hears.[b]

4 It was he who sent his messenger[c]
    and took me from my father's sheep,
    and anointed me with his anointing
        oil.

5 My brothers were handsome and tall,
    but the Lord was not pleased with
        them.

6 I went out to meet the Philistine,[d]
    and he cursed me by his idols.

7 But I drew his own sword;
    I beheaded him, and took away disgrace
        from the people of Israel.

---

[a] Other ancient authorities add *of the one hundred fifty* (psalms)   [b] Other ancient authorities add *everything*; others add *me*; others read *who will hear me*   [c] Or *angel*   [d] Or *foreigner*

3 MACCABEES

The Battle of Raphia

1 When Philopator learned from those who returned that the regions that he had controlled had been seized by Antiochus, he gave orders to all his forces, both infantry and cavalry, took with him his sister Arsinoë, and marched out to the region near Raphia, where the army of Antiochus was encamped. [2]But a certain Theodotus, determined to carry out the plot he had devised, took with him the best of the Ptolemaic arms that had been previously issued to him,[a] and crossed over by night to the tent of Ptolemy, intending single-handed to kill him and thereby end the war. [3]But Dositheus, known as the son of Drimylus, a Jew by birth who later changed his religion and apostatized from the ancestral traditions, had led the king away and arranged that a certain insignificant man should sleep in the tent; and so it turned out that this man incurred the vengeance meant for the king.[b] [4]When a bitter fight resulted, and matters were turning out rather in favor of Antiochus, Arsinoë went to the troops with wailing and tears, her locks all disheveled, and exhorted them to defend themselves and their children and wives bravely, promising to give them each two minas of gold if they won the battle. [5]And so it came about that the enemy was routed in the action, and many captives also were taken. [6]Now that he had foiled the plot, Ptolemy[c] decided to visit the neighboring cities and encourage them. [7]By doing this, and by endowing their sacred enclosures with gifts, he strengthened the morale of his subjects.

Philopator Attempts to Enter the Temple

8 Since the Jews had sent some of their council and elders to greet him, to bring him gifts of welcome, and to congratulate him on what had happened, he was all the more eager to visit them as soon as possible. [9]After he had arrived in Jerusalem, he offered sacrifice to the supreme God[d] and made thank offerings and did what was fitting for the holy place.[e] Then, upon entering the place and being impressed by its excellence and its beauty, [10]he marveled at the good order of the temple, and conceived a desire to enter the sanctuary. [11]When they said that this was not permitted, because not even members of their own nation were allowed to enter, not even all of the priests, but only the high priest who was pre-eminent over all—and he only once a year—the king was by no means persuaded. [12]Even after the law had been read to him, he did not cease to maintain that he ought to enter, saying, "Even if those men are deprived of this honor, I ought not to be." [13]And he inquired why, when he entered every other temple,[f] no one there had stopped him. [14]And someone answered thoughtlessly that it was wrong to take that as a portent.[g] [15]"But since this has happened," the king[c] said, "why should not I at least enter, whether they wish it or not?"

Jewish Resistance to Ptolemy

16 Then the priests in all their vestments prostrated themselves and entreated the supreme God[d] to aid in the present situation and to avert the violence of this evil design, and they filled the temple with cries and tears; [17]those who remained behind in the city were agitated and hurried out, supposing that something mysterious was occurring. [18]Young women who had been secluded in their chambers rushed out with their mothers, sprinkled their hair with dust,[h] and filled the streets with groans and lamentations. [19]Those women who had recently been arrayed for marriage abandoned the bridal chambers[i] prepared for wedded union, and, neglecting proper modesty, in a disorderly rush flocked together in the city. [20]Mothers and nurses abandoned even newborn children here and there, some in houses and some in the streets, and without a backward look they crowded together at the most high temple. [21]Various were the supplications of those gathered there because of what the king was profanely plotting. [22]In addition, the bolder of the citizens would not tolerate the completion of his plans or

---

[a] Or the best of the Ptolemaic soldiers previously put under his command   [b] Gk that one   [c] Gk he   [d] Gk the greatest God   [e] Gk the place   [f] Or entered the temple precincts   [g] Or to boast of this   [h] Other ancient authorities add and ashes   [i] Or the canopies

the fulfillment of his intended purpose. [23]They shouted to their compatriots to take arms and die courageously for the ancestral law, and created a considerable disturbance in the holy place;[j] and being barely restrained by the old men and the elders,[k] they resorted to the same posture of supplication as the others. [24]Meanwhile the crowd, as before, was engaged in prayer, [25]while the elders near the king tried in various ways to change his arrogant mind from the plan that he had conceived. [26]But he, in his arrogance, took heed of nothing, and began now to approach, determined to bring the aforesaid plan to a conclusion. [27]When those who were around him observed this, they turned, together with our people, to call upon him who has all power to defend them in the present trouble and not to overlook this unlawful and haughty deed. [28]The continuous, vehement, and concerted cry of the crowds[l] resulted in an immense uproar; [29]for it seemed that not only the people but also the walls and the whole earth around echoed, because indeed all at that time[m] preferred death to the profanation of the place.

The Prayer of the High Priest Simon

2 Then the high priest Simon, facing the sanctuary, bending his knees and extending his hands with calm dignity, prayed as follows:[n] [2]"Lord, Lord, king of the heavens, and sovereign of all creation, holy among the holy ones, the only ruler, almighty, give attention to us who are suffering grievously from an impious and profane man, puffed up in his audacity and power. [3]For you, the creator of all things and the governor of all, are a just Ruler, and you judge those who have done anything in insolence and arrogance. [4]You destroyed those who in the past committed injustice, among whom were even giants who trusted in their strength and boldness, whom you destroyed by bringing on them a boundless flood. [5]You consumed with fire and sulfur the people of Sodom who acted arrogantly, who were notorious for their vices;[o] and you made them an example to those who should come afterward. [6]You made known your mighty power by inflicting many and varied punishments on the

audacious Pharaoh who had enslaved your holy people Israel. [7]And when he pursued them with chariots and a mass of troops, you overwhelmed him in the depths of the sea, but carried through safely those who had put their confidence in you, the Ruler over the whole creation. [8]And when they had seen works of your hands, they praised you, the Almighty. [9]You, O King, when you had created the boundless and immeasurable earth, chose this city and sanctified this place for your name, though you have no need of anything; and when you had glorified it by your magnificent manifestation,[p] you made it a firm foundation for the glory of your great and honored name. [10]And because you love the house of Israel, you promised that if we should have reverses and tribulation should overtake us, you would listen to our petition when we come to this place and pray. [11]And indeed you are faithful and true. [12]And because oftentimes when our fathers were oppressed you helped them in their humiliation, and rescued them from great evils, [13]see now, O holy King, that because of our many and great sins we are crushed with suffering, subjected to our enemies, and overtaken by helplessness. [14]In our downfall this audacious and profane man undertakes to violate the holy place on earth dedicated to your glorious name. [15]For your dwelling is the heaven of heavens, unapproachable by human beings. [16]But because you graciously bestowed your glory on your people Israel, you sanctified this place. [17]Do not punish us for the defilement committed by these men, or call us to account for this profanation, otherwise the transgressors will boast in their wrath and exult in the arrogance of their tongue, saying, [18]'We have trampled down the house of the sanctuary as the houses of the abominations are trampled down.' [19]Wipe away our sins and disperse our errors, and reveal your mercy at this hour. [20]Speedily let your mercies overtake us, and put praises in the mouth of those who are downcast and broken in spirit, and give us peace."

God's Punishment of Ptolemy

21 Thereupon God, who oversees all things, the first Father of all, holy among

---

[j] Gk *the place* [k] Other ancient authorities read *priests* [l] Other ancient authorities read *vehement cry of the assembled crowds* [m] Other ancient authorities lack *at that time* [n] Other ancient authorities lack verse 1 [o] Other ancient authorities read *secret in their vices* [p] Or *epiphany*

the holy ones, having heard the lawful supplication, scourged him who had exalted himself in insolence and audacity. [22]He shook him on this side and that as a reed is shaken by the wind, so that he lay helpless on the ground and, besides being paralyzed in his limbs, was unable even to speak, since he was smitten[q] by a righteous judgment. [23]Then both friends and bodyguards, seeing the severe punishment that had overtaken him, and fearing that he would lose his life, quickly dragged him out, panic-stricken in their exceedingly great fear. [24]After a while he recovered, and though he had been punished, he by no means repented, but went away uttering bitter threats.

Hostile Measures against the Jews

25 When he arrived in Egypt, he increased in his deeds of malice, abetted by the previously mentioned drinking companions and comrades, who were strangers to everything just. [26]He was not content with his uncounted licentious deeds, but even continued with such audacity that he framed evil reports in the various localities; and many of his friends, intently observing the king's purpose, themselves also followed his will. [27]He proposed to inflict public disgrace on the Jewish community,[r] and he set up a stone[s] on the tower in the courtyard with this inscription: [28]"None of those who do not sacrifice shall enter their sanctuaries, and all Jews shall be subjected to a registration involving poll tax and to the status of slaves. Those who object to this are to be taken by force and put to death; [29]those who are registered are also to be branded on their bodies by fire with the ivy-leaf symbol of Dionysus, and they shall also be reduced to their former limited status." [30]In order that he might not appear to be an enemy of all, he inscribed below: "But if any of them prefer to join those who have been initiated into the mysteries, they shall have equal citizenship with the Alexandrians."

31 Now some, however, with an obvious abhorrence of the price to be exacted for maintaining the religion of their city,[t] readily gave themselves up, since they expected to enhance their reputation by their future association with the king. [32]But the majority acted firmly with a courageous spirit and did not abandon their religion; and by paying money in exchange for life they

confidently attempted to save themselves from the registration. [33]They remained resolutely hopeful of obtaining help, and they abhorred those who separated themselves from them, considering them to be enemies of the Jewish nation,[r] and depriving them of companionship and mutual help.

The Jews and Their Neighbors

3 When the impious king comprehended this situation, he became so infuriated that not only was he enraged against those Jews who lived in Alexandria, but was still more bitterly hostile toward those in the countryside; and he ordered that all should promptly be gathered into one place, and put to death by the most cruel means. [2]While these matters were being arranged, a hostile rumor was circulated against the Jewish nation by some who conspired to do them ill, a pretext being given by a report that they hindered others[u] from the observance of their customs. [3]The Jews, however, continued to maintain goodwill and unswerving loyalty toward the dynasty; [4]but because they worshiped God and conducted themselves by his law, they kept their separateness with respect to foods. For this reason they appeared hateful to some; [5]but since they adorned their style of life with the good deeds of upright people, they were established in good repute with everyone. [6]Nevertheless those of other races paid no heed to their good service to their nation, which was common talk among all; [7]instead they gossiped about the differences in worship and foods, alleging that these people were loyal neither to the king nor to his authorities, but were hostile and greatly opposed to his government. So they attached no ordinary reproach to them.

8 The Greeks in the city, though wronged in no way, when they saw an unexpected tumult around these people and the crowds that suddenly were forming, were not strong enough to help them, for they lived under tyranny. They did try to console them, being grieved at the situation, and expected that matters would change; [9]for such a great community ought not be left to its fate when it had committed no offense. [10]And already some of their neighbors and friends and business associates had taken some of them aside privately and were pledging to protect them and to exert more earnest efforts for their assistance.

---

[q] Other ancient authorities read *pierced*   [r] Gk *the nation*   [s] Gk *stele*   [t] Meaning of Gk uncertain   [u] Gk *them*

Ptolemy's Decree That All Jews Be Arrested
11 Then the king, boastful of his present good fortune, and not considering the might of the supreme God,ᵛ but assuming that he would persevere constantly in his same purpose, wrote this letter against them:
12 "King Ptolemy Philopator to his generals and soldiers in Egypt and all its districts, greetings and good health:
13 "I myself and our government are faring well. ¹⁴When our expedition took place in Asia, as you yourselves know, it was brought to conclusion, according to plan, by the gods' deliberate alliance with us in battle, ¹⁵and we considered that we should not rule the nations inhabiting Coelesyria and Phoenicia by the power of the spear, but should cherish them with clemency and great benevolence, gladly treating them well. ¹⁶And when we had granted very great revenues to the temples in the cities, we came on to Jerusalem also, and went up to honor the temple of those wicked people, who never cease from their folly. ¹⁷They accepted our presence by word, but insincerely by deed, because when we proposed to enter their inner temple and honor it with magnificent and most beautiful offerings, ¹⁸they were carried away by their traditional arrogance, and excluded us from entering; but they were spared the exercise of our power because of the benevolence that we have toward all. ¹⁹By maintaining their manifest ill-will toward us, they become the only people among all nations who hold their heads high in defiance of kings and their own benefactors, and are unwilling to regard any action as sincere.
20 "But we, when we arrived in Egypt victorious, accommodated ourselves to their folly and did as was proper, since we treat all nations with benevolence. ²¹Among other things, we made known to all our amnesty toward their compatriots here, both because of their alliance with us and the myriad affairs liberally entrusted to them from the beginning; and we ventured to make a change, by deciding both to deem them worthy of Alexandrian citizenship and to make them participants in our regular religious rites.ʷ ²²But in their innate malice they took this in a contrary spirit, and disdained what is good. Since they incline constantly to evil, ²³they not only spurn the

priceless citizenship, but also both by speech and by silence they abominate those few among them who are sincerely disposed toward us; in every situation, in accordance with their infamous way of life, they secretly suspect that we may soon alter our policy. ²⁴Therefore, fully convinced by these indications that they are ill-disposed toward us in every way, we have taken precautions so that, if a sudden disorder later arises against us, we shall not have these impious people behind our backs as traitors and barbarous enemies. ²⁵Therefore we have given orders that, as soon as this letter arrives, you are to send to us those who live among you, together with their wives and children, with insulting and harsh treatment, and bound securely with iron fetters, to suffer the sure and shameful death that befits enemies. ²⁶For when all of these have been punished, we are sure that for the remaining time the government will be established for ourselves in good order and in the best state. ²⁷But those who shelter any of the Jews, whether old people or children or even infants, will be tortured to death with the most hateful torments, together with their families. ²⁸Any who are willing to give information will receive the property of those who incur the punishment, and also two thousand drachmas from the royal treasury, and will be awarded their freedom.ˣ ²⁹Every place detected sheltering a Jew is to be made unapproachable and burned with fire, and shall become useless for all time to any mortal creature." ³⁰The letter was written in the above form.

The Jews Deported to Alexandria
4 In every place, then, where this decree arrived, a feast at public expense was arranged for the Gentiles with shouts and gladness, for the inveterate enmity that had long ago been in their minds was now made evident and outspoken. ²But among the Jews there was incessant mourning, lamentation, and tearful cries; everywhere their hearts were burning, and they groaned because of the unexpected destruction that had suddenly been decreed for them. ³What district or city, or what habitable place at all, or what streets were not filled with mourning and wailing for them? ⁴For with such a harsh and ruthless spirit were they

ᵛ Gk *the greatest God*   ʷ Other ancient authorities read *partners of our regular priests*   ˣ Gk *crowned with freedom*

197

being sent off, all together, by the generals in the several cities, that at the sight of their unusual punishments, even some of their enemies, perceiving the common object of pity before their eyes, reflected on the uncertainty of life and shed tears at the most miserable expulsion of these people. [5]For a multitude of gray-headed old men, sluggish and bent with age, was being led away, forced to march at a swift pace by the violence with which they were driven in such a shameful manner. [6]And young women who had just entered the bridal chamber[u] to share married life exchanged joy for wailing, their myrrh-perfumed hair sprinkled with ashes, and were carried away unveiled, all together raising a lament instead of a wedding song, as they were torn by the harsh treatment of the heathen.[z] [7]In bonds and in public view they were violently dragged along as far as the place of embarkation. [8]Their husbands, in the prime of youth, their necks encircled with ropes instead of garlands, spent the remaining days of their marriage festival in lamentations instead of good cheer and youthful revelry, seeing death immediately before them.[a] [9]They were brought on board like wild animals, driven under the constraint of iron bonds; some were fastened by the neck to the benches of the boats, others had their feet secured by unbreakable fetters, [10]and in addition they were confined under a solid deck, so that, with their eyes in total darkness, they would undergo treatment befitting traitors during the whole voyage.

The Jews Imprisoned at Schedia

11 When these people had been brought to the place called Schedia, and the voyage was concluded as the king had decreed, he commanded that they should be enclosed in the hippodrome that had been built with a monstrous perimeter wall in front of the city, and that was well suited to make them an obvious spectacle to all coming back into the city and to those from the city[b] going out into the country, so that they could neither communicate with the king's forces nor in any way claim to be inside the circuit of the city.[c] [12]And when this had happened, the king, hearing that the Jews' compatriots from the city frequently went out in secret

to lament bitterly the ignoble misfortune of their kindred, [13]ordered in his rage that these people be dealt with in precisely the same fashion as the others, not omitting any detail of their punishment. [14]The entire race was to be registered individually, not for the hard labor that has been briefly mentioned before, but to be tortured with the outrages that he had ordered, and at the end to be destroyed in the space of a single day. [15]The registration of these people was therefore conducted with bitter haste and zealous intensity from the rising of the sun until its setting, coming to an end after forty days but still uncompleted.

16 The king was greatly and continually filled with joy, organizing feasts in honor of all his idols, with a mind alienated from truth and with a profane mouth, praising speechless things that are not able even to communicate or to come to one's help, and uttering improper words against the supreme God.[d] [17]But after the previously mentioned interval of time the scribes declared to the king that they were no longer able to take the census of the Jews because of their immense number, [18]though most of them were still in the country, some still residing in their homes, and some at the place;[e] the task was impossible for all the generals in Egypt. [19]After he had threatened them severely, charging that they had been bribed to contrive a means of escape, he was clearly convinced about the matter [20]when they said and proved that both the paper[f] and the pens they used for writing had already given out. [21]But this was an act of the invincible providence of him who was aiding the Jews from heaven.

Execution of the Jews Is Twice Thwarted

5 Then the king, completely inflexible, was filled with overpowering anger and wrath; so he summoned Hermon, keeper of the elephants, [2]and ordered him on the following day to drug all the elephants—five hundred in number—with large handfuls of frankincense and plenty of unmixed wine, and to drive them in, maddened by the lavish abundance of drink, so that the Jews might meet their doom. [3]When he had given these orders he returned to his feasting, together with those of his Friends and

---

[u] Or *the canopy*   [z] Other ancient authorities read *as though torn by heathen whelps*   [a] Gk *seeing Hades already lying at their feet*   [b] Gk *those of them*   [c] Or *claim protection of the walls*; meaning of Gk uncertain   [d] Gk *the greatest God*   [e] Other ancient authorities read *on the way*   [f] Or *paper factory*

of the army who were especially hostile toward the Jews. [4]And Hermon, keeper of the elephants, proceeded faithfully to carry out the orders. [5]The servants in charge of the Jews[g] went out in the evening and bound the hands of the wretched people and arranged for their continued custody through the night, convinced that the whole nation would experience its final destruction. [6]For to the Gentiles it appeared that the Jews were left without any aid, [7]because in their bonds they were forcibly confined on every side. But with tears and a voice hard to silence they all called upon the Almighty Lord and Ruler of all power, their merciful God and Father, praying [8]that he avert with vengeance the evil plot against them and in a glorious manifestation rescue them from the fate now prepared for them. [9]So their entreaty ascended fervently to heaven.

10 Hermon, however, when he had drugged the pitiless elephants until they had been filled with a great abundance of wine and satiated with frankincense, presented himself at the courtyard early in the morning to report to the king about these preparations. [11]But the Lord[h] sent upon the king a portion of sleep, that beneficence that from the beginning, night and day, is bestowed by him who grants it to whomever he wishes. [12]And by the action of the Lord he was overcome by so pleasant and deep a sleep[i] that he quite failed in his lawless purpose and was completely frustrated in his inflexible plan. [13]Then the Jews, since they had escaped the appointed hour, praised their holy God and again implored him who is easily reconciled to show the might of his all-powerful hand to the arrogant Gentiles.

14 But now, since it was nearly the middle of the tenth hour, the person who was in charge of the invitations, seeing that the guests were assembled, approached the king and nudged him. [15]And when he had with difficulty roused him, he pointed out that the hour of the banquet was already slipping by, and he gave him an account of the situation. [16]The king, after considering this, returned to his drinking, and ordered those present for the banquet to recline opposite him. [17]When this was done he urged them to give themselves over to revelry and to

make the present[j] portion of the banquet joyful by celebrating all the more. [18]After the party had been going on for some time, the king summoned Hermon and with sharp threats demanded to know why the Jews had been allowed to remain alive through the present day. [19]But when he, with the corroboration of the king's[k] Friends, pointed out that while it was still night he had carried out completely the order given him, [20]the king,[h] possessed by a savagery worse than that of Phalaris, said that the Jews[l] were benefited by today's sleep, "but," he added, "tomorrow without delay prepare the elephants in the same way for the destruction of the lawless Jews!" [21]When the king had spoken, all those present readily and joyfully with one accord gave their approval, and all went to their own homes. [22]But they did not so much employ the duration of the night in sleep as in devising all sorts of insults for those they thought to be doomed.

23 Then, as soon as the cock had crowed in the early morning, Hermon, having equipped[m] the animals, began to move them along in the great colonnade. [24]The crowds of the city had been assembled for this most pitiful spectacle and they were eagerly waiting for daybreak. [25]But the Jews, at their last gasp—since the time had run out—stretched their hands toward heaven and with most tearful supplication and mournful dirges implored the supreme God[n] to help them again at once. [26]The rays of the sun were not yet shed abroad, and while the king was receiving his Friends, Hermon arrived and invited him to come out, indicating that what the king desired was ready for action. [27]But he, on receiving the report and being struck by the unusual invitation to come out—since he had been completely overcome by incomprehension—inquired what the matter was for which this had been so zealously completed for him. [28]This was the act of God who rules over all things, for he had implanted in the king's mind a forgetfulness of the things he had previously devised. [29]Then Hermon and all the king's Friends[o] pointed out that the animals and the armed forces were ready, "O king, according to your eager purpose."[p] [30]But at these words he was filled with an overpowering wrath, because by the provi-

dence of God his whole mind had been deranged concerning these matters; and with a threatening look he said, [31]"If your parents or children were present, I would have prepared them to be a rich feast for the savage animals instead of the Jews, who give me no ground for complaint and have exhibited to an extraordinary degree a full and firm loyalty to my ancestors. [32]In fact you would have been deprived of life instead of these, if it were not for an affection arising from our nurture in common and your usefulness." [33]So Hermon suffered an unexpected and dangerous threat, and his eyes wavered and his face fell. [34]The king's Friends one by one sullenly slipped away and dismissed[q] the assembled people to their own occupations. [35]Then the Jews, on hearing what the king had said, praised the manifest Lord God, King of kings, since this also was his aid that they had received.

36 The king, however, reconvened the party in the same manner and urged the guests to return to their celebrating. [37]After summoning Hermon he said in a threatening tone, "How many times, you poor wretch, must I give you orders about these things? [38]Equip[r] the elephants now once more for the destruction of the Jews tomorrow!" [39]But the officials who were at table with him, wondering at his instability of mind, remonstrated as follows: [40]"O king, how long will you put us to the test, as though we are idiots, ordering now for a third time that they be destroyed, and again revoking your decree in the matter?[s] [41]As a result the city is in a tumult because of its expectation; it is crowded with masses of people, and also in constant danger of being plundered."

42 At this the king, a Phalaris in everything and filled with madness, took no account of the changes of mind that had come about within him for the protection of the Jews, and he firmly swore an irrevocable oath that he would send them to death[t] without delay, mangled by the knees and feet of the animals, [43]and would also march against Judea and rapidly level it to the ground with fire and spear, and by burning to the ground the temple inaccessible to him[u] would quickly render it forever empty of those who offered sacrifices there. [44]Then the Friends and officers departed with great joy, and they confidently posted the armed forces at the places in the city most favorable for keeping guard.

45 Now when the animals had been brought virtually to a state of madness, so to speak, by the very fragrant draughts of wine mixed with frankincense and had been equipped with frightful devices, the elephant keeper [46]entered at about dawn into the courtyard—the city now being filled with countless masses of people crowding their way into the hippodrome—and urged the king on to the matter at hand. [47]So he, when he had filled his impious mind with a deep rage, rushed out in full force along with the animals, wishing to witness, with invulnerable heart and with his own eyes, the grievous and pitiful destruction of the aforementioned people.

48 When the Jews saw the dust raised by the elephants going out at the gate and by the following armed forces, as well as by the trampling of the crowd, and heard the loud and tumultuous noise, [49]they thought that this was their last moment of life, the end of their most miserable suspense, and giving way to lamentation and groans they kissed each other, embracing relatives and falling into one another's arms[v]—parents and children, mothers and daughters, and others with babies at their breasts who were drawing their last milk. [50]Not only this, but when they considered the help that they had received before from heaven, they prostrated themselves with one accord on the ground, removing the babies from their breasts, [51]and cried out in a very loud voice, imploring the Ruler over every power to manifest himself and be merciful to them, as they stood now at the gates of death.[t]

The Prayer of Eleazar

6 Then a certain Eleazar, famous among the priests of the country, who had attained a ripe old age and throughout his life had been adorned with every virtue, directed the elders around him to stop calling upon the holy God, and he prayed as follows: [2]"King of great power, Almighty God Most High, governing all creation with mercy, [3]look upon the descendants of Abraham, O Father, upon the children of the sainted Jacob, a people of your consecrated portion who are perishing as foreigners in a foreign land. [4]Pharaoh with his

---

[q] Other ancient authorities read *he dismissed*   [r] Or *Arm*   [s] Other ancient authorities read *when the matter is in hand*   [t] Gk *Hades*   [u] Gk *us*   [v] Gk *falling upon their necks*

abundance of chariots, the former ruler of this Egypt, exalted with lawless insolence and boastful tongue, you destroyed together with his arrogant army by drowning them in the sea, manifesting the light of your mercy on the nation of Israel. [5]Sennacherib exulting in his countless forces, oppressive king of the Assyrians, who had already gained control of the whole world by the spear and was lifted up against your holy city, speaking grievous words with boasting and insolence, you, O Lord, broke in pieces, showing your power to many nations. [6]The three companions in Babylon who had voluntarily surrendered their lives to the flames so as not to serve vain things, you rescued unharmed, even to a hair, moistening the fiery furnace with dew and turning the flame against all their enemies. [7]Daniel, who through envious slanders was thrown down into the ground to lions as food for wild animals, you brought up to the light unharmed. [8]And Jonah, wasting away in the belly of a huge, sea-born monster, you, Father, watched over and restored[w] unharmed to all his family. [9]And now, you who hate insolence, all-merciful and protector of all, reveal yourself quickly to those of the nation of Israel[x]—who are being outrageously treated by the abominable and lawless Gentiles.

10 "Even if our lives have become entangled in impieties in our exile, rescue us from the hand of the enemy, and destroy us, Lord, by whatever fate you choose. [11]Let not the vain-minded praise their vanities[y] at the destruction of your beloved people, saying, 'Not even their god has rescued them.' [12]But you, O Eternal One, who have all might and all power, watch over us now and have mercy on us who by the senseless insolence of the lawless are being deprived of life in the manner of traitors. [13]And let the Gentiles cower today in fear of your invincible might, O honored One, who have power to save the nation of Jacob. [14]The whole throng of infants and their parents entreat you with tears. [15]Let it be shown to all the Gentiles that you are with us, O Lord, and have not turned your face from us; but just as you have said, 'Not even when they were in the land of their enemies did I neglect them,' so accomplish it, O Lord."

Two Angels Rescue the Jews

16 Just as Eleazar was ending his prayer, the king arrived at the hippodrome with the animals and all the arrogance of his forces. [17]And when the Jews observed this they raised great cries to heaven so that even the nearby valleys resounded with them and brought an uncontrollable terror upon the army. [18]Then the most glorious, almighty, and true God revealed his holy face and opened the heavenly gates, from which two glorious angels of fearful aspect descended, visible to all but the Jews. [19]They opposed the forces of the enemy and filled them with confusion and terror, binding them with immovable shackles. [20]Even the king began to shudder bodily, and he forgot his sullen insolence. [21]The animals turned back upon the armed forces following them and began trampling and destroying them.

22 Then the king's anger was turned to pity and tears because of the things that he had devised beforehand. [23]For when he heard the shouting and saw them all fallen headlong to destruction, he wept and angrily threatened his Friends, saying, [24]"You are committing treason and surpassing tyrants in cruelty; and even me, your benefactor, you are now attempting to deprive of dominion and life by secretly devising acts of no advantage to the kingdom. [25]Who has driven from their homes those who faithfully kept our country's fortresses, and foolishly gathered every one of them here? [26]Who is it that has so lawlessly encompassed with outrageous treatment those who from the beginning differed from[z] all nations in their goodwill toward us and often have accepted willingly the worst of human dangers? [27]Loose and untie their unjust bonds! Send them back to their homes in peace, begging pardon for your former actions![a] [28]Release the children of the almighty and living God of heaven, who from the time of our ancestors until now has granted an unimpeded and notable stability to our government." [29]These then were the things he said; and the Jews, immediately released, praised their holy God and Savior, since they now had escaped death.

The Jews Celebrate Their Deliverance

30 Then the king, when he had returned to the city, summoned the official in charge

---

[w] Other ancient authorities read *rescued and restored*; others, *mercifully restored*   [x] Other ancient authorities read *to the saints of Israel*   [y] Or *bless their vain gods*   [z] Or *excelled above*   [a] Other ancient authorities read *revoking your former commands*

of the revenues and ordered him to provide to the Jews both wines and everything else needed for a festival of seven days, deciding that they should celebrate their rescue with all joyfulness in that same place in which they had expected to meet their destruction. [31]Accordingly those disgracefully treated and near to death,[b] or rather, who stood at its gates, arranged for a banquet of deliverance instead of a bitter and lamentable death, and full of joy they apportioned to celebrants the place that had been prepared for their destruction and burial. [32]They stopped their chanting of dirges and took up the song of their ancestors, praising God, their Savior and worker of wonders.[c] Putting an end to all mourning and wailing, they formed choruses[d] as a sign of peaceful joy. [33]Likewise also the king, after convening a great banquet to celebrate these events, gave thanks to heaven unceasingly and lavishly for the unexpected rescue that he[e] had experienced. [34]Those who had previously believed that the Jews would be destroyed and become food for birds, and had joyfully registered them, groaned as they themselves were overcome by disgrace, and their fire-breathing boldness was ignominiously[f] quenched.

35 The Jews, as we have said before, arranged the aforementioned choral group[g] and passed the time in feasting to the accompaniment of joyous thanksgiving and psalms. [36]And when they had ordained a public rite for these things in their whole community and for their descendants, they instituted the observance of the aforesaid days as a festival, not for drinking and gluttony, but because of the deliverance that had come to them through God. [37]Then they petitioned the king, asking for dismissal to their homes. [38]So their registration was carried out from the twenty-fifth of Pachon to the fourth of Epeiph,[h] for forty days; and their destruction was set for the fifth to the seventh of Epeiph,[i] the three days [39]on which the Lord of all most gloriously revealed his mercy and rescued them all together and unharmed. [40]Then they feasted, being provided with everything by the king, until the fourteenth day,[j] on which also they made the petition for their dismissal. [41]The king granted their request at once

and wrote the following letter for them to the generals in the cities, magnanimously expressing his concern:

Ptolemy's Letter on Behalf of the Jews

7 "King Ptolemy Philopator to the generals in Egypt and all in authority in his government, greetings and good health: 2 "We ourselves and our children are faring well, the great God guiding our affairs according to our desire. [3]Certain of our friends, frequently urging us with malicious intent, persuaded us to gather together the Jews of the kingdom in a body and to punish them with barbarous penalties as traitors; [4]for they declared that our government would never be firmly established until this was accomplished, because of the ill-will that these people had toward all nations. [5]They also led them out with harsh treatment as slaves, or rather as traitors, and, girding themselves with a cruelty more savage than that of Scythian custom, they tried without any inquiry or examination to put them to death. [6]But we very severely threatened them for these acts, and in accordance with the clemency that we have toward all people we barely spared their lives. Since we have come to realize that the God of heaven surely defends the Jews, always taking their part as a father does for his children, [7]and since we have taken into account the friendly and firm goodwill that they had toward us and our ancestors, we justly have acquitted them of every charge of whatever kind. [8]We also have ordered all people to return to their own homes, with no one in any place[k] doing them harm at all or reproaching them for the irrational things that have happened. [9]For you should know that if we devise any evil against them or cause them any grief at all, we always shall have not a mortal but the Ruler over every power, the Most High God, in everything and inescapably as an antagonist to avenge such acts. Farewell."

The Jews Return Home with Joy

10 On receiving this letter the Jews[l] did not immediately hurry to make their departure, but they requested of the king that at

---

[b] Gk *Hades*　[c] Other ancient authorities read *praising Israel and the wonder-working God*; or *praising Israel's Savior, the wonder-working God*　[d] Or *dances*　[e] Other ancient authorities read *they*　[f] Other ancient authorities read *completely*　[g] Or *dance*　[h] July 7—August 15　[i] August 16—18　[j] August 25　[k] Other ancient authorities read *way*　[l] Gk *they*

their own hands those of the Jewish nation who had willfully transgressed against the holy God and the law of God should receive the punishment they deserved. ¹¹They declared that those who for the belly's sake had transgressed the divine commandments would never be favorably disposed toward the king's government. ¹²The king*ᵐ* then, admitting and approving the truth of what they said, granted them a general license so that freely, and without royal authority or supervision, they might destroy those everywhere in his kingdom who had transgressed the law of God. ¹³When they had applauded him in fitting manner, their priests and the whole multitude shouted the Hallelujah and joyfully departed. ¹⁴And so on their way they punished and put to a public and shameful death any whom they met of their compatriots who had become defiled. ¹⁵In that day they put to death more than three hundred men; and they kept the day as a joyful festival, since they had destroyed the profaners. ¹⁶But those who had held fast to God even to death and had received the full enjoyment of deliverance began their departure from the city, crowned with all sorts of very fragrant flowers, joyfully and loudly giving thanks to the one God of their ancestors, the eternal Savior*ⁿ* of Israel, in words of praise and all kinds of melodious songs.

17 When they had arrived at Ptolemais, called "rose-bearing" because of a characteristic of the place, the fleet waited for them, in accordance with the common desire, for seven days. ¹⁸There they celebrated their deliverance,*ᵒ* for the king had generously provided all things to them for their journey until all of them arrived at their own houses. ¹⁹And when they had all landed in peace with appropriate thanksgiving, there too in like manner they decided to observe these days as a joyous festival during the time of their stay. ²⁰Then, after inscribing them as holy on a pillar and dedicating a place of prayer at the site of the festival, they departed unharmed, free, and overjoyed, since at the king's command they had all of them been brought safely by land and sea and river to their own homes. ²¹They also possessed greater prestige among their enemies, being held in honor and awe; and they were not subject at all to confiscation of their belongings by anyone. ²²Besides, they all recovered all of their property, in accordance with the registration, so that those who held any of it restored it to them with extreme fear.*ᵖ* So the supreme God perfectly performed great deeds for their deliverance. ²³Blessed be the Deliverer of Israel through all times! Amen.

ᵐ Gk He   *ⁿ* Other ancient authorities read *the holy Savior*; others, *the holy one*   *ᵒ* Gk *they made a cup of deliverance*   *ᵖ* Other ancient authorities read *with a very large supplement*

(c) The following book is included in the Slavonic Bible as 3 Esdras, but is not found in the Greek. It is included in the Appendix to the Latin Vulgate Bible as 4 Esdras.

2 ESDRAS

Comprising what is sometimes called 5 Ezra (chapters 1–2), 4 Ezra (chapters 3–14), and 6 Ezra (chapters 15–16)

The Genealogy of Ezra

1 The book[a] of the prophet Ezra son of Seraiah, son of Azariah, son of Hilkiah, son of Shallum, son of Zadok, son of Ahitub, [2]son of Ahijah, son of Phinehas, son of Eli, son of Amariah, son of Azariah, son of Meraimoth, son of Arna, son of Uzzi, son of Borith, son of Abishua, son of Phinehas, son of Eleazar, [3]son of Aaron, of the tribe of Levi, who was a captive in the country of the Medes in the reign of Artaxerxes, king of the Persians.[b]

Ezra's Prophetic Call

4 The word of the Lord came to me, saying, [5]"Go, declare to my people their evil deeds, and to their children the iniquities that they have committed against me, so that they may tell[c] their children's children [6]that the sins of their parents have increased in them, for they have forgotten me and have offered sacrifices to strange gods. [7]Was it not I who brought them out of the land of Egypt, out of the house of bondage? But they have angered me and despised my counsels. [8]Now you, pull out the hair of your head and hurl[d] all evils upon them, for they have not obeyed my law—they are a rebellious people. [9]How long shall I endure them, on whom I have bestowed such great benefits? [10]For their sake I have overthrown many kings; I struck down Pharaoh with his servants and all his army. [11]I destroyed all nations before them, and scattered in the east the peoples of two provinces,[e] Tyre and Sidon; I killed all their enemies.

God's Mercies to Israel

12 "But speak to them and say, Thus says the Lord: [13]Surely it was I who brought you through the sea, and made safe highways for you where there was no road; I gave you Moses as leader and Aaron as priest; [14]I provided light for you from a pillar of fire, and did great wonders among you. Yet you have forgotten me, says the Lord.

15 "Thus says the Lord Almighty:[f] The quails were a sign to you; I gave you camps for your protection, and in them you complained. [16]You have not exulted in my name at the destruction of your enemies, but to this day you still complain.[g] [17]Where are the benefits that I bestowed on you? When you were hungry and thirsty in the wilderness, did you not cry out to me, [18]saying, 'Why have you led us into this wilderness to kill us? It would have been better for us to serve the Egyptians than to die in this wilderness.' [19]I pitied your groanings and gave you manna for food; you ate the bread of angels. [20]When you were thirsty, did I not split the rock so that waters flowed in abundance? Because of the heat I clothed you with the leaves of trees.[h] [21]I divided fertile lands among you; I drove out the Canaanites, the Perizzites, and the Philistines[i] before you. What more can I do for you? says the Lord. [22]Thus says the Lord Almighty:[j] When you were in the wilderness, at the bitter stream, thirsty and blaspheming my name, [23]I did not send fire on you for your blasphemies, but threw a tree into the water and made the stream sweet.

Israel's Disobedience and Rejection

24 "What shall I do to you, O Jacob? You, Judah, would not obey me. I will turn to other nations and will give them my

---

[a] Other ancient authorities read *The second book*   [b] Other ancient authorities, which place chapters 1 and 2 after 16.78, lack verses 1–3 and begin the chapter: *The word of the Lord that came to Ezra son of Chusi in the days of King Nebuchadnezzar, saying, "Go*   [c] Other ancient authorities read *nourish*   [d] Other ancient authorities read *and shake out*   [e] Other ancient authorities read *Did I not destroy the city of Bethsaida because of you, and to the south burn two cities . . . ?*   [f] Other ancient authorities lack *Almighty*   [g] Other ancient authorities read verse 16, *Your pursuer with his army I sank in the sea, but still the people complain also concerning their own destruction.*   [h] Other ancient authorities read *I made for you trees with leaves*   [i] Other ancient authorities read *Perizzites and their children*   [j] Other ancient authorities lack *Almighty*

name, so that they may keep my statutes. ²⁵Because you have forsaken me, I also will forsake you. When you beg mercy of me, I will show you no mercy. ²⁶When you call to me, I will not listen to you; for you have defiled your hands with blood, and your feet are swift to commit murder. ²⁷It is not as though you had forsaken me; you have forsaken yourselves, says the Lord.

28 "Thus says the Lord Almighty: Have I not entreated you as a father entreats his sons or a mother her daughters or a nurse her children, ²⁹so that you should be my people and I should be your God, and that you should be my children and I should be your father? ³⁰I gathered you as a hen gathers her chicks under her wings. But now, what shall I do to you? I will cast you out from my presence. ³¹When you offer oblations to me, I will turn my face from you; for I have rejected your*k* festal days, and new moons, and circumcisions of the flesh.*l* ³²I sent you my servants the prophets, but you have taken and killed them and torn their bodies*m* in pieces; I will require their blood of you, says the Lord.*n*

33 "Thus says the Lord Almighty: Your house is desolate; I will drive you out as the wind drives straw; ³⁴and your sons will have no children, because with you*o* they have neglected my commandment and have done what is evil in my sight. ³⁵I will give your houses to a people that will come, who without having heard me will believe. Those to whom I have shown no signs will do what I have commanded. ³⁶They have seen no prophets, yet will recall their former state.*p* ³⁷I call to witness the gratitude of the people that is to come, whose children rejoice with gladness;*q* though they do not see me with bodily eyes, yet with the spirit they will believe the things I have said.

38 "And now, father,*r* look with pride and see the people coming from the east; ³⁹to them I will give as leaders Abraham, Isaac, and Jacob, and Hosea and Amos and Micah and Joel and Obadiah and Jonah ⁴⁰and Nahum and Habakkuk, Zephaniah, Haggai, Zechariah and Malachi, who is also called the messenger of the Lord.*s*

God's Judgment on Israel

2 "Thus says the Lord: I brought this people out of bondage, and I gave them commandments through my servants the prophets; but they would not listen to them, and made my counsels void. ²The mother who bore them*t* says to them, 'Go, my children, because I am a widow and forsaken. ³I brought you up with gladness; but with mourning and sorrow I have lost you, because you have sinned before the Lord God and have done what is evil in my sight.*u* ⁴But now what can I do for you? For I am a widow and forsaken. Go, my children, and ask for mercy from the Lord.' ⁵Now I call upon you, father, as a witness in addition to the mother of the children, because they would not keep my covenant, ⁶so that you may bring confusion on them and bring their mother to ruin, so that they may have no offspring. ⁷Let them be scattered among the nations; let their names be blotted out from the earth, because they have despised my covenant.

8 "Woe to you, Assyria, who conceal the unrighteous within you! O wicked nation, remember what I did to Sodom and Gomorrah, ⁹whose land lies in lumps of pitch and heaps of ashes.*v* That is what I will do to those who have not listened to me, says the Lord Almighty."

10 Thus says the Lord to Ezra: "Tell my people that I will give them the kingdom of Jerusalem, which I was going to give to

---

k Other ancient authorities read *I have not commanded for you* *l* Other ancient authorities lack *of the flesh* *m* Other ancient authorities read *the bodies of the apostles* *n* Other ancient authorities add *Thus says the Lord Almighty: Recently you also laid hands on me, crying out before the judge's seat for him to deliver me to you. You took me as a sinner, not as a father who freed you from slavery, and you delivered me to death by hanging me on the tree; these are the things you have done. Therefore, says the Lord, let my Father and his angels return and judge between you and me; if I have not kept the commandment of the Father, if I have not nourished you, if I have not done the things my Father commanded, I will contend in judgment with you, says the Lord.* *o* Other ancient authorities lack *with you* *p* Other ancient authorities read *their iniquities* *q* Other ancient authorities read *The apostles bear witness to the coming people with joy* *r* Other ancient authorities read *brother* *s* Other ancient authorities read *and Jacob, Elijah and Enoch, Zechariah and Hosea, Amos, Joel, Micah, Obadiah, Zephaniah,* ⁴⁰*Nahum, Jonah, Mattia (or Mattathias), Habakkuk, and twelve angels with flowers* *t* Other ancient authorities read *They begat for themselves a mother who* *u* Other ancient authorities read *in his sight* *v* Other ancient authorities read *Gomorrah, whose land descends to hell*

Israel. [11]Moreover, I will take back to myself their glory, and will give to these others the everlasting habitations, which I had prepared for Israel.[w] [12]The tree of life shall give them fragrant perfume, and they shall neither toil nor become weary. [13]Go[x] and you will receive; pray that your days may be few, that they may be shortened. The kingdom is already prepared for you; be on the watch! [14]Call, O call heaven and earth to witness: I set aside evil and created good; for I am the Living One, says the Lord.

Exhortation to Good Works

15 "Mother, embrace your children; bring them up with gladness, as does a dove; strengthen their feet, because I have chosen you, says the Lord. [16]And I will raise up the dead from their places, and bring them out from their tombs, because I recognize my name in them. [17]Do not fear, mother of children, for I have chosen you, says the Lord. [18]I will send you help, my servants Isaiah and Jeremiah. According to their counsel I have consecrated and prepared for you twelve trees loaded with various fruits, [19]and the same number of springs flowing with milk and honey, and seven mighty mountains on which roses and lilies grow; by these I will fill your children with joy.

20 "Guard the rights of the widow, secure justice for the ward, give to the needy, defend the orphan, clothe the naked, [21]care for the injured and the weak, do not ridicule the lame, protect the maimed, and let the blind have a vision of my splendor. [22]Protect the old and the young within your walls; [23]When you find any who are dead, commit them to the grave and mark it,[y] and I will give you the first place in my resurrection. [24]Pause and be quiet, my people, because your rest will come.

25 "Good nurse, nourish your children; strengthen their feet. [26]Not one of the servants[z] whom I have given you will perish, for I will require them from among your number. [27]Do not be anxious, for when the day of tribulation and anguish comes, others shall weep and be sorrowful, but you shall rejoice and have abundance. [28]The nations shall envy you, but they shall not be able to do anything against you, says the Lord. [29]My power will protect[a] you, so

that your children may not see hell.[b]

30 "Rejoice, O mother, with your children, because I will deliver you, says the Lord. [31]Remember your children that sleep, because I will bring them out of the hiding places of the earth, and will show mercy to them; for I am merciful, says the Lord Almighty. [32]Embrace your children until I come, and proclaim mercy to them; because my springs run over, and my grace will not fail."

Ezra on Mount Horeb

33 I, Ezra, received a command from the Lord on Mount Horeb to go to Israel. When I came to them they rejected me and refused the Lord's commandment. [34]Therefore I say to you, O nations that hear and understand, "Wait for your shepherd; he will give you everlasting rest, because he who will come at the end of the age is close at hand. [35]Be ready for the rewards of the kingdom, because perpetual light will shine on you forevermore. [36]Flee from the shadow of this age, receive the joy of your glory; I publicly call on my savior to witness.[c] [37]Receive what the Lord has entrusted to you and be joyful, giving thanks to him who has called you to the celestial kingdoms. [38]Rise, stand erect and see the number of those who have been sealed at the feast of the Lord. [39]Those who have departed from the shadow of this age have received glorious garments from the Lord. [40]Take again your full number, O Zion, and close the list of your people who are clothed in white, who have fulfilled the law of the Lord. [41]The number of your children, whom you desired, is now complete; implore the Lord's authority that your people, who have been called from the beginning, may be made holy."

Ezra Sees the Son of God

42 I, Ezra, saw on Mount Zion a great multitude that I could not number, and they all were praising the Lord with songs. [43]In their midst was a young man of great stature, taller than any of the others, and on the head of each of them he placed a crown, but he was more exalted than they. And I was held spellbound. [44]Then I asked

---

[w] Lat *for those*   [x] Other ancient authorities read *Seek*   [y] Or *seal it*; or *mark them and commit them to the grave*
[z] Or *slaves*   [a] Lat *hands will cover*   [b] Lat *Gehenna*   [c] Other ancient authorities read *I testify that my savior has been commissioned by the Lord*

an angel, "Who are these, my lord?" [45]He answered and said to me, "These are they who have put off mortal clothing and have put on the immortal, and have confessed the name of God. Now they are being crowned, and receive palms." [46]Then I said to the angel, "Who is that young man who is placing crowns on them and putting palms in their hands?" [47]He answered and said to me, "He is the Son of God, whom they confessed in the world." So I began to praise those who had stood valiantly for the name of the Lord.[d] [48]Then the angel said to me, "Go, tell my people how great and how many are the wonders of the Lord God that you have seen."

Ezra's Prayer of Complaint

3 In the thirtieth year after the destruction of the city, I was in Babylon—I, Salathiel, who am also called Ezra. I was troubled as I lay on my bed, and my thoughts welled up in my heart, [2]because I saw the desolation of Zion and the wealth of those who lived in Babylon. [3]My spirit was greatly agitated, and I began to speak anxious words to the Most High, and said, [4]"O sovereign Lord, did you not speak at the beginning when you planted[e] the earth—and that without help—and commanded the dust[f] [5]and it gave you Adam, a lifeless body? Yet he was the creation of your hands, and you breathed into him the breath of life, and he was made alive in your presence. [6]And you led him into the garden that your right hand had planted before the earth appeared. [7]And you laid upon him one commandment of yours; but he transgressed it, and immediately you appointed death for him and for his descendants. From him there sprang nations and tribes, peoples and clans without number. [8]And every nation walked after its own will; they did ungodly things in your sight and rejected your commands, and you did not hinder them. [9]But again, in its time you brought the flood upon the inhabitants of the world and destroyed them. [10]And the same fate befell all of them: just as death came upon Adam, so the flood upon them. [11]But you left one of them, Noah with his household, and all the righteous who have descended from him.

12 "When those who lived on earth began to multiply, they produced children and peoples and many nations, and again they began to be more ungodly than were their ancestors. [13]And when they were committing iniquity in your sight, you chose for yourself one of them, whose name was Abraham; [14]you loved him, and to him alone you revealed the end of the times, secretly by night. [15]You made an everlasting covenant with him, and promised him that you would never forsake his descendants; and you gave him Isaac, and to Isaac you gave Jacob and Esau. [16]You set apart Jacob for yourself, but Esau you rejected; and Jacob became a great multitude. [17]And when you led his descendants out of Egypt, you brought them to Mount Sinai. [18]You bent down the heavens and shook[g] the earth, and moved the world, and caused the depths to tremble, and troubled the times. [19]Your glory passed through the four gates of fire and earthquake and wind and ice, to give the law to the descendants of Jacob, and your commandment to the posterity of Israel.

20 "Yet you did not take away their evil heart from them, so that your law might produce fruit in them. [21]For the first Adam, burdened with an evil heart, transgressed and was overcome, as were also all who were descended from him. [22]Thus the disease became permanent; the law was in the hearts of the people along with the evil root; but what was good departed, and the evil remained. [23]So the times passed and the years were completed, and you raised up for yourself a servant, named David. [24]You commanded him to build a city for your name, and there to offer you oblations from what is yours. [25]This was done for many years; but the inhabitants of the city transgressed, [26]in everything doing just as Adam and all his descendants had done, for they also had the evil heart. [27]So you handed over your city to your enemies.

Babylon Compared with Zion
28 "Then I said in my heart, Are the deeds of those who inhabit Babylon any better? Is that why it has gained dominion over Zion? [29]For when I came here I saw ungodly deeds without number, and my soul has seen many sinners during these

---

[d]Other ancient authorities read *to praise and glorify the Lord*   [e]Other ancient authorities read *formed*   [f]Syr Ethiop: Lat *people* or *world*   [g]Syr Ethiop Arab 1 Georg: Lat *set fast*

thirty years.[h] And my heart failed me, [30]because I have seen how you endure those who sin, and have spared those who act wickedly, and have destroyed your people, and protected your enemies, [31]and have not shown to anyone how your way may be comprehended.[i] Are the deeds of Babylon better than those of Zion? [32]Or has another nation known you besides Israel? Or what tribes have so believed the covenants as these tribes of Jacob? [33]Yet their reward has not appeared and their labor has borne no fruit. For I have traveled widely among the nations and have seen that they abound in wealth, though they are unmindful of your commandments. [34]Now therefore weigh in a balance our iniquities and those of the inhabitants of the world; and it will be found which way the turn of the scale will incline. [35]When have the inhabitants of the earth not sinned in your sight? Or what nation has kept your commandments so well? [36]You may indeed find individuals who have kept your commandments, but nations you will not find."

Limitations of the Human Mind

4 Then the angel that had been sent to me, whose name was Uriel, answered [2]and said to me, "Your understanding has utterly failed regarding this world, and do you think you can comprehend the way of the Most High?" [3]Then I said, "Yes, my lord." And he replied to me, "I have been sent to show you three ways, and to put before you three problems. [4]If you can solve one of them for me, then I will show you the way you desire to see, and will teach you why the heart is evil."

[5]I said, "Speak, my lord."

And he said to me, "Go, weigh for me the weight of fire, or measure for me a blast[j] of wind, or call back for me the day that is past."

[6]I answered and said, "Who of those that have been born can do that, that you should ask me about such things?"

[7]And he said to me, "If I had asked you, 'How many dwellings are in the heart of the sea, or how many streams are at the source of the deep, or how many streams are above the firmament, or which are the

exits of Hades, or which are the entrances[k] of paradise?' [8]perhaps you would have said to me, 'I never went down into the deep, nor as yet into Hades, neither did I ever ascend into heaven.' [9]But now I have asked you only about fire and wind and the day—things that you have experienced and from which you cannot be separated, and you have given me no answer about them." [10]He said to me, "You cannot understand the things with which you have grown up; [11]how then can your mind comprehend the way of the Most High? And how can one who is already worn out[l] by the corrupt world understand incorruption?"[m] When I heard this, I fell on my face[n] [12]and said to him, "It would have been better for us not to be here than to come here and live in ungodliness, and to suffer and not understand why."

Parable of the Forest and the Sea

13 He answered me and said, "I went into a forest of trees of the plain, and they made a plan [14]and said, 'Come, let us go and make war against the sea, so that it may recede before us and so that we may make for ourselves more forests.' [15]In like manner the waves of the sea also made a plan and said, 'Come, let us go up and subdue the forest of the plain so that there also we may gain more territory for ourselves.' [16]But the plan of the forest was in vain, for the fire came and consumed it; [17]likewise also the plan of the waves of the sea was in vain,[o] for the sand stood firm and blocked it. [18]If now you were a judge between them, which would you undertake to justify, and which to condemn?"

19 I answered and said, "Each made a foolish plan, for the land has been assigned to the forest, and the locale of the sea a place to carry its waves."

20 He answered me and said, "You have judged rightly, but why have you not judged so in your own case? [21]For as the land has been assigned to the forest and the sea to its waves, so also those who inhabit the earth can understand only what is on the earth, and he who is[p] above the heavens can understand what is above the height of the heavens."

---

[h] Ethiop Arab 1 Arm: Lat Syr *in this thirtieth year*   [i] Syr; compare Ethiop: Lat *how this way should be forsaken*   [j] Syr Ethiop Arab 1 Arab 2 Georg *a measure*   [k] Syr Compare Ethiop Arab 2 Arm: Lat lacks *of Hades, or which are the entrances*   [l] Meaning of Lat uncertain   [m] Syr Ethiop *the way of the incorruptible?*   [n] Syr Ethiop Arab 1: Meaning of Lat uncertain   [o] Lat lacks *was in vain*   [p] Or *those who are*

The New Age Will Make All Things Clear

22 Then I answered and said, "I implore you, my lord, why*q* have I been endowed with the power of understanding? ²³For I did not wish to inquire about the ways above, but about those things that we daily experience: why Israel has been given over to the Gentiles in disgrace; why the people whom you loved has been given over to godless tribes, and the law of our ancestors has been brought to destruction and the written covenants no longer exist. ²⁴We pass from the world like locusts, and our life is like a mist,*r* and we are not worthy to obtain mercy. ²⁵But what will he do for his*s* name that is invoked over us? It is about these things that I have asked."

26 He answered me and said, "If you are alive, you will see, and if you live long,*t* you will often marvel, because the age is hurrying swiftly to its end. ²⁷It will not be able to bring the things that have been promised to the righteous in their appointed times, because this age is full of sadness and infirmities. ²⁸For the evil about which*u* you ask me has been sown, but the harvest of it has not yet come. ²⁹If therefore that which has been sown is not reaped, and if the place where the evil has been sown does not pass away, the field where the good has been sown will not come. ³⁰For a grain of evil seed was sown in Adam's heart from the beginning, and how much ungodliness it has produced until now—and will produce until the time of threshing comes! ³¹Consider now for yourself how much fruit of ungodliness a grain of evil seed has produced. ³²When heads of grain without number are sown, how great a threshing floor they will fill!"

When Will the New Age Come?

33 Then I answered and said, "How long?*u* When will these things be? Why are our years few and evil?" ³⁴He answered me and said, "Do not be in a greater hurry than the Most High. You, indeed, are in a hurry for yourself,*v* but the Highest is in a hurry on behalf of many. ³⁵Did not the souls of the righteous in their chambers ask about these matters, saying, 'How long are we to remain here?*w* And when will the harvest of our reward come?' ³⁶And the archangel Jeremiel answered and said, 'When the number of those like yourselves is completed;*x* for he has weighed the age in the balance, ³⁷and measured the times by measure, and numbered the times by number; and he will not move or arouse them until that measure is fulfilled.' "

38 Then I answered and said, "But, O sovereign Lord, all of us also are full of ungodliness. ³⁹It is perhaps on account of us that the time of threshing is delayed for the righteous—on account of the sins of those who inhabit the earth."

40 He answered me and said, "Go and ask a pregnant woman whether, when her nine months have been completed, her womb can keep the fetus within her any longer."

41 And I said, "No, lord, it cannot."

He said to me, "In Hades the chambers of the souls are like the womb. ⁴²For just as a woman who is in labor makes haste to escape the pangs of birth, so also do these places hasten to give back those things that were committed to them from the beginning. ⁴³Then the things that you desire to see will be disclosed to you."

How Much Time Remains?

44 I answered and said, "If I have found favor in your sight, and if it is possible, and if I am worthy, ⁴⁵show me this also: whether more time is to come than has passed, or whether for us the greater part has gone by. ⁴⁶For I know what has gone by, but I do not know what is to come."

47 And he said to me, "Stand at my right side, and I will show you the interpretation of a parable."

48 So I stood and looked, and lo, a flaming furnace passed by before me, and when the flame had gone by I looked, and lo, the smoke remained. ⁴⁹And after this a cloud full of water passed before me and poured down a heavy and violent rain, and when the violent rainstorm had passed, drops still remained in the cloud.*y*

50 He said to me, "Consider it for yourself; for just as the rain is more than the drops, and the fire is greater than the smoke, so the quantity that passed was far greater; but drops and smoke remained."

51 Then I prayed and said, "Do you think that I shall live until those days? Or

---

q Syr Ethiop Arm: Meaning of Lat uncertain   *r* Syr Ethiop Arab Georg: Lat *a trembling*   *s* Ethiop adds *holy*
t Syr: Lat *live*   *u* Syr Ethiop: Meaning of Lat uncertain   *v* Syr Ethiop Arab Arm: Meaning of Lat uncertain
w Syr Ethiop Arab 2 Georg: Lat *How long do I hope thus?*   *x* Syr Ethiop Arab 2: Lat *number of seeds is completed*
for you   *y* Lat *in it*

who will be alive in those days?"

52 He answered me and said, "Concerning the signs about which you ask me, I can tell you in part; but I was not sent to tell you concerning your life, for I do not know.

Signs of the End

5 "Now concerning the signs: lo, the days are coming when those who inhabit the earth shall be seized with great terror,[z] and the way of truth shall be hidden, and the land shall be barren of faith. [2]Unrighteousness shall be increased beyond what you yourself see, and beyond what you heard of formerly. [3]And the land that you now see ruling shall be a trackless waste, and people shall see it desolate. [4]But if the Most High grants that you live, you shall see it thrown into confusion after the third period;[a]

and the sun shall suddenly begin to
        shine at night,
    and the moon during the day.
[5] Blood shall drip from wood,
    and the stone shall utter its voice;
the peoples shall be troubled,
    and the stars shall fall.[b]

[6]And one shall reign whom those who inhabit the earth do not expect, and the birds shall fly away together; [7]and the Dead Sea[c] shall cast up fish; and one whom the many do not know shall make his voice heard by night, and all shall hear his voice.[d] [8]There shall be chaos also in many places, fire shall often break out, the wild animals shall roam beyond their haunts, and menstruous women shall bring forth monsters. [9]Salt waters shall be found in the sweet, and all friends shall conquer one another; then shall reason hide itself, and wisdom shall withdraw into its chamber, [10]and it shall be sought by many but shall not be found, and unrighteousness and unrestraint shall increase on earth. [11]One country shall ask its neighbor, 'Has righteousness, or anyone who does right, passed through you?' And it will answer, 'No.' [12]At that time people shall hope but not obtain; they shall labor, but their ways shall not prosper. [13]These are the signs that I am permitted to tell you, and if you pray again, and weep as you do now, and fast

for seven days, you shall hear yet greater things than these."

Conclusion of the Vision

14 Then I woke up, and my body shuddered violently, and my soul was so troubled that it fainted. [15]But the angel who had come and talked with me held me and strengthened me and set me on my feet.

16 Now on the second night Phaltiel, a chief of the people, came to me and said, "Where have you been? And why is your face sad? [17]Or do you not know that Israel has been entrusted to you in the land of their exile? [18]Rise therefore and eat some bread, and do not forsake us, like a shepherd who leaves the flock in the power of savage wolves."

19 Then I said to him, "Go away from me and do not come near me for seven days; then you may come to me." He heard what I said and left me. [20]So I fasted seven days, mourning and weeping, as the angel Uriel had commanded me.

Ezra's Second Prayer of Complaint

21 After seven days the thoughts of my heart were very grievous to me again. [22]Then my soul recovered the spirit of understanding, and I began once more to speak words in the presence of the Most High. [23]I said, "O sovereign Lord, from every forest of the earth and from all its trees you have chosen one vine, [24]and from all the lands of the world you have chosen for yourself one region,[e] and from all the flowers of the world you have chosen for yourself one lily, [25]and from all the depths of the sea you have filled for yourself one river, and from all the cities that have been built you have consecrated Zion for yourself, [26]and from all the birds that have been created you have named for yourself one dove, and from all the flocks that have been made you have provided for yourself one sheep, [27]and from all the multitude of peoples you have gotten for yourself one people; and to this people, whom you have loved, you have given the law that is approved by all. [28]And now, O Lord, why have you handed the one over to the many, and dishonored[f] the one root

---

[z] Syr Ethiop: Meaning of Lat uncertain [a] Literally *after the third*; Ethiop *after three months*; Arm *after the third vision*; Georg *after the third day*   [b] Ethiop Compare Syr and Arab: Meaning of Lat uncertain   [c] Lat *Sea of Sodom*   [d] Cn: Lat *fish; and it shall make its voice heard by night, which the many have not known, but all shall hear its voice.*   [e] Ethiop: Lat *pit*   [f] Syr Ethiop Arab: Lat *prepared*

beyond the others, and scattered your only one among the many? [29]And those who opposed your promises have trampled on those who believed your covenants. [30]If you really hate your people, they should be punished at your own hands."

Response to Ezra's Complaints

31 When I had spoken these words, the angel who had come to me on a previous night was sent to me. [32]He said to me, "Listen to me, and I will instruct you; pay attention to me, and I will tell you more."

33 Then I said, "Speak, my lord." And he said to me, "Are you greatly disturbed in mind over Israel? Or do you love him more than his Maker does?"

34 I said, "No, my lord, but because of my grief I have spoken; for every hour I suffer agonies of heart, while I strive to understand the way of the Most High and to search out some part of his judgment."

35 He said to me, "You cannot." And I said, "Why not, my lord? Why then was I born? Or why did not my mother's womb become my grave, so that I would not see the travail of Jacob and the exhaustion of the people of Israel?"

36 He said to me, "Count up for me those who have not yet come, and gather for me the scattered raindrops, and make the withered flowers bloom again for me; [37]open for me the closed chambers, and bring out for me the winds shut up in them, or show me the picture of a voice; and then I will explain to you the travail that you ask to understand."[g]

38 I said, "O sovereign Lord, who is able to know these things except him whose dwelling is not with mortals? [39]As for me, I am without wisdom, and how can I speak concerning the things that you have asked me?"

40 He said to me, "Just as you cannot do one of the things that were mentioned, so you cannot discover my judgment, or the goal of the love that I have promised to my people."

Why Successive Generations Have Been Created

41 I said, "Yet, O Lord, you have charge of those who are alive at the end, but what will those do who lived before me, or we, ourselves, or those who come after us?"

42 He said to me, "I shall liken my judgment to a circle;[h] just as for those who are last there is no slowness, so for those who are first there is no haste."

43 Then I answered and said, "Could you not have created at one time those who have been and those who are and those who will be, so that you might show your judgment the sooner?"

44 He replied to me and said, "The creation cannot move faster than the Creator, nor can the world hold at one time those who have been created in it."

45 I said, "How have you said to your servant that you[i] will certainly give life at one time to your creation? If therefore all creatures will live at one time[j] and the creation will sustain them, it might even now be able to support all of them present at one time."

46 He said to me, "Ask a woman's womb, and say to it, 'If you bear ten[k] children, why one after another?' Request it therefore to produce ten at one time."

47 I said, "Of course it cannot, but only each in its own time."

48 He said to me, "Even so I have given the womb of the earth to those who from time to time are sown in it. [49]For as an infant does not bring forth, and a woman who has become old does not bring forth any longer, so I have made the same rule for the world that I created."

When and How Will the End Come?

50 Then I inquired and said, "Since you have now given me the opportunity, let me speak before you. Is our mother, of whom you have told me, still young? Or is she now approaching old age?"

51 He replied to me, "Ask a woman who bears children, and she will tell you. [52]Say to her, 'Why are those whom you have borne recently not like those whom you bore before, but smaller in stature?' [53]And she herself will answer you, 'Those born in the strength of youth are different from those born during the time of old age, when the womb is failing.' [54]Therefore you also should consider that you and your contemporaries are smaller in stature than those who were before you, [55]and those who

[g] Lat *see* [h] Or *crown* [i] Syr Ethiop Arab 1: Meaning of Lat uncertain [j] Lat lacks *If . . . one time* [k] Syr Ethiop Arab 2 Arm: Meaning of Lat uncertain

come after you will be smaller than you, as born of a creation that already is aging and passing the strength of youth."

56 I said, "I implore you, O Lord, if I have found favor in your sight, show your servant through whom you will visit your creation."

6 He said to me, "At the beginning of the circle of the earth, before[^j] the portals of the world were in place, and before the assembled winds blew, [2]and before the rumblings of thunder sounded, and before the flashes of lightning shone, and before the foundations of paradise were laid, [3]and before the beautiful flowers were seen, and before the powers of movements[^m] were established, and before the innumerable hosts of angels were gathered together, [4]and before the heights of the air were lifted up, and before the measures of the firmaments were named, and before the footstool of Zion was established, [5]and before the present years were reckoned and before the imaginations of those who now sin were estranged, and before those who stored up treasures of faith were sealed— [6]then I planned these things, and they were made through me alone and not through another; just as the end shall come through me alone and not through another."

The Dividing of the Times

7 I answered and said, "What will be the dividing of the times? Or when will be the end of the first age and the beginning of the age that follows?"

8 He said to me, "From Abraham to Isaac,[^n] because from him were born Jacob and Esau, for Jacob's hand held Esau's heel from the beginning. [9]Now Esau is the end of this age, and Jacob is the beginning of the age that follows. [10]The beginning of a person is the hand, and the end of a person is the heel;[^o] seek for nothing else, Ezra, between the heel and the hand, Ezra!"

More Signs of the End

11 I answered and said, "O sovereign Lord, if I have found favor in your sight,

[12]show your servant the last of your signs of which you showed me a part on a previous night."

13 He answered and said to me, "Rise to your feet and you will hear a full, resounding voice. [14]And if the place where you are standing is greatly shaken [15]while the voice is speaking, do not be terrified; because the word concerns the end, and the foundations of the earth will understand [16]that the speech concerns them. They will tremble and be shaken, for they know that their end must be changed."

17 When I heard this, I got to my feet and listened; a voice was speaking, and its sound was like the sound of mighty[^p] waters. [18]It said, "The days are coming when I draw near to visit the inhabitants of the earth, [19]and when I require from the doers of iniquity the penalty of their iniquity, and when the humiliation of Zion is complete. [20]When the seal is placed upon the age that is about to pass away, then I will show these signs: the books shall be opened before the face of the firmament, and all shall see my judgment[^q] together. [21]Children a year old shall speak with their voices, and pregnant women shall give birth to premature children at three and four months, and these shall live and leap about. [22]Sown places shall suddenly appear unsown, and full storehouses shall suddenly be found to be empty; [23]the trumpet shall sound aloud, and when all hear it, they shall suddenly be terrified. [24]At that time friends shall make war on friends like enemies, the earth and those who inhabit it shall be terrified, and the springs of the fountains shall stand still, so that for three hours they shall not flow.

25 "It shall be that whoever remains after all that I have foretold to you shall be saved and shall see my salvation and the end of my world. [26]And they shall see those who were taken up, who from their birth have not tasted death; and the heart of the earth's[^r] inhabitants shall be changed and converted to a different spirit. [27]For evil shall be blotted out, and deceit shall be quenched; [28]faithfulness shall flourish, and corruption shall be overcome, and the truth, which has been so long without fruit, shall be revealed."

[^j]: Meaning of Lat uncertain: Compare Syr *The beginning by the hand of humankind, but the end by my own hands. For as before the land of the world existed there, and before*; Ethiop: *At first by the Son of Man, and afterwards I myself. For before the earth and the lands were created, and before*   [^m]: Or *earthquakes*   [^n]: Other ancient authorities read *to Abraham*   [^o]: Syr: Meaning of Lat uncertain   [^p]: Lat *many*   [^q]: Syr: Lat lacks *my judgment*   [^r]: Syr Compare Ethiop Arab 1 Arm: Lat lacks *earth's*

Conclusion of the Second Vision

29 While he spoke to me, little by little the place where I was standing began to rock to and fro.[s] [30]And he said to me, "I have come to show you these things this night.[t] [31]If therefore you will pray again and fast again for seven days, I will again declare to you greater things than these,[u] [32]because your voice has surely been heard by the Most High; for the Mighty One has seen your uprightness and has also observed the purity that you have maintained from your youth. [33]Therefore he sent me to show you all these things, and to say to you: 'Believe and do not be afraid! [34]Do not be quick to think vain thoughts concerning the former times; then you will not act hastily in the last times.' "

The Third Vision

35 Now after this I wept again and fasted seven days in the same way as before, in order to complete the three weeks that had been prescribed for me. [36]Then on the eighth night my heart was troubled within me again, and I began to speak in the presence of the Most High. [37]My spirit was greatly aroused, and my soul was in distress.

God's Work in Creation

38 I said, "O Lord, you spoke at the beginning of creation and said on the first day, 'Let heaven and earth be made,' and your word accomplished the work. [39]Then the spirit was blowing, and darkness and silence embraced everything; the sound of human voices was not yet there.[v] [40]Then you commanded a ray of light to be brought out from your store-chambers, so that your works could be seen.

41 "Again, on the second day, you created the spirit of the firmament, and commanded it to divide and separate the waters, so that one part might move upward and the other part remain beneath.

42 "On the third day you commanded the waters to be gathered together in a seventh part of the earth; six parts you dried up and kept so that some of them might be planted and cultivated and be of service before you. [43]For your word went forth, and

at once the work was done. [44]Immediately fruit came forth in endless abundance and of varied appeal to the taste, and flowers of inimitable color, and odors of inexpressible fragrance. These were made on the third day.

45 "On the fourth day you commanded the brightness of the sun, the light of the moon, and the arrangement of the stars to come into being; [46]and you commanded them to serve humankind, about to be formed.

47 "On the fifth day you commanded the seventh part, where the water had been gathered together, to bring forth living creatures, birds, and fishes; and so it was done. [48]The dumb and lifeless water produced living creatures, as it was commanded, so that therefore the nations might declare your wondrous works.

49 "Then you kept in existence two living creatures;[w] the one you called Behemoth[x] and the name of the other Leviathan. [50]And you separated one from the other, for the seventh part where the water had been gathered together could not hold them both. [51]And you gave Behemoth[x] one of the parts that had been dried up on the third day, to live in it, where there are a thousand mountains; [52]but to Leviathan you gave the seventh part, the watery part; and you have kept them to be eaten by whom you wish, and when you wish.

53 "On the sixth day you commanded the earth to bring forth before you cattle, wild animals, and creeping things; [54]and over these you placed Adam, as ruler over all the works that you had made; and from him we have all come, the people whom you have chosen.

Why Do God's People Suffer?

55 "All this I have spoken before you, O Lord, because you have said that it was for us that you created this world.[y] [56]As for the other nations that have descended from Adam, you have said that they are nothing, and that they are like spittle, and you have compared their abundance to a drop from a bucket. [57]And now, O Lord, these nations, which are reputed to be as nothing, domineer over us and devour us. [58]But we your

---

[s] Syr Ethiop Compare Arab Arm: Meaning of Lat uncertain   [t] Syr Compare Ethiop: Meaning of Lat uncertain   [u] Syr Ethiop Arab 1 Arm: Lat adds *by day*   [v] Syr Ethiop: Lat *was not yet from you*   [w] Syr Ethiop: Lat *two souls*   [x] Other Lat authorities read *Enoch*   [y] Syr Ethiop Arab 2: Lat *the firstborn world* Compare Arab 1 *first world*

213

people, whom you have called your first-born, only begotten, zealous for you,[z] and most dear, have been given into their hands. [59]If the world has indeed been created for us, why do we not possess our world as an inheritance? How long will this be so?"

Response to Ezra's Questions

7 When I had finished speaking these words, the angel who had been sent to me on the former nights was sent to me again. [2]He said to me, "Rise, Ezra, and listen to the words that I have come to speak to you."

3 I said, "Speak, my lord." And he said to me, "There is a sea set in a wide expanse so that it is deep and vast, [4]but it has an entrance set in a narrow place, so that it is like a river. [5]If there are those who wish to reach the sea, to look at it or to navigate it, how can they come to the broad part unless they pass through the narrow part? [6]Another example: There is a city built and set on a plain, and it is full of all good things; [7]but the entrance to it is narrow and set in a precipitous place, so that there is fire on the right hand and deep water on the left. [8]There is only one path lying between them, that is, between the fire and the water, so that only one person can walk on the path. [9]If now the city is given to someone as an inheritance, how will the heir receive the inheritance unless by passing through the appointed danger?"

10 I said, "That is right, lord." He said to me, "So also is Israel's portion. [11]For I made the world for their sake, and when Adam transgressed my statutes, what had been made was judged. [12]And so the entrances of this world were made narrow and sorrowful and toilsome; they are few and evil, full of dangers and involved in great hardships. [13]But the entrances of the greater world are broad and safe, and yield the fruit of immortality. [14]Therefore unless the living pass through the difficult and futile experiences, they can never receive those things that have been reserved for them. [15]Now therefore why are you disturbed, seeing that you are to perish? Why are you moved, seeing that you are mortal? [16]Why have you not considered in your mind what is to come, rather than what is now present?"

The Fate of the Ungodly

17 Then I answered and said, "O sovereign Lord, you have ordained in your law that the righteous shall inherit these things, but that the ungodly shall perish. [18]The righteous, therefore, can endure difficult circumstances while hoping for easier ones; but those who have done wickedly have suffered the difficult circumstances and will never see the easier ones."

19 He said to me, "You are not a better judge than the Lord,[a] or wiser than the Most High! [20]Let many perish who are now living, rather than that the law of God that is set before them be disregarded! [21]For the Lord[b] strictly commanded those who came into the world, when they came, what they should do to live, and what they should observe to avoid punishment. [22]Nevertheless they were not obedient, and spoke against him;

they devised for themselves vain thoughts,

23   and proposed to themselves wicked frauds;

they even declared that the Most High does not exist,

and they ignored his ways.

24 They scorned his law,

and denied his covenants;

they have been unfaithful to his statutes,

and have not performed his works.

[25]That is the reason, Ezra, that empty things are for the empty, and full things are for the full.

The Temporary Messianic Kingdom

26 "For indeed the time will come, when the signs that I have foretold to you will come to pass, that the city that now is not seen shall appear,[c] and the land that now is hidden shall be disclosed. [27]Everyone who has been delivered from the evils that I have foretold shall see my wonders. [28]For my son the Messiah[d] shall be revealed with those who are with him, and those who remain shall rejoice four hundred years. [29]After those years my son the Messiah shall die, and all who draw human breath.[e] [30]Then

---

[z] Meaning of Lat uncertain   [a] Other ancient authorities read *God*; Ethiop Georg *the only One*   [b] Other ancient authorities read *God*   [c] Arm: Lat Syr *that the bride shall appear, even the city appearing*   [d] Syr Arab 1: Ethiop *my Messiah*; Arab 2 *the Messiah*; Arm *the Messiah of God*; Lat *my son Jesus*   [e] Arm *all who have continued in faith and in patience*

the world shall be turned back to primeval silence for seven days, as it was at the first beginnings, so that no one shall be left. [31]After seven days the world that is not yet awake shall be roused, and that which is corruptible shall perish. [32]The earth shall give up those who are asleep in it, and the dust those who rest there in silence; and the chambers shall give up the souls that have been committed to them. [33]The Most High shall be revealed on the seat of judgment, and compassion shall pass away, and patience shall be withdrawn.*f* [34]Only judgment shall remain, truth shall stand, and faithfulness shall grow strong. [35]Recompense shall follow, and the reward shall be manifested; righteous deeds shall awake, and unrighteous deeds shall not sleep.*g* [36] The pit*h* of torment shall appear, and opposite it shall be the place of rest; and the furnace of hell*i* shall be disclosed, and opposite it the paradise of delight. [37] Then the Most High will say to the nations that have been raised from the dead, 'Look now, and understand whom you have denied, whom you have not served, whose commandments you have despised. [38] Look on this side and on that; here are delight and rest, and there are fire and torments.' Thus he will*j* speak to them on the day of judgment— [39] a day that has no sun or moon or stars, [40] or cloud or thunder or lightning, or wind or water or air, or darkness or evening or morning, [41] or summer or spring or heat or winter*k* or frost or cold, or hail or rain or dew, [42] or noon or night, or dawn or shining or brightness or light, but only the splendor of the glory of the Most High, by which all shall see what has been destined. [43] It will last as though for a week of years. [44] This is my judgment and its prescribed order; and to you alone I have shown these things."

Only a Few Will Be Saved

45 I answered and said, "O sovereign Lord, I said then and*l* I say now: Blessed are those who are alive and keep your commandments! [46] But what of those for whom I prayed? For who among the living is there

that has not sinned, or who is there among mortals that has not transgressed your covenant? [47] And now I see that the world to come will bring delight to few, but torments to many. [48] For an evil heart has grown up in us, which has alienated us from God,*m* and has brought us into corruption and the ways of death, and has shown us the paths of perdition and removed us far from life—and that not merely for a few but for almost all who have been created."

49 He answered me and said, "Listen to me, Ezra,*n* and I will instruct you, and will admonish you once more. [50] For this reason the Most High has made not one world but two. [51] Inasmuch as you have said that the righteous are not many but few, while the ungodly abound, hear the explanation for this.

52 "If you have just a few precious stones, will you add to them lead and clay?"*o* [53] I said, "Lord, how could that be?" [54] And he said to me, "Not only that, but ask the earth and she will tell you; defer to her, and she will declare it to you. [55] Say to her, 'You produce gold and silver and bronze, and also iron and lead and clay; [56]but silver is more abundant than gold, and bronze than silver, and iron than bronze, and lead than iron, and clay than lead.' [57]Judge therefore which things are precious and desirable, those that are abundant or those that are rare?"

58 I said, "O sovereign Lord, what is plentiful is of less worth, for what is more rare is more precious."

59 He answered me and said, "Consider within yourself*p* what you have thought, for the person who has what is hard to get rejoices more than the person who has what is plentiful. [60] So also will be the judgment*q* that I have promised; for I will rejoice over the few who shall be saved, because it is they who have made my glory to prevail now, and through them my name has now been honored. [61] I will not grieve over the great number of those who perish; for it is they who are now like a mist, and are similar to a flame and smoke—they are set on fire and burn hotly, and are extinguished."

---

f Lat *shall gather together* *g* The passage from verse 36 to verse 105, formerly missing, has been restored to the text *h* Syr Ethiop: Lat *place* *i* Lat Syr Ethiop *Gehenna* *j* Syr Ethiop Arab 1: Lat *you shall* *k* Or *storm* *l* Syr: Lat *And I answered, "I said then, O Lord, and* *m* Cn: Lat Syr Ethiop *from these* *n* Syr Arab 1 Georg: Lat Ethiop lack *Ezra* *o* Arab 1: Meaning of Lat Syr Ethiop uncertain *p* Syr Ethiop Arab 1: Meaning of Lat uncertain *q* Syr Arab 1: Lat *creation*

Lamentation of Ezra, with Response

62 I replied and said, "O earth, what have you brought forth, if the mind is made out of the dust like the other created things? 63 For it would have been better if the dust itself had not been born, so that the mind might not have been made from it. 64 But now the mind grows with us, and therefore we are tormented, because we perish and we know it. 65 Let the human race lament, but let the wild animals of the field be glad; let all who have been born lament, but let the cattle and the flocks rejoice. 66 It is much better with them than with us; for they do not look for a judgment, and they do not know of any torment or salvation promised to them after death. 67 What does it profit us that we shall be preserved alive but cruelly tormented? 68 For all who have been born are entangled in[r] iniquities, and are full of sins and burdened with transgressions. 69 And if after death we were not to come into judgment, perhaps it would have been better for us."

70 He answered me and said, "When the Most High made the world and Adam and all who have come from him, he first prepared the judgment and the things that pertain to the judgment. 71 But now, understand from your own words—for you have said that the mind grows with us. 72For this reason, therefore, those who live on earth shall be tormented, because though they had understanding, they committed iniquity; and though they received the commandments, they did not keep them; and though they obtained the law, they dealt unfaithfully with what they received. 73What, then, will they have to say in the judgment, or how will they answer in the last times? 74 How long the Most High has been patient with those who inhabit the world!—and not for their sake, but because of the times that he has foreordained."

State of the Dead before Judgment

75 I answered and said, "If I have found favor in your sight, O Lord, show this also to your servant: whether after death, as soon as everyone of us yields up the soul, we shall be kept in rest until those times come when you will renew the creation, or whether we shall be tormented at once?"

76 He answered me and said, "I will show you that also, but do not include yourself with those who have shown scorn, or number yourself among those who are tormented. 77 For you have a treasure of works stored up with the Most High, but it will not be shown to you until the last times. 78 Now concerning death, the teaching is: When the decisive decree has gone out from the Most High that a person shall die, as the spirit leaves the body to return again to him who gave it, first of all it adores the glory of the Most High. 79 If it is one of those who have shown scorn and have not kept the way of the Most High, who have despised his law and hated those who fear God— 80 such spirits shall not enter into habitations, but shall immediately wander about in torments, always grieving and sad, in seven ways. 81 The first way, because they have scorned the law of the Most High. 82 The second way, because they cannot now make a good repentance so that they may live. 83 The third way, they shall see the reward laid up for those who have trusted the covenants of the Most High. 84 The fourth way, they shall consider the torment laid up for themselves in the last days. 85 The fifth way, they shall see how the habitations of the others are guarded by angels in profound quiet. 86 The sixth way, they shall see how some of them will cross over[s] into torments. 87 The seventh way, which is worse[t] than all the ways that have been mentioned, because they shall utterly waste away in confusion and be consumed with shame,[u] and shall wither with fear at seeing the glory of the Most High in whose presence they sinned while they were alive, and in whose presence they are to be judged in the last times.

88 "Now this is the order of those who have kept the ways of the Most High, when they shall be separated from their mortal body.[v] 89 During the time that they lived in it,[u] they laboriously served the Most High, and withstood danger every hour so that they might keep the law of the Lawgiver perfectly. 90 Therefore this is the teaching concerning them: 91 First of all, they shall see with great joy the glory of him who receives them, for they shall have rest in seven orders. 92 The first order, because they have striven with great effort to overcome the evil thought that was formed with them, so that it might not lead them astray from

---

[r] Syr *defiled with*   [s] Cn: Meaning of Lat uncertain   [t] Lat Syr Ethiop *greater*   [u] Syr Ethiop: Meaning of Lat uncertain   [v] Lat *the corruptible vessel*

life into death. *93* The second order, because they see the perplexity in which the souls of the ungodly wander and the punishment that awaits them. *94* The third order, they see the witness that he who formed them bears concerning them, that throughout their life they kept the law with which they were entrusted. *95* The fourth order, they understand the rest that they now enjoy, being gathered into their chambers and guarded by angels in profound quiet, and the glory waiting for them in the last days. *96* The fifth order, they rejoice that they have now escaped what is corruptible and shall inherit what is to come; and besides they see the straits and toil*ᵂ* from which they have been delivered, and the spacious liberty that they are to receive and enjoy in immortality. *97* The sixth order, when it is shown them how their face is to shine like the sun, and how they are to be made like the light of the stars, being incorruptible from then on. *98* The seventh order, which is greater than all that have been mentioned, because they shall rejoice with boldness, and shall be confident without confusion, and shall be glad without fear, for they press forward to see the face of him whom they served in life and from whom they are to receive their reward when glorified. *99* This is the order of the souls of the righteous, as henceforth is announced;*ˣ* and the previously mentioned are the ways of torment that those who would not give heed shall suffer hereafter."

100 Then I answered and said, "Will time therefore be given to the souls, after they have been separated from the bodies, to see what you have described to me?"

101 He said to me, "They shall have freedom for seven days, so that during these seven days they may see the things of which you have been told, and afterwards they shall be gathered in their habitations."

No Intercession for the Ungodly

102 I answered and said, "If I have found favor in your sight, show further to me, your servant, whether on the day of judgment the righteous will be able to intercede for the ungodly or to entreat the Most High for them— *103* fathers for sons or sons for parents, brothers for brothers, relatives for their kindred, or friends for those who are most dear."

104 He answered me and said, "Since you have found favor in my sight, I will show you this also. The day of judgment is decisive*ʸ* and displays to all the seal of truth. Just as now a father does not send his son, or a son his father, or a master his servant, or a friend his dearest friend, to be ill*ᶻ* or sleep or eat or be healed in his place, *105* so no one shall ever pray for another on that day, neither shall anyone lay a burden on another;*ᵃ* for then all shall bear their own righteousness and unrighteousness."

36 *106* I answered and said, "How then do we find that first Abraham prayed for the people of Sodom, and Moses for our ancestors who sinned in the desert, 37 *107* and Joshua after him for Israel in the days of Achan, 38 *108* and Samuel in the days of Saul,*ᵇ* and David for the plague, and Solomon for those at the dedication, 39 *109* and Elijah for those who received the rain, and for the one who was dead, that he might live, 40 *110* and Hezekiah for the people in the days of Sennacherib, and many others prayed for many? 41 *111* So if now, when corruption has increased and unrighteousness has multiplied, the righteous have prayed for the ungodly, why will it not be so then as well?"

42 *112* He answered me and said, "This present world is not the end; the full glory does not*ᶜ* remain in it;*ᵈ* therefore those who were strong prayed for the weak. 43 *113* But the day of judgment will be the end of this age and the beginning*ᵉ* of the immortal age to come, in which corruption has passed away, 44 *114* sinful indulgence has come to an end, unbelief has been cut off, and righteousness has increased and truth has appeared. 45 *115* Therefore no one will then be able to have mercy on someone who has been condemned in the judgment, or to harm*ᶠ* someone who is victorious."

Lamentation over the Fate of Most People

46 *116* I answered and said, "This is my first and last comment: it would have been better if the earth had not produced Adam, or else, when it had produced him, had

ᵂ Syr Ethiop: Lat *fullness*   *ˣ* Syr: Meaning of Lat uncertain   *ʸ* Lat *bold*   *ᶻ* Syr Ethiop Arm: Lat *to understand*   *ᵃ* Syr Ethiop: Lat lacks *on that . . . another*   *ᵇ* Syr Ethiop Arab 1: Lat Arab 2 Arm lack *in the days of Saul*   *ᶜ* Lat lacks *not*   *ᵈ* Or *the glory does not continuously abide in it*   *ᵉ* Syr Ethiop: Lat lacks *the beginning*   *ᶠ* Syr Ethiop: Lat *overwhelm*

restrained him from sinning. [47] [117] For what good is it to all that they live in sorrow now and expect punishment after death? [48] [118] O Adam, what have you done? For though it was you who sinned, the fall was not yours alone, but ours also who are your descendants. [49] [119] For what good is it to us, if an immortal time has been promised to us, but we have done deeds that bring death? [50] [120] And what good is it that an everlasting hope has been promised to us, but we have miserably failed? [51] [121] Or that safe and healthful habitations have been reserved for us, but we have lived wickedly? [52] [122] Or that the glory of the Most High will defend those who have led a pure life, but we have walked in the most wicked ways? [53] [123] Or that a paradise shall be revealed, whose fruit remains unspoiled and in which are abundance and healing, but we shall not enter it [54] [124] because we have lived in perverse ways?[g] [55] [125] Or that the faces of those who practiced self-control shall shine more than the stars, but our faces shall be blacker than darkness? [56] [126] For while we lived and committed iniquity we did not consider what we should suffer after death."

[57] [127] He answered and said, "This is the significance of the contest that all who are born on earth shall wage: [58] [128] if they are defeated they shall suffer what you have said, but if they are victorious they shall receive what I have said.[h] [59] [129] For this is the way of which Moses, while he was alive, spoke to the people, saying, 'Choose life for yourself, so that you may live!' [60] [130] But they did not believe him or the prophets after him, or even myself who have spoken to them. [61] [131] Therefore there shall not be[i] grief at their destruction, so much as joy over those to whom salvation is assured."

Ezra Appeals to God's Mercy

[62] [132] I answered and said, "I know, O Lord, that the Most High is now called merciful, because he has mercy on those who have not yet come into the world; [63] [133] and gracious, because he is gracious to those who turn in repentance to his law; [64] [134] and patient, because he shows patience toward those who have sinned, since they are his own creatures; [65] [135] and bountiful, because he would rather give than take

away;[j] [66] [136] and abundant in compassion, because he makes his compassions abound more and more to those now living and to those who are gone and to those yet to come— [67] [137] for if he did not make them abound, the world with those who inhabit it would not have life— [68] [138] and he is called the giver, because if he did not give out of his goodness so that those who have committed iniquities might be relieved of them, not one ten-thousandth of humankind could have life; [69] [139] and the judge, because if he did not pardon those who were created by his word and blot out the multitude of their sins,[k] [70] [140] there would probably be left only very few of the innumerable multitude."

8 He answered me and said, "The Most High made this world for the sake of many, but the world to come for the sake of only a few. [2]But I tell you a parable, Ezra. Just as, when you ask the earth, it will tell you that it provides a large amount of clay from which earthenware is made, but only a little dust from which gold comes, so is the course of the present world. [3]Many have been created, but only a few shall be saved."

Ezra Again Appeals to God's Mercy

[4] I answered and said, "Then drink your fill of understanding,[l] O my soul, and drink wisdom, O my heart. [5]For not of your own will did you come into the world,[m] and against your will you depart, for you have been given only a short time to live. [6]O Lord above us, grant to your servant that we may pray before you, and give us a seed for our heart and cultivation of our understanding so that fruit may be produced, by which every mortal who bears the likeness[n] of a human being may be able to live. [7]For you alone exist, and we are a work of your hands, as you have declared. [8]And because you give life to the body that is now fashioned in the womb, and furnish it with members, what you have created is preserved amid fire and water, and for nine months the womb[o] endures your creature that has been created in it. [9]But that which keeps and that which is kept shall both be kept by your keeping.[m] And when the womb gives up again what has been created in it, [10]you have commanded that from the

---

[g] Cn: Lat Syr *places*   [h] Syr Ethiop Arab 1: Lat *what I say*   [i] Syr: Lat *there was not*   [j] Or *he is ready to give according to requests*   [k] Lat *contempts*   [l] Syr: Lat *Then release understanding*   [m] Syr: Meaning of Lat uncertain   [n] Syr: Lat *place*   [o] Lat *what you have formed*

members themselves (that is, from the breasts) milk, the fruit of the breasts, should be supplied, [11]so that what has been fashioned may be nourished for a time; and afterwards you will still guide it in your mercy. [12]You have nurtured it in your righteousness, and instructed it in your law, and reproved it in your wisdom. [13]You put it to death as your creation, and make it live as your work. [14]If then you will suddenly and quickly[p] destroy what with so great labor was fashioned by your command, to what purpose was it made? [15]And now I will speak out: About all humankind you know best; but I will speak about your people, for whom I am grieved, [16]and about your inheritance, for whom I lament, and about Israel, for whom I am sad, and about the seed of Jacob, for whom I am troubled. [17]Therefore I will pray before you for myself and for them, for I see the failings of us who inhabit the earth; [18]and now also[q] I have heard of the swiftness of the judgment that is to come. [19]Therefore hear my voice and understand my words, and I will speak before you."

Ezra's Prayer

The beginning of the words of Ezra's prayer,[r] before he was taken up. He said: [20]"O Lord, you who inhabit eternity,[s] whose eyes are exalted[t] and whose upper chambers are in the air, [21]whose throne is beyond measure and whose glory is beyond comprehension, before whom the hosts of angels stand trembling [22]and at whose command they are changed to wind and fire,[u] whose word is sure and whose utterances are certain, whose command is strong and whose ordinance is terrible, [23]whose look dries up the depths and whose indignation makes the mountains melt away, and whose truth is established[v] forever— [24]hear, O Lord, the prayer of your servant, and give ear to the petition of your creature; attend to my words. [25]For as long as I live I will speak, and as long as I have understanding I will answer. [26]O do not look on the sins of your people, but on those who serve you in truth. [27]Do not take note of the endeavors of those who act wickedly, but of the endeavors of those

who have kept your covenants amid afflictions. [28]Do not think of those who have lived wickedly in your sight, but remember those who have willingly acknowledged that you are to be feared. [29]Do not will the destruction of those who have the ways of cattle, but regard those who have gloriously taught your law.[w] [30]Do not be angry with those who are deemed worse than wild animals, but love those who have always put their trust in your glory. [31]For we and our ancestors have passed our lives in ways that bring death;[x] but it is because of us sinners that you are called merciful. [32]For if you have desired to have pity on us, who have no works of righteousness, then you will be called merciful. [33]For the righteous, who have many works laid up with you, shall receive their reward in consequence of their own deeds. [34]But what are mortals, that you are angry with them; or what is a corruptible race, that you are so bitter against it? [35]For in truth there is no one among those who have been born who has not acted wickedly; among those who have existed[y] there is no one who has not done wrong. [36]For in this, O Lord, your righteousness and goodness will be declared, when you are merciful to·those who have no store of good works."

Response to Ezra's Prayer

37 He answered me and said, "Some things you have spoken rightly, and it will turn out according to your words. [38]For indeed I will not concern myself about the fashioning of those who have sinned, or about their death, their judgment, or their destruction; [39]but I will rejoice over the creation of the righteous, over their pilgrimage also, and their salvation, and their receiving their reward. [40]As I have spoken, therefore, so it shall be.

41 "For just as the farmer sows many seeds in the ground and plants a multitude of seedlings, and yet not all that have been sown will come up[z] in due season, and not all that were planted will take root; so also those who have been sown in the world will not all be saved."

42 I answered and said, "If I have found

---

[p] Syr: Lat *will with a light command* [q] Syr: Lat *but* [r] Syr Ethiop; Lat *beginning of Ezra's words* [s] Or *you who abide forever* [t] Another Lat text reads *whose are the highest heavens* [u] Syr: Lat *they whose service takes the form of wind and fire* [v] Arab 2: Other authorities read *truth bears witness* [w] Syr *have received the brightness of your law* [x] Syr Ethiop: Meaning of Lat uncertain [y] Syr: Meaning of Lat uncertain [z] Syr Ethiop *will live; Lat will be saved*

favor in your sight, let me speak. [43]If the farmer's seed does not come up, because it has not received your rain in due season, or if it has been ruined by too much rain, it perishes.[a] [44]But people, who have been formed by your hands and are called your own image because they are made like you, and for whose sake you have formed all things—have you also made them like the farmer's seed? [45]Surely not, O Lord[b] above! But spare your people and have mercy on your inheritance, for you have mercy on your own creation."

Ezra's Final Appeal for Mercy

46 He answered me and said, "Things that are present are for those who live now, and things that are future are for those who will live hereafter. [47]For you come far short of being able to love my creation more than I love it. But you have often compared yourself[c] to the unrighteous. Never do so! [48]But even in this respect you will be praiseworthy before the Most High, [49]because you have humbled yourself, as is becoming for you, and have not considered yourself to be among the righteous. You will receive the greatest glory, [50]for many miseries will affect those who inhabit the world in the last times, because they have walked in great pride. [51]But think of your own case, and inquire concerning the glory of those who are like yourself, [52]because it is for you that paradise is opened, the tree of life is planted, the age to come is prepared, plenty is provided, a city is built, rest is appointed,[d] goodness is established and wisdom perfected beforehand. [53]The root of evil[e] is sealed up from you, illness is banished from you, and death[f] is hidden; Hades has fled and corruption has been forgotten;[g] [54]sorrows have passed away, and in the end the treasure of immortality is made manifest. [55]Therefore do not ask any more questions about the great number of those who perish. [56]For when they had opportunity to choose, they despised the Most High, and were contemptuous of his law, and abandoned his ways. [57]Moreover, they have even trampled on his righteous ones, [58]and said in their hearts that there is no God—though

they knew well that they must die. [59]For just as the things that I have predicted await[h] you, so the thirst and torment that are prepared await them. For the Most High did not intend that anyone should be destroyed; [60]but those who were created have themselves defiled the name of him who made them, and have been ungrateful to him who prepared life for them now. [61]Therefore my judgment is now drawing near; [62]I have not shown this to all people, but only to you and a few like you."

Then I answered and said, [63]"O Lord, you have already shown me a great number of the signs that you will do in the last times, but you have not shown me when you will do them."

More about the Signs of the End

9 He answered me and said, "Measure carefully in your mind, and when you see that some of the predicted signs have occurred, [2]then you will know that it is the very time when the Most High is about to visit the world that he has made. [3]So when there shall appear in the world earthquakes, tumult of peoples, intrigues of nations, wavering of leaders, confusion of princes, [4]then you will know that it was of these that the Most High spoke from the days that were of old, from the beginning. [5]For just as with everything that has occurred in the world, the beginning is evident,[i] and the end manifest; [6]so also are the times of the Most High: the beginnings are manifest in wonders and mighty works, and the end in penalties[j] and in signs.

7 "It shall be that all who will be saved and will be able to escape on account of their works, or on account of the faith by which they have believed, [8]will survive the dangers that have been predicted, and will see my salvation in my land and within my borders, which I have sanctified for myself from the beginning. [9]Then those who have now abused my ways shall be amazed, and those who have rejected them with contempt shall live in torments. [10]For as many as did not acknowledge me in their lifetime, though they received my benefits, [11]and as many as scorned my law while they still

---

[a] Cn: Compare Syr Arab 1 Arm Georg 2: Meaning of Lat uncertain   [b] Ethiop Arab Compare Syr: Lat lacks *O Lord*   [c] Syr Ethiop: Lat *brought yourself near*   [d] Syr Ethiop: Lat *allowed*   [e] Lat lacks *of evil*   [f] Syr Ethiop Arm: Lat lacks *death*   [g] Syr: Lat *Hades and corruption have fled into oblivion*; or *corruption has fled into Hades to be forgotten*   [h] Syr: Lat *will receive*   [i] Syr: Ethiop *is in the word*; Meaning of Lat uncertain   [j] Syr: Lat Ethiop *in effects*

had freedom, and did not understand but despised it[k] while an opportunity of repentance was still open to them, [12]these must in torment acknowledge it[k] after death. [13]Therefore, do not continue to be curious about how the ungodly will be punished; but inquire how the righteous will be saved, those to whom the age belongs and for whose sake the age was made."[l]

The Argument Recapitulated

14 I answered and said, [15]"I said before, and I say now, and will say it again: there are more who perish than those who will be saved, [16]as a wave is greater than a drop of water."

17 He answered me and said, "As is the field, so is the seed; and as are the flowers, so are the colors; and as is the work, so is the product; and as is the farmer, so is the threshing floor. [18]For there was a time in this age when I was preparing for those who now exist, before the world was made for them to live in, and no one opposed me then, for no one existed; [19]but now those who have been created in this world, which is supplied both with an unfailing table and an inexhaustible pasture,[m] have become corrupt in their ways. [20]So I considered my world, and saw that it was lost. I saw that my earth was in peril because of the devices of those who[n] had come into it. [21]And I saw and spared some[o] with great difficulty, and saved for myself one grape out of a cluster, and one plant out of a great forest.[p] [22]So let the multitude perish that has been born in vain, but let my grape and my plant be saved, because with much labor I have perfected them.

23 "Now, if you will let seven days more pass—do not, however, fast during them, [24]but go into a field of flowers where no house has been built, and eat only of the flowers of the field, and taste no meat and drink no wine, but eat only flowers—[25]and pray to the Most High continually, then I will come and talk with you."

The Abiding Glory of the Mosaic Law

26 So I went, as he directed me, into the field that is called Ardat;[q] there I sat among the flowers and ate of the plants of the field,

and the nourishment they afforded satisfied me. [27]After seven days, while I lay on the grass, my heart was troubled again as it was before. [28]Then my mouth was opened, and I began to speak before the Most High, and said, [29]"O Lord, you showed yourself among us, to our ancestors in the wilderness when they came out from Egypt and when they came into the untrodden and unfruitful wilderness; [30]and you said, 'Hear me, O Israel, and give heed to my words, O descendants of Jacob. [31]For I sow my law in you, and it shall bring forth fruit in you, and you shall be glorified through it forever.' [32]But though our ancestors received the law, they did not keep it and did not observe the[r] statutes; yet the fruit of the law did not perish—for it could not, because it was yours. [33]Yet those who received it perished, because they did not keep what had been sown in them. [34]Now this is the general rule that, when the ground was received seed, or the sea a ship, or any dish food or drink, and when it comes about that what was sown or what was launched or what was put in is destroyed, [35]they are destroyed, but the things that held them remain; yet with us it has not been so. [36]For we who have received the law and sinned will perish, as well as our hearts that received it; [37]the law, however, does not perish but survives in its glory."

The Vision of a Weeping Woman

38 When I said these things in my heart, I looked around,[s] and on my right I saw a woman; she was mourning and weeping with a loud voice, and was deeply grieved at heart; her clothes were torn, and there were ashes on her head. [39]Then I dismissed the thoughts with which I had been engaged, and turned to her [40]and said to her, "Why are you weeping, and why are you grieved at heart?"

41 She said to me, "Let me alone, my lord, so that I may weep for myself and continue to mourn, for I am greatly embittered in spirit and deeply distressed."

42 I said to her, "What has happened to you? Tell me."

43 And she said to me, "Your servant was barren and had no child, though I lived with my husband for thirty years. [44]Every

---

[k] Or me   [l] Syr: Lat *saved, and whose is the age and for whose sake the age was made and when*   [m] Cn: Lat *law*
[n] Cn: Lat *devices that*   [o] Lat *them*   [p] Syr Ethiop Arab 1: Lat *tribe*   [q] Syr Ethiop *Arpad*; Arm *Ardab*   [r] Lat *my*
[s] Syr Arab Arm: Lat *I looked about me with my eyes*

221

hour and every day during those thirty years I prayed to the Most High, night and day. [45]And after thirty years God heard your servant, and looked upon my low estate, and considered my distress, and gave me a son. I rejoiced greatly over him, I and my husband and all my neighbors;[t] and we gave great glory to the Mighty One. [46]And I brought him up with much care. [47]So when he grew up and I came to take a wife for him, I set a day for the marriage feast.

10 "But it happened that when my son entered his wedding chamber, he fell down and died. [2]So all of us put out our lamps, and all my neighbors[t] attempted to console me; I remained quiet until the evening of the second day. [3]But when all of them had stopped consoling me, encouraging me to be quiet, I got up in the night and fled, and I came to this field, as you see. [4]And now I intend not to return to the town, but to stay here; I will neither eat nor drink, but will mourn and fast continually until I die."

5 Then I broke off the reflections with which I was still engaged, and answered her in anger and said, [6]"You most foolish of women, do you not see our mourning, and what has happened to us? [7]For Zion, the mother of us all, is in deep grief and great distress. [8]It is most appropriate to mourn now, because we are all mourning, and to be sorrowful, because we are all sorrowing; you are sorrowing for one son, but we, the whole world, for our mother.[u] [9]Now ask the earth, and she will tell you that it is she who ought to mourn over so many who have come into being upon her. [10]From the beginning all have been born of her, and others will come; and, lo, almost all go[v] to perdition, and a multitude of them will come to doom. [11]Who then ought to mourn the more, she who lost so great a multitude, or you who are grieving for one alone? [12]But if you say to me, 'My lamentation is not like the earth's, for I have lost the fruit of my womb, which I brought forth in pain and bore in sorrow; [13]but it is with the earth according to the way of the earth—the multitude that is now in it goes as it came'; [14]then I say to you, 'Just as you brought forth in sorrow, so the earth also has from the beginning given her fruit, that is, humankind, to him who made her.'

[15]Now, therefore, keep your sorrow to yourself, and bear bravely the troubles that have come upon you. [16]For if you acknowledge the decree of God to be just, you will receive your son back in due time, and will be praised among women. [17]Therefore go into the town to your husband."

18 She said to me, "I will not do so; I will not go into the city, but I will die here."

19 So I spoke again to her, and said, [20]"Do not do that, but let yourself be persuaded—for how many are the adversities of Zion?—and be consoled because of the sorrow of Jerusalem. [21]For you see how our sanctuary has been laid waste, our altar thrown down, our temple destroyed; [22]our harp has been laid low, our song has been silenced, and our rejoicing has been ended; the light of our lampstand has been put out, the ark of our covenant has been plundered, our holy things have been polluted, and the name by which we are called has been almost profaned; our children[w] have suffered abuse, our priests have been burned to death, our Levites have gone into exile, our virgins have been defiled, and our wives have been ravished; our righteous men[x] have been carried off, our little ones have been cast out, our young men have been enslaved and our strong men made powerless. [23]And, worst of all, the seal of Zion has been deprived of its glory, and given over into the hands of those that hate us. [24]Therefore shake off your great sadness and lay aside your many sorrows, so that the Mighty One may be merciful to you again, and the Most High may give you rest, a respite from your troubles."

25 While I was talking to her, her face suddenly began to shine exceedingly; her countenance flashed like lightning, so that I was too frightened to approach her, and my heart was terrified. While[y] I was wondering what this meant, [26]she suddenly uttered a loud and fearful cry, so that the earth shook at the sound. [27]When I looked up, the woman was no longer visible to me, but a city was being built,[z] and a place of huge foundations showed itself. I was afraid, and cried with a loud voice and said, [28]"Where is the angel Uriel, who came to me at first? For it was he who brought me into this overpowering bewilderment; my end has become corruption, and my prayer a reproach."

---

[t] Literally *all my citizens*   [u] Compare Syr: Meaning of Lat uncertain   [v] Literally *walk*   [w] Ethiop *free men*
[x] Syr *our seers*   [y] Syr Ethiop Arab 1: Lat lacks *I was too . . . terrified. While*   [z] Lat: Syr Ethiop Arab 1 Arab 2 Arm *but there was an established city*

Uriel's Interpretation of the Vision

29 While I was speaking these words, the angel who had come to me at first came to me, and when he saw me ³⁰lying there like a corpse, deprived of my understanding, he grasped my right hand and strengthened me and set me on my feet, and said to me, ³¹"What is the matter with you? And why are you troubled? And why are your understanding and the thoughts of your mind troubled?"

32 I said, "It was because you abandoned me. I did as you directed, and went out into the field, and lo, what I have seen, and can still see, I am unable to explain."

33 He said to me, "Stand up like a man, and I will instruct you."

34 I said, "Speak, my lord; only do not forsake me, so that I may not die before my time.ᵃ ³⁵For I have seen what I did not know, and I hearᵇ what I do not understand ³⁶—or is my mind deceived, and my soul dreaming? ³⁷Now therefore I beg you to give your servant an explanation of this bewildering vision."

38 He answered me and said, "Listen to me, and I will teach you, and tell you about the things that you fear; for the Most High has revealed many secrets to you. ³⁹He has seen your righteous conduct, and that you have sorrowed continually for your people and mourned greatly over Zion. ⁴⁰This therefore is the meaning of the vision. ⁴¹The woman who appeared to you a little while ago, whom you saw mourning and whom you began to console ⁴²(you do not now see the form of a woman, but there appeared to you a city being built)ᶜ ⁴³and who told you about the misfortune of her son—this is the interpretation: ⁴⁴The woman whom you saw is Zion, which you now behold as a city being built.ᵈ ⁴⁵And as for her telling you that she was barren for thirty years, the reason is that there were three thousandᵉ years in the world before any offering was offered in it.ᶠ ⁴⁶And after three thousandᵍ years Solomon built the city, and offered offerings; then it was that the barren woman bore a son. ⁴⁷And as for her telling you that she brought him up with much care, that was the period of residence in Jerusalem. ⁴⁸And as for her saying to you, 'My son died as he entered his

wedding chamber,' and that misfortune had overtaken her,ʰ this was the destruction that befell Jerusalem. ⁴⁹So you saw her likeness, how she mourned for her son, and you began to console her for what had happened.ⁱ ⁵⁰For now the Most High, seeing that you are sincerely grieved and profoundly distressed for her, has shown you the brilliance of her glory, and the loveliness of her beauty. ⁵¹Therefore I told you to remain in the field where no house had been built, ⁵²for I knew that the Most High would reveal these things to you. ⁵³Therefore I told you to go into the field where there was no foundation of any building, ⁵⁴because no work of human construction could endure in a place where the city of the Most High was to be revealed.

55 "Therefore do not be afraid, and do not let your heart be terrified; but go in and see the splendor orʲ the vastness of the building, as far as it is possible for your eyes to see it, ⁵⁶and afterward you will hear as much as your ears can hear. ⁵⁷For you are more blessed than many, and you have been called to be withᵏ the Most High as few have been. ⁵⁸But tomorrow night you shall remain here, ⁵⁹and the Most High will show you in those dream visions what the Most High will do to those who inhabit the earth in the last days."

So I slept that night and the following one, as he had told me.

The Vision of the Eagle

11 On the second night I had a dream: I saw rising from the sea an eagle that had twelve feathered wings and three heads. ²I saw it spread its wings overˡ the whole earth, and all the winds of heaven blew upon it, and the clouds were gathered around it.ᵐ ³I saw that out of its wings there grew opposing wings; but they became little, puny wings. ⁴But its heads were at rest; the middle head was larger than the other heads, but it too was at rest with them. ⁵Then I saw that the eagle flew with its wings, and it reigned over the earth and over those who inhabit it. ⁶And I saw how all things under heaven were subjected to

---

ᵃ Syr Ethiop Arab: Lat *die to no purpose*   ᵇ Other ancient authorities read *have heard*   ᶜ Lat: Syr Ethiop Arab 1 Arab 2 Arm *an established city*   ᵈ Cn: Lat *an established city*   ᵉ Most Lat Mss read *three*   ᶠ Cn: Lat Syr Arab Arm *her*   ᵍ Syr Ethiop Arab Arm: Lat *three*   ʰ Or *him*   ⁱ Most Lat Mss and Arab 1 add *These were the things to be opened to you*   ʲ Other ancient authorities read *and*   ᵏ Or *been named by*   ˡ Arab 2 Arm: Lat Syr Ethiop *in*   ᵐ Syr: Compare Ethiop Arab: Lat lacks *the clouds* and *around it*

it, and no one spoke against it—not a single creature that was on the earth. [7]Then I saw the eagle rise upon its talons, and it uttered a cry to its wings, saying, [8]"Do not all watch at the same time; let each sleep in its own place, and watch in its turn; [9]but let the heads be reserved for the last."

10 I looked again and saw that the voice did not come from its heads, but from the middle of its body. [11]I counted its rival wings, and there were eight of them. [12]As I watched, one wing on the right side rose up, and it reigned over all the earth. [13]And after a time its reign came to an end, and it disappeared, so that even its place was no longer visible. Then the next wing rose up and reigned, and it continued to reign a long time. [14]While it was reigning its end came also, so that it disappeared like the first. [15]And a voice sounded, saying to it, [16]"Listen to me, you who have ruled the earth all this time; I announce this to you before you disappear. [17]After you no one shall rule as long as you have ruled, not even half as long."

18 Then the third wing raised itself up, and held the rule as the earlier ones had done, and it also disappeared. [19]And so it went with all the wings; they wielded power one after another and then were never seen again. [20]I kept looking, and in due time the wings that followed[n] also rose up on the right[o] side, in order to rule. There were some of them that ruled, yet disappeared suddenly; [21]and others of them rose up, but did not hold the rule.

22 And after this I looked and saw that the twelve wings and the two little wings had disappeared, [23]and nothing remained on the eagle's body except the three heads that were at rest and six little wings.

24 As I kept looking I saw that two little wings separated from the six and remained under the head that was on the right side; but four remained in their place. [25]Then I saw that these little wings[p] planned to set themselves up and hold the rule. [26]As I kept looking, one was set up, but suddenly disappeared; [27]a second also, and this disappeared more quickly than the first. [28]While I continued to look the two that remained were planning between themselves to reign together; [29]and while they were planning, one of the heads that were at rest (the one that was in the middle) suddenly awoke; it

was greater than the other two heads. [30]And I saw how it allied the two heads with itself, [31]and how the head turned with those that were with it and devoured the two little wings[p] that were planning to reign. [32]Moreover this head gained control of the whole earth, and with much oppression dominated its inhabitants; it had greater power over the world than all the wings that had gone before.

33 After this I looked again and saw the head in the middle suddenly disappear, just as the wings had done. [34]But the two heads remained, which also in like manner ruled over the earth and its inhabitants. [35]And while I looked, I saw the head on the right side devour the one on the left.

A Lion Roused from the Forest

36 Then I heard a voice saying to me, "Look in front of you and consider what you see." [37]When I looked, I saw what seemed to be a lion roused from the forest, roaring; and I heard how it uttered a human voice to the eagle, and spoke, saying, [38]"Listen and I will speak to you. The Most High says to you, [39]'Are you not the one that remains of the four beasts that I had made to reign in my world, so that the end of my times might come through them? [40]You, the fourth that has come, have conquered all the beasts that have gone before; and you have held sway over the world with great terror, and over all the earth with grievous oppression; and for so long you have lived on the earth with deceit.[q] [41]You have judged the earth, but not with truth, [42]for you have oppressed the meek and injured the peaceable; you have hated those who tell the truth, and have loved liars; you have destroyed the homes of those who brought forth fruit, and have laid low the walls of those who did you no harm. [43]Your insolence has come up before the Most High, and your pride to the Mighty One. [44]The Most High has looked at his times; now they have ended, and his ages have reached completion. [45]Therefore you, eagle, will surely disappear, you and your terrifying wings, your most evil little wings, your malicious heads, your most evil talons, and your whole worthless body, [46]so that the whole earth, freed from your violence, may be refreshed and relieved, and may

---

[n] Syr Arab 2 *the little wings*   [o] Some Ethiop Mss read *left*   [p] Syr: Lat *underwings*   [q] Syr Arab Arm: Lat Ethiop *The fourth came, however, and conquered . . . and held sway . . . and for so long lived*

hope for the judgment and mercy of him who made it.' "

12 While the lion was saying these words to the eagle, I looked ²and saw that the remaining head had disappeared. The two wings that had gone over to it rose up and^r set themselves up to reign, and their reign was brief and full of tumult. ³When I looked again, they were already vanishing. The whole body of the eagle was burned, and the earth was exceedingly terrified.

Then I woke up in great perplexity of mind and great fear, and I said to my spirit, ⁴"You have brought this upon me, because you search out the ways of the Most High. ⁵I am still weary in mind and very weak in my spirit, and not even a little strength is left in me, because of the great fear with which I have been terrified tonight. ⁶Therefore I will now entreat the Most High that he may strengthen me to the end."

The Interpretation of the Vision

7 Then I said, "O sovereign Lord, if I have found favor in your sight, and if I have been accounted righteous before you beyond many others, and if my prayer has indeed come up before your face, ⁸strengthen me and show me, your servant, the interpretation and meaning of this terrifying vision so that you may fully comfort my soul. ⁹For you have judged me worthy to be shown the end of the times and the last events of the times."

10 He said to me, "This is the interpretation of this vision that you have seen: ¹¹The eagle that you saw coming up from the sea is the fourth kingdom that appeared in a vision to your brother Daniel. ¹²But it was not explained to him as I now explain to you or have explained it. ¹³The days are coming when a kingdom shall rise on earth, and it shall be more terrifying than all the kingdoms that have been before it. ¹⁴And twelve kings shall reign in it, one after another. ¹⁵But the second that is to reign shall hold sway for a longer time than any other one of the twelve. ¹⁶This is the interpretation of the twelve wings that you saw.

17 "As for your hearing a voice that spoke, coming not from the eagle's^s heads

but from the midst of its body, this is the interpretation: ¹⁸In the midst of^t the time of that kingdom great struggles shall arise, and it shall be in danger of falling; nevertheless it shall not fall then, but shall regain its former power.^u ¹⁹As for your seeing eight little wings^v clinging to its wings, this is the interpretation: ²⁰Eight kings shall arise in it, whose times shall be short and their years swift; ²¹two of them shall perish when the middle of its time draws near; and four shall be kept for the time when its end approaches, but two shall be kept until the end.

22 "As for your seeing three heads at rest, this is the interpretation: ²³In its last days the Most High will raise up three kings,^w and they^x shall renew many things in it, and shall rule the earth ²⁴and its inhabitants more oppressively than all who were before them. Therefore they are called the heads of the eagle, ²⁵because it is they who shall sum up his wickedness and perform his last actions. ²⁶As for your seeing that the large head disappeared, one of the kings^y shall die in his bed, but in agonies. ²⁷But as for the two who remained, the sword shall devour them. ²⁸For the sword of one shall devour him who was with him; but he also shall fall by the sword in the last days.

29 "As for your seeing two little wings^z passing over to^a the head which was on the right side, ³⁰this is the interpretation: It is these whom the Most High has kept for the eagle's^b end; this was the reign which was brief and full of tumult, as you have seen.

31 "And as for the lion whom you saw rousing up out of the forest and roaring and speaking to the eagle and reproving him for his unrighteousness, and as for all his words that you have heard, ³²this is the Messiah^c whom the Most High has kept until the end of days, who will arise from the offspring of David, and will come and speak^d with them. He will denounce them for their ungodliness and for their wickedness, and will display before them their contemptuous dealings. ³³For first he will bring them alive before his judgment seat, and when he has reproved them, then he will destroy them. ³⁴But in mercy he will set free the remnant of my people, those who have been saved

---

^r Ethiop: Lat lacks *rose up and*   ^s Lat *his*   ^t Syr Arm: Lat *After*   ^u Ethiop Arab 1 Arm: Lat Syr *its beginning*   ^v Syr: Lat *underwings*   ^w Syr Ethiop Arab Arm: Lat *kingdoms*   ^x Syr Ethiop Arm: Lat *he*   ^y Lat *them*   ^z Arab 1: Lat *underwings*   ^a Syr Ethiop: Lat lacks *to*   ^b Lat *his*   ^c Literally *anointed one*   ^d Syr: Lat lacks *of days . . . and speak*

throughout my borders, and he will make them joyful until the end comes, the day of judgment, of which I spoke to you at the beginning. [35]This is the dream that you saw, and this is its interpretation. [36]And you alone were worthy to learn this secret of the Most High. [37]Therefore write all these things that you have seen in a book, put it[e] in a hidden place; [38]and you shall teach them to the wise among your people, whose hearts you know are able to comprehend and keep these secrets. [39]But as for you, wait here seven days more, so that you may be shown whatever it pleases the Most High to show you." Then he left me.

The People Come to Ezra

40 When all the people heard that the seven days were past and I had not returned to the city, they all gathered together, from the least to the greatest, and came to me and spoke to me, saying, [41]"How have we offended you, and what harm have we done you, that you have forsaken us and sit in this place? [42]For of all the prophets you alone are left to us, like a cluster of grapes from the vintage, and like a lamp in a dark place, and like a haven for a ship saved from a storm. [43]Are not the disasters that have befallen us enough? [44]Therefore if you forsake us, how much better it would have been for us if we also had been consumed in the burning of Zion. [45]For we are no better than those who died there." And they wept with a loud voice.

Then I answered them and said, [46]"Take courage, O Israel; and do not be sorrowful, O house of Jacob; [47]for the Most High has you in remembrance, and the Mighty One has not forgotten you in your struggle. [48]As for me, I have neither forsaken you nor withdrawn from you; but I have come to this place to pray on account of the desolation of Zion, and to seek mercy on account of the humiliation of our[f] sanctuary. [49]Now go to your homes, every one of you, and after these days I will come to you." [50]So the people went into the city, as I told them to do. [51]But I sat in the field seven days, as the angel[g] had commanded me; and I ate only of the flowers of the field, and my food was of plants during those days.

The Man from the Sea

13 After seven days I dreamed a dream in the night. [2]And lo, a wind arose from the sea and stirred up[h] all its waves. [3]As I kept looking the wind made something like the figure of a man come up out of the heart of the sea. And I saw[i] that this man flew[j] with the clouds of heaven; and wherever he turned his face to look, everything under his gaze trembled, [4]and whenever his voice issued from his mouth, all who heard his voice melted as wax melts[k] when it feels the fire.

5 After this I looked and saw that an innumerable multitude of people were gathered together from the four winds of heaven to make war against the man who came up out of the sea. [6]And I looked and saw that he carved out for himself a great mountain, and flew up on to it. [7]And I tried to see the region or place from which the mountain was carved, but I could not.

8 After this I looked and saw that all who had gathered together against him, to wage war with him, were filled with fear, and yet they dared to fight. [9]When he saw the onrush of the approaching multitude, he neither lifted his hand nor held a spear or any weapon of war; [10]but I saw only how he sent forth from his mouth something like a stream of fire, and from his lips a flaming breath, and from his tongue he shot forth a storm of sparks.[l] [11]All these were mingled together, the stream of fire and the flaming breath and the great storm, and fell on the onrushing multitude that was prepared to fight, and burned up all of them, so that suddenly nothing was seen of the innumerable multitude but only the dust of ashes and the smell of smoke. When I saw it, I was amazed.

12 After this I saw the same man come down from the mountain and call to himself another multitude that was peaceable. [13]Then many people[m] came to him, some of whom were joyful and some sorrowful; some of them were bound, and some were bringing others as offerings.

The Interpretation of the Vision

Then I woke up in great terror, and prayed to the Most High, and said, [14]"From

---

[e] Ethiop Arab 1 Arab 2 Arm: Lat Syr *them*   [f] Syr Ethiop: Lat *your*   [g] Literally *he*   [h] Other ancient authorities read *I saw a wind arise from the sea and stir up*   [i] Syr: Lat lacks *the wind . . . I saw*   [j] Syr Ethiop Arab Arm: Lat *grew strong*   [k] Syr: Lat *burned as the earth rests*   [l] Meaning of Lat uncertain   [m] Lat Syr Arab 2 literally *the faces of many people*

the beginning you have shown your servant these wonders, and have deemed me worthy to have my prayer heard by you; [15]now show me the interpretation of this dream also. [16]For as I consider it in my mind, alas for those who will be left in those days! And still more, alas for those who are not left! [17]For those who are not left will be sad [18]because they understand the things that are reserved for the last days, but cannot attain them. [19]But alas for those also who are left, and for that very reason! For they shall see great dangers and much distress, as these dreams show. [20]Yet it is better" to come into these things,[o] though incurring peril, than to pass from the world like a cloud, and not to see what will happen in the last days."

He answered me and said, [21]"I will tell you the interpretation of the vision, and I will also explain to you the things that you have mentioned. [22]As for what you said about those who survive, and concerning those who do not survive,[p] this is the interpretation: [23]The one who brings the peril at that time will protect those who fall into peril, who have works and faith toward the Almighty. [24]Understand therefore that those who are left are more blessed than those who have died.

25 "This is the interpretation of the vision: As for your seeing a man come up from the heart of the sea, [26]this is he whom the Most High has been keeping for many ages, who will himself deliver his creation; and he will direct those who are left. [27]And as for your seeing wind and fire and a storm coming out of his mouth, [28]and as for his not holding a spear or weapon of war, yet destroying the onrushing multitude that came to conquer him, this is the interpretation: [29]The days are coming when the Most High will deliver those who are on the earth. [30]And bewilderment of mind shall come over those who inhabit the earth. [31]They shall plan to make war against one another, city against city, place against place, people against people, and kingdom against kingdom. [32]When these things take place and the signs occur that I showed you before, then my Son will be revealed, whom you saw as a man coming up from the sea.[q]

33 "Then, when all the nations hear his voice, all the nations shall leave their own lands and the warfare that they have against one another; [34]and an innumerable multitude shall be gathered together, as you saw, wishing to come and conquer him. [35]But he shall stand on the top of Mount Zion. [36]And Zion shall come and be made manifest to all people, prepared and built, as you saw the mountain carved out without hands. [37]Then he, my Son, will reprove the assembled nations for their ungodliness (this was symbolized by the storm), [38]and will reproach them to their face with their evil thoughts and the torments with which they are to be tortured (which were symbolized by the flames), and will destroy them without effort by means of the law[r] (which was symbolized by the fire).

39 "And as for your seeing him gather to himself another multitude that was peaceable, [40]these are the nine[s] tribes that were taken away from their own land into exile in the days of King Hoshea, whom Shalmaneser, king of the Assyrians, made captives; he took them across the river, and they were taken into another land. [41]But they formed this plan for themselves, that they would leave the multitude of the nations and go to a more distant region, where no human beings had ever lived, [42]so that there at least they might keep their statutes that they had not kept in their own land. [43]And they went in by the narrow passages of the Euphrates river. [44]For at that time the Most High performed signs for them, and stopped the channels of the river until they had crossed over. [45]Through that region there was a long way to go, a journey of a year and a half; and that country is called Arzareth.[t]

46 "Then they lived there until the last times; and now, when they are about to come again, [47]the Most High will stop[u] the channels of the river again, so that they may be able to cross over. Therefore you saw the multitude gathered together in peace. [48]But those who are left of your people, who are found within my holy borders, shall be saved.[v] [49]Therefore when he destroys the multitude of the nations that are gathered together, he will defend the people who remain. [50]And then he will show them very many wonders."

" Ethiop Compare Arab 2: Lat *easier*   *o* Syr: Lat *this*   *p* Syr Arab 1: Lat lacks *and . . . not survive*   *q* Syr and most Lat Mss lack *from the sea*   *r* Syr: Lat *effort and the law*   *s* Other Lat Mss *ten*; Syr Ethiop Arab 1 Arm *nine and a half*   *t* That is *Another Land*   *u* Syr: Lat *stops*   *v* Syr: Lat lacks *shall be saved*

51 I said, "O sovereign Lord, explain this to me: Why did I see the man coming up from the heart of the sea?"

52 He said to me, "Just as no one can explore or know what is in the depths of the sea, so no one on earth can see my Son or those who are with him, except in the time of his day.^{w} ^{53}This is the interpretation of the dream that you saw. And you alone have been enlightened about this, ^{54}because you have forsaken your own ways and have applied yourself to mine, and have searched out my law; ^{55}for you have devoted your life to wisdom, and called understanding your mother. ^{56}Therefore I have shown you these things; for there is a reward laid up with the Most High. For it will be that after three more days I will tell you other things, and explain weighty and wondrous matters to you."

57 Then I got up and walked in the field, giving great glory and praise to the Most High for the wonders that he does^x from time to time, ^{58}and because he governs the times and whatever things come to pass in their seasons. And I stayed there three days.

The Lord Commissions Ezra

14 On the third day, while I was sitting under an oak, suddenly a voice came out of a bush opposite me and said, "Ezra, Ezra!" ^{2}And I answered, "Here I am, Lord," and I rose to my feet. ^{3}Then he said to me, "I revealed myself in a bush and spoke to Moses when my people were in bondage in Egypt; ^{4}and I sent him and led^y my people out of Egypt; and I led him up on Mount Sinai, where I kept him with me many days. ^{5}I told him many wondrous things, and showed him the secrets of the times and declared to him^z the end of the times. Then I commanded him, saying, ^{6}'These words you shall publish openly, and these you shall keep secret.' ^{7}And now I say to you: ^{8}Lay up in your heart the signs that I have shown you, the dreams that you have seen, and the interpretations that you have heard; ^{9}for you shall be taken up from among humankind, and henceforth you shall live with my Son and with those who are like you, until the times

are ended. ^{10}The age has lost its youth, and the times begin to grow old. ^{11}For the age is divided into twelve parts, and nine^a of its parts have already passed, ^{12}as well as half of the tenth part; so two of its parts remain, besides half of the tenth part.^{b} ^{13}Now therefore, set your house in order, and reprove your people; comfort the lowly among them, and instruct those that are wise.^{c} And now renounce the life that is corruptible, ^{14}and put away from you mortal thoughts; cast away from you the burdens of humankind, and divest yourself now of your weak nature; ^{15}lay to one side the thoughts that are most grievous to you, and hurry to escape from these times. ^{16}For evils worse than those that you have now seen happen shall take place hereafter. ^{17}For the weaker the world becomes through old age, the more shall evils be increased upon its inhabitants. ^{18}Truth shall go farther away, and falsehood shall come near. For the eagle^d that you saw in the vision is already hurrying to come."

Ezra's Concern to Restore the Scriptures

19 Then I answered and said, "Let me speak^e in your presence, Lord. ^{20}For I will go, as you have commanded me, and I will reprove the people who are now living; but who will warn those who will be born hereafter? For the world lies in darkness, and its inhabitants are without light. ^{21}For your law has been burned, and so no one knows the things which have been done or will be done by you. ^{22}If then I have found favor with you, send the holy spirit into me, and I will write everything that has happened in the world from the beginning, the things that were written in your law, so that people may be able to find the path, and that those who want to live in the last days may do so."

23 He answered me and said, "Go and gather the people, and tell them not to seek you for forty days. ^{24}But prepare for yourself many writing tablets, and take with you Sarea, Dabria, Selemia, Ethanus, and Asiel— these five, who are trained to write rapidly; ^{25}and you shall come here, and I will light in your heart the lamp of understanding,

---

^{w} Syr: Ethiop *except when his time and his day have come.* Lat lacks *his* ^{x} Lat *did* ^{y} Syr Arab 1 Arab 2 *he led* ^{z} Syr Ethiop Arab Arm: Lat lacks *declared to him* ^{a} Cn: Lat Ethiop *ten* ^{b} Syr lacks verses 11, 12: Ethiop *For the world is divided into ten parts, and has come to the tenth, and half of the tenth remains. Now . . .* ^{c} Lat lacks *and . . . wise* ^{d} Syr Ethiop Arab Arm: Meaning of Lat uncertain ^{e} Most Lat Mss lack *Let me speak*

which shall not be put out until what you are about to write is finished. ²⁶And when you have finished, some things you shall make public, and some you shall deliver in secret to the wise; tomorrow at this hour you shall begin to write."

Ezra's Last Words to the People

27 Then I went as he commanded me, and I gathered all the people together, and said, ²⁸"Hear these words, O Israel. ²⁹At first our ancestors lived as aliens in Egypt, and they were liberated from there ³⁰and received the law of life, which they did not keep, which you also have transgressed after them. ³¹Then land was given to you for a possession in the land of Zion; but you and your ancestors committed iniquity and did not keep the ways that the Most High commanded you. ³²And since he is a righteous judge, in due time he took from you what he had given. ³³And now you are here, and your people*ᶠ* are farther in the interior.*ᵍ* ³⁴If you, then, will rule over your minds and discipline your hearts, you shall be kept alive, and after death you shall obtain mercy. ³⁵For after death the judgment will come, when we shall live again; and then the names of the righteous shall become manifest, and the deeds of the ungodly shall be disclosed. ³⁶But let no one come to me now, and let no one seek me for forty days."

The Restoration of the Scriptures

37 So I took the five men, as he commanded me, and we proceeded to the field, and remained there. ³⁸And on the next day a voice called me, saying, "Ezra, open your mouth and drink what I give you to drink." ³⁹So I opened my mouth, and a full cup was offered to me; it was full of something like water, but its color was like fire. ⁴⁰I took it and drank; and when I had drunk it, my heart poured forth understanding, and wisdom increased in my breast, for my spirit retained its memory, ⁴¹and my mouth

was opened and was no longer closed. ⁴²Moreover, the Most High gave understanding to the five men, and by turns they wrote what was dictated, using characters that they did not know.*ʰ* They sat forty days; they wrote during the daytime, and ate their bread at night. ⁴³But as for me, I spoke in the daytime and was not silent at night. ⁴⁴So during the forty days, ninety-four*ⁱ* books were written. ⁴⁵And when the forty days were ended, the Most High spoke to me, saying, "Make public the twenty-four*ʲ* books that you wrote first, and let the worthy and the unworthy read them; ⁴⁶but keep the seventy that were written last, in order to give them to the wise among your people. ⁴⁷For in them is the spring of understanding, the fountain of wisdom, and the river of knowledge." ⁴⁸And I did so.*ᵏ*

Vengeance on the Wicked

15 *ˡ* Speak in the ears of my people the words of the prophecy that I will put in your mouth, says the Lord, ²and cause them to be written on paper; for they are trustworthy and true. ³Do not fear the plots against you, and do not be troubled by the unbelief of those who oppose you. ⁴For all unbelievers shall die in their unbelief.*ᵐ*

5 Beware, says the Lord, I am bringing evils upon the world, the sword and famine, death and destruction, ⁶because iniquity has spread throughout every land, and their harmful doings have reached their limit. ⁷Therefore, says the Lord, ⁸I will be silent no longer concerning their ungodly acts that they impiously commit, neither will I tolerate their wicked practices. Innocent and righteous blood cries out to me, and the souls of the righteous cry out continually. ⁹I will surely avenge them, says the Lord, and will receive to myself all the innocent blood from among them. ¹⁰See, my people are being led like a flock to the slaughter; I will not allow them to live any longer in the land of Egypt, ¹¹but I will bring them

---

*ᶠ*Lat *brothers*   *ᵍ*Syr Ethiop Arm: Lat *are among you*   *ʰ*Syr Compare Ethiop Arab 2 Arm: Meaning of Lat uncertain   *ⁱ*Syr Ethiop Arab 1 Arm: Meaning of Lat uncertain   *ʲ*Syr Arab 1: Lat lacks *twenty-four*   *ᵏ*Syr adds *in the seventh year of the sixth week, five thousand years and three months and twelve days after creation. At that time Ezra was caught up, and taken to the place of those who are like him, after he had written all these things. And he was called the scribe of the knowledge of the Most High for ever and ever.* Ethiop Arab 1 Arm have a similar ending   *ˡ*Chapters 15 and 16 (except 15.57–59, which has been found in Greek) are extant only in Lat   *ᵐ*Other ancient authorities add *and all who believe shall be saved by their faith*

229

out with a mighty hand and with an uplifted arm, and will strike Egypt with plagues, as before, and will destroy all its land. 12 Let Egypt mourn, and its foundations, because of the plague of chastisement and castigation that the Lord will bring upon it. [13]Let the farmers that till the ground mourn, because their seed shall fail to grow[n] and their trees shall be ruined by blight and hail and by a terrible tempest. [14]Alas for the world and for those who live in it! [15]For the sword and misery draw near them, and nation shall rise up to fight against nation, with swords in their hands. [16]For there shall be unrest among people; growing strong against one another, they shall in their might have no respect for their king or the chief of their leaders. [17]For a person will desire to go into a city, and shall not be able to do so. [18]Because of their pride the cities shall be in confusion, the houses shall be destroyed, and people shall be afraid. [19]People shall have no pity for their neighbors, but shall make an assault upon[o] their houses with the sword, and plunder their goods, because of hunger for bread and because of great tribulation.

20 See how I am calling together all the kings of the earth to turn to me, says God, from the rising sun and from the south, from the east and from Lebanon; to turn and repay what they have given them. [21]Just as they have done to my elect until this day, so I will do, and will repay into their bosom. Thus says the Lord God: [22]My right hand will not spare the sinners, and my sword will not cease from those who shed innocent blood on earth. [23]And a fire went forth from his wrath, and consumed the foundations of the earth and the sinners, like burnt straw. [24]Alas for those who sin and do not observe my commandments, says the Lord;[p] [25]I will not spare them. Depart, you faithless children! Do not pollute my sanctuary. [26]For God[q] knows all who sin against him; therefore he will hand them over to death and slaughter. [27]Already calamities have come upon the whole earth, and you shall remain in them; God[q] will not deliver you, because you have sinned against him.

A Terrifying Vision of Warfare

28 What a terrifying sight, appearing from the east! [29]The nations of the dragons of Arabia shall come out with many chariots, and from the day that they set out, their hissing shall spread over the earth, so that all who hear them will fear and tremble. [30]Also the Carmonians, raging in wrath, shall go forth like wild boars[r] from the forest, and with great power they shall come and engage them in battle, and with their tusks they shall devastate a portion of the land of the Assyrians with their teeth. [31]And then the dragons,[s] remembering their origin, shall become still stronger; and if they combine in great power and turn to pursue them, [32]then these shall be disorganized and silenced by their power, and shall turn and flee.[t] [33]And from the land of the Assyrians an enemy in ambush shall attack them and destroy one of them, and fear and trembling shall come upon their army, and indecision upon their kings.

Judgment on Babylon

34 See the clouds from the east, and from the north to the south! Their appearance is exceedingly threatening, full of wrath and storm. [35]They shall clash against one another and shall pour out a heavy tempest on the earth, and their own tempest;[u] and there shall be blood from the sword as high as a horse's belly [36]and a man's thigh and a camel's hock. [37]And there shall be fear and great trembling on the earth; those who see that wrath shall be horror-stricken, and they shall be seized with trembling. [38]After that, heavy storm clouds shall be stirred up from the south, and from the north, and another part from the west. [39]But the winds from the east shall prevail over the cloud that was[v] raised in wrath, and shall dispel it; and the tempest[u] that was to cause destruction by the east wind shall be driven violently toward the south and west. [40]Great and mighty clouds, full of wrath and tempest, shall rise and destroy all the earth and its inhabitants, and shall pour out upon every high and lofty place[w] a terrible tempest, [41]fire and hail and flying

---

[n] Lat lacks *to grow*   [o] Cn: Lat *shall empty*   [p] Other ancient authorities read *God*   [q] Other ancient authorities read *the Lord*   [r] Other ancient authorities lack *like wild boars*   [s] Cn: Lat *dragon*   [t] Other ancient authorities read *turn their face to the north*   [u] Meaning of Lat uncertain   [v] Literally *that he*   [w] Or *eminent person*

swords and floods of water, so that all the fields and all the streams shall be filled with the abundance of those waters. ⁴²They shall destroy cities and walls, mountains and hills, trees of the forests, and grass of the meadows, and their grain. ⁴³They shall go on steadily to Babylon and blot it out. ⁴⁴They shall come to it and surround it; they shall pour out on it the tempest* and all its fury;ʸ then the dust and smoke shall reach the sky, and all who are around it shall mourn for it. ⁴⁵And those who survive shall serve those who have destroyed it.

Judgment on Asia

46 And you, Asia, who share in the splendor of Babylon and the glory of her person— ⁴⁷woe to you, miserable wretch! For you have made yourself like her; you have decked out your daughters for prostitution to please and glory in your lovers, who have always lusted after you. ⁴⁸You have imitated that hateful one in all her deeds and devices.ᶻ Therefore Godᵃ says, ⁴⁹I will send evils upon you: widowhood, poverty, famine, sword, and pestilence, bringing ruin to your houses, bringing destruction and death. ⁵⁰And the glory of your strength shall wither like a flower when the heat shall rise that is sent upon you. ⁵¹You shall be weakened like a wretched woman who is beaten and wounded, so that you cannot receive your mighty lovers. ⁵²Would I have dealt with you so violently, says the Lord, ⁵³if you had not killed my chosen people continually, exulting and clapping your hands and talking about their death when you were drunk?

54 Beautify your face! ⁵⁵The reward of a prostitute is in your lap; therefore you shall receive your recompense. ⁵⁶As you will do to my chosen people, says the Lord, so God will do to you, and will hand you over to adversities. ⁵⁷Your children shall die of hunger, and you shall fall by the sword; your cities shall be wiped out, and all your people who are in the open country shall fall by the sword. ⁵⁸Those who are in the mountains and highlandsᵇ shall perish of hunger, and they shall eat their own flesh

in hunger for bread and drink their own blood in thirst for water. ⁵⁹Unhappy above all others, you shall come and suffer fresh miseries. ⁶⁰As they pass by they shall crush the hatefulᶜ city, and shall destroy a part of your land and abolish a portion of your glory, when they return from devastated Babylon. ⁶¹You shall be broken down by them like stubble,ᵈ and they shall be like fire to you. ⁶²They shall devour you and your cities, your land and your mountains; they shall burn with fire all your forests and your fruitful trees. ⁶³They shall carry your children away captive, plunder your wealth, and mar the glory of your countenance.

Further Denunciations

16 Woe to you, Babylon and Asia! Woe to you, Egypt and Syria! ²Bind on sackcloth and cloth of goats' hair,ᵉ and wail for your children, and lament for them; for your destruction is at hand. ³The sword has been sent upon you, and who is there to turn it back? ⁴A fire has been sent upon you, and who is there to quench it? ⁵Calamities have been sent upon you, and who is there to drive them away? ⁶Can one drive off a hungry lion in the forest, or quench a fire in the stubble once it has started to burn?ᶠ ⁷Can one turn back an arrow shot by a strong archer? ⁸The Lord God sends calamities, and who will drive them away? ⁹Fire will go forth from his wrath, and who is there to quench it? ¹⁰He will flash lightning, and who will not be afraid? He will thunder, and who will not be terrified? ¹¹The Lord will threaten, and who will not be utterly shattered at his presence? ¹²The earth and its foundations quake, the sea is churned up from the depths, and its waves and the fish with them shall be troubled at the presence of the Lord and the glory of his power. ¹³For his right hand that bends the bow is strong, and his arrows that he shoots are sharp and when they are shot to the ends of the world will not miss once. ¹⁴Calamities are sent forth and shall not return until they come over the earth. ¹⁵The fire is kindled, and shall not be put out until it consumes the

---

ˣ Meaning of Lat uncertain   ʸ Other ancient authorities add *until they destroy it to its foundations*   ᶻ Other ancient authorities add *devices, and you have followed after that one about to gratify her magnates and leaders so that you may be made proud and be pleased by her fornications*   ᵃ Other ancient authorities read *the Lord*   ᵇ Gk: Lat omits *and highlands*   ᶜ Another reading is *idle* or *unprofitable*   ᵈ Other ancient authorities read *like dry straw*   ᵉ Other ancient authorities lack *cloth of goats' hair*   ᶠ Other ancient authorities read *fire when dry straw has been set on fire*

foundations of the earth. [16]Just as an arrow shot by a mighty archer does not return, so the calamities that are sent upon the earth shall not return. [17]Alas for me! Alas for me! Who will deliver me in those days?

The Horror of the Last Days

18 The beginning of sorrows, when there shall be much lamentation; the beginning of famine, when many shall perish; the beginning of wars, when the powers shall be terrified; the beginning of calamities, when all shall tremble. What shall they do, when the calamities come? [19]Famine and plague, tribulation and anguish are sent as scourges for the correction of humankind. [20]Yet for all this they will not turn from their iniquities, or ever be mindful of the scourges. [21]Indeed, provisions will be so cheap upon earth that people will imagine that peace is assured for them, and then calamities shall spring up on the earth—the sword, famine, and great confusion. [22]For many of those who live on the earth shall perish by famine; and those who survive the famine shall die by the sword. [23]And the dead shall be thrown out like dung, and there shall be no one to console them; for the earth shall be left desolate, and its cities shall be demolished. [24]No one shall be left to cultivate the earth or to sow it. [25]The trees shall bear fruit, but who will gather it? [26]The grapes shall ripen, but who will tread them? For in all places there shall be great solitude; [27]a person will long to see another human being, or even to hear a human voice. [28]For ten shall be left out of a city; and two, out of the field, those who have hidden themselves in thick groves and clefts in the rocks. [29]Just as in an olive orchard three or four olives may be left on every tree, [30]or just as, when a vineyard is gathered, some clusters may be left[g] by those who search carefully through the vineyard, [31]so in those days three or four shall be left by those who search their houses with the sword. [32]The earth shall be left desolate, and its fields shall be plowed up,[h] and its roads and all its paths shall bring forth thorns, because no sheep will go along them. [33]Virgins shall mourn because they have no bridegrooms; women shall mourn because they have no husbands; their daughters shall mourn, because they have no help. [34]Their bridegrooms shall be killed in war, and their husbands shall perish of famine.

God's People Must Prepare for the End

35 Listen now to these things, and understand them, you who are servants of the Lord. [36]This is the word of the Lord; receive it and do not disbelieve what the Lord says.[i] [37]The calamities draw near, and are not delayed. [38]Just as a pregnant woman, in the ninth month when the time of her delivery draws near, has great pains around her womb for two or three hours beforehand, but when the child comes forth from the womb, there will not be a moment's delay, [39]so the calamities will not delay in coming upon the earth, and the world will groan, and pains will seize it on every side.

40 Hear my words, O my people; prepare for battle, and in the midst of the calamities be like strangers on the earth. [41]Let the one who sells be like one who will flee; let the one who buys be like one who will lose; [42]let the one who does business be like one who will not make a profit; and let the one who builds a house be like one who will not live in it; [43]let the one who sows be like one who will not reap; so also the one who prunes the vines, like one who will not gather the grapes; [44]those who marry, like those who will have no children; and those who do not marry, like those who are widowed. [45]Because of this, those who labor, labor in vain; [46]for strangers shall gather their fruits, and plunder their goods, overthrow their houses, and take their children captive; for in captivity and famine they will produce their children.[j] [47]Those who conduct business do so only to have it plundered; the more they adorn their cities, their houses and possessions, and their persons, [48]the more angry I will be with them for their sins, says the Lord. [49]Just as a respectable and virtuous woman abhors a prostitute, [50]so righteousness shall abhor iniquity, when she decks herself out, and shall accuse her to her face when he comes who will defend the one who searches out every sin on earth.

---

[g] Other ancient authorities read *a cluster may remain exposed*   [h] Other ancient authorities read *be for briers*
[i] Cn: Lat *do not believe the gods of whom the Lord speaks*   [j] Other ancient authorities read *therefore those who are married may know that they will produce children for captivity and famine*

The Power and Wisdom of God

51 Therefore do not be like her or her works. [52]For in a very short time iniquity will be removed from the earth, and righteousness will reign over us. [53]Sinners must not say that they have not sinned;[k] for God[l] will burn coals of fire on the head of everyone who says, "I have not sinned before God and his glory." [54]The Lord[m] certainly knows everything that people do; he knows their imaginations and their thoughts and their hearts. [55]He said, "Let the earth be made," and it was made, and "Let the heaven be made," and it was made. [56]At his word the stars were fixed in their places, and he knows the number of the stars. [57]He searches the abyss and its treasures; he has measured the sea and its contents; [58]he has confined the sea in the midst of the waters;[n] and by his word he has suspended the earth over the water. [59]He has spread out the heaven like a dome and made it secure upon the waters; [60]he has put springs of water in the desert, and pools on the tops of the mountains, so as to send rivers from the heights to water the earth. [61]He formed human beings and put a heart in the midst of each body, and gave each person breath and life and understanding [62]and the spirit[o] of Almighty God,[p] who surely made all things and searches out hidden things in hidden places. [63]He knows your imaginations and what you think in your hearts! Woe to those who sin and want to hide their sins! [64]The Lord will strictly examine all their works, and will make a public spectacle of all of you. [65]You shall be put to shame when your sins come out before others, and your own iniquities shall stand as your accusers on that day. [66]What will you do? Or how will you hide your sins before the Lord and his glory? [67]Indeed, God[q] is the judge; fear him! Cease from your sins, and forget your iniquities, never to commit them again; so God[q] will lead you forth and deliver you from all tribulation.

Impending Persecution of God's People

68 The burning wrath of a great multitude is kindled over you; they shall drag some of you away and force you to eat what was sacrificed to idols. [69]And those who consent to eat shall be held in derision and contempt, and shall be trampled under foot. [70]For in many places[r] and in neighboring cities there shall be a great uprising against those who fear the Lord. [71]They shall[s] be like maniacs, sparing no one, but plundering and destroying those who continue to fear the Lord.[t] [72]For they shall destroy and plunder their goods, and drive them out of house and home. [73]Then the tested quality of my elect shall be manifest, like gold that is tested by fire.

Promise of Divine Deliverance

74 Listen, my elect ones, says the Lord; the days of tribulation are at hand, but I will deliver you from them. [75]Do not fear or doubt, for God[q] is your guide. [76]You who keep my commandments and precepts, says the Lord God, must not let your sins weigh you down, or your iniquities prevail over you. [77]Woe to those who are choked by their sins and overwhelmed by their iniquities! They are like a field choked with underbrush and its path[u] overwhelmed with thorns, so that no one can pass through. [78]It is shut off and given up to be consumed by fire.

---

[k] Other ancient authorities add *or the unjust done injustice* [l] Lat *for he* [m] Other ancient authorities read *Lord God* [n] Other ancient authorities read *confined the world between the waters and the waters* [o] Or *breath* [p] Other ancient authorities read *of the Lord Almighty* [q] Other ancient authorities read *the Lord* [r] Meaning of Lat uncertain [s] Other ancient authorities read *For people, because of their misfortunes, shall* [t] Other ancient authorities read *fear God* [u] Other ancient authorities read *seed*

4 MACCABEES

The Author's Definition of His Task

1 The subject that I am about to discuss is most philosophical, that is, whether devout reason is sovereign over the emotions. So it is right for me to advise you to pay earnest attention to philosophy. ²For the subject is essential to everyone who is seeking knowledge, and in addition it includes the praise of the highest virtue—I mean, of course, rational judgment. ³If, then, it is evident that reason rules over those emotions that hinder self-control, namely, gluttony and lust, ⁴it is also clear that it masters the emotions that hinder one from justice, such as malice, and those that stand in the way of courage, namely anger, fear, and pain. ⁵Some might perhaps ask, "If reason rules the emotions, why is it not sovereign over forgetfulness and ignorance?" Their attempt at argument is ridiculous!ᵃ ⁶For reason does not rule its own emotions, but those that are opposed to justice, courage, and self-control;ᵇ and it is not for the purpose of destroying them, but so that one may not give way to them.

7 I could prove to you from many and various examples that reasonᶜ is dominant over the emotions, ⁸but I can demonstrate it best from the noble bravery of those who died for the sake of virtue, Eleazar and the seven brothers and their mother. ⁹All of these, by despising sufferings that bring death, demonstrated that reason controls the emotions. ¹⁰On this anniversaryᵈ it is fitting for me to praise for their virtues those who, with their mother, died for the sake of nobility and goodness, but I would also call them blessed for the honor in which they are held. ¹¹All people, even their torturers, marveled at their courage and endurance, and they became the cause of the downfall of tyranny over their nation. By their endurance they conquered the tyrant, and thus their native land was purified through them. ¹²I shall shortly have an opportunity to speak of this; but, as my custom is, I shall begin by stating my main principle, and then I shall turn to their story, giving glory to the all-wise God.

The Supremacy of Reason

13 Our inquiry, accordingly, is whether reason is sovereign over the emotions. ¹⁴We shall decide just what reason is and what emotion is, how many kinds of emotions there are, and whether reason rules over all these. ¹⁵Now reason is the mind that with sound logic prefers the life of wisdom. ¹⁶Wisdom, next, is the knowledge of divine and human matters and the causes of these. ¹⁷This, in turn, is education in the law, by which we learn divine matters reverently and human affairs to our advantage. ¹⁸Now the kinds of wisdom are rational judgment, justice, courage, and self-control. ¹⁹Rational judgment is supreme over all of these, since by means of it reason rules over the emotions. ²⁰The two most comprehensive typesᵉ of the emotions are pleasure and pain; and each of these is by nature concerned with both body and soul. ²¹The emotions of both pleasure and pain have many consequences. ²²Thus desire precedes pleasure and delight follows it. ²³Fear precedes pain and sorrow comes after. ²⁴Anger, as a person will see by reflecting on this experience, is an emotion embracing pleasure and pain. ²⁵In pleasure there exists even a malevolent tendency, which is the most complex of all the emotions. ²⁶In the soul it is boastfulness, covetousness, thirst for honor, rivalry, and malice; ²⁷in the body, indiscriminate eating, gluttony, and solitary gormandizing.

28 Just as pleasure and pain are two plants growing from the body and the soul, so there are many offshoots of these plants,ᶠ ²⁹each of which the master cultivator, reason, weeds and prunes and ties up and waters and thoroughly irrigates, and so tames the jungle of habits and emotions. ³⁰For reason is the guide of the virtues, but over the emotions it is sovereign.

Observe now, first of all, that rational judgment is sovereign over the emotions by virtue of the restraining power of self-control. ³¹Self-control, then, is dominance over the desires. ³²Some desires are mental, others are physical, and reason obviously rules over both. ³³Otherwise, how is it that when

---

ᵃ Or *They are attempting to make my argument ridiculous!*   ᵇ Other ancient authorities add *and rational judgment*   ᶜ Other ancient authorities read *devout reason*   ᵈ Gk *At this time*   ᵉ Or *sources*   ᶠ Other ancient authorities read *these emotions*

we are attracted to forbidden foods we abstain from the pleasure to be had from them? Is it not because reason is able to rule over appetites? I for one think so. ³⁴Therefore when we crave seafood and fowl and animals and all sorts of foods that are forbidden to us by the law, we abstain because of domination by reason. ³⁵For the emotions of the appetites are restrained, checked by the temperate mind, and all the impulses of the body are bridled by reason.

Compatibility of the Law with Reason

2 And why is it amazing that the desires of the mind for the enjoyment of beauty are rendered powerless? ²It is for this reason, certainly, that the temperate Joseph is praised, because by mental effort*ᵍ* he overcame sexual desire. ³For when he was young and in his prime for intercourse, by his reason he nullified the frenzy*ʰ* of the passions. ⁴Not only is reason proved to rule over the frenzied urge of sexual desire, but also over every desire.*ⁱ* ⁵Thus the law says, "You shall not covet your neighbor's wife or anything that is your neighbor's." ⁶In fact, since the law has told us not to covet, I could prove to you all the more that reason is able to control desires.

Just so it is with the emotions that hinder one from justice. ⁷Otherwise how could it be that someone who is habitually a solitary gormandizer, a glutton, or even a drunkard can learn a better way, unless reason is clearly lord of the emotions? ⁸Thus, as soon as one adopts a way of life in accordance with the law, even though a lover of money, one is forced to act contrary to natural ways and to lend without interest to the needy and to cancel the debt when the seventh year arrives. ⁹If one is greedy, one is ruled by the law through reason so that one neither gleans the harvest nor gathers the last grapes from the vineyard.

In all other matters we can recognize that reason rules the emotions. ¹⁰For the law prevails even over affection for parents, so that virtue is not abandoned for their sakes. ¹¹It is superior to love for one's wife, so that one rebukes her when she breaks the law. ¹²It takes precedence over love for children, so that one punishes them for misdeeds. ¹³It is sovereign over the relationship of friends, so that one rebukes friends

when they act wickedly. ¹⁴Do not consider it paradoxical when reason, through the law, can prevail even over enmity. The fruit trees of the enemy are not cut down, but one preserves the property of enemies from marauders and helps raise up what has fallen.*ʲ*

15 It is evident that reason rules even*ᵏ* the more violent emotions: lust for power, vainglory, boasting, arrogance, and malice. ¹⁶For the temperate mind repels all these malicious emotions, just as it repels anger— for it is sovereign over even this. ¹⁷When Moses was angry with Dathan and Abiram, he did nothing against them in anger, but controlled his anger by reason. ¹⁸For, as I have said, the temperate mind is able to get the better of the emotions, to correct some, and to render others powerless. ¹⁹Why else did Jacob, our most wise father, censure the households of Simeon and Levi for their irrational slaughter of the entire tribe of the Shechemites, saying, "Cursed be their anger"? ²⁰For if reason could not control anger, he would not have spoken thus. ²¹Now when God fashioned human beings, he planted in them emotions and inclinations, ²²but at the same time he enthroned the mind among the senses as a sacred governor over them all. ²³To the mind he gave the law; and one who lives subject to this will rule a kingdom that is temperate, just, good, and courageous.

24 How is it then, one might say, that if reason is master of the emotions, it does not control forgetfulness and ignorance?

3 ¹But this argument is entirely ridiculous; for it is evident that reason rules not over its own emotions, but over those of the body. ²No one of us*ⁱ* can eradicate that kind of desire, but reason can provide a way for us not to be enslaved by desire. ³No one of us can eradicate anger from the mind, but reason can help to deal with anger. ⁴No one of us can eradicate malice, but reason can fight at our side so that we are not overcome by malice. ⁵For reason does not uproot the emotions but is their antagonist.

King David's Thirst

6 Now this can be explained more clearly by the story of King David's thirst. ⁷David had been attacking the Philistines all day

---

ᵍ Other ancient authorities add *in reasoning* *ʰ* Or *gadfly* *ⁱ* Or *all covetousness* *ʲ* Or *the beasts that have fallen*
ᵏ Other ancient authorities read *through* *ⁱ* Gk *you*

long, and together with the soldiers of his nation had killed many of them. [8]Then when evening fell, he[m] came, sweating and quite exhausted, to the royal tent, around which the whole army of our ancestors had encamped. [9]Now all the rest were at supper, [10]but the king was extremely thirsty, and though springs were plentiful there, he could not satisfy his thirst from them. [11]But a certain irrational desire for the water in the enemy's territory tormented and inflamed him, undid and consumed him. [12]When his guards complained bitterly because of the king's craving, two staunch young soldiers, respecting[n] the king's desire, armed themselves fully, and taking a pitcher climbed over the enemy's ramparts. [13]Eluding the sentinels at the gates, they went searching throughout the enemy camp [14]and found the spring, and from it boldly brought the king a drink. [15]But David,[o] though he was burning with thirst, considered it an altogether fearful danger to his soul to drink what was regarded as equivalent to blood. [16]Therefore, opposing reason to desire, he poured out the drink as an offering to God. [17]For the temperate mind can conquer the drives of the emotions and quench the flames of frenzied desires; [18]it can overthrow bodily agonies even when they are extreme, and by nobility of reason spurn all domination by the emotions.

An Attempt on the Temple Treasury

19 The present occasion now invites us to a narrative demonstration of temperate reason.

20 At a time when our ancestors were enjoying profound peace because of their observance of the law and were prospering, so that even Seleucus Nicanor, king of Asia, had both appropriated money to them for the temple service and recognized their commonwealth— [21]just at that time certain persons attempted a revolution against the public harmony and caused many and various disasters.

4 Now there was a certain Simon, a political opponent of the noble and good man, Onias, who then held the high priesthood for life. When despite all manner of slander he was unable to injure Onias in the eyes of the nation, he fled the country with the purpose of betraying it. [2]So he came to Apollonius, governor of Syria,

Phoenicia, and Cilicia, and said, [3]"I have come here because I am loyal to the king's government, to report that in the Jerusalem treasuries there are deposited tens of thousands in private funds, which are not the property of the temple but belong to King Seleucus." [4]When Apollonius learned the details of these things, he praised Simon for his service to the king and went up to Seleucus to inform him of the rich treasure. [5]On receiving authority to deal with this matter, he proceeded quickly to our country accompanied by the accursed Simon and a very strong military force. [6]He said that he had come with the king's authority to seize the private funds in the treasury. [7]The people indignantly protested his words, considering it outrageous that those who had committed deposits to the sacred treasury should be deprived of them, and did all that they could to prevent it. [8]But, uttering threats, Apollonius went on to the temple. [9]While the priests together with women and children were imploring God in the temple to shield the holy place that was being treated so contemptuously, [10]and while Apollonius was going up with his armed forces to seize the money, angels on horseback with lightning flashing from their weapons appeared from heaven, instilling in them great fear and trembling. [11]Then Apollonius fell down half dead in the temple area that was open to all, stretched out his hands toward heaven, and with tears begged the Hebrews to pray for him and propitiate the wrath of the heavenly army. [12]For he said that he had committed a sin deserving of death, and that if he were spared he would praise the blessedness of the holy place before all people. [13]Moved by these words, the high priest Onias, although otherwise he had scruples about doing so, prayed for him so that King Seleucus would not suppose that Apollonius had been overcome by human treachery and not by divine justice. [14]So Apollonius,[o] having been saved beyond all expectations, went away to report to the king what had happened to him.

Antiochus's Persecution of the Jews

15 When King Seleucus died, his son Antiochus Epiphanes succeeded to the throne, an arrogant and terrible man, [16]who removed Onias from the priesthood and appointed Onias's[p] brother Jason as high

---

[m] Other ancient authorities read *he hurried and*   [n] Or *embarrassed because of*   [o] Gk *he*   [p] Gk *his*

priest. [17]Jason[q] agreed that if the office were conferred on him he would pay the king three thousand six hundred sixty talents annually. [18]So the king appointed him high priest and ruler of the nation. [19]Jason[q] changed the nation's way of life and altered its form of government in complete violation of the law, [20]so that not only was a gymnasium constructed at the very citadel[r] of our native land, but also the temple service was abolished. [21]The divine justice was angered by these acts and caused Antiochus himself to make war on them. [22]For when he was warring against Ptolemy in Egypt, he heard that a rumor of his death had spread and that the people of Jerusalem had rejoiced greatly. He speedily marched against them, [23]and after he had plundered them he issued a decree that if any of them were found observing the ancestral law they should die. [24]When, by means of his decrees, he had not been able in any way to put an end to the people's observance of the law, but saw that all his threats and punishments were being disregarded [25]—even to the extent that women, because they had circumcised their sons, were thrown headlong from heights along with their infants, though they had known beforehand that they would suffer this— [26]when, I say, his decrees were despised by the people, he himself tried through torture to compel everyone in the nation to eat defiling foods and to renounce Judaism.

Antiochus's Encounter with Eleazar

5 The tyrant Antiochus, sitting in state with his counselors on a certain high place, and with his armed soldiers standing around him, [2]ordered the guards to seize each and every Hebrew and to compel them to eat pork and food sacrificed to idols. [3]If any were not willing to eat defiling food, they were to be broken on the wheel and killed. [4]When many persons had been rounded up, one man, Eleazar by name, leader of the flock, was brought[s] before the king. He was a man of priestly family, learned in the law, advanced in age, and known to many in the tyrant's court because of his philosophy.[t]

[5] When Antiochus saw him he said, [6]"Before I begin to torture you, old man, I would advise you to save yourself by eating pork, [7]for I respect your age and your gray hairs. Although you have had them for so long a time, it does not seem to me that you are a philosopher when you observe the religion of the Jews. [8]When nature has granted it to us, why should you abhor eating the very excellent meat of this animal? [9]It is senseless not to enjoy delicious things that are not shameful, and wrong to spurn the gifts of nature. [10]It seems to me that you will do something even more senseless if, by holding a vain opinion concerning the truth, you continue to despise me to your own hurt. [11]Will you not awaken from your foolish philosophy, dispel your futile reasonings, adopt a mind appropriate to your years, philosophize according to the truth of what is beneficial, [12]and have compassion on your old age by honoring my humane advice? [13]For consider this: if there is some power watching over this religion of yours, it will excuse you from any transgression that arises out of compulsion."

[14] When the tyrant urged him in this fashion to eat meat unlawfully, Eleazar asked to have a word. [15]When he had received permission to speak, he began to address the people as follows: [16]"We, O Antiochus, who have been persuaded to govern our lives by the divine law, think that there is no compulsion more powerful than our obedience to the law. [17]Therefore we consider that we should not transgress it in any respect. [18]Even if, as you suppose, our law were not truly divine and we had wrongly held it to be divine, not even so would it be right for us to invalidate our reputation for piety. [19]Therefore do not suppose that it would be a petty sin if we were to eat defiling food; [20]to transgress the law in matters either small or great is of equal seriousness, [21]for in either case the law is equally despised. [22]You scoff at our philosophy as though living by it were irrational, [23]but it teaches us self-control, so that we master all pleasures and desires, and it also trains us in courage, so that we endure any suffering willingly; [24]it instructs us in justice, so that in all our dealings we act impartially,[u] and it teaches us piety, so that with proper reverence we worship the only living God.

[25] "Therefore we do not eat defiling food; for since we believe that the law was established by God, we know that in the nature

[q] Gk *He*   [r] Or *high place*   [s] Or *was the first of the flock to be brought*   [t] Other ancient authorities read *his advanced age*   [u] Or *so that we hold in balance all our habitual inclinations*

of things the Creator of the world in giving us the law has shown sympathy toward us. [26]He has permitted us to eat what will be most suitable for our lives,[v] but he has forbidden us to eat meats that would be contrary to this. [27]It would be tyrannical for you to compel us not only to transgress the law, but also to eat in such a way that you may deride us for eating defiling foods, which are most hateful to us. [28]But you shall have no such occasion to laugh at me, [29]nor will I transgress the sacred oaths of my ancestors concerning the keeping of the law, [30]not even if you gouge out my eyes and burn my entrails. [31]I am not so old and cowardly as not to be young in reason on behalf of piety. [32]Therefore get your torture wheels ready and fan the fire more vehemently! [33]I do not so pity my old age as to break the ancestral law by my own act. [34]I will not play false to you, O law that trained me, nor will I renounce you, beloved self-control. [35]I will not put you to shame, philosophical reason, nor will I reject you, honored priesthood and knowledge of the law. [36]You, O king,[w] shall not defile the honorable mouth of my old age, nor my long life lived lawfully. [37]My ancestors will receive me as pure, as one who does not fear your violence even to death. [38]You may tyrannize the ungodly, but you shall not dominate my religious principles, either by words or through deeds."

Martyrdom of Eleazar

6 When Eleazar in this manner had made eloquent response to the exhortations of the tyrant, the guards who were standing by dragged him violently to the instruments of torture. [2]First they stripped the old man, though he remained adorned with the gracefulness of his piety. [3]After they had tied his arms on each side they flogged him, [4]while a herald who faced him cried out, "Obey the king's commands!" [5]But the courageous and noble man, like a true Eleazar, was unmoved, as though being tortured in a dream; [6]yet while the old man's eyes were raised to heaven, his flesh was being torn by scourges, his blood flowing, and his sides were being cut to pieces. [7]Although he fell to the ground because his body could not endure the agonies, he kept his reason upright and unswerving. [8]One of the cruel guards

rushed at him and began to kick him in the side to make him get up again after he fell. [9]But he bore the pains and scorned the punishment and endured the tortures. [10]Like a noble athlete the old man, while being beaten, was victorious over his torturers; [11]in fact, with his face bathed in sweat, and gasping heavily for breath, he amazed even his torturers by his courageous spirit.

12 At that point, partly out of pity for his old age, [13]partly out of sympathy from their acquaintance with him, partly out of admiration for his endurance, some of the king's retinue came to him and said, [14]"Eleazar, why are you so irrationally destroying yourself through these evil things? [15]We will set before you some cooked meat; save yourself by pretending to eat pork."

16 But Eleazar, as though more bitterly tormented by this counsel, cried out: [17]"Never may we, the children of Abraham,[x] think so basely that out of cowardice we feign a role unbecoming to us! [18]For it would be irrational if having lived in accordance with truth up to old age and having maintained in accordance with law the reputation of such a life, we should now change our course [19]and ourselves become a pattern of impiety to the young by setting them an example in the eating of defiling food. [20]It would be shameful if we should survive for a little while and during that time be a laughingstock to all for our cowardice, [21]and be despised by the tyrant as unmanly by not contending even to death for our divine law. [22]Therefore, O children of Abraham, die nobly for your religion! [23]And you, guards of the tyrant, why do you delay?"

24 When they saw that he was so courageous in the face of the afflictions, and that he had not been changed by their compassion, the guards brought him to the fire. [25]There they burned him with maliciously contrived instruments, threw him down, and poured stinking liquids into his nostrils. [26]When he was now burned to his very bones and about to expire, he lifted up his eyes to God and said, [27]"You know, O God, that though I might have saved myself, I am dying in burning torments for the sake of the law. [28]Be merciful to your people, and let our punishment suffice for them. [29]Make my blood their purification, and take my life in exchange for theirs." [30]After he said this, the holy man died nobly in his tortures; even in the tortures of death he

[v] Or *souls*   [w] Gk lacks *O king*   [x] Or *O children of Abraham*

resisted, by virtue of reason, for the sake of the law.

31 Admittedly, then, devout reason is sovereign over the emotions. [32]For if the emotions had prevailed over reason, we would have testified to their domination. [33]But now that reason has conquered the emotions, we properly attribute to it the power to govern. [34]It is right for us to acknowledge the dominance of reason when it masters even external agonies. It would be ridiculous to deny it.[y] [35]I have proved not only that reason has mastered agonies, but also that it masters pleasures and in no respect yields to them.

An Encomium on Eleazar

7 For like a most skillful pilot, the reason of our father Eleazar steered the ship of religion over the sea of the emotions, [2]and though buffeted by the stormings of the tyrant and overwhelmed by the mighty waves of tortures, [3]in no way did he turn the rudder of religion until he sailed into the haven of immortal victory. [4]No city besieged with many ingenious war machines has ever held out as did that most holy man. Although his sacred life was consumed by tortures and racks, he conquered the besiegers with the shield of his devout reason. [5]For in setting his mind firm like a jutting cliff, our father Eleazar broke the maddening waves of the emotions. [6]O priest, worthy of the priesthood, you neither defiled your sacred teeth nor profaned your stomach, which had room only for reverence and purity, by eating defiling foods. [7]O man in harmony with the law and philosopher of divine life! [8]Such should be those who are administrators of the law, shielding it with their own blood and noble sweat in sufferings even to death. [9]You, father, strengthened our loyalty to the law through your glorious endurance, and you did not abandon the holiness that you praised, but by your deeds you made your words of divine[z] philosophy credible. [10]O aged man, more powerful than tortures; O elder, fiercer than fire; O supreme king over the passions, Eleazar! [11]For just as our father Aaron, armed with the censer, ran through the multitude of the people and conquered the fiery[a] angel, [12]so the descendant of Aaron, Eleazar, though being consumed by the fire,

remained unmoved in his reason. [13]Most amazing, indeed, though he was an old man, his body no longer tense and firm,[b] his muscles flabby, his sinews feeble, he became young again [14]in spirit through reason; and by reason like that of Isaac he rendered the many-headed rack ineffective. [15]O man of blessed age and of venerable gray hair and of law-abiding life, whom the faithful seal of death has perfected!

16 If, therefore, because of piety an aged man despised tortures even to death, most certainly devout reason is governor of the emotions. [17]Some perhaps might say, "Not all have full command of their emotions, because not all have prudent reason." [18]But as many as attend to religion with a whole heart, these alone are able to control the passions of the flesh, [19]since they believe that they, like our patriarchs Abraham and Isaac and Jacob, do not die to God, but live to God. [20]No contradiction therefore arises when some persons appear to be dominated by their emotions because of the weakness of their reason. [21]What person who lives as a philosopher by the whole rule of philosophy, and trusts in God, [22]and knows that it is blessed to endure any suffering for the sake of virtue, would not be able to overcome the emotions through godliness? [23]For only the wise and courageous are masters of their emotions.

Seven Brothers Defy the Tyrant

8 For this is why even the very young, by following a philosophy in accordance with devout reason, have prevailed over the most painful instruments of torture. [2]For when the tyrant was conspicuously defeated in his first attempt, being unable to compel an aged man to eat defiling foods, then in violent rage he commanded that others of the Hebrew captives be brought, and that any who ate defiling food would be freed after eating, but if any were to refuse, they would be tortured even more cruelly.

3 When the tyrant had given these orders, seven brothers—handsome, modest, noble, and accomplished in every way— were brought before him along with their aged mother. [4]When the tyrant saw them, grouped about their mother as though a chorus, he was pleased with them. And

Syr: Meaning of Gk uncertain   *z Other ancient authorities lack divine*   *a Other ancient authorities lack fiery*   *b Gk the tautness of the body already loosed*

struck by their appearance and nobility, he smiled at them, and summoned them nearer and said, ⁵"Young men, with favorable feelings I admire each and every one of you, and greatly respect the beauty and the number of such brothers. Not only do I advise you not to display the same madness as that of the old man who has just been tortured, but I also exhort you to yield to me and enjoy my friendship. ⁶Just as I am able to punish those who disobey my orders, so I can be a benefactor to those who obey me. ⁷Trust me, then, and you will have positions of authority in my government if you will renounce the ancestral tradition of your national life. ⁸Enjoy your youth by adopting the Greek way of life and by changing your manner of living. ⁹But if by disobedience you rouse my anger, you will compel me to destroy each and every one of you with dreadful punishments through tortures. ¹⁰Therefore take pity on yourselves. Even I, your enemy, have compassion for your youth and handsome appearance. ¹¹Will you not consider this, that if you disobey, nothing remains for you but to die on the rack?"

12 When he had said these things, he ordered the instruments of torture to be brought forward so as to persuade them out of fear to eat the defiling food. ¹³When the guards had placed before them wheels and joint-dislocators, rack and hooks*ᶜ* and catapults*ᵈ* and caldrons, braziers and thumbscrews and iron claws and wedges and bellows, the tyrant resumed speaking: ¹⁴"Be afraid, young fellows; whatever justice you revere will be merciful to you when you transgress under compulsion."

15 But when they had heard the inducements and saw the dreadful devices, not only were they not afraid, but they also opposed the tyrant with their own philosophy, and by their right reasoning nullified his tyranny. ¹⁶Let us consider, on the other hand, what arguments might have been used if some of them had been cowardly and unmanly. Would they not have been the following? ¹⁷"O wretches that we are and so senseless! Since the king has summoned and exhorted us to accept kind treatment if we obey him, ¹⁸why do we take pleasure in vain resolves and venture upon a disobedience that brings death? ¹⁹O men and brothers, should we not fear the

instruments of torture and consider the threats of torments, and give up this vain opinion and this arrogance that threatens to destroy us? ²⁰Let us take pity on our youth and have compassion on our mother's age; ²¹and let us seriously consider that if we disobey we are dead! ²²Also, divine justice will excuse us for fearing the king when we are under compulsion. ²³Why do we banish ourselves from this most pleasant life and deprive ourselves of this delightful world? ²⁴Let us not struggle against compulsion*ᵉ* or take hollow pride in being put to the rack. ²⁵Not even the law itself would arbitrarily put us to death for fearing the instruments of torture. ²⁶Why does such contentiousness excite us and such a fatal stubbornness please us, when we can live in peace if we obey the king?"

27 But the youths, though about to be tortured, neither said any of these things nor even seriously considered them. ²⁸For they were contemptuous of the emotions and sovereign over agonies, ²⁹so that as soon as the tyrant had ceased counseling them to eat defiling food, all with one voice together, as from one mind, said:

9 "Why do you delay, O tyrant? For we are ready to die rather than transgress our ancestral commandments; ²we are obviously putting our forebears to shame unless we should practice ready obedience to the law and to Moses*ᶠ* our counselor. ³Tyrant and counselor of lawlessness, in your hatred for us do not pity us more than we pity ourselves.*ᶜ* ⁴For we consider this pity of yours, which insures our safety through transgression of the law, to be more grievous than death itself. ⁵You are trying to terrify us by threatening us with death by torture, as though a short time ago you learned nothing from Eleazar. ⁶And if the aged men of the Hebrews because of their religion lived piously*ᵍ* while enduring torture, it would be even more fitting that we young men should die despising your coercive tortures, which our aged instructor also overcame. ⁷Therefore, tyrant, put us to the test; and if you take our lives because of our religion, do not suppose that you can injure us by torturing us. ⁸For we, through this severe suffering and endurance, shall have the prize of virtue and shall be with God, on whose account we suffer; ⁹but you, because of your bloodthirstiness toward us,

---

*ᶜ Meaning of Gk uncertain   *ᵈ* Here and elsewhere in 4 Macc an instrument of torture   *ᵉ* Or *fate*   *ᶠ* Other ancient authorities read *knowledge*   *ᵍ* Other ancient authorities read *died*

will deservedly undergo from the divine justice eternal torment by fire."

The Torture of the First and Second Brothers

10 When they had said these things, the tyrant was not only indignant, as at those who are disobedient, but also infuriated, as at those who are ungrateful. ¹¹Then at his command the guards brought forward the eldest, and having torn off his tunic, they bound his hands and arms with thongs on each side. ¹²When they had worn themselves out beating him with scourges, without accomplishing anything, they placed him upon the wheel. ¹³When the noble youth was stretched out around this, his limbs were dislocated, ¹⁴and with every member disjointed he denounced the tyrant, saying, ¹⁵"Most abominable tyrant, enemy of heavenly justice, savage of mind, you are mangling me in this manner, not because I am a murderer, or as one who acts impiously, but because I protect the divine law." ¹⁶And when the guards said, "Agree to eat so that you may be released from the tortures," ¹⁷he replied, "You abominable lackeys, your wheel is not so powerful as to strangle my reason. Cut my limbs, burn my flesh, and twist my joints; ¹⁸through all these tortures I will convince you that children of the Hebrews alone are invincible where virtue is concerned." ¹⁹While he was saying these things, they spread fire under him, and while fanning the flames*ʰ* they tightened the wheel further. ²⁰The wheel was completely smeared with blood, and the heap of coals was being quenched by the drippings of gore, and pieces of flesh were falling off the axles of the machine. ²¹Although the ligaments joining his bones were already severed, the courageous youth, worthy of Abraham, did not groan, ²²but as though transformed by fire into immortality, he nobly endured the rackings. ²³"Imitate me, brothers," he said. "Do not leave your post in my struggle*ⁱ* or renounce our courageous family ties. ²⁴Fight the sacred and noble battle for religion. Thereby the just Providence of our ancestors may become merciful to our nation and take vengeance on the accursed

tyrant." ²⁵When he had said this, the saintly youth broke the thread of life.

26 While all were marveling at his courageous spirit, the guards brought in the next eldest, and after fitting themselves with iron gauntlets having sharp hooks, they bound him to the torture machine and catapult. ²⁷Before torturing him, they inquired if he were willing to eat, and they heard his noble decision.*ʲ* ²⁸These leopard-like beasts tore out his sinews with the iron hands, flayed all his flesh up to his chin, and tore away his scalp. But he steadfastly endured this agony and said, ²⁹"How sweet is any kind of death for the religion of our ancestors!" ³⁰To the tyrant he said, "Do you not think, you most savage tyrant, that you are being tortured more than I, as you see the arrogant design of your tyranny being defeated by our endurance for the sake of religion? ³¹I lighten my pain by the joys that come from virtue, ³²but you suffer torture by the threats that come from impiety. You will not escape, you most abominable tyrant, the judgments of the divine wrath."

The Torture of the Third and Fourth Brothers

10 When he too had endured a glorious death, the third was led in, and many repeatedly urged him to save himself by tasting the meat. ²But he shouted, "Do you not know that the same father begot me as well as those who died, and the same mother bore me, and that I was brought up on the same teachings? ³I do not renounce the noble kinship that binds me to my brothers."*ᵏ* ⁵Enraged by the man's boldness, they disjointed his hands and feet with their instruments, dismembering him by prying his limbs from their sockets, ⁶and breaking his fingers and arms and legs and elbows. ⁷Since they were not able in any way to break his spirit,*ˡ* they abandoned the instruments*ᵐ* and scalped him with their fingernails in a Scythian fashion. ⁸They immediately brought him to the wheel, and while his vertebrae were being dislocated by this, he saw his own flesh torn all around and drops of blood flowing from his entrails. ⁹When he was about to die, he said, ¹⁰"We, most abominable tyrant, are suffering

---

ʰ Meaning of Gk uncertain   *ⁱ* Other ancient authorities read *post forever*   *ʲ* Other ancient authorities read *having heard his noble decision, they tore him to shreds*   *ᵏ* Other ancient authorities add verse 4, *So if you have any instrument of torture, apply it to my body; for you cannot touch my soul, even if you wish."*   *ˡ* Gk *to strangle him*   *ᵐ* Other ancient authorities read *they tore off his skin*

because of our godly training and virtue, [11]but you, because of your impiety and bloodthirstiness, will undergo unceasing torments."

12 When he too had died in a manner worthy of his brothers, they dragged in the fourth, saying, [13]"As for you, do not give way to the same insanity as your brothers, but obey the king and save yourself." [14]But he said to them, "You do not have a fire hot enough to make me play the coward. [15]No—by the blessed death of my brothers, by the eternal destruction of the tyrant, and by the everlasting life of the pious, I will not renounce our noble family ties. [16]Contrive tortures, tyrant, so that you may learn from them that I am a brother to those who have just now been tortured." [17]When he heard this, the bloodthirsty, murderous, and utterly abominable Antiochus gave orders to cut out his tongue. [18]But he said, "Even if you remove my organ of speech, God hears also those who are mute. [19]See, here is my tongue; cut it off, for in spite of this you will not make our reason speechless. [20]Gladly, for the sake of God, we let our bodily members be mutilated. [21]God will visit you swiftly, for you are cutting out a tongue that has been melodious with divine hymns."

The Torture of the Fifth and Sixth Brothers

11 When he too died, after being cruelly tortured, the fifth leaped up, saying, [2]"I will not refuse, tyrant, to be tortured for the sake of virtue. [3]I have come of my own accord, so that by murdering me you will incur punishment from the heavenly justice for even more crimes. [4]Hater of virtue, hater of humankind, for what act of ours are you destroying us in this way? [5]Is it because[n] we revere the Creator of all things and live according to his virtuous law? [6]But these deeds deserve honors, not tortures."[o] [9]While he was saying these things, the guards bound him and dragged him to the catapult; [10]they tied him to it on his knees, and fitting iron clamps on them, they twisted his back[p] around the wedge on the wheel,[q] so that he was completely curled back like a scorpion, and all his members were disjointed. [11]In this condition, gasping for breath and in anguish of body, [12]he said,

"Tyrant, they are splendid favors that you grant us against your will, because through these noble sufferings you give us an opportunity to show our endurance for the law."

13 When he too had died, the sixth, a mere boy, was led in. When the tyrant inquired whether he was willing to eat and be released, he said, [14]"I am younger in age than my brothers, but I am their equal in mind. [15]Since to this end we were born and bred, we ought likewise to die for the same principles. [16]So if you intend to torture me for not eating defiling foods, go on torturing!" [17]When he had said this, they led him to the wheel. [18]He was carefully stretched tight upon it, his back was broken, and he was roasted[r] from underneath. [19]To his back they applied sharp spits that had been heated in the fire, and pierced his ribs so that his entrails were burned through. [20]While being tortured he said, "O contest befitting holiness, in which so many of us brothers have been summoned to an arena of sufferings for religion, and in which we have not been defeated! [21]For religious knowledge, O tyrant, is invincible. [22]I also, equipped with nobility, will die with my brothers, [23]and I myself will bring a great avenger upon you, you inventor of tortures and enemy of those who are truly devout. [24]We six boys have paralyzed your tyranny. [25]Since you have not been able to persuade us to change our mind or to force us to eat defiling foods, is not this your downfall? [26]Your fire is cold to us, and the catapults painless, and your violence powerless. [27]For it is not the guards of the tyrant but those of the divine law that are set over us; therefore, unconquered, we hold fast to reason."

The Torture of the Seventh Brother

12 When he too, thrown into the caldron, had died a blessed death, the seventh and youngest of all came forward. [2]Even though the tyrant had been vehemently reproached by the brothers, he felt strong compassion for this child when he saw that he was already in fetters. He summoned him to come nearer and tried to persuade him, saying, [3]"You see the result of your brothers' stupidity, for they died in

---

[n] Other ancient authorities read *Or does it seem evil to you that you but understood human feelings and had hope of salvation from God—* [o] Other authorities add verses 7 and 8, [7]*If* [8]*but, as it is, you are a stranger to God and persecute those who serve him."* [p] Gk *loins* [q] Meaning of Gk uncertain [r] Other ancient authorities add *by fire*

torments because of their disobedience. ⁴You too, if you do not obey, will be miserably tortured and die before your time, ⁵but if you yield to persuasion you will be my friend and a leader in the government of the kingdom." ⁶When he had thus appealed to him, he sent for the boy's mother to show compassion on her who had been bereaved of so many sons and to influence her to persuade the surviving son to obey and save himself. ⁷But when his mother had exhorted him in the Hebrew language, as we shall tell a little later, ⁸he said, "Let me loose, let me speak to the king and to all his friends that are with him." ⁹Extremely pleased by the boy's declaration, they freed him at once. ¹⁰Running to the nearest of the braziers, ¹¹he said, "You profane tyrant, most impious of all the wicked, since you have received good things and also your kingdom from God, were you not ashamed to murder his servants and torture on the wheel those who practice religion? ¹²Because of this, justice has laid up for you intense and eternal fire and tortures, and these throughout all time*ˢ* will never let you go. ¹³As a man, were you not ashamed, you most savage beast, to cut out the tongues of men who have feelings like yours and are made of the same elements as you, and to maltreat and torture them in this way? ¹⁴Surely they by dying nobly fulfilled their service to God, but you will wail bitterly for having killed without cause the contestants for virtue." ¹⁵Then because he too was about to die, he said, ¹⁶"I do not desert the excellent example*ᵗ* of my brothers, ¹⁷and I call on the God of our ancestors to be merciful to our nation;*ᵘ* ¹⁸but on you he will take vengeance both in this present life and when you are dead." ¹⁹After he had uttered these imprecations, he flung himself into the braziers and so ended his life.*ᵛ*

Reason's Sovereignty in the Seven

13 Since, then, the seven brothers despised sufferings even unto death, everyone must concede that devout reason is sovereign over the emotions. ²For if they had been slaves to their emotions and had eaten defiling food, we would say that they had been conquered by these emotions. ³But in fact it was not so. Instead, by reason, which is praised before God, they prevailed over their emotions. ⁴The supremacy of the mind over these cannot be overlooked, for the brothers*ʷ* mastered both emotions and pains. ⁵How then can one fail to confess the sovereignty of right reason over emotion in those who were not turned back by fiery agonies? ⁶For just as towers jutting out over harbors hold back the threatening waves and make it calm for those who sail into the inner basin, ⁷so the seven-towered right reason of the youths, by fortifying the harbor of religion, conquered the tempest of the emotions. ⁸For they constituted a holy chorus of religion and encouraged one another, saying, ⁹"Brothers, let us die like brothers for the sake of the law; let us imitate the three youths in Assyria who despised the same ordeal of the furnace. ¹⁰Let us not be cowardly in the demonstration of our piety." ¹¹While one said, "Courage, brother," another said, "Bear up nobly," ¹²and another reminded them, "Remember whence you came, and the father by whose hand Isaac would have submitted to being slain for the sake of religion." ¹³Each of them and all of them together looking at one another, cheerful and undaunted, said, "Let us with all our hearts consecrate ourselves to God, who gave us our lives,*ˣ* and let us use our bodies as a bulwark for the law. ¹⁴Let us not fear him who thinks he is killing us, ¹⁵for great is the struggle of the soul and the danger of eternal torment lying before those who transgress the commandment of God. ¹⁶Therefore let us put on the full armor of self-control, which is divine reason. ¹⁷For if we so die,*ʸ* Abraham and Isaac and Jacob will welcome us, and all the fathers will praise us." ¹⁸Those who were left behind said to each of the brothers who were being dragged away, "Do not put us to shame, brother, or betray the brothers who have died before us."

19 You are not ignorant of the affection of family ties, which the divine and all-wise Providence has bequeathed through the fathers to their descendants and which was implanted in the mother's womb. ²⁰There each of the brothers spent the same length of time and was shaped during the same period of time; and growing from the same blood and through the same life, they were brought to the light of day. ²¹When they

were born after an equal time of gestation, they drank milk from the same fountains. From such embraces brotherly-loving souls are nourished; [22]and they grow stronger from this common nurture and daily companionship, and from both general education and our discipline in the law of God. 23 Therefore, when sympathy and brotherly affection had been so established, the brothers were the more sympathetic to one another. [24]Since they had been educated by the same law and trained in the same virtues and brought up in right living, they loved one another all the more. [25]A common zeal for nobility strengthened their goodwill toward one another, and their concord, [26]because they could make their brotherly love more fervent with the aid of their religion. [27]But although nature and companionship and virtuous habits had augmented the affection of family ties, those who were left endured for the sake of religion, while watching their brothers being maltreated and tortured to death.

14 Furthermore, they encouraged them to face the torture, so that they not only despised their agonies, but also mastered the emotions of brotherly love.

2 O reason,[z] more royal than kings and freer than the free! [3]O sacred and harmonious concord of the seven brothers on behalf of religion! [4]None of the seven youths proved coward or shrank from death, [5]but all of them, as though running the course toward immortality, hastened to death by torture. [6]Just as the hands and feet are moved in harmony with the guidance of the mind, so those holy youths, as though moved by an immortal spirit of devotion, agreed to go to death for its sake. [7]O most holy seven, brothers in harmony! For just as the seven days of creation move in choral dance around religion, [8]so these youths, forming a chorus, encircled the sevenfold fear of tortures and dissolved it. [9]Even now, we ourselves shudder as we hear of the suffering of these young men; they not only saw what was happening, not only heard the direct word of threat, but also bore the sufferings patiently, and in agonies of fire at that. [10]What could be more excruciatingly painful than this? For the power of fire is intense and swift, and it consumed their bodies quickly.

An Encomium on the Mother of the Seven

11 Do not consider it amazing that reason had full command over these men in their tortures, since the mind of woman despised even more diverse agonies, [12]for the mother of the seven young men bore up under the rackings of each one of her children.

13 Observe how complex is a mother's love for her children, which draws everything toward an emotion felt in her inmost parts. [14]Even unreasoning animals, as well as human beings, have a sympathy and parental love for their offspring. [15]For example, among birds, the ones that are tame protect their young by building on the housetops, [16]and the others, by building in precipitous chasms and in holes and tops of trees, hatch the nestlings and ward off the intruder. [17]If they are not able to keep the intruder[a] away, they do what they can to help their young by flying in circles around them in the anguish of love, warning them with their own calls. [18]And why is it necessary to demonstrate sympathy for children by the example of unreasoning animals, [19]since even bees at the time for making honeycombs defend themselves against intruders and, as though with an iron dart, sting those who approach their hive and defend it even to the death? [20]But sympathy for her children did not sway the mother of the young men; she was of the same mind as Abraham.

15 O reason of the children, tyrant over the emotions! O religion, more desirable to the mother than her children! [2]Two courses were open to this mother, that of religion, and that of preserving her seven sons for a time, as the tyrant had promised. [3]She loved religion more, the religion that preserves them for eternal life according to God's promise.[b] [4]In what manner might I express the emotions of parents who love their children? We impress upon the character of a small child a wondrous likeness both of mind and of form. Especially is this true of mothers, who because of their birth pangs have a deeper sympathy toward their offspring than do the fathers. [5]Considering that mothers are the weaker sex and give birth to many, they are more devoted to their children.[c] [6]The mother of the seven boys, more than any other mother, loved

---

[z] Or *O minds*   [a] Gk *it*   [b] Gk *according to God*   [c] Or *For to the degree that mothers are weaker and the more children they bear, the more they are devoted to their children.*

her children. In seven pregnancies she had implanted in herself tender love toward them, [7]and because of the many pains she suffered with each of them she had sympathy for them; [8]yet because of the fear of God she disdained the temporary safety of her children. [9]Not only so, but also because of the nobility of her sons and their ready obedience to the law, she felt a greater tenderness toward them. [10]For they were righteous and self-controlled and brave and magnanimous, and loved their brothers and their mother, so that they obeyed her even to death in keeping the ordinances.

11 Nevertheless, though so many factors influenced the mother to suffer with them out of love for her children, in the case of none of them were the various tortures strong enough to pervert her reason. [12]But each child separately and all of them together the mother urged on to death for religion's sake. [13]O sacred nature and affection of parental love, yearning of parents toward offspring, nurture and indomitable suffering by mothers! [14]This mother, who saw them tortured and burned one by one, because of religion did not change her attitude. [15]She watched the flesh of her children being consumed by fire, their toes and fingers scattered[d] on the ground, and the flesh of the head to the chin exposed like masks.

16 O mother, tried now by more bitter pains than even the birth pangs you suffered for them! [17]O woman, who alone gave birth to such complete devotion! [18]When the firstborn breathed his last, it did not turn you aside, nor when the second in torments looked at you piteously nor when the third expired; [19]nor did you weep when you looked at the eyes of each one in his tortures gazing boldly at the same agonies, and saw in their nostrils the signs of the approach of death. [20]When you saw the flesh of children burned upon the flesh of other children, severed hands upon hands, scalped heads upon heads, and corpses fallen on other corpses, and when you saw the place filled with many spectators of the torturings, you did not shed tears. [21]Neither the melodies of sirens nor the songs of swans attract the attention of their hearers as did the voices of the children in torture calling to their mother. [22]How great and how many torments the mother then suffered as her sons were tortured on the wheel and with the hot irons! [23]But devout reason, giving her heart a man's courage in the very midst of her emotions, strengthened her to disregard, for the time, her parental love.

24 Although she witnessed the destruction of seven children and the ingenious and various rackings, this noble mother disregarded all these[e] because of faith in God. [25]For as in the council chamber of her own soul she saw mighty advocates— nature, family, parental love, and the rackings of her children— [26]this mother held two ballots, one bearing death and the other deliverance for her children. [27]She did not approve the deliverance that would preserve the seven sons for a short time, [28]but as the daughter of God-fearing Abraham she remembered his fortitude.

29 O mother of the nation, vindicator of the law and champion of religion, who carried away the prize of the contest in your heart! [30]O more noble than males in steadfastness, and more courageous than men in endurance! [31]Just as Noah's ark, carrying the world in the universal flood, stoutly endured the waves, [32]so you, O guardian of the law, overwhelmed from every side by the flood of your emotions and the violent winds, the torture of your sons, endured nobly and withstood the wintry storms that assail religion.

16 If, then, a woman, advanced in years and mother of seven sons, endured seeing her children tortured to death, it must be admitted that devout reason is sovereign over the emotions. [2]Thus I have demonstrated not only that men have ruled over the emotions, but also that a woman has despised the fiercest tortures. [3]The lions surrounding Daniel were not so savage, nor was the raging fiery furnace of Mishael so intensely hot, as was her innate parental love, inflamed as she saw her seven sons tortured in such varied ways. [4]But the mother quenched so many and such great emotions by devout reason.

5 Consider this also: If this woman, though a mother, had been fainthearted, she would have mourned over them and perhaps spoken as follows: [6]"O how wretched am I and many times unhappy! After bearing seven children, I am now the mother of none! [7]O seven childbirths all in vain, seven profitless pregnancies, fruitless nurturings and wretched nursings! [8]In vain, my sons,

---

[d] Or *quivering*   [e] Other ancient authorities read *having bidden them farewell, surrendered them*

I endured many birth pangs for you, and the more grievous anxieties of your upbringing. ⁹Alas for my children, some unmarried, others married and without offspring.ᶠ I shall not see your children or have the happiness of being called grandmother. ¹⁰Alas, I who had so many and beautiful children am a widow and alone, with many sorrows.ᵍ ¹¹And when I die, I shall have none of my sons to bury me."

12 Yet that holy and God-fearing mother did not wail with such a lament for any of them, nor did she dissuade any of them from dying, nor did she grieve as they were dying. ¹³On the contrary, as though having a mind like adamant and giving rebirth for immortality to the whole number of her sons, she implored them and urged them on to death for the sake of religion. ¹⁴O mother, soldier of God in the cause of religion, elder and woman! By steadfastness you have conquered even a tyrant, and in word and deed you have proved more powerful than a man. ¹⁵For when you and your sons were arrested together, you stood and watched Eleazar being tortured, and said to your sons in the Hebrew language, ¹⁶"My sons, noble is the contest to which you are called to bear witness for the nation. Fight zealously for our ancestral law. ¹⁷For it would be shameful if, while an aged man endures such agonies for the sake of religion, you young men were to be terrified by tortures. ¹⁸Remember that it is through God that you have had a share in the world and have enjoyed life, ¹⁹and therefore you ought to endure any suffering for the sake of God. ²⁰For his sake also our father Abraham was zealous to sacrifice his son Isaac, the ancestor of our nation; and when Isaac saw his father's hand wielding a knifeʰ and descending upon him, he did not cower. ²¹Daniel the righteous was thrown to the lions, and Hananiah, Azariah, and Mishael were hurled into the fiery furnace and endured it for the sake of God. ²²You too must have the same faith in God and not be grieved. ²³It is unreasonable for people who have religious knowledge not to withstand pain."

24 By these words the mother of the seven encouraged and persuaded each of her sons to die rather than violate God's commandment. ²⁵They knew also that those who die for the sake of God live to God, as do Abraham and Isaac and Jacob and all the patriarchs.

17 Some of the guards said that when she also was about to be seized and put to death she threw herself into the flames so that no one might touch her body.

2 O mother, who with your seven sons nullified the violence of the tyrant, frustrated his evil designs, and showed the courage of your faith! ³Nobly set like a roof on the pillars of your sons, you held firm and unswerving against the earthquake of the tortures. ⁴Take courage, therefore, O holy-minded mother, maintaining firm an enduring hope in God. ⁵The moon in heaven, with the stars, does not stand so august as you, who, after lighting the way of your star-like seven sons to piety, stand in honor before God and are firmly set in heaven with them. ⁶For your children were true descendants of father Abraham.ⁱ

The Effect of the Martyrdoms

7 If it were possible for us to paint the history of your religion as an artist might, would not those who first beheld it have shuddered as they saw the mother of the seven children enduring their varied tortures to death for the sake of religion? ⁸Indeed it would be proper to inscribe on their tomb these words as a reminder to the people of our nation:ʲ

9 "Here lie buried an aged priest and an aged woman and seven sons, because of the violence of the tyrant who wished to destroy the way of life of the Hebrews. ¹⁰They vindicated their nation, looking to God and enduring torture even to death."

11 Truly the contest in which they were engaged was divine, ¹²for on that day virtue gave the awards and tested them for their endurance. The prize was immortality in endless life. ¹³Eleazar was the first contestant, the mother of the seven sons entered the competition, and the brothers contended. ¹⁴The tyrant was the antagonist, and the world and the human race were the spectators. ¹⁵Reverence for God was victor and gave the crown to its own athletes. ¹⁶Who did not admire the athletes of the divineᵏ legislation? Who were not amazed? 17 The tyrant himself and all his council

---

ᶠ Gk *without benefit*   ᵍ Or *much to be pitied*   ʰ Gk *sword*   ⁱ Gk *For your childbearing was from Abraham the father*; other ancient authorities read *For . . . Abraham the servant*   ʲ Or *as a memorial to the heroes of our people*   ᵏ Other ancient authorities read *true*

marveled at their[l] endurance, [18]because of which they now stand before the divine throne and live the life of eternal blessedness. [19]For Moses says, "All who are consecrated are under your hands." [20]These, then, who have been consecrated for the sake of God,[m] are honored, not only with this honor, but also by the fact that because of them our enemies did not rule over our nation, [21]the tyrant was punished, and the homeland purified—they having become, as it were, a ransom for the sin of our nation. [22]And through the blood of those devout ones and their death as an atoning sacrifice, divine Providence preserved Israel that previously had been mistreated.

23 For the tyrant Antiochus, when he saw the courage of their virtue and their endurance under the tortures, proclaimed them to his soldiers as an example for their own endurance, [24]and this made them brave and courageous for infantry battle and siege, and he ravaged and conquered all his enemies.

18 O Israelite children, offspring of the seed of Abraham, obey this law and exercise piety in every way, [2]knowing that devout reason is master of all emotions, not only of sufferings from within, but also of those from without.

3 Therefore those who gave over their bodies in suffering for the sake of religion were not only admired by mortals, but also were deemed worthy to share in a divine inheritance. [4]Because of them the nation gained peace, and by reviving observance of the law in the homeland they ravaged the enemy. [5]The tyrant Antiochus was both punished on earth and is being chastised after his death. Since in no way whatever was he able to compel the Israelites to become pagans and to abandon their ancestral customs, he left Jerusalem and marched against the Persians.

The Mother's Address to Her Children

6 The mother of seven sons expressed also these principles to her children: [7]"I was a pure virgin and did not go outside my father's house; but I guarded the rib from which woman was made.[n] [8]No seducer corrupted me on a desert plain, nor did the destroyer, the deceitful serpent, defile the purity of my virginity. [9]In the time of my maturity I remained with my husband, and when these sons had grown up their father died. A happy man was he, who lived out his life with good children, and did not have the grief of bereavement. [10]While he was still with you, he taught you the law and the prophets. [11]He read to you about Abel slain by Cain, and Isaac who was offered as a burnt offering, and about Joseph in prison. [12]He told you of the zeal of Phinehas, and he taught you about Hananiah, Azariah, and Mishael in the fire. [13]He praised Daniel in the den of the lions and blessed him. [14]He reminded you of the scripture of Isaiah, which says, 'Even though you go through the fire, the flame shall not consume you.' [15]He sang to you songs of the psalmist David, who said, 'Many are the afflictions of the righteous.' [16]He recounted to you Solomon's proverb, 'There is a tree of life for those who do his will.' [17]He confirmed the query of Ezekiel, 'Shall these dry bones live?' [18]For he did not forget to teach you the song that Moses taught, which says, [19]'I kill and I make alive: this is your life and the length of your days.' "

20 O bitter was that day—and yet not bitter—when that bitter tyrant of the Greeks quenched fire with fire in his cruel caldrons, and in his burning rage brought those seven sons of the daughter of Abraham to the catapult and back again to more[o] tortures, [21]pierced the pupils of their eyes and cut out their tongues, and put them to death with various tortures. [22]For these crimes divine justice pursued and will pursue the accursed tyrant. [23]But the sons of Abraham with their victorious mother are gathered together into the chorus of the fathers, and have received pure and immortal[p] souls from God, [24]to whom be glory forever and ever. Amen.

---

[l] Other ancient authorities add *virtue and that was built*   [m] Other ancient authorities lack *for the sake of God*   [n] Gk *the rib*   [o] Other ancient authorities read *to all his*   [p] Other ancient authorities read *victorious*